*Reading Food
in Modern
Japanese
Literature*

Reading Food in Modern Japanese Literature

Tomoko Aoyama

University of Hawai'i Press
Honolulu

Printed in the United States of America

13 12 11 10 09 08 6 5 4 3 2 1

LIBRARY OF CONGRESS CATALOGING-IN-PUBLICATION DATA

Aoyama, Tomoko.
Reading food in modern Japanese literature / Tomoko Aoyama.
p. cm.
Includes bibliographical references and index.
ISBN 978-0-8248-3285-8 (hard cover : alk. paper)
1. Japanese literature—20th century—History and criticism. 2. Food in literature. I. Title.
PL726.57.F65A59 2008
808.8'0355—dc22

2008022150

Four illustrations by Mizuno Toshikata (1866–1908) are reproduced from the 1976 reprint of Murai Gensai's 1903 novel *Kuidōraku* with the permission of Shibata Shoten.

Figure 1: "Natsu no maki" (vol. 2, Summer), pp. 88–89
Figure 2: "Aki no maki" (vol. 3, Fall), pp. 246–247
Figure 3: "Natsu no maki" (vol. 2, Summer), pp. 156–157
Figure 4: "Aki no maki" (vol. 3, Fall), pp. 68–69

University of Hawai'i Press books are printed on acid-free paper and meet the guidelines for permanence and durability of the Council on Library Resources.

Designed by the University of Hawai'i Press production staff
Printed by The Maple-Vail Book Manufacturing Group

Contents

Acknowledgments

A number of people and organizations have given me generous support and inspiration for this project. In the early days the Australian Research Council's Small Grant in 1998 assisted me in a way that was not at all small. So did each of the University of Queensland's fellowships: Promoting Women Fellowship (2001) and Centre for Critical and Cultural Studies Faculty Fellowship (2002). For this latter opportunity I would like to express my special thanks to the director of the CCCS, Professor Graeme Turner, for his generous encouragement. The preparation of chapter 6 of this book has greatly benefited from the Australian Research Council Discovery Project "From *musume* (daughter) to *shōjo* (girl)." Throughout the project my immediate colleagues at the School of Languages and Comparative Cultural Studies, and its predecessor the Department of Asian Languages and Studies, have supported me enormously in giving both moral and practical support. As I cannot fill this page with the names of all my former and current colleagues, I will name just one: Professor Nanette Gottlieb, who has always been strongly supportive, from the earliest stage of this project through to its final stage.

As noted in detail in each chapter, some sections of this book are based on my earlier publications in multiauthored volumes edited by Elise Tipton and John Clark, Kam Louie and Morris Low, Mark McLelland and Romit Dasgupta, and also in journals such as *US-Japan Women's Journal, Japanstudien,* and *Japanese Studies.* I am grateful to all the editors and readers at these publications for nurturing these earlier projects and allowing me to reproduce some parts of them in the present book. Above all, however, it is the University of Hawai'i Press, and especially Pamela Kelley and the anonymous readers, whose patient and constructive guidance and advice have made it possible for this project to grow into a book.

One of the most enjoyable things about this project has been that so many people have taken a genuine interest in what I have been struggling to do. At every conference presentation and staff seminar at which I have presented the work in progress, I have received excellent feedback and hints for further studies. The interest has often lasted well after the occasion and has often alerted me to new and old publications, conferences, and other events that extend beyond my immediate specialty of modern Japanese literary studies. The conviviality around the subject of food has certainly assisted me in creating a network of helpful fellow scholars. While it would be impossible to name everyone, there are several colleagues who have generously spared their own time to assist me with insightful feedback. I thank Dr. Erik Lofgren of Bucknell University for his helpful comments on an early and still very messy draft of the cannibalism chapter. David Kelly (University of Western Sydney) has given me wonderful support through a close reading of some early chapter drafts. Dr. Barbara Hartley (University of Tasmania) deserves special thanks for her enthusiastic support and acute comments. This project could not have been completed without a series of able and efficient editorial assistants: Anne Platt, Bill Fryer, and Cory Taylor. Finally, I thank my husband, James Wheatley, for all his support (and cooking). He certainly deserves a nice supper with plenty to drink, ideally at a place like Tōzentei, the utopian establishment that appears in Aoki Masaru's story (see chapter 5).

Introduction

Why Read *Food* in Modern
Japanese Literature?

Towards the end of Tanizaki Jun'ichirō's novel *Tade kuu mushi* (1929, trans. *Some Prefer Nettles*, 1955) the protagonist Kaname and his wife, Misako, visit Misako's father in Kyoto to discuss their marriage, which has been on the rocks. After years of inertia and hesitation, the couple has finally decided to make a move towards formal separation and divorce. Realizing this, Misako's father wants to talk to Kaname first, then take his daughter to a restaurant for a quiet chat. Before leaving Kaname in the house, the old man asks his young, "doll-like" mistress, O-Hisa, to ensure that his son-in-law is looked after well.

> "What can you offer your guest?"
> "Nothing decent."
> "The salmon roe?"
> "I thought I might deep-fry the salmon roe."
> "And what else?"
> "Baked trout—"
> "And?"
> "And a salad."
> "Well, Kaname, the food to go with it doesn't sound very promising, but maybe you could stay and have a few drinks."
> "Poor Kaname gets the booby prize."
> "Really, now," Kaname protested, "the cook is better than the cook at the Hyōtei. I'll have myself a feast."[1]

I begin this book on food, eating, and cooking in modern Japanese literature by quoting this passage not because at first sight it contains anything breathtaking or illuminating, but because it refers to food that seems quite simple and yet has many things to tell us. In fact, as we shall see shortly, the seemingly simple and ordinary may turn out to be surprisingly complex, once we pay attention to it.

When food appears in literature, what can we read in it? And how much can we, and should we, read *into* it? How has that food in the text been read by various readers over time? What factors affect our reading? Why, indeed, should we bother to pay attention to food in literature? These are the questions this book attempts to answer by examining wide-ranging examples taken from Japanese literary texts written since the beginning of the twentieth century. The food we read may well be closely related to the food in the actual, physical world. Or it may be symbolic or metaphysical food.

That food is no simple matter has been widely recognized—in fields such as anthropology, sociology, food science, semiotics, history, political science, and economics, as well as in literary, film, and cultural studies. Food nourishes and poisons; it soothes and tortures, divides as well as unites individuals and groups of people. Food is essential, but it can also be seen as optional, superfluous, or extravagant. Food plays important roles in various types of rituals. It also serves as a means of communicating and acting out our religious, political, philosophical, and cultural views or of expressing a range of emotions. Food may be an object of intense desire, admiration, addiction, craving, fear, disgust, and loathing, or it may be ignored or rejected either intentionally or unintentionally. Food involves production, distribution, preparation, and consumption, and in each process there are rules, taboos, structures, order, customs, styles, fashions, and conventions to create, to follow, or to break. Food has been discovered, invented, classified, and scrutinized, as well as enjoyed, consumed, and devoured. It is, to borrow Gaye Poole's words, "a polysemous signifier that articulates in concrete terms what is very often internal, vague, abstract."[2]

The situation becomes more complicated when the subject is not actual food but food within literary texts, for literature, like food, is "endlessly interpretable," to quote Terry Eagleton, and food, like literature, "looks like an object but is actually a relationship."[3] It lends itself to no finite or definitive interpretations. The relationship implied within activities surrounding food covers a variety of areas and dimensions both concrete and abstract—not merely interpersonal relations but also the relation between nature and culture, the physical and the spiritual as well as between the individual and society and between production and reception. Food is "a window on the political," for "food practices are implicated in a complex field of relationships, expectations, and choices that are contested, negotiated, and often unequal."[4]

Such relations are often discussed as binary pairs "such as cooked/raw, center/periphery, voice/writing, spirit/flesh, art (culture)/nature, male/female, content/form, proper/improper, literal/metaphorical, public/private, work/home, production/consumption, author/reader, host/guest, familiar/foreign, classic/grotesque, high/low, autonomy/relatedness," as Maggie Kilgour lists them in her study of metaphors of incorporation *From Communion to Cannibalism*, along with the pair she herself focuses on: "inside/outside."[5] These binary pairs themselves, however, are not the focus of this book; rather, I seek, among other things, to contribute to the questioning of such dichotomies by studying examples of ambiguity and merging where the hierarchy habitually implied in these pairs—the presumption that the first member of each pair is in some way prior to, or privileged over, the second—is subverted and undone. In this focus on food, readers will discover "the surprising and intriguing variety of ways that food and eating may function as a code, a sign system, a leitmotif of fascinating complexity, to expand the possible repertoire of readings."[6] Needless to say, if some prior sociocultural and linguistic knowledge is needed to understand a text, this is also the case if we are to understand the complex relationships involved in the particular food in the text.

The Subtle Taste of Nettles

Let us see how this is so in the case of *Tade kuu mushi*, the title of which symbolically indicates the importance of multiplicity and relativity: there is no such thing as absolute or universal values or criteria for taste and desire. Even the short passage quoted above suggests multiple relationships involving food. To appreciate the complexity fully, it is essential to understand not only intratextual but extratextual (e.g., sociohistorical and cultural) contexts. Hyōtei, for instance, the restaurant Misako's father is taking her to, is an existing traditional Japanese-style restaurant in Nanzenji, the up-market part of Kyoto containing the famous Zen temple of the same name. Even if the reader has never heard of the restaurant,[7] at least it is clear from the text that it is a famous restaurant in Kyoto, and within walking distance of Misako's father's house. The old man tells his mistress, O-Hisa, to phone the restaurant, expecting that a nice quiet room will be available for him for that same evening. He is obviously a regular customer. The novel does not include the actual dining scene at the restaurant because the primary focus is placed on Kaname rather than on Misako, her father, or O-Hisa. The reader can assume, however, that on this occasion, with such an atmosphere of doom hanging over her marriage, like the very weather on that evening, thick and oppressive, neither father nor daughter is likely to enjoy what the famous restaurant has to offer—the delicacies, the fine pottery, the elegant interior, the garden, the service, the tranquility, all of which are in any case not new to this privileged pair.

O-Hisa says she cannot offer Kaname anything "decent." However, from a number of earlier episodes the reader knows that the young woman has been trained meticulously by Misako's father according to his peculiarly and stubbornly old-fashioned taste. As we shall see in later chapters, a man teaching a woman how to cook is by no means an uncommon motif, and in many cases it is also linked to a sexual relationship. The link is evident in this text, too, although it never goes beyond allusion and implication. Even if the food O-Hisa cooks for the evening will not be as elaborate as the dinner served at Hyōtei, it undoubtedly is going to be more than "decent," with carefully selected ingredients cooked and served efficiently and with care. Kaname is more and more attracted to this young woman, not as a specific individual, but as a type.[8] This is indeed a "feast" for him.

The reader of the English version, however, may find the menu odd because the significance of local specialities is lost in translation.[9] What is sacrificed is of course the important cultural specificity (Kyoto) of the original items, as discussed below.

Tanizaki is a devoted advocate and a champion practitioner of ambiguity, or to use the key term in his "how to write" book,[10] *ganchiku* (implications, overtones, connotations). His writing and the food *in* his writing are both certainly "polysemous" and "endlessly interpretable." What is interesting, as we shall see, is that Tanizakian ambiguity emerges not out of chaos and disorder but out of the way the seemingly neat and schematic dichotomies he presents or implies (thus, at least at first sight, confirming Kilgour's "binary pairs"!) are actually subverted. David Pollack proposes two major defining axes in this novel: "a traditional opposition between the Kantō (Eastern) and Kansai (Western) regions of Japan" on the one hand and on the other the cultural difference within Kansai, from the "traditional morality" of Kyoto to its opposite, "the modern and entirely amoral 'foreign' culture of Kobe."[11] O-Hisa represents the old aesthetic, that of traditional and overtly submissive Japan, associated with Kyoto and its language and culture, including music, theater, and cooking. She cooks and serves—if she does not herself eat—Kyoto-style food, as instructed by Misako's father. The lengths they both go to and the pride he takes in her cooking are evident in the following passage, in which the father wants the couple to stay longer.

> "And O-Hisa spent all yesterday evening and this morning getting the lunch ready," the old man persisted. "We can't possibly eat it by ourselves."
>
> "It's nothing, really. Don't stay just for that." O-Hisa had been quite outside the conversation, listening as a child would listen to grownups, but at the old man's remark she somewhat uncomfortably readjusted the lid to hide the mosaic-like array inside the square box. Even the boiling of an egg was likely to call forth a lecture from the old man, and the training of his young mistress had involved a long course in cooking. Now, however, no one except O-Hisa could cook a decent meal, and he was clearly anxious to show her off.[12]

Again, this cuisine, though this is hidden by the translation, is in Kyoto style; what is given as "the boiling of an egg" in the translation is in the original text the cooking of another Kansai product, *Kōya dōfu* (diced tofu frozen and then dried to preserve it, named after Kōyasan, where it originated).[13]

In contrast, Misako represents, according to Pollack's schema, the "modern inauthentic Japan" associated with Tokyo, rather than with the "entirely amoral" Kobe, the topos that is represented by Louise, a Eurasian prostitute Kaname regularly visits. The food Misako eats, however, suggests that she has connections—superficially but regularly—with "amoral" and "foreign" Kobe. Her usual breakfast consists of toast and, perhaps to most readers' surprise, liver sausages from a German butcher in Kobe. While eating her late breakfast cooked and served by her maid, she flirts—or pretends to flirt—with Kaname's cousin and old family friend Takanatsu, who happens to be staying with them.[14] The food associated with Takanatsu, by the way, is garlic, indicating his close connection with China, or more specifically, Shanghai. Misako cannot stand the houseguest's odor, and openly complains to him about it.

Both food and literature, then, are intimately, perhaps inextricably, connected to specific cultures and societies. At the same time there would seem to be some apparently fundamental or "natural" aspects of both that are universal. The line between culture and "nature," between the specific and the universal, however, is often vague and ambiguous. Similarly, the supposedly clear boundaries between two cultures also become blurred. In *Tade kuu mushi* food is used almost as a stereotypical sociocultural identifier in the binary pairs of Kantō/Kansai, East/West, Japan/China, traditional/modern, sexual/asexual, vegetarian/carnivorous, young/old, and so on. As many critics have noted,[15] however, binaries such as these are merged, transgressed, and redefined or reinvented in Tanizaki's literature. A foreign land becomes a new home (Kyoto in the case of Misako's father, China in the case of Takanatsu), and past and future may become present (e.g., Misako's father reconstructing and living the past; Kaname possibly following in his footsteps).[16] Some parts of Kansai remind Kaname of the old Tokyo of his childhood, thus blurring the Kantō/Kansai division. We may also note that even though Misako eats German liver sausages with a knife and a fork, to do so she sits at *chabudai*, a low table, in a Japanese-style room. Even the authentic-seeming O-Hisa, the "doll-like" Kyoto woman, is in fact a creation of Misako's father, who, though a Tokyoite, teaches the native Kyoto woman how to cook Kyoto dishes and generally how to behave like an ideal premodern Kyoto woman. Kaname thinks that O-Hisa must surely have an occasional urge for a movie instead of the puppet theater and a steak instead of braised bracken.[17]

Food and cooking are also linked closely to gender and sexuality. Referring to Freud and others, Carole Counihan reminds us that "food and sex are analogous instinctive needs," both connoting intimacy as well as danger, and that therefore they are "surrounded with rules and taboos." Counihan also asserts, "In all cultures, women's primary responsibilities involve food provisioning and the bearing and rearing of children. . . . Women *are* food to the fetus and infant, and the breasts can be sources of both sexual pleasure and food."[18] In *Tade kuu mushi* we see clearly marked gender roles that are linked to sex. Most prominently in the case of Misako's father and O-Hisa, the roles are carefully planned, studied, rehearsed, and performed—in this case under the direction of the old man, and with the full cooperation of the young woman. Furthermore, social norms and boundaries are often blurred or transgressed. O-Hisa, younger than any of the other main characters, may look like an asexual child or a classic doll, yet at the same time she plays the roles of concubine, mother (to the old man rather than to Misako or Kaname), housekeeper, entertainer, and many others. Misako, too, has to fill contesting roles and positions. While her husband finds her sexually uninteresting, her lover, Aso,[19] obviously has a different opinion. Takanatsu, who knows about Misako's ongoing affair and her husband's full sanction, sees her as "a chaste wife and a virtuous mother" underneath, and only pretending to be flirtatious when she offers him a piece of sausage by directly putting it into his mouth with her fork.[20] The novel tells us again and again that simple dichotomy never works.

Misako's father's plans for the evening in the last part of the novel include the use of food as a gift that he hopes may work to solve the marital problem between Kaname and Misako. By taking his daughter to Hyōtei while letting O-Hisa entertain Kaname, the father hopes not only to talk to Misako privately but also to detain her for long enough to make it too late for the younger couple to go home:[21] they will have to sleep in the same room in Misako's father's house. The reader knows, however, that the father's scheme will not work; Kaname simply enjoys O-Hisa's "feast." Perhaps it is an overreading to note that one of the dishes, the grilled *ayu*, is almost always garnished with *tade*.

Neglected Dishes

The above discussion is a very small sample of what we can read in food in *Tade kuu mushi*, and yet this novel is no more food-oriented than others of Tanizaki's. More generally, food abounds in modern Japanese literature—though not every sample may be appetizing. Despite this abundance, and despite its diversity, the theme of food in Japanese literature has been neglected for decades, primarily because food and eating have only recently begun to attract serious academic attention. "Food and eating have not until very recently generally merited a 'sociology of' to themselves."[22] This historical neglect is based on disgust, on a fear of food and eating, on a view that they are banal, feminine, embodied, impure, unclean, and uncivilized.[23] The perception of food as a "feminine" concern is also noted by a number of scholars.[24]

Sociology is by no means alone in neglecting food.[25] Kilgour attributes the origin of her book *From Communion to Cannibalism* to a discovery she made as an undergraduate student: "I happened to read Ovid, Dante, and Melville at the same time and began wondering why there were so many cannibals running around literature, and even more, why no one else had seemed to notice."[26] Even food and eating in Chinese literature, which one might expect to have been studied in great detail, remained an "unexplored topic"[27] until the appearance of Gang Yue's study *The Mouth That Begs* in 1999. While the last two examples might be considered to be special cases of silence and neglect rooted specifically in the taboo on cannibalism, Gaye Poole remarks that the neglect is much more general. She says that despite the fact that food "plays much more than an accidental or incidental role, . . . it is rarely referred to in critical discussions of theatre, performance or film."[28] Why? Poole suggests that "because food is *so* embedded in life . . . and therefore may be taken for granted, the multiplicity of meanings generated by its inclusion may not always be fully conscious."[29]

In addition to these general factors, there seems to be another set of reasons for the neglect of food in Japanese literature, as the following comment by writer and renowned gastronome Kaikō Takeshi suggests. In "Nihon no sakka-tachi no shokuyoku" (The Appetite of Japanese Writers), written in the late 1970s, Kaikō laments the fact that eating, unlike drinking, has tended to be treated "as an illegitimate child, or as a concubine or a mistress" in literature.[30] The significance of the thematic of drinking is certainly evident in both modern and classic Japanese literature. In contrast, eating has enjoyed much less prominence; for centuries it was regarded as vulgar and unmanly to talk about food, let alone to celebrate the pleasures of eating or cooking. Kaikō is by no means alone in finding this regrettable.[31] One might read Kaikō's metaphor of illegitimacy as implicitly, and perhaps inadvertently, supporting the notion of "serious" or "legitimate" literature as being the domain of the adult male rather than of women and children. The other side of the same coin is the notion that food and cooking belong to women. Clearly, the marginalization of food as a serious subject in the academic and literary worlds has had to do with gender issues. Intertwined with these issues, other important factors have brought about the general neglect of food in Japanese literature. These concern the development of the *shōsetsu* and its language, and *bundan* (literary world)[32] politics.

In his *Shōsetsu shinzui* (The Essence of the Novel, 1885) Tsubouchi Shōyō (1859–1935) adopts the term *shōsetsu* as the translation for "the novel" in its (arguably) European sense. What he had in mind here was the realistic novel as opposed to romance and fantasy. Adopting a Sino-Japanese word (or even inventing one) as an equivalent for a European term was common practice in the discourse of Meiji intellectuals.[33] On the surface it seems to indicate a double cultural borrowing—first from China and then from Europe. When one sees a cultural product such as the *shōsetsu*, and in fact, some food such as Japanese "curry," "hamburger," and "croquette" merely as an adaptation of an external model, it may seem an unauthentic, inaccurate, and distorted imitation. From another perspective, however, it can be regarded as an innovation, and even as evidence of the flexibility of Japanese culture in adapting itself to new needs and circumstances. Hence what may seem to be merely imitative about Japanese culture (including food and literature) may just as easily appear to constitute its originality—and vice versa.

In fact, Shōyō's use of the term *shōsetsu* does not necessarily correspond neatly to "the novel" in the European sense. Furthermore, his juxtaposition (see note 33) of existing terms such as *monogatari* not only blurs the difference between traditional prose fiction and the *shōsetsu* but also symbolically predicts, on the one hand, the continuity with the past, despite Shōyō's advocacy of the modernization of Japanese literature, and on the other hand, the almost amorphous open-endedness of this new genre. As we shall see, the actual works subsumed under the term *shōsetsu* in the twentieth century include not only novels but short stories and fiction in general, as well as works that might be categorized in the European sense as (auto)biographies, essays, travelogues, journals, and so on. Indeed, Noguchi concludes his *Ichigo no jiten: shōsetsu* (A Dictionary of One Word: Shōsetsu) with the following remarks:

> [*Shōsetsu*] is printed literature for reading (as opposed to *monogatari*); with no metric or rhythmic constraints (as opposed to poetry); and with the freedom to use the imagination (as opposed to documentary); moreover *through predation it has ingested* essays, criticism, biography and other neighboring genres. With the continuous modification of its form according to its environment, this prose art has enjoyed a favorable reception in bourgeois society to date.[34]

One cannot but notice Noguchi's food metaphor: "predation," "ingested"—texts eating and incorporating other texts.

One of the key issues in this book is the notion of "textual cannibalism" and other intertextual relationships. The Brazilian critic Haroldo de Campos writes, "In Latin America as well as in Europe, writing will increasingly mean rewriting, digesting, masticating."[35] This, presumably, is true of other literatures, and it is certainly true of modern Japanese literature. Some critics, of course, see this negatively. Fredric Jameson, for example, laments that literature "no longer produces monumental works of the modernist type, but ceaselessly reshuffles the fragments of preexistent texts . . . in some new and heightened bricolage: metabooks which cannibalize other books."[36] My position here is to recognize the significance of the textual cannibalism, and more broadly intertextuality, which includes not merely quotation, allusion, parody, and pastiche (itself a culinary term)[37] but also critical reading and creative transformation within the text. I noted earlier that in our reading of food in literature it is important to pay attention to various intratextual and extratextual relationships. It is equally important, and rewarding, too, to consider intertextual relationships, or, to use Genette's term, transtextuality, that is, everything that situates one text in relation to other texts.[38] The texts that are rewritten, digested, and masticated include not only published literary texts but also oral or visual texts, private texts, nonliterary texts, and discourses. Texts within texts (i.e., consumed by other texts) also contain other sets of texts, which in their turn have incorporated other texts, and so on.[39] Our reading, then, reveals *some* of the texts embedded and transformed within other texts—but, it goes without saying, only some, since it would be impossible (and in any event pointless) to try to trace this "textual food chain" back to the original act of ingestion.

Despite this "predatory" and in fact omnivorous nature of the *shōsetsu*, food and eating, both in concrete and metaphorical senses, have long been neglected and marginalized in Japan, as Kaikō claimed. The single most important reason for this seems to be the central position given in the *hundan* and in conventional literary history to the kind of *shōsetsu* proposed by Shōyō and produced, with modifications, by other writers in late Meiji and Taishō. As Noguchi notes, the *shōsetsu* in fact includes and incorporates an extremely wide variety of writing. For decades, however, only some of this writing has been treated as real, serious, and legitimate *shōsetsu*.

Shōyō advocated the modern Japanese *shōsetsu*, which, under his guidance and with careful planning on the part of the writers, would "finally surpass the European novel and take a glorious place on the altar of the arts along with painting, music and poetry."[40] What Shōyō identified as the "essence" of the novel is the realistic, or mimetic, depiction of "human emotions" and the supposedly objective and unembellished depiction of life "as it is." It is not difficult to see in this focus on human emotions, rather than on society, the harbinger of an unengaged, apolitical tendency to accept the status quo, if only by default. Shōyō's idea of the *shōsetsu* was passed down to what has long been regarded as the mainstream of modern Japanese literature, namely so-called naturalist (*shizen shugi*) writing and the *shishōsetsu* (or *watakushi shōsetsu*, usually translated as the "I novel"). Of particular importance is the shared emphasis on the realistic depiction of life. The principle of objective depiction was combined with a series of popular *shizen shugi* motifs such as the discovery of "self" or "interiority," the dissection of unpalatable "truths" such as carnal desire, loneliness, disappointment, and "confession."

Just as *shōsetsu* was given by Shōyō as a translated term for the novel, *shizen shugi* (literally, "nature" + "ism") had models in various types of European naturalism. Nevertheless, as many have pointed out, *shizen shugi* is remarkably different from (or, according to some critics, inferior to) European, especially Zolaist naturalism, just as the *shōsetsu* is different from the novel. One of the major differences is the lesser degree of interest in the natural and social sciences. With a few exceptions *shizen shugi* texts were little concerned, for instance, with the institution of the family or other aspects of the social system; instead their focus was on the immediate milieu of the writer-protagonist and his (his, since both the author of the text and the protagonist, who is usually very much like his creator, are almost invariably male) search for self. The "self" supposedly discovered by *shizen shugi* writers is enclosed in the even narrower and more immediately recognizable surroundings of the writer, and exposed in detail to the reader in the Taishō *shishōsetsu*. Noguchi calls this genre "the *shōsetsu* of *watakushi* by *watakushi* for *watakushi*," with a note that the *watakushi* is neither an "implied I" nor a simple "explicit I" but a "displayed I," so to speak.[41]

Another characteristic common to *shizen shugi* and *shishōsetsu* is the disdain for clear plot, structure, dramatic events, arresting metaphor, and generally what one might regard as novelistic devices and techniques. Any attempt to entertain the reader is frowned upon. In his famous (or notorious) 1925 apologia for the *shishōsetsu*, Kume Masao (1891–1952) insisted that *War and Peace, Crime and Punishment*, and *Madame Bovary* are, after all, great pieces of popular (and vulgar) fiction and that however skillful Balzac, for example, may be, his works of fiction are nothing but fabrications and are therefore less trustworthy than his personal comments about the difficulty of writing.[42] The rejection of "fabrication" is sometimes[43] likened to a rejection of elaborate and systematic cooking: ordinary raw ingredients are presented with little or no cooking, and the chef seems to pride himself on the total absence of sugar, spices, and other taste enhancers from his dishes. "The expert in depicting unsavory dishes" is the title awarded to the naturalist Shimazaki Tōson (1872–1943) by the literary and culinary commentator Arashiyama Kōzaburō in his collection of essays on eccentric eating habits among modern Japanese writers. Arashiyama's chapter on Tōson is subtitled "Wizened Apples," the special taste of which Tōson admired.[44] Arashiyama's jocose award not only foregrounds the elements of food and cooking in *shizen shugi–shishōsetsu* writing but also recognizes Tōson's mastery of this particular kind of writing. The reference to wizened apples urges the reader to contrast them with the fresh and juicy apple in Tōson's prenaturalist poem "Hatsukoi" (First Love, 1896),[45] one of the most celebrated poems in modern Japanese literature. Tōson, however, abandoned the romantic and poetic apple and instead developed a taste for wizened apples. It is not that the fresh apple and the youthful love became faded and wizened with age; it was Tōson's choice and his mission to pursue the seemingly prosaic and unappetizing.

Unsurprisingly, the kind of writing/cooking advocated and practiced by the *shizen shugi–shishōsetsu* writers is not "to everyone's taste." As a matter of fact, as we shall see, both contemporaries of writers affiliated with these literary modes and later critics have leveled scathing criticism at them, often sparking full-scale literary debates. Nevertheless, one must reiterate that the Shōyō–*shizen shugi–shishōsetsu* lineage has been regarded, if sometimes grudgingly, as forming the very core of modern Japanese fiction. Paradoxically, many of the canonical *shizen shugi* and *shishōsetsu* texts have been forgotten by the reading public, while writers such as Sōseki, Ōgai, and Tanizaki, who were labeled nonnaturalists or antinaturalists at the time and were regarded by their detractors as being popular (i.e., vulgar), pedantic, or insincere, are still read widely.

The *shizen shugi–shishōsetsu* debate is in fact much more complex than my outline would suggest, and has been the subject of a number of major works by scholars such as Karatani Kōjin, Edward Fowler, Irmela Hijiya-Kirschnereit, Tomi Suzuki, and Suzuki Sadami. For our purposes, it will suffice to say that the construct (however controversial) of what counts as "mainstream" has worked against reading and writing about food. And such is the autobiographizing nature of the *shizen shugi–shishōsetsu*, which constitutes the "mainstream," that even when critics do interest themselves in a textualized food, the urge to explain biographically takes over. The fresh apple of the much beloved "First Love" has not escaped such an approach on the part of Tōson specialists: "diligent research has revealed that when Tōson was nine or ten the lady in the house next door used to pick apples and throw them to him."[46] Even Kaikō's essay drawing attention to food in Japanese literature is titled "Nihon no sakka-tachi no shokuyoku" (The Appetite of Japanese Writers), betraying the highly conventional author-centered interest. Arashiyama's book also adheres to the tradition: ultimately he is interested in what and how each writer ate (and lived) rather than in what and how they wrote about food or eating.[47] My reservations about this sort of exegesis do not mean that biographical considerations will be absent from the chapters that follow. Biographical interest, however, does not lie at the center, biography being only one of the many tools available to contextualize food in literature.

The Menu

The chapters that follow set out to show the diverse ways in which the *shōsetsu* genre has dealt with the themes of food, eating, and cooking. Despite the neglect outlined above, food, as I have said, is everywhere in Japanese literature. The texts I consider have been selected not for their canonicity but for their relevance to the particular issue under discussion. A careful balance has had to be struck between texts that are readily available in translation and those that are obscure and inaccessible. I shall also discuss their reception—how other readers have read a particular text and how these readings have varied synchronically and have changed over time. I do not adhere to one or two particular theories or methods, for I am more interested in multiplicity than in unity. To quote Louis Marin's Introduction to *Food for Thought*:

> I have not been primarily concerned in these readings with erecting a general theory of power, language or representation; that task has already been

admirably undertaken in several disciplines. . . . I have instead sought to transmit the surprise and amazement that may be derived from a careful and attentive description, summary, or reading of certain texts. . . .[48]

In the first five chapters, texts dating from Meiji to present will be examined to illustrate historical changes and variations in the treatment of a specific topic relating to food. The topic of the first chapter is food and eating in various "literary" diaries, which range from the nonfictive to fictive, from private to public, and from poetic to prosaic. The texts examined reveal how the physical and financial conditions of the diarists, their gender, and sociohistorical factors shape or affect their desire to eat and to write. At the same time, this first chapter shows numerous instances of multiple, often conflicting, readings of the same text, proving that there are many approaches other than the conventional author-centered one.

The second and third chapters focus on "down-to-earth eating and writing," or the notion of food and literature as a necessity for all rather than a luxury for the few. The advocacy of the "down-to-earth" appears again and again throughout the century, with specific historical and ideological implications. Some texts clearly exhibit certain naturalist characteristics, and yet they present what is absent from the *shizen shugi–shishōsetsu* "mainstream" in both political and literary senses. Chapter 2 concentrates on prewar texts, including examples of late-Meiji "peasant" literature and the "proletarian" writings as well as children's literature of the 1920s and 1930s. I show how food in the prewar examples is a marker of class divisions. The recurrent motif is of workers engaged in food production being starved, and devoured, by capitalists. Chapter 3 examines gender-specific hunger in women's texts, the survival strategies of marginalized people both during and after the war, and warnings against the affluence and environmental destruction of postindustrialized Japan.

Chapter 4 turns to the theme of cannibalism in serious and popular novels. Some of the texts are based, if loosely, on historical cases of survival or pathological cannibalism, while others are purely imaginative. Key issues in these stories include ethical questions about the drive to survive, colonization, and cultural identity. The treatment of these issues, the style, and the form vary greatly, but almost all of these texts show clear signs of texts "eating" other texts, a tendency that is closely related to another common and prominent element—the question of cross-cultural contact.

Chapter 5 looks at a number of texts, mainly fictional, in which the quest for gastronomic gratification is a dominant theme. As we have already seen, the existence of such literature had long been completely overlooked; it is only in the last few decades that both contemporary and earlier, long-forgotten "gourmet novels" have attracted some attention.[49] What is evident here, particularly in prewar stories of this type, is the tendency to subvert the "mainstream" *shishō-setsu* and to present a variety of alternatives. Postwar examples, on the other hand, either advocate or resist the democratization and popularization of the gastronomic quest (to adopt a shorthand term for it). Like cannibalism, the gastronomic quest as a literary theme is deeply implicated with cultural identity, and a certain textual cannibalism is also evident.

Although each of the above chapters touches on issues concerning gender, such as how women's appetite for eating and writing was affected by modernization, nationalism, and democratization, chapter 6 deals specifically with food and eating in contemporary women's texts. Some of these texts celebrate the inclusiveness of eating (and of writing), while others deal with the fear of eating. This fear or disgust can be seen as a warning against what the complacent "gourmet boom" of the 1980s and 1990s concealed: the dangers of the market economy, environmental destruction, and continuing gender biases. Intertextual criticism frequently appears in these texts: just as eating can distort or destroy the body, the discourse on food in the canonical literature and media can be manipulative and unreliable. Bulimia and anorexia not only appear as the afflictions of some of the female protagonists but also symbolically indicate their craving for, or rejection of, knowledge and information as food.

Chapter One

Food in the Diary

[September 3, 1901]

Change of dressing in morning. Bowel movement at about 10.

[...]

Breakfast: 2 bowls steamed rice, *tsukudani*,[1] some pickled plums, 1/2 cup of milk with cocoa, a few sweet buns.

Lunch: 3 bowls rice gruel, half of bonito sashimi (half because it contained some fly eggs). Had the little yellowtail bought for supper made into sashimi, but did not eat it as it wasn't nice. 1 bowl miso soup, 3 pieces of rice cracker, one helping shaved ice with lemon syrup.

Supper: 2 bowls rice gruel, cooked yellowtail (no good), beans, potatoes, a little bit of sushi, *konnyaku* noodles. None tasted good. Had to eat with more *tsukudani*. 1 pear.[2]

The diarist is Masaoka Shiki (1867–1902), the poet-critic celebrated as the key figure in the radical modernization of the haiku and the tanka, the close friend of Natsume Sōseki, and the literary ally of Tsubouchi Shōyō.[3] He is in the last year of his life and is bedridden, being slowly consumed by tuberculosis of the spine. This process is recorded in two diaries,[4] one of them "private," the other "public." What we have just seen is a part of the private diary, which, as we will see more closely below, is a frank and honest record of, among other things, the dying man's desire, frustration, irritation, anger, pain, and worry.

To Eat, to Write, and to Live

In considering food as a thematic in modern Japanese literature, where better to begin than with the diary, which is, by definition—though admittedly a rather simplistic definition—a record of everyday activities and concerns, among which the consumption of food must necessarily have a place. This is certainly true of Shiki's diary: in it he records diligently—and obsessively—what he has eaten on each day as well as what he would like to eat or could not eat. His passion for, or concerns about, food is combined with his urge and impulse to write. The two activities, writing and eating, are both means and ends. They are also seen, and treated, as proofs of living. In his study of diaries written between 1860 and 1920, Donald Keene comments that the impulsion to keep a diary "was as natural [. . .] as it is for Japanese today to take group photographs as souvenirs of an occasion."[5] Perhaps in the age of the Internet blog (and of the digital camera and the mobile phone video), the analogy of a photograph may no longer seem as apt as it once was; the passion for blogging seems "global" rather than specifically "Japanese." It is true, however, that the diary (*nikki*) is one of the most venerable of Japanese literary genres, dating back to Heian and the *Tosa nikki* (The Tosa Diary, c. 935), the first example of the *kana nikki* (a diary written in kana as opposed to Chinese or Sino-Japanese).[6] Its content, too, tending, if we are to accept Keene's summation, towards the introspective, the personal, the emotional, the private, the intuitive, and the feminine, is seen as autochthonous in contrast to Chinese literature.[7]

The diaries I shall discuss in this chapter are, with the exception of Shiki's private diary, *Gyōga manroku*, in many respects rather different from the classical *nikki*, being either a hybrid between the *nikki* and the *shōsetsu* (and some other genres) or *nikki* (both historical and fictive) incorporated into *shōsetsu*. As mentioned in the Introduction, the *shōsetsu* is, in Noguchi's explanation, a genre that has "ingested" many other genres "through predation." The diary is certainly one of those genres "ingested" by the *shōsetsu*—an excellent example of this, as we shall see, being Ibuse Masuji's *Black Rain*. In this chapter we will also encounter various cases of the diary ingesting other texts. Hayashi Fumiko's *Diary of a Vagabond*, for example, incorporates both prose and verse texts, and both her own and someone else's. Inoue Hisashi's *Tokyo Seven Roses*, which will also be discussed in this chapter, presents a rather extreme case of numerous public and private (and even highly confidential) documents copied into a private citizen's diary.

Within the broad and amorphous genre of the *shōsetsu*, the *shishōsetsu*, in particular, shares the "introspective, personal, emotional and private" nature of the *nikki*. This *shishōsetsu* is, in Noguchi's words, the *shōsetsu* of, by, and for *watakushi*, that is, the "displayed I" (quoted in the Introduction). While neither *Black Rain* nor *Tokyo Seven Roses* is a *shishōsetsu*, *Diary of a Vagabond* seems to fit neatly into Noguchi's definition. However, Hayashi's text is not generally thought of as representative of the *shishōsetsu* because the gender of the "I" has traditionally been taken for granted to be male. This has created problems both at production and reception levels, but as Janice Brown remarks, Hayashi has successfully "made her mark writing from the position of female outsider."[8] Besides gender issues, other areas that have been the focus of studies of the *shishōsetsu* are relevant to our discussion here. Edward Fowler, for example, notes that the raison d'être of the genre "rests on the powerful *illusion* of its textual transparency—its sincerity—which lets the reader view the author's experience 'unmediated' by forms, shapes, structures, or other 'trappings' of fiction."[9] If this can be said of the *shishōsetsu*, it would seem to be all the more true of any diary, whose function and primary interest as a published text is surely to provide the reader with the experience, illusory or not—and perhaps never entirely innocent of a certain voyeurism—of viewing a private reality.

The diary as, or within, a literary text is a nexus of intersecting ambiguities. The term "literary" itself raises the question of the diary's claim to literarity. The "Diary of the Illness of Yasuko Takamaru"[10] within *Black Rain*, for example, is in itself an unassuming record of the progress of a young woman's illness, jotted down by her aunt for entirely practical purposes. One might argue that it is only the fact that it appears in the context of an undeniably literary text, and is framed by that environment, that gives it "literarity." But one might also argue that it constitutes a literary text simply because it is, in fact, an invention—a work of fiction—and works of fiction (including those in the form of diaries) are by definition literature, even if the reverse, of course, is not necessarily true—a consideration that might raise questions about the status of some other diaries incorporated in Ibuse's novel as well as of Shiki's "private" diary.

This consideration leads us to the second of the ambiguities inherent in the published diary, an ambiguity or at least an uncertainty already alluded to in the quotation from Fowler. Diaries, at least diaries that have been published, are not likely to fall neatly and unambiguously into one of two categories—on the one hand, the "authentic" diary that presents "unmediated," unadorned and unedited, "warts and all" the author's experience, and on the other, the purely fictive (whether or not openly so). They are much more likely to be positioned somewhere on a continuum that stretches from the totally unmediated through the mediated to the totally fictive. To add to the complexity of possibilities, their exact place on the continuum may be determined in a variety of ways—in other words, what makes a diary fictive at all, and determines the extent to which it is in fact so, is not necessarily predictable.

Moreover, a diary's position on the continuum is always provisional and subject, at least in theory, to revision, as in the celebrated case of Bashō's sunshine haiku in his travel diary *Oku no hosomichi* (The Narrow Road of Oku):

ara tōto	How awe-inspiring,
aoba wakaba no	On the green leaves, the young leaves,
hi no hikari	The light of the sun![11]

For two and a half centuries it was taken for granted that Bashō did indeed see the sun's rays shining on the fresh green leaves in the forest of the famous Nikkō (literally, "sunshine") mausoleum. Only when the parallel diary of Bashō's disciple and travelling companion was published (in 1943!) did it emerge that on the day of their visit it was actually raining.[12]

It is difficult to imagine (although such texts may exist) a diary that occupies the fictive end of the continuum and at the same time is seriously intended to be private, and here we come to the third ambiguity inherent in the genre. How private is any diary really intended to be? The very writing of a diary would seem inevitably to imply a reader—even if not as overtly as in Tanizaki's *Kagi* (The Key, 1956) or in the case of online diaries.[13] Does not even a thirteen-year-old diarist write, if for no one else, at least for his or her future, older self as reader? But if that is so, it is also true that a diary, even when published or at least made accessible to others, retains as an integral part of its performance the notion of its privacy and, with that, a consciousness on the part of the reader—a pleasurable consciousness—of trespassing upon another's secret space, a generic feature that leaves the diary reader curiously open to the manipulations of the diarist.

With these general considerations in mind, let us return to Shiki's diary.

A Dying Man's Appetite

I have already mentioned that the last months of Shiki's life are recorded in two separate texts, one public and the other private. The public one was serialized as *Byōshō rokushaku* (A Six-foot Sickbed) in the *Nihon shinbun* from May to September 1902, the final extract appearing just two days before Shiki's death. The text was intended for the newspaper audience who knew Shiki as the leading poet tragically being devoured by his illness. The writing of *Byōshō rokushaku* involved, as a matter of fact required—because of the seriousness of Shiki's conditions—the collaboration of people around the author, especially Shiki's sister

Ritsu (1870–1941) and his friend and disciple Takahama Kyoshi (1874–1959). The overtly public nature of this text, which was dictated daily to either Ritsu or Kyoshi, is reflected in its modern, colloquial style (*de aru, genbun itchi*) and in the choice of hiragana and kanji. Shiki's acute observations and humor, combined with his strong will to keep on writing, certainly move the reader. The overall impression of *Byōshō rokushaku*, however, is still of a public text, impersonal and masculine, qualities it shares with Shiki's critical essays. In this diary he is, in a sense, Shiki the public figure, and there is no conflict or discrepancy between the intended effect and its reception.

The private diary, on the other hand, written in the katakana-kanji combination that was the norm for men's diaries before the war,[14] and in plain, traditional *bungo* style, seems genuinely to have been intended as such: none of Shiki's family, intimate friends, or disciples had access to it, at least until after his death. Given Shiki's literary celebrity, it was inevitable that it would find its way into the public domain, though it did so only in 1918, when it was published under the title *Gyōga manroku* (Stray Notes While Lying on My Back).

Both diaries record the dying man's observations and thoughts on topics ranging from politics to poetry, and are thus in a sense also scrapbooks, containing pieces of literary criticism as boldly opinionated and humorous as those in his polemical essays, as well as passages of prose or transcriptions of poems that embody the kind of realism Shiki famously espoused and termed *shasei*.[15] But it is in *Gyōga manroku* that Shiki applies his *shasei* to his illness in all its physicality—in fact, so much so that it often jeopardizes the calm equilibrium associated with the *shasei*. Intermingled with records of visitors and conversations, his thoughts on poetry, haiku and tanka of his own or others' composition, sketches, watercolors, and ink-brush drawings, the often harrowing details of Shiki's physical condition are recorded religiously, even obsessively, in the form of simple lists or notes that can either be brief or extend over a few pages: his pain, his medication, the treatments he undergoes, and—most strikingly and even bizarrely—his daily diet.

It is astonishing just how much the invalid consumes. For example, for someone so seriously ill, two bowls of rice plus a few "sweet buns," as recorded in the above-quoted September 3, 1901 entry, would seem, to say the least, a hearty breakfast. Even if we allow for the fact that at that time rice consumption was more than twice what it was to be at the end of the century,[16] Shiki's eating does appear surprising. To cite another example, what are we to think of the seven skewered eels—along with oysters—he consumed for supper on the twelfth? Or of the *eighteen* grilled sardines he ate—among other things—for supper four days earlier? (Shiki puts small circles beside the number eighteen to emphasize it, which Yamada Yūsaku suggests is an expression of Shiki's "victorious atti-tude toward life."[17]) What is also notable is that Shiki's diet is much richer in protein than that of the average middle-class Japanese of the time. Yet he was by no means wealthy; what made this diet possible was the dedicated support of his family and friends—the latter often brought him presents of delicacies. One presumes that all this nutrition was provided and consumed in the hope of prolonging his life, if not of curing his disease.

Such an appetite may also have been a symptom of morbidity. Certainly it is evident from the beginning of the diary that Shiki's food intake is causing prob-lems and that his digestive system cannot cope. In the very first entry in the di-ary, undated but presumably that for the second of September, after listing what he has eaten that day (no fewer than four bowls of steamed rice or rice gruel at *each* meal), Shiki acknowledges that he is overeating and that this overeating is the cause of his stomach pains and vomiting. As the diary continues, his condi-tion worsens, but his eating and his obsession with eating do not diminish as his despair intensifies: he admits to prolonged bouts of bitter crying.

Despite the deeply depressing facts, the diary maintains—perhaps in keep-ing with Shiki's insistence on *shasei*—a realistic, observational tone. If it reflects the self-absorption of the invalid, this self-absorption is not of the confessional kind. The "eighteen sardines" entry is not so much an admission to bulimic eat-ing but rather, as Yamada suggests, Shiki reassuring himself that he is still alive and able—if he wants—to eat this much. His devotion to food is sometimes treated with wry humor. If his eating days are numbered, he writes, he would love to have one final feast, brought from the best restaurant in Tokyo, and he would do anything to be able to afford it—write still more essays perhaps, or sell his personal library (although to have his books, imprinted with his personal seal, browsed through by the customers of some secondhand bookshop would be embarrassing). This topic is aired at several points in the diary, although Shiki knows it is but a dream.

By late October his "only pleasure" is about to forsake him: his digestive system is finally failing, and whatever he eats gives him pain and is excreted un-digested. The diary itself breaks off at the end of November 1902, the remaining pages being taken up with poetry occasionally copied or composed and—dur-ing the following June and July—a record of morphine doses.

Compared with those of this literally painfully honest diary, the food descrip-tions in *Byōshō rokushaku* are much fewer in number and more constrained in style and content. Only a small number of the 127 entries include a dietary record, which is usually brief and simple. There are some short essays and para-graphs on topics related to food. Some of these express the author's personal preferences, but they are mostly general and impersonal observations on such matters as the etymology of food names, the difference between men's food preferences and those of women, commercial catering services, and fashions in fruit. Although the diary does include some descriptions of Shiki's physical condition, the readers of the *Nihon shinbun* are, not surprisingly, spared the harrowing details that abound in *Gyōga manroku*.

How is one to read *Gyōga manroku*? How do we read what was never (presumably) intended for our eyes? Why are we tempted to treat it as literature, if it was not intended as literature? And if it was not intended as such, why do at least some of us find it more powerful as literature than *Byōshō rokushaku*?[18] Is it the victory of unmodified, unmediated fact over the depersonalization of *shasei*? Commentators generally seem to have treated *Gyōga manroku* as supplementary to the public diary, and it is clear that it provides a detailed account of Shiki's day-to-day existence against the background of which the *Byōshō rokushaku* can be read. But only *can* be read. Is *Gyōga manroku* essential to an understanding of the public text?

An alternative approach, that of treating the two diaries as equal and mutually complementary, is adopted by the poet-psychiatrist Saitō Mokichi (1879–1953), although it is his reading of the private diary that is of the greater interest. Mokichi believed that it is vital to know Shiki's view of his illness, death, and life in order to understand the "calm, clear-eyed, and *outpouring* nature of his literary output."[19]

> In such agony Shiki found his only consolation in what he called "the pleasure of eating and the freedom of writing." In his resignation he wailed, and in his wailing he was resigned, and at times reached beyond resignation. This state of mind beyond resignation means to enjoy the natural life that remains, after submitting to destiny. [. . .] Thus Shiki enjoyed eating and drinking, as we see in *Gyōga manroku*, and took pleasure in writing and sketching flowers and plants, as we see in *Gyōga manroku*, *Bokujū itteki*, and *Byōshō rokushaku*. He also pondered objectively on death.[20]

Mokichi notes that while many other writers who suffered from tuberculosis turned in their desperation to religion and the metaphysical world, Shiki remained in the ordinary physical world and continued to observe it. This may be Mokichi's public reading of Shiki's diaries and of his eating: his rather less public—though published, and obviously more related to his other interest as a psychiatrist—interpretation seems to be that Shiki's obsession with eating was a compensation for the loss of his libido or at least his inability to satisfy it because of his illness.[21] Ironically, Mokichi himself was to become the object of a literary-journalistic examination of *his* private desires as revealed in his own diaries, notably his obsession with eels.[22] It is hard to see how the number of eels Mokichi consumed in his life could contribute to the understanding of his tanka. By the same token, one might wonder what the invalid Shiki's compulsive eating has to tell us, but it does seem to have been treated as a legitimate and even essential element in understanding his work.

Such "public" readings of the "private" diary in the aftermath of its publication tended to pass over the more disturbing and unsightly details of eating, vomiting, and excreting. It is only relatively recently that literary journalists have started to discuss openly the manic appetite of the dying Shiki. Arashiyama Kōzaburō reads it as a somewhat lurid drama of the will:

> Eating for Shiki was an expedition into his own desire. Knowing well that eating would lead to infernal agony, he insisted on eating, with great determination. He ate and he listened to the voice of his emaciated body. [. . .] Just as a boundless, searching mind drives the scholar into the intellectual labyrinth, Shiki throws his dying body into the very crucible of human desire.[23]

For Arashiyama, then, Shiki's eating is not the defeat of the will in the face of an uncontrollable physical compulsion but a triumph of his will over his body's incapacity. This tenacious will, in Arashiyama's view, made it possible for Shiki to face and observe the aggression and self-destructiveness of appetite.[24] Whereas *Byōshō rokushaku* was written for the self in others, continues Arashiyama, *Gyōga manroku* was written to discover and examine the other within the self.

Mokichi and Arashiyama, like most other commentators, read *Gyōga manroku* as part of a critical enterprise, that of understanding, or reimagining, Shiki's life and art. Whether they are justified in doing so may be left undecided here, and it is interesting to turn to Kanai Keiko, who offers a very different reading.[25] The focus of her attention is not Shiki but his sister, Masaoka Ritsu. Ritsu, three years her brother's junior, looked after him for several years. Changing his dressings (mentioned in the first line of the quoted September 3 entry) was but one of the numerous routine tasks assigned to her. It was (Shiki tells us) a highly demanding and distressing task, for even the most careful and gentle touch on Shiki's diseased back, which oozed blood and pus, made him scream in agony.

As Kanai notes, in two consecutive entries in *Gyōga manroku* Shiki attacks his sister viciously. Ritsu, he writes on September 20, is a coldhearted woman of reason, who cares for the sick out of obligation and without real sympathy. It is not clear what has actually triggered this rage, but Kanai seems to be right in relating it to the "*dango* incident" of September 4. The food list for September 4 includes sweet *dango*; Shiki adds a brusque note in brackets about a "dispute" caused by these small dumplings. The reader can gather the nature of this dispute from the following, part of the September 20 indictment of his sister as coldhearted:

> For example, even when the invalid repeatedly expresses his wish to eat some *dango*, she takes no notice. Anyone with any sympathy would immediately go out and buy some for him. The idea would never occur to Ritsu. So if one feels like eating *dango*, one needs to tell her directly to go and get some. She does obey orders.[26]

He continues to complain about his sister, who, in his opinion, cares more about her pet canaries than about her brother. As Kanai remarks, Shiki sounds like a child, demanding sweets and crying for undivided attention. On the following day he again grumbles about his sister's stubbornness and bad temper. His rage over the *dango*, however, seems to have subsided somewhat, as he also acknowledges the demanding nature and vital importance of her work, as well as her selfless devotion to this completely unpaid work.

> Ritsu is not just a nurse; she is at the same time a cook, a housekeeper, and my secretary. She acts as my librarian, and she prepares fair (though not perfect) copies of my manuscripts. With all this work, she spends not even a tenth of what a nurse would ask as wages. Her meals consist of [rice and] only one dish, vegetables or pickles. She seems never to dream of buying meat or fish for herself.[27]

Shiki is well aware of the highly contagious nature of his illness, and he fears that his sister, who is in the closest contact with him, may one day come down with it. He writes that he would prefer to die before this happens.

Kanai tells us that after Shiki's death Ritsu managed to further her education and have her own career, as a teacher of sewing at a technical college for women.[28] Unlike her celebrated brother, Ritsu left no diary, private or public. We know of the life of this evidently brave and resilient woman only through her brother's writing and through the memoirs of others. Ritsu was, to borrow Kanai's phrase, "a woman who saw but did not write."[29] She looked daily upon the oozing holes in her brother's back, which he himself could not see, and witnessed many other things that neither he nor his friends saw; but what she saw is unrecorded. Only with the advent of women writers such as Kōda Aya (see chapter 3) would the perspective of women as domestic cooks and carers find expression in autobiography and fiction.

To be fair to the invalid at the center of *Gyōga manroku*, Shiki was—as we have glimpsed—well aware of his sister's sacrifice as cook and carer. The frustration of his "six-foot confinement" might drive him to rage and binge eating,[30] but he always returned to a fairer understanding of the situation. On October 27, 1901, the family of three celebrated his birthday with a five-course dinner—for two—delivered from a restaurant. After recording the full menu, Shiki comments:

> People often say that nothing is as boring as restaurant food, as it is always the same. To me, who eat the same old sashimi in my sickbed day in and day out, it is unusual and enjoyable. To my mother and sister, who usually eat their pickles in the kitchen corner, it must be even more unusual and enjoyable.[31]

This awareness, however, does not quite lead to a change of attitude toward his sister, let alone to any concern for gender equality; he shows sympathy toward women who are obliged to take all the responsibility for housework and nursing, but the perspective is always that of a male patient. Many of the thoughts expressed in *Gyōga manroku* appear in *Byōshō rokushaku*, in a greatly modified and extended form. On July 17, 1902, for instance, Shiki discusses the importance of education for women who are caring for invalids. He suggests simplifying housework: there is no need to clean the house every day or for all meals to be homemade. The most important thing, he insists, is to allow the carer to devote herself to respecting and satisfying the patient's needs and wishes. He also adds that few women are capable of this because most lack the knowledge and common sense required.[32] We can detect here the reverberation of the *dango* incident, but now the personal attack has been transformed into a general discourse, one based on clearly patriarchal ideas.

A Vagabond's Appetite

It is perhaps a relief to move from the frank record of a dying man's appetite to the equally unvarnished record of the hungers of a healthy young woman: Hayashi Fumiko's *Hōrōki* (Diary of a Vagabond).[33] Hayashi is known for her assertion that to eat and to write are the only two reasons for living.[34] *Hōrōki* is generally read as an autobiographical novel in the form of Hayashi's diary, which covered the years from 1922 to 1926. The complete edition of *Hōrōki* is divided into three parts, each of which was published as a separate volume (parts 1 and 2 in 1930, part 3 in 1949). As we shall see, the history of the novel's publication turned out to have significant consequences for the private-public relationship of each part to the others. Within each part, entries appear to be arranged in chronological order,[35] although only the month is given, with no indication of the day or the year. Notably, the three parts do not represent three consecutive periods; what Keene has called the "ready-made structure" of diaries—namely, "the passage of the days"[36]—is only partially retained in this text. As Kanai Keiko remarks, a reader of the complete version who expected something in the nature of a Bildungsroman involving the linear progress of time "would be perplexed by the mere cycling of seasons and the sudden reappearance of those who are supposed to have departed from the narrative."[37]

The mere cycling of seasons is suggestive of the classical genre of *monogatari* or *uta monogatari*. Like the early-tenth-century *Ise monogatari* (The Tale of Ise), *Hōrōki* relates scenes and episodes from the life of one person. Whereas the classic tale, also known as *Zaigo ga chūjō nikki* (The Diary of Ariwara no Narihira), was written not by the renowned poet and expert in amorous affairs Narihira himself but by an anonymous writer, *Hōrōki* expects the reader to treat its narrator-diarist as identical with its author. The poems in *Ise monogatari* are mostly Narihira's own, although some are anonymous or composed by others. In Hayashi's *Hōrōki* we find popular songs of the time, together with poems ranging from well-known tanka and other types of poetry by Ishikawa Takuboku, Kitahara Hakushū, Murō Saisei, and Tagore to lesser-known works by the modernist poet-artist Murayama Kaita (1896–1919) and finally Hayashi's own poems, which strongly reflect the avant-garde movement of the period.[38] These songs and poems are interspersed with accounts of the daily struggle of the narrator to eat (and to write) and of seasonal and other changes—jobs, houses, and lovers.

It has often been noted that the charm of *Hōrōki* and the secret of its commercial success lie in the seemingly unmodified, frank style adopted by the female narrator and the strength of her will to survive. Hayashi first emerged from obscurity with the 1928 serialization of some of the *Hōrōki* segments in the feminist literary magazine *Nyonin geijutsu* (Women's Arts), and then shot to celebrity status after the 1930 publication of *Hōrōki* parts 1 and 2. Overnight, so to speak, Hayashi's writing had solved (at least partly) her economic problems, and her "private" diary had become a commodity and a literary text for public consumption. The success and fame patently affected the reception and further production (i.e., the third part) of *Hōrōki*. Once part 1 was a best-seller, Hayashi's writing became a vital source of income for her family. At the end of part 2 Hayashi regards her present (1930) life as "cutting [her]self up into pieces like advertisements and blowing them away in all directions."[39] For readers, too, the narrator of the diary is no longer an unknown young woman but a famous writer with well-known literary and Marxist friends. The driving hunger that forms the core of the first part, if present at all, loses much of its power and urgency in the second part, despite the fact that the sequel contains, as Joan Ericson points out, "more graphic elaboration and incriminating detail" of other matters such as abortion and physical abuse.[40] It is instructive to examine this transformation a little more closely.

It is well known that Hayashi was inspired to write this text by Knut Hamsun's *Hunger* (1890). If, as Akutagawa Ryūnosuke wrote, Hamsun was the first in world literature to discover and present how appetite contains poetry,[41] the first part of *Hōrōki* can certainly claim pioneering status in modern Japanese literature for its treatment of hunger from a woman's perspective. *Hōrōki* is reminiscent of Colette's *La Vagabonde* (1911) in more than just its title: even if Colette's Renée is a bourgeoise fleeing the pain of a broken love affair whereas Hayashi's narrator is battling real deprivation, there are, interestingly, many common elements in these two autobiographical texts. Each is narrated by a woman who strives to find independence. Both narratives include lyric monologues on the subjects of loneliness, love, sadness, and joy, as well as vivid descriptions of a metropolis and its cafés and music halls where the narrators find work, and of the wide range of people they meet and interact with as friends, admirers, lovers, co-workers, neighbors and patrons.

But for the narrator of *Hōrōki* starvation threatens herself and her family; she can never "get used to eating nothing" as Renée says she can.[42] Her being a "vagabond" is a consequence of this perpetual hunger. Since childhood she has had to move from one place to another, from one job to another, and from one relationship to another in search of an escape from poverty and starvation. This is completely different from Renée's "lately acquired liking for uprootings and travel [which] fits in happily with the peaceful fatalism natural to the *bourgeoise* that [she is]."[43] Another fundamental difference between the two vagabond narrators is that one has a successful writing career that has been temporarily interrupted for personal reasons, while the other has not yet gained recognition. Renée has already proved herself as a fiction writer and knows that her readers are waiting for her next novel. Hayashi's narrator, on the other hand, has difficulty selling her manuscripts and supporting herself.

The long list of the jobs the narrator takes in *Hōrōki* begins with peddling cheap merchandise such as food, fans, and underwear on the streets with her mother. Although hardly profitable, she considers this much better than her previous job at a candy factory.[44] The narrator's curriculum vitae continues to expand: she works as a shop assistant, a waitress in cheap cafés, a babysitter, an office clerk, a housemaid, and so on. This may give the reader the impression that the narrator, in chronic destitution in both childhood and early adulthood, did not receive proper schooling, but Hayashi's biography shows that she completed both primary and secondary education. Neither the first two parts nor the brief introductory section, "Hōrōki izen" (Before *Hōrōki*), which is placed at the beginning of part 1, mentions the narrator's school days. Only in part 3 is it briefly mentioned that her teacher used to call her hands *dinpuru hando* (dimpled hands).[45] Even in this recollection the emphasis is placed on the narrator's poverty, with youth her only possession, rather than on nostalgia for the "good old days." Nevertheless, the reader realizes for the first time here that the narrator as a young woman was not completely deprived of bourgeois culture and education. Thus, while the struggles of the working girl that are depicted in *Hōrōki* are no doubt based on Hayashi's own experience, they are not depicted without mediation and editing.

Hayashi, unlike Sata Ineko (1904–1998) or their mutual friend Hirabayashi Taiko (1905–1972), who appears in later entries in *Hōrōki* as "Taiko-san," was not directly or seriously involved in the Marxist movement or in the production of so-called proletarian literature. However, her text does depict her firsthand experience as a working woman and expresses her deep sympathy for her fellow workers and neighbors, some of whom are key figures in left-wing activities. Through these experiences and associations, and through her avid reading, Hayashi is aware of many of the things that her activist friends are fighting for. She is, as is clear in part 3, much more interested in and sympathetic towards anarchism and Dadaism than in communism. What actually motivates her, however, is neither a sociopolitical cause nor an ideological conviction; it is her own survival and her search for an independence that will allow her to eat and write to her heart's content:

> I haven't had anything since this morning. Selling a few children's stories and poems did not provide money enough for a month's white rice. Hunger makes me dizzy and it makes my ideology grow moldy. There isn't any proletariat or bourgeoisie in my head. All I long for is a handful of white rice.[46]

Similarly, the narrator does not advocate the emancipation of women, though a recurrent theme is her aversion to being "fed" (*kuwashite morau*) by a man. Early in part 1, in an entry dated "December x," she is working for meager wages in a factory that manufactures celluloid toys. An admirer, a worker in a printing factory who is boarding in the same house as she is, offers financial help. His courting present is not the expensive bunch of flowers that Renée's admirer sends, but meat. Though far from impressed by him, and finding his request that she chop up some spring onions simply impertinent, she cannot help but feel some sympathy for this kind but unattractive man called Matsuda. After helping him to cook, she notes, "What kind of feelings the meat he gave me on a plate provoked, as it passed through my throat! I pictured in my mind all kinds of people. Everything seemed meaningless. And I thought I wouldn't mind getting married to Matsuda."[47]

When she visits his room for the first time after this meal, however, the sight of him putting rice cakes in a basket in preparation for the New Year makes her feel an even stronger aversion to him than before. It is clear to her that marriage would not be a solution. She reconsiders her plan to change jobs yet again: "working in a sushi restaurant would be boring, too."[48]

The entry immediately after this includes the line "I am a woman with a weakness for men."[49] The context of this entry dated "April x," however, clearly shows that the man in question here is not Matsuda but someone involved in the theater, who has a wife and also seems to be having an affair with a young actress. Two entries later, still in April, she writes:

> This is my first day at work. *To be fed by a man is harder than to chew mud.* The work I have found—and I didn't worry about respectability—is a job as a waitress in a sukiyaki house. "One sirloin!" Sashaying up the steps, I felt like singing a beautiful song with all my heart. Every face in the crowd in the hall looked like part of an interesting film. Going up and down the stairs with plates of meat in my hands, the inside of my sash gradually gets a bit fatter with money. Inside the room there's no whiff of poverty. Instead, it's filled with the pleasant smell of meat being cooked.[50]

This new place of work is indeed the same kind of restaurant that the poet-artist Takamura Kōtarō (1883–1956) passionately admired in his 1921 poem "Yonekyū no bansan" (Dinner at Yonekyū), part of which reads:

> An August evening steams up now in Yonekyū.
>
> My friend and I—in a trance,
> Praising the nutritious, mountainous beef at Yonekyū,

Hearing in this vigorous human appetite and bestiality the irrepressible voice of
  nature,
Feeling the unfathomable mind of the one who gave such a blind element to the
  motive power of this world,
With tears at each little omnipresent sight of pure and beautiful human nature,
Sending our embraced and embracing love
Even to the serenely world-wise reticent greetings of the old head-waitress,
Showering as members of this crowd our sincere passion over their carefree
  heads,
With mysterious energy growing inside us—calmly left our table.

An August evening steams up now in Yonekyū.[51]

Takamura's poem, "the best sukiyaki song ever written," as Kaikō Takeshi puts
it,[52] captures the essence of happy, energetic, and uninhibited eating, free from
fear, anger, guilt or morbid obsession.

This kind of beef restaurant began to appear at the beginning of Meiji. The
Japanese enthusiastically embraced beef, the consumption of which, together
with that of other four-footed animals, had been prohibited by Buddhism.[53] Sukiyaki quickly became a popular dish, the new taste of "civilization." Notably,
although beef itself was regarded as a Western food, sukiyaki was a Japanese
invention, which used the traditional seasonings of soy sauce, sake, and sugar
and other ingredients such as spring onions, tofu, and konnyaku noodles. Kanagaki Robun (1829–1894) captures the early-Meiji enthusiasm for beef in his
Edo-style illustrated comic fiction Agura nabe (Sitting around the Cooking Pot,
1871–1872),[54] which takes the form of the monologues of customers at a beef
restaurant. These customers include all sorts of people, from samurai to prostitutes, from the fashionable to the unsophisticated. Although Robun made full
use of these differences among the customers for his comic ends, the beef restaurant really did offer the setting for a form of modern and inclusive eating. By
Takamura's and Hayashi's time the novelty value of eating beef had dissipated,
but the warm, happy, and inclusive atmosphere remained.[55]

The narrator of Hōrōki feels this happiness and energy and is fascinated by
the crowd, each person with a different face and background, echoing Robun's
comic prose and Takamura's poem. But she is there not to sit and join in this
seemingly all-inclusive eating experience but to work in order to eat. By the end
of the evening she is exhausted from constantly going up and down the stairs.
The last tram has long gone, and she has to walk home through the dark streets,
to be with her actor lover, a "man as cold as goods."[56]

Going back to the beginning of this entry, one notices that the first sentence describes the narrator's parting from the actor on a street corner "in a cold fashion, like strangers."[57] The parting, obviously, is only temporary; he goes to his rehearsal and she goes to work. The last sentence describes her hurrying home to be with this "cold" man. The middle section of the entry begins with the passage quoted above, with the declaration that "*to be fed by a man is harder than to chew mud*," and depicts the narrator's initial elation at her new work, followed by physical hardship and the misery of going home alone. This forms a clear triadic structure, beginning with the cold parting and ending with the cold homecoming, with the steamy, lively restaurant scene in between. It is also obvious that this passage was written not on the day the events occurred but on the following day or some time later, as the demanding work and late homecoming must have left the narrator exhausted. Such an interval between an event and its recording is common enough in the process of diary writing, yet the structuredness here seems to suggest the shift from personal diary to *monogatari*.

There is another prominent sign of this shift. The italicized sentence "*to be fed by . . .*" is distinguished in this way because it ends in *desu*, while all other sentences are in plain style. This happens frequently in *Hōrōki*. Whenever the narrator makes an important statement, one she wishes to highlight, even if it is in self-mockery, as is often the case, she tends to use the polite *desu-masu* style or the humble *de gozaimasu*. "I am a woman with a weakness for men," for example, ends in *desu*. Similarly, "An empty woman—that is me" (*de gozaimasu*), "After all I am soiled by this world" (*de gozaimasu*), "I am a great fool to interpret [. . .]" (*desu*), and "This is all I have as ammunition for my desperate fight" (*de gozaimasu*).[58] The use of these forms in the otherwise plain-style writing is clearly intentional; it draws the reader's attention and creates the effect that the narrator is talking, rather than writing, to an audience. The question of who constitutes this audience may not produce a simple answer. Assuming that this occurs in the *ur*text—the personal diary written at different times—it may have been the author's alter ego, or the diary itself, as its symbol ("Dear Diary, . . ."). It is not impossible, however, that the narrator of the *ur*diary had somewhere in mind the hope or intention to publish it one day. It is not clear whether the *desu* and *de gozaimasu* endings were added in the process of editing the *ur*diary for publication or what kind of modifications were made in that process, except that we do have the following remark, attached to the end of part 2: "This *Hōrōki* is just my surface; my [real] diary is endlessly filled with descriptions of suffering too desperate to face."[59]

What we do know, however, is that the use of *desu* and *de gozaimasu* in fiction gives an orality to the written narrative, and that they are often used in children's stories and fiction narrated by (pseudo-)historical characters.[60] The above examples differ from these common uses of *desu* and *de gozaimasu* in that they stand out from the rest of the text. Apart from emphatic and self-mocking examples such as we saw above, the use of these endings is limited strictly to the narrator's directly addressing someone specific, perhaps a character in the book to whom she would like to explain something (or whom she would like to rebuke, encourage, or console) but to whom for various reasons she cannot actually speak. All other instances occur within quoted dialogues or letters. Interestingly, however, the epilogue of part 2 mixes the plain and *desu-masu* styles almost indiscriminately, as we see in the following passages, in which *desu-masu* sentences are italicized:

> *I love my kitchen.* Needless to say I love my family. And I resign myself with my eyes closed to the fate of growing old peacefully among them.
>   [. . .]
> —I do not trust my blood relations. They are much harder to deal with than strangers. It is painful to think that they love me because I work hard. *Painful as it is, in the end I nestle close to them and chop daikon and carrots.*[61]

Even here it may be possible to find some pattern; yet the frequent switching between the polite and plain styles and the seemingly self-contradictory statements seem to suggest that the narrator, who has carefully constructed the "unmediated" style of *Hōrōki* parts 1 and 2, has been exhausted by the long battle to eat and write and by the effect of the commercial success of her writing upon her relationship with her family. And yet we also sense that this kind of stylistic confusion and this fatigue must be an integral component of the "unmediated" narrative of the now public figure that is Hayashi Fumiko.

Given this epilogue to part 2, the selection of entries in each part seems to suggest a slightly different artistic intention in each case. While the theme of part 1 is undoubtedly the narrator's eating and writing for survival, part 2 seems to place more weight on her relationships with other people. This is despite the fact that each part covers different episodes from more or less the same period and regardless of the fact that many of the people mentioned in part 1 reappear in parts 2 and 3. The first half of part 2 hardly mentions hunger; instead the relational problems between the narrator and her lover/admirer/husband and family or between her friends and their lovers and relations occupy much more space than in part 1.

Part 3 is usually explained as comprising material that was omitted from the prewar publications for fear of censorship. Indeed, there are some references to the "madness of His Imperial Majesty,"[62] anarchism,[63] and women's sexual desire, all of which would have caused a problem in 1930. If one expected something dramatically different or new, however, part 3 would disappoint. It is another cycling of seasons, to use Kanai Keiko's phrase, and what we see is seemingly endless variations on the familiar themes: hunger and problematic relationships, especially the "weakness for men." This is by no means to imply that part 3 is less effective than the previous parts. The oft-quoted poem (?) of four short lines, "Ude-tamago tonde koi" (Fly to Me, Boiled Eggs),[64] is found in this part. The complexity of the narrator's love for her mother, too, is much more vividly present in this part than in the others. As regards style and content, however, there is no great difference between the prewar and postwar publications.

What *is* dramatically different about part 3 is, quite apart from the literary position of Hayashi, the general social situation; if the hunger and poverty of the *Hōrōki* narrator were not uncommon in the 1920s, hers was still an extreme case. The war brought hunger closer to everyone, as we shall see shortly, even to those who had previously experienced no fear of deprivation. Hayashi does not attach any preface or epilogue to part 3 to relate its content to her prewar publications or her present conditions. The reader is expected to read this as a sequel to parts 1 and 2, even though it does not "progress" in chronological terms. Furthermore, despite the fact that the gap between the events described and the time of publication now extends to more than twenty years, and despite the author's 1930 remarks that the published *Hōrōki* consisted of the mere "surface" of her *ur*diary, the reader is expected to treat this third part as the frank and honest diary of a young woman—in fact even franker and more honest than the previous parts, given the postwar freedom of speech. It is tempting to say, however, that for Hayashi, an established and popular prewar writer, and one whose association with wartime propaganda attracted severe criticism, the publication of this third part functioned as a source of new energy and impetus for her postwar writing. It may be that by returning to the very beginning of her writing career—to those hungry days characterized by resilience and hope—she managed to write such important works as "Bangiku" (Late Chrysanthemum, 1948) and *Ukigumo* (Drifting Clouds, 1951) in the short period between the publication of part 3 and her death in 1951.[65] Her unfinished novel, her most ambitious in the opinion of many critics, is titled *Meshi* (Food, Meals).[66]

Food, War, and Diaries: *Black Rain*

So far we have seen food, appetite, and eating in both private and public diaries, with or without modification for publication. Ibuse Masuji's *Kuroi ame* (Black Rain, 1966) clearly differs in that it is a nonautobiographical novel, has no poet or novelist as its narrator, and is a compilation of actual and fictive texts. Readings of this text, widely recognized as a powerful literary account of the devastation brought by the atomic bomb to ordinary people in Hiroshima, have understandably focused primarily on the historic events and secondly on the personal tragedy of the protagonist's niece. It has been widely known that the protagonist, Shizuma Shigematsu, was modeled on a historical, if obscure, person named Shigematsu Shizuma.[67] Embedded in the novel are Shigematsu's diary and many other diaries and documents, some of which are quoted from or based on existing documents, that is, the *urtexts*. The fictional diary form had been adopted by Ibuse in earlier works such as *Sazanami gunki* (The Waves, 1930) and "Aru shōjo no senji nikki" (A Young Girl's Wartime Diary, 1943), but never before *Kuroi ame* had he incorporated so many different diaries in one work. Within these secondary narratives some other voices and writings are included. While this polyphonic aspect of the novel—and the humor and understatement that are quintessentially Ibuse's[68]—have been discussed by many critics, it was Sakaki Atsuko's careful and insightful reading that drew attention for the first time to the significance of what she calls the "web of interactions of intentions and effects of the narrative performance":[69]

> We are moved not only by the significance of the incident that is retold but also by the passion and persistence of the writers and readers inside the text, which are so conspicuous in this narrative. It is not simply a conglomeration of secondary narratives connected by the omniscient narrator's remarks. Rather, the text consists of acts of writing and reading by which incorporated texts come into the action. It is with the particular circumstances under which people write and read that texts are generated.[70]

In contrast to the texts discussed above, and also to some historical diaries written during the war such as those of Furukawa Roppa (1903–1961) and Uchida Hyakken (1889–1971),[71] food is by no means a central issue here. Rather—and this is what makes this text special among Japanese war literature—food operates as an important signifier of ordinariness in the midst of extraordinary circumstances.[72]

The most striking instance of this is the document "Hiroshima nite senjika ni okeru shoku-seikatsu" (Diet in Wartime Hiroshima), written in mid-1950 by Shigematsu's wife, Shigeko,[73] at his request and incorporated into the primary narrative of the novel. Shigematsu has been copying his own wartime diary in order to donate it to a local school library and has come up with the idea of attaching Shigeko's document as an appendix to his "history."[74] Notably, Shigematsu's copying of his personal diary is also motivated by the need to clear up a "rumor" about the health of his niece, Yasuko; before submitting it to the school library, he intends to show the copy to Yasuko's go-between together with Yasuko's own diary, which has been copied by Shigeko. This is all for the purpose of proving that Yasuko was not in the directly affected area at the time of the bombing and that she has no signs of radiation sickness. The private diaries of Yasuko and Shigematsu are thus to be used by the couple for the personal but social purpose of removing obstacles to the desirable and desired marriage of their niece. Shigeko's document, however, has no such specific or ulterior social purpose; it is intended merely as a record of the food situation, written by an ordinary housewife. In copying the diaries, Shigematsu and Shigeko inevitably face the dilemma of whether or not they should omit some parts—namely the description of Yasuko being rained on by black rain—that would raise further suspicion about her condition. This dilemma also functions within the primary narrative as an important clue to the curious absence of the person in question, Yasuko, from the scenes of copying and reading her own diary, as well as to her tragic destiny. In contrast, writing about the wartime food shortage does not affect anyone personally.

The intended audience of Shigeko's record is a public one, but she is not a professional writer. Her choice of paper (letter pad) and the "quasi-epistolary" *desu-masu* (and occasional *de gozaimasu*) style suggest, as Sakaki points out, that she is "conscious of herself and how she writes"; she does not "pretend to be objective" or try to conform to the discursive conventions expected in public documents.[75] That she is not a great stylist is obvious from the awkward title; a teacher of composition would probably suggest that the phrase order should be changed to "Senjika no Hiroshima ni okeru shoku-seikatsu" or something similar.

Paradoxically, this awkwardness and total lack of literary aspirations or experience in writing for the public qualify Shigeko to be an authentic representative of ordinary women. Unlike Shiki and Hayashi Fumiko, she has no passion or obsession about her own eating or writing; she has simply been urged by her husband to write about what they were eating in wartime Hiroshima because in his opinion "what the family eats is really [her] affair, as mistress of the house."[76] Shigeko understands this, and includes in her document exactly what is expected: "the unbelievably meager diet of the Shizuma family in wartime,"[77] as her husband puts it. What Shigematsu initially wanted were some notes about their family's meals or "better still" a list of all their menus. He knows, however, that such a list would be difficult to make, as it has to be produced almost five years after the event.

What Shigeko writes, then, is not a diary but a memoir, or a report of food consumed by her family—herself, Shigematsu, and Yasuko. She knows, however, that it will be treated as an appendix to her husband's "history," his diary. However personal the content of their documents may be, they are to become public property. And this change of status from private to public is intended by these ordinary writers to contribute to the public memory of the extraordinary. On a private level the couple is deeply concerned about their niece's future; on a public level they feel obliged to leave an accurate record of what they know.

That the public is intertwined with the private is evident in the wartime food situation; the private sphere cannot be separated from the public. Shigeko begins her document by explaining the general situation and the workings of food rationing, the neighborhood association, and the black market. Under the wartime circumstances it is impossible for a private citizen to live and to eat as such. One literally needs to share rationed food and information about it not only with one's family but also with other members of the association. Food from the black market has to be cooked and consumed discreetly—boiling rather than broiling, for example, to keep the appetizing smell in the house—so that it will not raise any suspicions (or jealousy) among the neighbors. The impossibility of maintaining one's privacy comes up again and again in Shigematsu's diary and those of others and is closely connected to the plot surrounding Yasuko's tragedy.

The descriptions of food in Shigeko's writing vividly demonstrate not only the extent of the "unspeakable" food shortage but also how ordinary people tried to cope with it, by using substitute ingredients, fuel, and seasonings; by planting vegetables in the backyard; and by collecting whatever was edible, from weeds to grubs. Despite the amateurish title of Shigeko's document, the reader immediately realizes that this is not an arid and boring record of the infamous wartime food shortage. It has an understated humor, satire, and social criticism—all Ibuse's specialties.[78] To give just a few examples, people, desperate for anything to eat, form queues without knowing what they are queuing for. In a textbook Miyazawa Kenji's famous poem is changed by teachers because the "four gō of unhulled rice a day"[79] mentioned in it as the diet for an ideally simple and frugal life exceeds the rationed amount, which has been reduced to three *gō*. And Mrs. Miyaji, a neighbor who publicly (on a train—on her way to buy black-market food) expresses her opinion about this, declaring it an insult to learning and that she "wouldn't be surprised if [children] even started getting ideas about the Japanese history they learn at school," is summoned by the authorities.

> "We know quite well you've been going to buy black-market goods," they said. "Such people have no business making impertinent remarks about textbooks. Irresponsible talk in wartime is a matter that's too serious for the ordinary civil or criminal code." The way they spoke, it was almost as though they were suggesting it was a breach of the National General Mobilization Law, which was a capital offense, of course. By that time, everybody was taking care what they said in front of others.[80]

Shigeko, unlike Mrs. Miyaji, never directly criticizes the wartime authorities, but her position is clear from the episodes she recounts and when she allows herself to wonder what kind of food was served at the Imperial Hotel to its VIP guests from the Greater East Asia Co-Prosperity Sphere and various organizations connected to the Foreign Ministry. Furthermore, her concluding words carry a clear and strong antiwar message:

> Before the war, Hiroshima was known as a place with plenty of produce both from the sea and the country, and although it was so big, there were no slums. But living in Hiroshima I realized, as they say, that in a long drawn out war it's a case of the larger the town, the shorter its inhabitants go of food. And I realized, too, that war's a sadistic killer of human beings, young and old, men and women alike.[81]

Writing in 1950, Shigeko does not need to fear the Japanese authorities, although the Allied Occupation continues. But the neighborhood watch is still very much alive in a different form, and she and her husband are especially cautious when it comes to the "rumor" about Yasuko. The generally understated tone of the document makes these final words stand out.

Shigematsu's diary, written in 1945, is more reserved about expressing antiwar sentiments or criticism of the military and the bureaucracy. Nevertheless, the shortage of food, fuel, and just about everything else and the arrogance and corruption of the authorities are recorded not only through his own experiences but through those related to him by others. In such episodes food often plays a pivotal role, indicating—both graphically and symbolically—the victimization of ordinary people. This is clear from Shigematsu's description of Yokogawa Station shortly after the blast, completely deserted and littered with numerous objects:

> The lunch-boxes were particularly numerous, and I was oddly shocked—no wonder, perhaps, when the food shortage made eating loom so large in one's mind—at the way their contents were all upset. The rice-balls were not good plain rice, but rice mixed with barley, rice mixed with soybeans from which all the oil had already been extracted, rice mixed with vegetables of a kind, rice mixed with the pressed-out leftovers from making bean curd. To go with the rice, pickled *daikon*, and nothing else. Everything testified to the mad scramble that had occurred a while ago.[82]

The sight makes Shigematsu utter the following, to the alarm of a cautious acquaintance:

> "I'd like the enemy to take a look at those lunch boxes lying there. If only they could see those rice-balls, I doubt if they'd bother to come raiding any more. There's been enough stupid waste like this! Why don't people realize how we feel?"[83]

And again, towards the end of the lengthy and detailed entry for August 6, Shigematsu includes an anecdote he heard from a fellow train passenger about an incident that had taken place two or three days earlier:

> [A]n army lieutenant had taken his boots off and was sprawled out over a whole seat, even though the train was jammed with passengers. The outrageousness of his conduct was plain, yet nobody took it upon himself to remonstrate with him. [...] Some time passed, and the train was drawing into Tokuyama, when one of the passengers tipped half a cooked rice-ball into each of the officer's boots, then proceeded to get off with the most innocent air in the world. At this, another passenger carefully shook each boot in turn, to make sure the rice had gone right down to the toes, before alighting from the train in his turn. He had shaken the boots, of course, to make sure that a sacrifice so noble—considering the scarcity of food—should have the very maximum effect. The army man remained fast asleep. The passengers standing nearby who had witnessed the scene looked at his sleeping form with grins on their faces, though several of them moved along to other coaches for fear of getting embroiled.[84]

This delightful story of a small act of revenge by ordinary people, using food as a weapon, certainly comes as light relief after a series of graphic descriptions of the horrendous scenes witnessed by Shigematsu that day. It also fits nicely with the theme of ordinariness within the extraordinary. That this is told by someone on a train that has stopped for a long time, and that his companion nudges him to remind him of the danger of telling such a story to strangers, echoes both the earlier lunch-box passage and the Mrs. Miyaji episode.

As noted earlier, food is an important signifier of the ordinary. It may cause jealousy, deceit, conflict, or bullying, but it may also support the needy and strengthen relationships. Diet also has an important significance in regard to radiation sickness. As no effective treatment has been found, all one can do is to take plenty of nutrition and rest. Food is therefore one of the last hopes for the victims and their families. Shigematsu, who has relatively mild symptoms of radiation sickness, chooses leisurely fishing and a small joint venture in carp farming. Three-quarters of the way through the novel, and with only three more entries to be copied, the reader discovers, first through a note at the end of the August 12 entry added by Shigematsu while copying the diary and then through the primary narrative, that Yasuko is indeed seriously ill. This revelation leads to the insertion of two further documents: "Diary of the Illness of Yasuko Taka-maru" and "Notes on the Bombing of Hiroshima, by Hiroshi Iwatake, Medical Reserve."[85] The first is jotted down by Shigeko to let her husband know the condition of their niece. This is necessary partly because Yasuko's symptoms include painful abscesses on her buttocks, which she was too ashamed to show to the doctor or tell Shigeko about for a long time. To spare her further embarrassment, Shigematsu decides it is better if he does not visit her sickroom too often. The diary is also a necessary means of communication because he and his wife cannot discuss the details of her illness without the fear of being overheard by Yasuko. So the diary is intended both to protect Yasuko's privacy and at the same time to deal with practical needs; hence it records not only Yasuko's condition and treatment but also her diet—almost as religiously as Shiki's diary did.

While the diary is kept from the patient herself, it is taken to Dr. Hosokawa, who has also been treating his own brother-in-law, another victim of the bomb. Dr. Hosokawa is reluctant to treat Yasuko, as he is really a specialist in hemorrhoids. Reading the diary, however, prompts him to send Shigematsu the notes of his brother-in-law, Iwatake, who miraculously recovered after being desperately ill. Unlike Shigeko's diary on Yasuko's condition, this document is to be read to Yasuko as encouragement and to be shown to another doctor who is treating her. In the same way as Shigeko's notes on food were attached to Shigematsu's diary, Mrs. Iwatake's reminiscences are appended to her husband's document.

Just as Shigeko wrote her food record in *desu-masu* form, Mrs. Iwatake's reminiscences, in which food is an important element, are also in polite spoken style, which Shigematsu thinks must be based on a stenographic record of her spoken words. Whereas Shigeko's document included criticism of the military regime, Mrs. Iwatake incorporates in her talk anecdotes of the arrogance and corruption of army doctors. Reading these, Shigematsu concludes:

> These reminiscences of Iwatake's wife, taken together with Iwatake's own
> account of his experiences, suggested that no proper treatment for radiation
> sickness had been discovered yet. The only measures taken in Iwatake's case were
> blood transfusions and large quantities of vitamin C, with a diet of peaches and
> raw egg. With him, that seemed to have done the trick—that, and an enormous
> will to beat the disease.[86]

We note that the treatment, after all, is not much different from what Shigematsu has been practicing himself. That Iwatake has recovered doubtless gives the best reason for Shigematsu and others to read his and his wife's writing. Thus food in *Kuroi ame* does not simply point to general shortages and difficulties; it also signals the dissent of ordinary people from the authorities and their last hope for survival amid the man-made disaster of war.

Food, War, and Inscription: *Tokyo Seven Roses*

There are many other historical and fictional diarists who are equally as obsessed with inscription[87] as Shigematsu. Among them, the narrator of Inoue Hisashi's novel *Tōkyō sebun rōzu*[88] (Tokyo Seven Roses, 1999) stands out. This 775-page novel, which mixes facts with (slapstick) comedy and fantasy, consists almost entirely of the diary of one Yamanaka Shinsuke, beginning on April 25, 1945, and ending on March 21, 1946. Shinsuke, like Shigematsu, is an ordinary citizen with an extraordinary passion for inscription. He keeps his diary religiously, often recording what he has heard and read that day. Shinsuke adopts an approach similar to Shigematsu's "stop-start" style, with entries of varying length.

Shinsuke's family business is the manufacturing and selling of fans—not the elegant folding type used for traditional dancing and the tea ceremony but the more run-of-the-mill and practical type called *uchiwa*, which usually have a round face and a long handle.[89] These fans are often used as a kind of advertising and as small gifts by companies and retailers. Hence, the printing of clients' names forms part of their manufacture. As the war drags on and even printing type is collected for recycling into bullets, Shinsuke decides to train himself at a leading mimeograph company in Tokyo so that he can print advertisements by hand. This special skill gives him opportunities to work as a mimeographist for the neighborhood association during the final stages of the war and after the war at police headquarters, while his real trade has been forced to shut down because of the lack of material for fans. Mimeographing for the police gives Shinsuke access to many confidential documents such as memos on legislative bills and the crimes of American soldiers, as well as letters from Japanese men and women to the "Moat-side Emperor" General MacArthur; and Shinsuke's mimeographic memory, so to speak, enables him to reproduce these in his diary. Thus his private diary contains public, and politically confidential, elements.

Shinsuke's obsessive diary keeping is closely connected to the main theme of the second half of the novel: how to save the written Japanese language. Here, the immediate and greatest enemy is an American lieutenant commander and chief of the language section of GHQ called Robert King Hall.[90] Hall here is depicted as an extremely gifted linguist[91] who has studied at four leading universities in America and has two doctorates. He firmly believes that in order to democratize Japan and the Japanese language it is necessary to change the writing system. The first part of his plan is to abolish kanji and hiragana and retain only katakana. The second step is to change the katakana to romanized Japanese. He also considers the possibility of making English or some other language, not necessarily European but perhaps something like Indonesian, the new national language. Just as Shinsuke is obsessed with inscription, Hall is obsessed with annihilating its essential tool, written Japanese, and possibly the spoken language as well.

Apart from this central theme, there are several others, including the American carpet bombing of civilian targets, the oppressive and corrupt Japanese military, the powerlessness of Japanese men in contrast to the resourcefulness of Japanese women, and the opportunism (both in wartime and postwar) of many Japanese. Even more than in *Kuroi ame*, food plays an extremely important role in this novel, a role closely associated with the depiction of survival techniques and the revolt of ordinary people in extraordinary situations. As we saw in Shigeko's record of diet in wartime Hiroshima, the shortage of food and other everyday needs was so serious and the ration allotments so meager that the black market and all forms of corruption were rampant. Inoue, who has long been deeply concerned about Japan's agricultural problems and has expressed his opinions not only in his essays and lectures but also in novels such as *Kirikirijin* (The People of Kirikiri, 1981) and *Yonsenman-po no otoko* (The Man of Forty Million Steps, 1986–1989), also includes an extensive range of topics related to food in this novel. One of the recurrent motifs is that governments, both wartime and postwar, are neither seriously committed to nor capable of feeding the population. Shinsuke's entry for October 12, 1945, for example, speaks of the worst famine since 1905, made more severe by the influx of his compatriots returning from abroad: "Despite this, the government has no policy to address this problem. [ ] Questioned by the press, the minister for agriculture replied, to our great fury, 'In short, all we can do is to bow our heads to the farmers. Then they might give us some.'"[92]

Shinsuke, like the "ordinary" people in *Kuroi ame*, is highly critical of the unproductive bureaucracy. Like everyone else, he knows that bartering and the black market are the only ways for people without military connections to obtain food to survive. As his fan-making business has been closed down, he begins a small transport business with an auto-tricycle. This new business brings him into close contact with a variety of people, including black marketeers. Seeing how people really appreciate what he delivers, he opines that they should be called not black marketeers (*yami-ya*) but "bright marketeers" (*hikari-ya*).[93]

Shinsuke, like Shigematsu, is a humane and decent man. There is, however, a certain ambiguity in his position. Compared to average families, Shinsuke's is privileged in terms of food and other matters both during and after the war. This privilege depends on something he does not wholeheartedly approve of, or of which he is even ashamed: his eldest daughter's marriage into the Furusawa family, which owns a well-established farming machinery business. As any business related to munitions or food prospers in wartime, the Furusawas experience no shortage of food or other necessities, and they have useful connections. They can afford an opulent wedding banquet (at least by 1945 Japanese standards) together with gifts such as light globes and soap, considered luxurious, for each wedding guest. Many things that would be an unattainable dream for ordinary citizens are readily available to this family. Embarrassed and uneasy as he is about their extravagance, Shinsuke cannot decline their offers of food and other items, not simply because they are needed but also because to do so (or at least to do so too often) would damage the relationship between the two families.

Postwar, Shinsuke's family finds itself if anything even more privileged, again thanks to the daughters. Their wartime benefactors, the Furusawas, are succeeded by none other than the Occupation army, the source of "luxury" items such as powdered eggs and real soap. The reader of *Tōkyō sebun rōzu* learns much earlier than does Shinsuke that his two surviving daughters (together with five other women, they make up the members of the eponymous Tokyo Seven Roses) work as mistresses or prostitutes for Americans. Their clients are officers rather than soldiers, and hence they are called "companions," distinguished from common *panpan* or streetwalkers.

It is through Shinsuke's own diary that we are led to suspect this long before the diarist himself does. Hints are scattered all through his entries, and he senses that there is something he does not know, but it takes him three weeks to realize how his daughters are able to bring such things home. This is partly because he has just been in prison for nearly four months (of which more below) and at one point even thought to be dead. On his return, everyone around him knows the truth, but no one tells him. When he questions his wife, she calmly tells him that nothing special has happened: "It's just that we looked for a way to escape starvation. How about an omelet for supper?"[94]

On a conscious level, Shinsuke is honest and sincere, and seemingly eager to find out the hidden truth, but his diary, which reveals more than its writer consciously realizes, strongly suggests his unconscious desire not to know the truth. His ignorance and his absence from the scene at the most crucial moments both in history (he is in prison when Japan surrenders) and in his family's life reinforce the theme of the novel: men are useless and women are the real strength. Shinsuke's imprisonment is based on the alleged offense of criticizing the authorities. While he did make the passing remark that "people of position tend to get fat from sucking the blood of young people"[95] during a private conversation with an opportunist neighbor, the real reason for his arrest was that this neighbor coveted Shinsuke's auto-tricycle. While in prison, Shinsuke meets fellow "political offenders," who have all been imprisoned on equally spurious grounds. However petty or ridiculous the alleged crimes may be, these prisoners are detained for months and forced to work in a factory inside the prison—processing sardines, which were at one time regarded as the "rubbish of the sea"[96] but have now become an important resource. Their task is not just to process the fish but to test new and ridiculous products such as sardine crackers, sardine jelly, and sardine buns. Their meals, of course, consist of sardines. The factory, the military, the police, and in fact the entire institution of the state are patently absurd.

Shinsuke is arrested again on October 19, the day after he finds out about the Seven Roses, and he remains in police custody for more than two months. Again, Shinsuke is treated as a political offender, his alleged crime this time being his involvement in a plan to sue the American government for its breach of the international agreement prohibiting the killing of noncombatants, and to seek compensation. All he actually did, however, was to attend a meeting and put his name to a founding document for the group. Before they achieve anything, all of the members of the group are arrested. Shinsuke is released after sixty-seven days partly because of the powerlessness of this group—they are regarded as practically harmless. His release also owes much to his daughter Fumiko, who urges her American officer, who is none other than Robert King Hall, to act on her father's behalf.

Shinsuke is arrested twice more. In all he spends two-thirds of the year covered by the novel in police or Allied military custody. He engages in a series of heated debates with Hall, but it is the Seven Roses who save the national language with their intelligence, careful and practical planning, and erotic charms. All Shinsuke achieves is writing the long diary, despite the prolonged gaps. The diary does nothing to provide food for the family, although his mimeographs and black-market transport do. On a practical level, he serves at best as a decoy to divert the attention of the Americans from a secret operation by the Seven Roses to save the language. The operation—which involves some erotic slapstick and blackmail—proves successful, and the American education mission's report to MacArthur, although recommending the use of romanized Japanese, includes a clause stating that any change to the language should come from the Japanese people.

The message of this novel seems to be summarized by the following remarks, by a friend of Shinsuke:

> "Since the war, it is women who have supported the essentials of living—rationing, marketing, and devices to provide our food and clothing. So they are indeed tough. In contrast, men were always absorbed in inventing brave words. We were in a way just blabbermouths. This was made clear on August 15 last year. Since then we have been paralyzed and dismayed. It's probably time for a change of players. Women will lead the world for quite some time. Or rather we have no choice but to depend on their toughness."[97]

The power of the women in this novel, however, depends primarily on their sexual charms; their own desires seem nonexistent. While accepting powdered eggs, chocolate, meat, coffee, cigarettes, and so on from their American lovers and clients in order to feed their families, they harbor a deep resentment towards America, as each of them has lost loved ones in the indiscriminate bombing. Once their mission is complete, they spend their savings on seven sewing machines, bought through the black market, and establish the Tokyo Seven Roses Clothing Recycling Company. They have used their sexual charms to protect their country, their language, and their families, including the powerless menfolk. When the threat is removed, they are happy to revert to their pure and humble lives.

Like *Byōshō rokushaku*, *Hōrōki*, and *Kuroi ame*, *Tōkyō sebun rōzu* was initially serialized in a magazine. The serialization continued from 1982 to 1997 with intervals in between—as in Shinsuke's diary. The complete version was published in 1999. That this story of women feeding their families and rescuing the language began its life at the height of the Japanese economic boom is worth noting. It can certainly be read as a warning against an affluent society in which the memory of starvation has long been forgotten. It also seems that the message of this novel is closely connected to Inoue's long-term campaign for the protection and improvement of Japanese agriculture. The American pressure to open up the Japanese rice market seems analogous to Hall's insistence upon romanization. Inoue's argument for the protection of domestic rice production is based both on environmental concerns and on the importance of self-sufficiency: rice production provides not only rice, but dams, in the form of rice paddies, and it preserves the soil, the vegetation, and the air. Emiko Ohnuki-Tierney suggests that rice "symbolizes *Japan itself*, its land, water, and air."[98] If rice is *self* in Inoue's polemic essays and lectures, the language too, particularly the use of kana and kanji, is regarded in this novel as being at the very core of Japanese identity. Indeed, one of the Roses, Tomoe, a widow and graduate of the Tokyo Women's Higher Normal School, comments, "How shall I put it—losing the kanji and the kana would seem to hurt me even more deeply than losing my husband. Maybe it's because it would affect the future of our children."[99] Language and children, then, are more important than husbands. Just as the rice paddies need to be protected for future generations, for their sake, too, the language needs to be defended against the enemy. It is not that Inoue tries to incite general anti-American sentiment; elsewhere, he has written that to him America is a country he "loves, hates, and loves" (*suki de kirai de suki*).[100] Nevertheless, given that the novel was written in the midst of the trade war between the two countries, it is tempting to read this story—ultimately a fantasy, with its obsessively detailed data on the war and the Occupation—in the context of the relationship between Japan and America in the late twentieth century.

It is doubtful whether Inoue's depiction of the strength of women appeals at all to contemporary Japanese readers, especially women. The Seven Roses, after all, return to their "pure, proper, and beautiful" (*kiyoku tadashiku utsukushii*) way of life, to borrow the catchphrase of the popular all-woman Takarazuka revue theater. None of them seems to be traumatized by her experience as a high-class *panpan*. The novel does not deal with cross-cultural contacts between Japanese women and American soldiers as, for instance, Ariyoshi Sawako's novel *Hishoku* (Non-Color, 1964) does. Tomoe, the Rose Shinsuke secretly admires, marries Shinsuke's neighbor and tailor, who has patiently waited until the Roses achieved their goal, just like "the lover of a courtesan (*oiran*) waiting for her contract to expire."[101] The courage, intelligence, and beauty of the Seven Roses are just like those of Edo courtesans in popular theater, fiction, and *rakugo* (comic raconteur). As the threat of romanization disappears, so does the threat of starvation—not from the Japan of 1946, but from the world of the *Tokyo Seven Roses*.

We began this chapter with the diaries of Masaoka Shiki, whose appetite caused problems but at the same time signaled his will to live. Similarly, hunger in Hayashi Fumiko's text indicates not only the difficulties of the young woman narrator but also her strong desire and vitality. In *Kuroi ame* and *Tōkyō sebun rōzu* hunger occurs on a national scale. The diary form was used in these novels about the war and its aftermath in order to attempt a detailed record of the everyday lives of ordinary people under extraordinary and devastating circumstances. We have also seen, however, that the diary may conceal some facts, or reveal facts that its writer does not know. The obsession for inscription evidenced in many of the diaries discussed above seems to consist of a variety of motives—to prove that one is still alive, to satisfy artistic aspirations, to leave a record for future generations, or to defend the very means of writing itself. In all of these texts, food functions both as a pleasure that brings people together and as a cause of conflict, struggle, compromise, oppression, manipulation, and corruption.

Each of the diaries discussed above also shows quite clearly the connection between food and gender. Our scope was limited, however, when it comes to this issue, and we will have to wait until later chapters to treat it more thoroughly. With the exception of *Hōrōki*, the writers of the published texts were men. In *Kuroi ame*, women's writing was inserted only as an "appendix" to the diaries of men, and it is in fact hard to imagine any woman writer creating the story of the Seven Roses, who are not only clever and sexy but also tough and pure in heart.

Chapter Two

Down-to-Earth Eating
and Writing (1)

"Poems to Eat" is my tentative title and derives from an advertisement I used to
see in streetcars which read "Beer to Eat." I use this title to refer to poetry written with both feet firmly planted on the ground, poetry written with feelings
that are inseparable from real life. Poems of this kind are "necessities." They are
neither delicacies nor a feast, but rather the pickles without which we cannot
enjoy our daily meal. This may well drag poetry down from its established
pedestal. But in my opinion it will ensure that poetry, which previously had no
impact whatsoever on our lives, becomes a necessity. And this is the only way
to justify its existence.[1]

Poet Ishikawa Takuboku (1886–1912) wrote this passage in his 1909 essay
"Kurau beki shi" (Poems to Eat). Takuboku's idea of "poems to eat" provides a prototype for the "earthy" and "down-to-earth" writing that is the subject of this and the following chapter; what he says about poetry can also be
applied to prose fiction. It is common to link food and literature on the grounds
of the vital importance of both in building, nurturing, and sustaining a healthy
mind and body. This view is often allied with a preference for the basic and the
ordinary, rather than special or luxurious delicacies or feasts. It rejects privileged
position or authoritarian attitude. A point to note is that the term "down-to-
earth" here signifies an approach that seeks to be not just honest, unembellished,
and frank, but also committed in some way to community and society, rather
than to the kind of personal struggle that we have seen in the texts discussed in
the previous chapter. This particular point is suggested in Takuboku's "Poems to
Eat" even though it is debatable whether his own poetry, though certainly loved

by generations of readers, may be regarded as good examples of "poems to eat."[2] It is worth looking a little more closely at his notion of such poems.

Poetry, he insists, should be written in everyday language, for life's sake rather than for poetry's sake. Likewise, poets should be ordinary men and women who in no way regard themselves as special beings. Here Takuboku is clearly criticizing both conventional poetry (which Shiki had earlier attacked) and more recent romantic and symbolist poetry. In this essay he also expresses sympathy for the Japanese naturalist movement, especially when he insists that poetry should be "a rigorous report, an honest diary, of man's emotional life."[3] However, there are other crucial elements in Takuboku's theory of down-to-earth poetics. He writes: "We demand poems written by a *Japanese* who lives in contemporary Japan, uses contemporary Japanese language, and *understands contemporary Japan*."[4] Reminiscent though it is of Tsubouchi Shōyō's *Shōsetsu shinzui*, Takuboku's emphasis on contemporary Japan does not seem to betray any sign of imperialist competitiveness such as we saw in Shōyō's hope that the modern Japanese *shōsetsu* would "finally surpass the European novel."[5] Rather than advocating a nationalistic desire to "surpass" the West in literature, Takuboku warns on the contrary that his contemporary intellectuals "idolize" imported knowledge to such an extent that they "forget to understand contemporary Japan." In other words, they "forget to plant their feet on the ground."[6]

Commitment to community does not necessarily mean *engagement* with a particular political ideology. Needless to say, community includes women, children, and elderly persons, all of whom, especially women and children, play central roles in the majority of the texts. Some of the texts discussed below may seem to avoid making any social comment, while others incorporate some advocacy for social change. Despite this, each text has a commitment to the here and now—local and contemporary language and society. Some texts actively adopt specific dialects even though this may not be clear in translation. We will also see the ways in which historical changes affect the forms, styles, and significance of commitment to particular issues and communities. Most of the examples we see in this chapter concern food production and distribution—starting with agriculture and moving to secondary and tertiary industries. Historical changes are also evident in the language and style of our example texts. Down-to-earth writing often rejects predominant literary conventions, but by no means does it reject narrative and rhetorical devices. One might assume that the commitment to here and now takes the form of realistic fiction or polemic essays and manifestos; as we see, however, there are many other possibilities including down-to-earth fantasy and "splatter-horror." Takuboku insisted that poems to eat should be an honest record. We have already seen, however, that diaries can be honest in many different ways and that the same event may be recorded in various ways in honest diaries produced by different observers, and sometimes even by the same observer writing at different times. My aim in this chapter, then, is to examine the variations on some recurrent themes and motifs concerning "earth," "eating," and "writing" in some representative prewar texts.

An Organic Novel: *Tsuchi*

Nagatsuka Takashi's (1879–1915) novel *Tsuchi* (serialized in the *Asahi shinbun* from June to December 1910, trans. *The Soil*, 1989) is a painstakingly detailed study of day-to-day life in a small farming village in Ibaraki Prefecture. The descriptions, based on the author's meticulous observation of his home village, are so realistic that the historian Ann Waswo emphasizes its value as "an informal ethnography of a rural community and its inhabitants in the early 1900s."[7] In other words, she regards it as a historical document. While few would now deny the significance of this work as a masterpiece of *nōmin bungaku* (peasant literature), its critical reception has passed through several noticeable phases. In the introduction to her English translation Waswo summarizes different readings of the novel as (1) representing bestiality, (2) exhibiting false consciousness, (3) exemplifying the healing powers of community, (4) being an ethnography (or social history), (5) showing a paradise lost, and (6) providing entrance examination fodder.[8] The first view, exemplified by Natsume Sōseki's comments, reveals the vast chasm between the nameless peasants depicted by Nagatsuka and the late-Meiji intellectuals who constituted the core of the contemporary reading public. The second reading represents the view of the "proletarian" critics of the 1920s and early 1930s. The third refers to the manner in which the stage and film adaptations of the novel made in the mid to late 1930s focused on the "villagers' collective wish to preserve harmony," thus creating the illusion that "by working together everything, even the New Order, was possible."[9] By the 1960s and early 1970s the value of the novel as ethnography had been recognized. With the rise of the postindustrial society of the late 1970s onwards, an additional reading arose based on a new nostalgia for the simple, earthy, rural life. Waswo adds one more element to these various readings based on the inclusion of the opening section of the novel in a 1986 university entrance examination, a development that "demonstrated, no doubt unwittingly, just how remote and marginal village life has become in today's highly urbanized and affluent Japan."[10]

Sōseki's opinion of this novel deserves a further examination. It was this great literary mentor who recognized Nagatsuka's talent from his earlier short stories and offered him the opportunity to serialize a full-length novel in the prestigious *Asahi shinbun*. Nevertheless, in his 1912 introduction to the book version of the novel, while praising the work's unique depiction of nature and local color, Sōseki also expresses his concern that the minute detail often interferes with the main story, which, in his view, is flat and dull, lacking suspense or climax. He also finds it difficult to follow the speech of the characters, who use authentic dialect as it is spoken in the author's home village. Sōseki concedes that these are relatively superficial problems. However, he goes on to argue that there is another more fundamental flaw in the novel:

> Tragedy, by definition, deals with something dreadful. Usually, however, a
> tragedy offers something that compensates for sorrow, and this is why the reader
> enjoys shedding tears. The painfulness depicted in *The Soil* does not even evoke
> our tears. It is the same kind of painfulness as having no rain and no prospect
> of sunshine for one's entire life. Our heart simply sinks beneath the earth; there
> is almost no compensation, emotionally and morally, for this pressing pain. We
> merely fall deep into the dark soil.[11]

Sōseki's negative reaction, which has attracted the criticism of later commentators,[12] is echoed in his use of terms such as "miserable," "maggot-like," and "beastly" elsewhere in his introduction in reference to the peasants depicted in the novel. However, these expressions might be more appropriate for another well-known, slightly earlier example of peasant literature—Mayama Seika's *Minamikoizumi-mura* (Minamikoizumi Village, 1907). Mayama's narrator, an obvious alter ego of the author, is a medical student working as a relief doctor in the eponymous village. He begins his narrative with the blunt declaration that "none are more miserable than the peasants"[13] and goes on to say how beastly, vulgar, dirty, ugly, sly, and imbecilic they are. So negative is it that Yoshida Seiichi, a pioneer in the study of Japanese naturalist literature, commented thus:

> One seeks in vain any explanation of where such ugliness, unhappiness, and
> meanness come from, let alone how any of these problems might be solved.
> There is no hint of cheerfulness or affection, such as we find in Nagatsuka
> Takashi's *The Soil*. The author is certainly skillful in drawing a powerful picture
> of brutal life in thick strong lines; nevertheless the question remains: why
> should anyone want to present such a shocking picture to others?[14]

It is interesting that Yoshida gives *Tsuchi* as an example of a text with cheerfulness and affection. It is worth noting, too, that Sōseki himself wrote a work depicting the lives of miners as miserable and beastly. *Kōfu* (The Miner, 1908), however, does not aim to present a realistic picture of the plight of the miners, despite its famous closing statement that everything is based on the narrator's own experience as a miner. Indeed, Sōseki's novel, or antinovel, presents an interesting journey into the nadir of human psychology as well as being experimental metafiction. Unlike the narrators of *Kōfu* and *Minamikoizumi-mura*, the *Tsuchi* narrator plays no active role in the story he narrates, preferring to conceal himself behind the landscape and people he depicts. Neither does he pass any overt moral judgment. While both Sōseki and Mayama have their narrators comment on the circumstances of the subjects they observe, in *Tsuchi* the narrator maintains a certain distance from his subject. The season changes and the characters grow older, but time is treated as more cyclical than linear, an effect emphasized by the fact that, in contrast to the other two narratives, *Tsuchi* has no beginning or end in the form of the narrator-protagonist's arrival and departure. This in itself is a statement.

Nagatsuka's text effectively presents multiple interrelated meanings. It is tempting to use the term "organic" to label these meanings: everything is natural and living, with each element linked to another. This may seem to reflect the notion of harmony in the third reading on Waswo's list, as well as the nostalgic idealization of the fifth reading. The term "organic" may also give rise to charges of false consciousness, a claim that might be considered valid from the perspectives of a class or gender analysis. The notion of the organic, however, allows the acknowledgment of the darker elements of the novel, those that attracted the accusation of "bestiality." Moreover, *Tsuchi* contains some subtle indications of the corroding and undermining aspects of the seemingly organic system. My aim, then, is neither to accept nor to reject the organic in Nagatsuka's novel but to try to clarify its limitations and achievements. A way of doing this is to approach *Tsuchi* as about food and eating.

The peasants in the novel work with the soil, the sun, water, and other natural elements, producing food in order to survive. However, their work is demanding and never ending, and most of the time eating is actually quite difficult. Food has a number of functions in the novel. It serves as an indicator of smooth or problematic relationships. It may also show the care and affection of one character for another, or highlight some conflict or lack of understanding. Some give food willingly, while others begrudge sharing. Offering food to others may be seen as a social gesture. However, it is often so deeply integrated into other aspects of daily life that no one involved in the act takes particular notice. Refusal to offer, share, or accept food, on the other hand, is more likely to attract attention. The novel deals with both collective and individual hunger, appetites, and eating practices among the young and old, men and women. Some observe unspoken rules about communal eating while others break those rules, stealing or deceiving. There are some bright and cheerful moments, usually corresponding to seasonal or natural changes. There are also a number of humble festivities and rituals in which food plays an important role.

The multiple practices of eating are closely related to nature, which of course is not always kind and nurturing: harsh winds, chills, scorching heat, drought, and floods torment the farmers and devastate their crops. Sōseki could not but be impressed by the novel's vivid description. Indeed, many critics regard this novel as a prose example of Nagatsuka's accomplishment in *shasei*, the art of sketching descriptions from real life, which was advocated, as we saw in the previous chapter, by Masaoka Shiki.[15] As one of Shiki's disciples, Nagatsuka developed his own way of sketching from life and nature in prose as well as tanka. The description of nature in *Tsuchi* combines the lyric with the scientific, as we can see, for example, in the following passage:

> Tall ungainly oak trees, planted years ago as a source of firewood and charcoal, bordered the path that Kanji and O-Tsugi followed. Every winter now, saws cut into the oak's limbs. As if in fear of what lay in store for them, they held on to their life-giving leaves long after all the other deciduous trees had shed theirs. Only after the wood-cutting season had ended and acorns nestled in shallow cups on their remaining branches did they give in to the cold and surrender their desiccated foliage. Their fear had disappeared just as thorns disappear from the trunk and branches of a grafted pear tree that no longer has any need to concern itself with progeny or self-protection. Whipped by the late winter wind the fallen oak leaves scurried for whatever cover they could find.[16]

Nature here is not some incomprehensible or unfathomable force, but is rather presented as having the same range of emotions as a human being. Many have pointed to the personification of nature in this text,[17] but it is hard to determine whether nature is being personified or human beings are being treated as part of nature. The soil, like the farmers themselves, becomes thin and emaciated without adequate nutrients. Poor farmers who cannot afford proper fertilizer thus end up with fewer crops, locking them into a vicious cycle of poverty. Tenant peasants, even poorer, are given more-difficult land to cultivate, and the soil they till can be rock hard, wet and muddy, or dry and dusty.

While it may yield crops and provide useful products, including building materials, the soil can also harm those in direct contact with it. In *Tsuchi*, the most brutal illustration of this is the death of O-Shina, the wife of the novel's protagonist, Kanji. O-Shina dies of tetanus after aborting her four-month-old fetus. With her husband away and no other adult to look after her, she forces herself to return to work in the field in order to hide the secret of her abortion from the neighbors:

> Still, how did she get the infection that killed her? [. . .] Perhaps the bacillus had been on the winter cherry root she had used to break through into her uterus. Or perhaps it was in the dust that covered everything in sight. The only thing one will ever know for certain is that it came originally from the soil.[18]

The bacillus from the soil may have been the direct cause of O-Shina's death, but Nagatsuka's text suggests another, more general, cause:

> It was the same for all poor farmers. They spent long hours in their fields doing all they could to raise enough food. Then after the harvest they had to part with most of what they had produced. Their crops were theirs only for as long as they stood rooted in the soil. Once the farmers had paid the rents they owed they were lucky to have enough left over to sustain them through the winter.[19]

In passages such as this, the novel describes the peasants' struggles in great detail. However, to the dissatisfaction of Marxist critics, it does not treat these difficulties as deriving from the exploitation and oppression of the peasantry by the landowners. On the contrary, Kanji's landlord, called simply East Neighbor in the novel, is generally kind and understanding. He understands, for example, how desperately needy Kanji's family is after O-Shina's death and agrees to let them bring only half the rice due as rent, giving them a one-year extension for the balance. Kanji, desperate to find extra food for the family, often steals produce. While working for East Neighbor, he hides some of the landlord's rice to take home. When the hidden rice is discovered, the mistress is not really interested in finding out who is responsible, preferring to turn a blind eye to such petty theft. However, one of her employees punishes the mysterious thief by replacing the rice with dirt. The symbolism is strong: those who cannot eat rice by honest means must eat mud. Kanji continues to steal for his hungry family—mainly from the master's fields but also from elsewhere. Ironically, it is Kanji's instruction to his young son Yokichi not to tell anyone that the family has eaten sweet potatoes that exposes his habitual stealing to everyone in the village. Yokichi is so excited about the sweet potatoes, especially delicious because East Neighbor can afford to use fish-meal fertilizer, that he cannot help mentioning the secret to a neighbor. When Kanji's stealing escalates and is finally reported to the police, once again it is East Neighbor master and mistress who patiently try to appease the angry villagers.

East Neighbor's exemplary mistress does not falter in her forgiving and caring attitude towards Kanji and his family, even after a fire, which starts in their hut, burns down the landlord's grand house and old cedar trees. Instead of making accusations or hurling abuse, she offers to help Kanji, and calmly inquires after his family. It is not surprising that while some readers find a wonderful sense of communal healing in this novel, others have detected a hollow "false consciousness." It might be noted that the better-off and better-educated landowners never play a central or romantic role in the novel: there is no Tolstoyan Levin or Sōsekian Yasu-san.[20] The focus is always firmly on the soil, and the peasantry, as represented by Kanji's family, and the fact that no matter what they do they simply cannot provide enough for their needs. While the novel does not offer a Marxist or any other systematic analysis or solution of their predicament, it is nevertheless rich in material on natural and social conditions.

Nagatsuka has been particularly successful in revealing the manner in which rural life in Japan at that time had, to some extent, become a function of modernity. For it is not just the contingencies of the soil that make life difficult for the villagers in *Tsuchi*. In order to survive, men such as Kanji need to leave the village for weeks in the farming off-season to work as laborers on construction sites. Even at the height of the farming season, they neglect their own fields to take casual work to earn extra money working for the landlords. Women, too, try to earn money by peddling foods—simple prepared foods such as tofu and *konnyaku*, as well as eggs—whenever they can between their work in the fields and in the house. The market economy has certainly made its way into farming villages. During one of his regular visit to Kanji's house, an egg wholesaler bemoans the drop in prices that has followed the flooding of the market with cheap eggs from Shanghai, claiming that growing crops is much safer than his own business. In fact, he claims, his only chance of making a profit lies in the possibility of a dysentery epidemic and the need for everyone to feed eggs to the sick. Ironically, at this stage O-Shina is already ill after her abortion, and even though Kanji, called back from the construction site, tells her to keep as many eggs as she likes for herself, she takes only the smallest two.[21]

While some villagers, like Kanji, are obliged to leave the village temporarily, others, like O-Shina's stepfather, Uhei, are required to do so for longer periods. As Nakayama Kazuko notes,[22] after the rapid stratification of the farming population in the 1880s, an increasing number of impoverished farmers were driven out of rural areas, providing cheap labor for city enterprises. Old people were no longer abandoned in the mountains as useless;[23] they could seldom afford, however, a quiet retirement. Uhei is already sixty-nine when he starts working as a live-in janitor in a soy sauce factory in Noda, a town known for this industry. Uhei works in order to provide for himself and to avoid friction with his son-in-law. When his health forces him to relinquish the night watchman's job, he returns to the village, presenting his son-in-law with an unwelcome extra mouth to feed. Food is both a cause and a sign of the antagonism between the two men. Although he refrains from doing so in Uhei's presence, Kanji complains bitterly to the young Yokichi about how quickly rice disappears since the old man's return. Yokichi, typically, finds it difficult to keep his mouth shut. However, this time it is a certain childish cunning rather than naivety that makes him pass on Kanji's words to Uhei: the boy expects some reward from the old man, some candy or small change from his hard-earned savings. As we shall see, the consequences of Yokichi's greed and lack of discretion play a pivotal role in the story.

Unlike the rest of the family, Uhei is accustomed to better rice, better soy sauce, and better bean paste than that available at Kanji's house. In addition to the tastes he developed during his years away from the village, his gums make it impossible for him to eat the same food as the rest of the family. Kanji's daughter, O-Tsugi, is sympathetic, but what she can do is limited. Uhei's solution to this problem is to build a small hut next to Kanji's where he cooks his own meals with the few provisions he receives from his reluctant son-in-law, supplemented by the occasional extra food he can afford. It is notable that Nagatsuka depicts the problems associated with aging in great detail here, long before aging became a major issue in literature.[24] Even more remarkable is that Uhei is presented not as some ugly, pathetic old man but as a man with his own tastes and feelings, as well as worries and regrets at his declining physical strength. Unlike, for example, the "mad old" connoisseur Utsugi Tokusuke in Tanizaki's *Diary of a Mad Old Man*, Uhei, whose favorite food is humble tofu or a small piece of salted salmon, displays nothing gross or grotesque in his tastes or appetites. The only dark element here is that in his younger days he killed and ate cats. This was partly to prevent stray cats from harming the chickens, but since eating four-legged animals was still taboo in the village, some villagers make the occasional joke about old Uhei's ailments deriving from a curse from the cats he ate.

Uhei's independence does not last long, however, as his health deteriorates and his meager savings diminish. And it is the combination of his physical condition and his grandson's uselessness that leads to the accidental fire that occurs while Kanji and O-Tsugi, the two healthy adults, are out in the fields. Completely shattered, and badly burned, Uhei cannot bear it when he receives yet another thoughtless report from Yokichi—that Kanji blames Uhei for the fire. Uhei decides to end his life. It is only after the feeble old man's attempt to hang himself fails that Kanji repents his ill treatment of his father-in-law. He removes the quilt from his son and covers Uhei, who has been found lying unconscious in the snow. When the old man regains consciousness, Kanji shows real concern for the first time in the novel as he offers him food, medicine, and warm words. The unseasonable snow has melted, and the family's temporary shack is illuminated by soft spring sunshine. There is also the suggestion that Kanji may return the money he found in the ashes of the fire to its owner, Uhei, thus finally curing himself of thieving. At least about this final scene, it would appear that, *pace* Sōseki, there is after all something here that compensates for the pain and sorrow.

Tsuchi provides an insight into intergenerational issues through the depiction of the relationship between Kanji and Uhei. It also sheds light on the issue of gender, particularly through its representation of the two women in the family, O-Shina and O-Tsugi. Waswo remarks that through this novel we can see "gender-role socialization in the home and the resultant emotional dependence of males on females in late Meiji Japan."[25] However, not all critics have responded positively to Nagatsuka's representation, and the portrayal of women in the novel has raised a number of issues, some of which are worth noting here.

Let us first revisit O-Shina's abortion and subsequent death, an event that greatly affects the lives of the other characters. It is central to the opening chapters of the novel and remains an important motif throughout the remainder of the text. As we have seen, the men of the village, including Kanji, need to leave for several weeks in winter to work as laborers and bring badly needed cash home to their families. Children who are old enough and are not needed either for work in the fields or in the house are sent to earn an income in factories and shops. Indeed, at the beginning of the novel, since the child Yokichi is now three and no longer requires constant care, Kanji and O-Shina have plans to send fifteen-year-old O-Tsugi, who until then had been looking after her infant brother, for bound service. The arrival of another baby would prevent this, with devastating consequences for the family. Since they are too busy with the harvest to discuss the matter before Kanji's departure, O-Shina is left alone to make the decision about the abortion. In fact, we are left to understand throughout that Kanji usually leaves all decision making and negotiations with others to his wife.[26]

Under Meiji criminal law, abortion was illegal, and those who violated this law were punished. Nakayama reminds us that despite this, and despite the great risk to their health and even their lives, many women opted for abortion, which was "regarded as a lesser evil than the financial and social burdens of bearing and raising a child."[27] Women who, unlike O-Shina, survived, suffered feelings of shame and guilt for the rest of their lives. Even for those lucky enough not to have to resort to abortion, there were numerous other risks associated with sexual activity. Uhei's first wife, for example, experienced repeated stillbirths, which were apparently caused by the syphilis Uhei had contracted years before their marriage. While this wife suffered ill health for most of their marriage, particularly during the last three years of her life, Uhei, although "never a wicked man" (*akunin*),[28] was more sympathetic towards O-Shina's poverty-stricken mother, a widow, and her toddler daughter than towards his own bedridden wife. The narrative makes no moral judgments. Nor is there any lamentation for the sad lot of women. Sōseki is right in saying that the sustained nature of these tragic episodes dries the reader's tears. Nevertheless, the calm, concise outline of Uhei's past in the few pages before the chapter about the fire provides many insights and leaves us in sympathy not only with Uhei's unfortunate wife, but also with Uhei himself and O-Shina's mother.

Apart from abortion and problems relating to childbirth, there are other dark naturalistic elements, the most serious and controversial of which is incest. There is a persistent rumor among the villagers that Kanji has an incestuous relationship with his daughter, O-Tsugi. Although the novel offers nothing to confirm this, opinion has been divided as to how we are to read it.[29] What is certain is that, since the death of her mother, O-Tsugi has had to take over her mother's role both inside the house and outside in the fields. She is growing into a healthy, caring, and attractive young woman, resembling her mother in the latter's youth. The incest rumor is prompted by Kanji's behavior towards his daughter. He is exceedingly jealous, strict, interfering, and even violent in matters involving the girl. Since Kanji is a widower and too poor to marry again, the villagers draw their own conclusions, which progress from nudges and whispers behind the backs of father and daughter to sniggers, innuendos, and jokes addressed directly to the pair. Nevertheless, O-Tsugi bears up and continues to play the role of woman of the house, repressing her own budding sexual desires.

How are we to read the ambiguous representation of this relationship? It seems reasonable to conclude that while there is no evidence of actual incest, Kanji does, at least subconsciously, have sexual feelings for his daughter. However, this is only one element of the situation. What, for instance, is O-Tsugi's actual position? To what extent is she aware of her father's hidden feelings? It is clear that she is neither too ignorant nor too timid to handle the unwanted advances and harassment of some of the men in the village. Does this indicate fear of her father's rage in the event that she has a relationship with a young man? In other matters she often manages to placate or even chide her father "with blunt words but in a sweet tone."[30] Why, then, would she be afraid of him in the matter of men? And how does she feel about being at the center of a horrible rumor for years in a small community? There are other kinds of questions, too. Should we risk committing an "intentional fallacy" and suggest, as Iwasa does,[31] that Nagatsuka's intention to deal with the incestuous theme must have been somewhat modified through consideration for his models? Or should we point out, as Nakayama does,[32] the myth of women's power in the portrayal of the ideally gentle, patient, and self-sacrificing mother and daughter? In other words, does the notion of O-Tsugi as compliant daughter merely entrench the illusory power forged and reinforced by the complicity of a male author and male critics? What we can say at least is that no matter how "organic" the treatment of nature, the soil, food, and people in this novel may seem, it is after all a construct that can be, and needs to be, destabilized.

Food, Class, and Children: Miyamoto Yuriko

Karatani Kōjin has noted in *Nihon kindai bungaku no kigen* (The Origins of Modern Japanese Literature, 1980) that "the discovery of the child" is one of the features of the emergence of modern Japanese literature.[33] Nagatsuka and many others writing in the late-Meiji and Taishō periods paid special attention to children and their appetites, and did so in works written for adult readers as well as for children. In *Tsuchi* the appetite of the protagonist's son, Yokichi, a boy whom Waswo reads as "pampered" and "unrelentingly self-centered,"[34] is significant in a number of ways. While in the early chapters his presence includes an element of innocence and frankness, it also provides unmistakable evidence of the privileged position of the boy in the impoverished household. Unlike his sister, he is not expected to contribute to either the farming or the household work until he finishes primary school. In Kanji's son, in contrast to the brave, wise, cheerful, hard-working, caring, and all-round admirable boy who typically appears in the popular boys' literature of late Meiji, we have a "down-to-earth"[35] portrayal of a distinctly unheroic child and his appetite, Yokichi's greed precluding him from having any heroic traits whatsoever. Rather, it results in comic misadventure for both himself and others (such as when he eats a lump of rock salt, believing it to be some unknown candy). Occasionally, as we have seen, it leads to more serious consequences.

Miyamoto Yuriko's (1899–1951) *Mazushiki hitobito no mure* (A Crowd of Poor Folks, 1917) is a portrayal of impoverished people, including children, in a small farming village. The narrator of this novel is, like its author, a privileged young woman consumed with idealism and compassion. Unlike the narrator of *Tsuchi*, this narrator plays an active role in the story, mingling with the "poor folks." She openly expresses her concern about the conditions of the peasantry and points out the hypocrisy of the town bourgeoisie. From the beginning of her narrative, we find adjectives similar to those used by the narrator of *Minamikoizumi–mura*: "dirty," "dark," "smelly," "miserable," "disgusting," and so on. However, Miyamoto's narrative does not aim merely to reveal these conditions; rather, it desperately seeks to find a solution both for those forced to live in destitution and for the narrator's conscience. We might even consider Miyamoto's text an example of *nōmin bungaku* and at the same time a Bildungsroman. The point of connection between the two is created by children's appetites.

The novel begins with a description of three children—brothers—in a dark, dirty house "more appropriately called a den."[36] The children are eagerly waiting for potatoes to cook. They are so absorbed in the prospect of eating that they take no notice when hens begin to help themselves to rice that is spilling onto the floor from a hole in a sack. When the potatoes are finally ready, the younger pair object as the oldest tries to put an extra serving into his bowl, and a fight breaks out. During the ensuing chaos the potatoes fall onto the floor. This brings the children to their senses, and after picking up the precious food, they begin to eat.

In this first chapter there is no overt trace of the narrator, who appears only at the beginning of the second chapter. Here she recounts how, happening to pass by this house, which belongs to a tenant farmer, she could not help but watch from behind a tree the scene depicted in the previous chapter. The focus of the narrative then shifts from the children to the effect they have on the narrator. Her initial reaction of disgust develops into fear, which in turn becomes pity and curiosity: "How much power a piece of potato has over those children! If possible, I thought, I would love to let them eat their fill. But even stronger was my curiosity: I just couldn't help wanting to make their acquaintance."[37]

This she does. However, she is stunned by the reaction of the children, never expecting that they will reject her somewhat patronizing overtures. When she approaches them, there is at first dead silence accompanied by intense staring. Then one of the boys comes behind her and screams right into her ear. They reply to her words of sympathy about their being left on their own in the house by telling her angrily and abusively that it is none of her business. This thoroughly shocks the well-meaning young woman, throwing her into an emotional tumult of anger, shame, pride, and a sense of powerlessness. The final humiliation comes when the children throw stones at her as she retreats. However, the incident serves as a catalyst for the narrator to begin to examine the cause of the suspicion and hostility she has aroused and to question her own privileged role and position—after all, she is the granddaughter of the landowner to whom the children's parents are indentured.

Before discussing this narrator's attempt to know the poor people better and embark on her journey *v narod*, we might compare her to another highly privileged character whose curiosity about and sympathy for the hunger of a lower-class boy form the basis of a story. In Shiga Naoya's celebrated short story "Kozō no kamisama" (The Errand Boy's God, 1920), a member of the House of Peers, known only as A, witnesses an embarrassing moment for a young shop boy at a sushi stall. In prewar Japan, sushi was regarded as a food of the common people rather than an expensive delicacy.[38] A parliamentary colleague tells A that a real connoisseur eats sushi with his fingers at a street stall rather than in a restaurant. Curious to try this for himself, A hesitantly stops at a popular stall. There he sees another novice customer, a twelve- or thirteen-year-old boy called Senkichi, trying to pretend that he is accustomed to eating in such a place. However, Senkichi is forced to return the piece of sushi he has picked because it costs more than he has in his pocket.

Shiga's story has prompted food and film critic Ogi Masahiro to suggest that the "suspect" foods consumed by the lower orders became fashionable among "snobs" at around the time of World War I,[39] when food was becoming an object of fashion in urban society. Just as A's curiosity was aroused by his colleague's account, Senkichi's desire to taste good sushi was the result of a conversation that took place among the senior shop assistants where he worked. While A can easily indulge his whim, however, the child cannot afford even one piece of sushi. That class divides appetites is evident in this story. Shiga's story, however, does not belong to what we have identified as down-to-earth writing. It does not deal with food as basic and essential. Senkichi is hungry but not starving. Neither Senkichi nor anyone else in the story expresses anger or frustration over social injustice; instead, the story focuses primarily on A's feelings, starting with his pity for the boy and finishing with a "strangely lonely, unpleasant feeling" (Shiga's signature emotion) and a sense of guilt about making Senkichi's dream come true. A does not have the "courage" to rescue the child from his embarrassing plight, but when he has another chance meeting with Senkichi, he takes the boy from his shop to a sushi restaurant, without revealing his intentions or identity. The benevolent A leaves the child in the restaurant, which happens to be the one mentioned favorably in the shop assistants' conversation, telling him that he can eat as much as he likes. This is exactly what Miyamoto's narrator-protagonist wanted to do in her encounter with the hungry boys. Alone in a private room, Senkichi eats three helpings, "like a starved, emaciated dog with unexpected food."[40] We must here depend on the omniscient narrator to observe and comment on how Senkichi eats in the room. Unlike the young woman in Miyamoto's novel, A has no desire to watch the child eat or to get to know him. Unaware of A's identity, the boy wonders who he was—could he be some kind of god, perhaps the god of the Inari shrine?—and from then on the thought of this mysterious benefactor brings him a sense of hope and deep-felt gratitude. The contrast is stark: the poor peasant boys in Miyamoto's story simply and emphatically reject the sympathetic narrator, while the errand boy happily and gratefully accepts the food provided by his unknown benefactor.

Shiga's story concludes with the palimpsest-like device of *misekechi* (showy erasure; canceling what is written in such a manner that the erased part remains visible): the "author" decides not to follow his initial plan to end the story with having Senkichi visit his benefactor's address only to find a small Inari shrine, because "it seems a little cruel to the shop boy."[41] (The thought that it might be even crueler to leave the boy believing in his "god" obviously does not occur to this "author.") A's misgivings after his philanthropic deed may simply seem like the guilt and embarrassment of the privileged, but they can also be interpreted as deriving from A's encounter with the naive, unfettered appetite of the child worker, which is to be satisfied only in a closed room, and A's absence.

Compared with the apotheosized A and the omniscient and technically accomplished narrator of the Shiga story, Miyamoto's young female narrator-protagonist is human, personal, and limited. She can be extremely precise and articulate, but she can also be a little careless and contradictory both as the heroine and as the narrator. The description of the three boys in the first chapter, for example, includes not only what the narrator can observe from behind the tree, but also things that it is impossible for her to know simply from watching: the almost painful sensation of the saliva that wets the boys' mouths, their perpetual hunger, and their father's repeated warning not to waste even one small grain of rice. Apart from these technical problems, there are incidents and expressions that reveal the narrator-protagonist's naivety, her naivety being an integral element in the novel. In the final chapter the narrator contemplates:

> I began to fear that most of what I did was actually to satisfy my own heart, which was starved for an opportunity to give. I gave them clothes, money, food, and sympathy, but what meaning did these things have in their lives? [. . .] I was not even as big as a poppy seed before you people. I have probably done many things you found disagreeable or stupid. [. . .]
> I am empty-handed. I have absolutely nothing. This small, miserable me,

completely at a loss, cannot do anything but mumble the question: what should I do?

But please do not hate me. I shall grasp something, I promise. However tiny it may be, I shall find something that you and I can be happy about. Please wait till then. Look after yourselves in your work, my sad friends!

I shall study even with tears in my eyes. I shall study hard.[42]

The narrative is unable to remain in the objective third person; it begins to address itself directly to the poor folks. This naive enthusiasm certainly fascinated many readers, including young and old anarchists, socialists, and communists.[43] One must also note, however, that the text includes some discerning analyses of the making of poor folks. The narrator, herself the granddaughter of the landlord who dedicated half his life to founding this small farming community in early Meiji, wonders whether it is really a good thing to cultivate fringe territory: "It is fine, of course, if it is a suitable place for human habitation and if there is hope for prosperity. But if it is somewhere with long winters and poor soil, is it still laudable to create a bunch of poor people?"[44]

She is also aware of the mechanism of exploitation and its impact upon children:

From an early age girls have to do the housework in place of their mothers, while boys are assigned to look after their little brothers and do some simple tasks in the field. Parents cannot afford to give their children the power to rise above their tenant status, and consequently tenant farmers' children end up as tenant farmers. That's almost a rule. Swarms of children grow only to enrich the landlords' dining tables, so to speak, by replacing their weakening parents.[45]

In a way, Miyamoto's narrative is the story of a privileged young woman's longing for the down-to-earth. Perhaps this explains why, unlike most other somber down-to-earth stories, it has some delightfully cheerful moments. In one instance, a child ventures into the narrator's grandmother's yard one night to steal some fruit. Completely entranced by the delicious apricots, the little intruder lets out a cry of joy. Then, frightened by the noise he has made and the prospect of being caught, he flees without picking up the fruit. Watching this incident, the narrator cannot help smiling: she understands and shares both the delight and the fear of this "lovable adventurer."[46] And as she smiles, many readers, and sometimes the villagers, smile (rather than snigger) at the blunders and emotional ups and downs of this narrator-protagonist, who herself is a lovable adventurer barely out of her adolescence.

Inevitably, perhaps, not every reader has found these adventures amusing or touching. Some, especially those who regarded themselves as "poor folks,"[47] found the text and its author offensively bourgeois. To complicate the matter further, it was not simply a class issue, that of a bourgeois writing about the peasantry. The narrator's age and gender also became issues. While some (like Tsubouchi Shōyō and Sakai Toshihiko) found it truly remarkable that a teenage girl could show such ideological and stylistic power and maturity, others attacked the alleged immaturity and arrogance of the work and its author. Evidently, regardless of whether reader response was positive or negative, the identification of the author with the narrator-protagonist seems to have strongly influenced the novel's reception.

Down-to-Earth Fantasy: Miyazawa Kenji

Many of our examples of down-to-earth eating and writing incorporate alarming issues and gruesome scenes.[48] Although these texts have differing degrees of lyrical, comic, satirical, grotesque, and polemical tones, it seems reasonable to say that realism is their common denominator. There is, however, a prominent exception in the writing of Miyazawa Kenji (1896–1933), who was deeply committed to the science, poetry, and ethics of food production and consumption. In his unpublished manifesto "Nōmin geijutsu gairon kōyō" (Outlines of Agrarian Art) Kenji writes, "Until the entire world attains happiness, there cannot be happiness for an individual."[49] As teacher, scientist, farmer, poet, and children's story writer he devoted his life and writing to that ideal of universal happiness and presented literally fantastic alternatives to the generally realistic, and often gloomy, down-to-earth eating and writing. "Down-to-earth fantasy" may seem an oxymoron. The following sample, though small, will demonstrate how such writing is possible. Kenji's writing has down-to-earth characteristics—such as the emphasis on the basic and essential and commitment to the here and now—but at the same time it is imaginary, in fact highly imaginative, and sublime, ethereal, spiritual, and even at times uncanny and perilous. That the primary audience of Kenji's stories and plays was children and adolescents by no means reduces the quality or the depth of his literature.

Let us look first at a delightful story, one of the most famous and beloved of all the stories Kenji wrote. At the time of its first publication "Chūmon no ōi ryōriten" (The Restaurant of Many Orders, 1924) was advertised as reflecting "the antagonism felt by village children with little food towards urban civilization and the self-indulgent classes."[50] This antagonism, we must say, is not entirely different from that encountered by the heroine of *Mazushiki hitobito no mure,* although the self-indulgent men in Kenji's story are obviously very different from the earnest sympathizer in Miyamoto's. Kenji's stories have no village urchins throwing stones at urban bourgeoisie; in fact in this particular story there are no child characters. And yet antagonism is certainly discernible in this story. The story blurs the division between food and the eater and even reverses the roles. Through effective use of onomatopoeia, repetition, irony, and other narrative and rhetorical devices, Kenji brings the fantastic world, which includes not only the beautiful and poetic but also some comic, absurd, as well as dangerous elements, to the mundane here and now.

Two snobbish gentlemen on a hunting expedition visit a restaurant called Yamanekoken (Wildcat House) and unwittingly prepare themselves to be eaten by the proprietor and staff of the restaurant: the prospect of eating lures these gullible philistines out of the safety and order of their everyday lives. Like Edogawa Ranpo's detective-horror story of cannibalism, which will be discussed in chapter 4, this story is set in the remote mountains, and like Ranpo's hotel, the restaurant in question is in the Western style. Unaware of what lurks beneath the modernity and sophistication, the visitors in both stories fall straight into the lethal trap that awaits them. The West as fashion plays an important role in "Chūmon no ōi ryōriten." The two men are attired "completely like English officers,"[51] and carry shiny new guns. They have neither hunting skills nor local knowledge. In short, they represent the complete opposite of the down-to-earth. They do not hunt for a living but for pleasure; if they cannot catch anything, they simply buy some game birds from the locals to take home (and probably to brag about, pretending that they have shot them). Their hunting dogs are valuable to them not as companions but as highly priced commodities. These men obviously have no qualms about killing and eating animals, which clearly goes against Kenji's Buddhist convictions and his vegetarian principles.

These vegetarian principles are elaborated on in another delightful but less well known story, "Bijiterian Taisai" (The Grand Festival of Vegetarians).[52] The story takes the form of a report on a world vegetarian convention held in a small village on the island of Newfoundland. In a series of debates vegetarians from all over the world refute the arguments of their opponents from the Chicago Stockbreeders' Union, and prove that their beliefs are correct from a wide range of perspectives, including those of taxonomy, animal psychology, comparative anatomy, dietetics, economics, ethics, and theology. Kenji incorporates all these viewpoints in a literally polyphonic manner. One Kenji scholar and aero physicist, Saitō Bun'ichi comments thus:

"The Grand Festival of Vegetarians" [...] is unusual among Kenji's works in that it centers on debates; it is almost like a thesis. And this displays Kenji's gifts in argumentation. What is really remarkable, however, is that such arguments are mixed with warning and lament in a narrative told in an easy fairy tale–like style. This is Kenji's testimony from his own life, and at the same time it provides the best kind of footnotes to understand that higher sphere that lies beyond ordinary people's imagination, namely the world that Kenji called "fantasy."[53]

While the story has the clear message not to harm, let alone eat, other living creatures, it certainly has multiple dimensions, and its ending presents problematic ambiguities. After all the arguments against vegetarianism are refuted carefully and completely, and all the opponents have been converted to vegetarians, it is revealed that everything has been a prepared act of entertainment to celebrate the occasion—all those "opponents" were indeed vegetarians playing the roles of the "heathen" carnivores and stockbreeders. In the midst of the festive, victorious mood of fellow vegetarians the narrator alone is disillusioned: "I was so aghast that the pleasant fantasy of the Grand Festival of Vegetarians was shattered. So I must ask you, everyone, to complete this as you wish, with a common dance scene from a movie or whatever."[54]

Many of Kenji's stories and plays do end on a happier note, however. In 1922, Kenji wrote a short operetta, "Kiga jin'ei" (The Camp of Starvation), which was performed under his direction the following year by his students at Hanamaki Agricultural School. The self-indulgent classes are represented in this play by General Bananan, who returns to his camp stuffed with food and drink, while his men are all starving. However, when his desperate sergeant and soldiers have eaten his precious banana epaulettes and his medals that are made of candy, the general, inspired by some divine revelation, invents "production exercises," a new kind of physical exercise that will produce fruit for everyone.[55] The military, identified as one of the three enemies of the workers in Kobayashi Takiji's text considered below, is in this musical fantasy given a second chance to change starvation into harvest, without the use of violence or aggression against human beings or any other living creature: the play is a celebration of communal and ethical food production. Similarly, the story "Yukiwatari" (Snow-Crossing, 1921) includes a wonderful example of the celebration of communal eating. Two human children are invited to a lantern-slide show organized by fox children, and accept what their hosts offer them despite the common folklore that foxes trick human beings into eating animal droppings. This act of eating is seen to establish mutual trust between innocent human and fox children who understand how to respect one another.

Kenji's alternative to down-to-earth writing may not have the kind of ethnographical or sociohistorical significance that many critics find in *Tsuchi*, and it does not urge the reader to act against oppression. Nevertheless, few would argue that his writing is less committed or less effective than the other texts discussed in this chapter and the next. Kenji's Preface to the collection of stories *Chūmon no ōi ryōriten* begins with the statement that "[w]e may not have as much sugar candy as we want, but we can eat the clear transparent wind and drink the beautiful pink rays of the morning."[56] While thus pointing out that we are surrounded by clean and magical foods and drinks that are the blessings of nature, he insists that all his stories are also "given" to him by nature, "the rainbow and the moonlight,"[57] and expresses the hope that "some pieces of these little stories will become genuine transparent food" for each reader.[58] "Transparent" may be interpreted in different ways here: as fresh and innocent, untainted by prejudice, greed, and other human vices, liberated from socioideological preconceptions, useless in worldly terms, and so on. Significantly, it is left to the reader to determine how to eat and digest this "transparent" food.

To illustrate this last point, it will be useful to quote a passage from Amazawa Taijirō's essay on *Chūmon no ōi ryōriten*. Amazawa, who is known as a poet, a translator, a writer of children's stories, and a leading scholar of Miyazawa Kenji studies, presents his reading of Kenji's book "as a restaurant." After a careful analysis of individual stories in the collection, Amazawa concludes thus:

> First, a restaurant makes its customers believe that it is going to provide food (or alternatively it may actually offer some food), but ultimately it is a device that eats the customers and gets fat.
>
> Second, generally speaking, stories are restaurants that survive for hundreds of years by eating readers.[59]

So far we have seen only a few examples of texts eating other texts; we will see many other cases in the following chapters, but here Amazawa draws our attention to a different kind of textual cannibalism: texts eating readers who believe that they are eating the texts. This interesting premise seems similar to the late-nineteenth-century European notion of the autonomy of art, and yet it also incorporates (or eats up) generations of readers and perhaps even the reception theory as well. In this sense it is a fitting conclusion to this discussion of Kenji's down-to-earth fantasy that continues to devour readers and grows fatter and fatter.

Proletarian Eating and Writing: Sata Ineko and Kobayashi Takiji

The division between those who can afford to eat and those who cannot has, of course, been a theme in literature unlimited to time or place. Nevertheless it was the so-called proletarian literature of the late 1920s and early 1930s that pioneered strategic representations of food as a sign of class distinction. While the social commitment of the narrator-protagonist of *Mazushiki hitobito no mure* does not really go beyond the bounds of a youthful dream, the two examples we will now consider focus on the class struggle itself rather than on the development of an individual. Another notable difference between these works and those of the previous decade involves the contemporaneous shift in economic focus from primary to secondary and tertiary industry. The recurring motif is one of workers being devoured by capitalists. I have chosen two texts for discussion. Both depict the exploitation of food industry workers.

The first is Sata Ineko's (1904–1998) short story "Kyarameru kōjō kara" (From the Caramel Factory, 1928). It is interesting in many respects to compare this work to that of Miyamoto. Each is the author's debut work, and each deals with the hunger and exploitation of children. Soon after the publication of Sata's story the two writers became friends and comrades, and both played a central role in the proletarian/communist movement. However, differences in their form, style, and approach are clear from the outset.

Sata's thirteen-year-old[60] heroine, Hiroko, barely has time for breakfast, which is an indispensable source of energy for her long hours at work. It is also the only source of warmth on a cold winter morning. Hiroko must rush each day to get to work on time because the factory gates close at seven sharp. Because management finds it too troublesome to calculate a penalty to deduct from their already meager wages, workers who arrive after seven are excluded for the day, thus denying them their badly needed day's wages. The tram Hiroko takes to the factory is full of workers and reeks of their hurried breakfasts. "Hiroko squeezed herself in between adult legs. She, too, was a worker—a fragile, little worker, like grass to be eaten by a horse."[61]

Unlike Miyamoto's narrator-protagonist, Sata's narrator, separate from the heroine Hiroko, never comes to the fore; there is no indication of the sex, age, ideology, or any other characteristics of this narrator. Nowhere in the story do we find direct comments or propaganda. And although the writing is simple and straightforward, with short, unembellished sentences, it is neither simplistic nor monotonous. The narrative consists mostly of external descriptions of events and conditions, interspersed with occasional dialogues. Only now and then is there a reference to Hiroko's thoughts and feelings. The entire story, which takes up only several pages, is roughly the same length as Shiga Naoya's story. Packed into these pages is a remarkable amount of information, not only about Hiroko's routines at the factory, working conditions, and her relations with her bosses and co-workers, but also about her extended family, their financial situation, and their educational backgrounds.

Hiroko has been forced to leave school, where she was in fifth grade and doing well. Obviously she would rather be at school than working in the factory, where she suffers the humiliation of being one of the least efficient. When the factory abolishes the fixed-wage system, her income is cut by two-thirds. Girls in the factory are allowed to eat broken fragments of caramel, but they must pay for their afternoon snack (always sweet potatoes) from their salaries. One of the few pleasures in the lives of these girls occurs on those days when the factory produces their favorite flavor. However, although these girls are children, just like the target consumers of their products, unlike the child consumers, these child workers are not allowed to eat caramel at home. At the end of the day's work, each girl is checked at the factory gate to ensure she has no caramel in her lunch box, pocket, or sleeve.

The story makes clear that the exploitation of child workers starts at home. It also gives us an image of a girl that is in sad contrast to the newly developed girls' culture of the time, represented by Yoshiya Nobuko's stories and Takarazuka, and the notion of the girl as consumer. It is Hiroko's father[62] who decides to send her to the factory, while apparently making no effort to find a job himself. The only faintly tendentious term in this story, "petty bourgeois," appears in an account of the father's pretentious aspirations to rise above his station. It is these pretensions that, combined with his irresponsible nature, make him abandon a steady but unglamorous job in a country town, fritter away all his assets and savings, and take his family to Tokyo without any clear plan for the future. It is purely at her father's whim (the job is with a well-known company) that Hiroko starts working at the factory, which is so far from their house that it takes not only a long time but also a good portion of her wages to commute by tram. He tells her about the job advertisement while the family is eating a meal, and suggests that she should apply. Hiroko is so surprised and upset that she can only respond by "silently stuff[ing] rice into her mouth," for when she tries to mention the word "school" tears well up in her eyes.[63] Her father, however, takes no notice of her reaction. Although at the end of the story he allows Hiroko to leave the factory, it is merely to take another menial job in a small noodle shop. He will not permit her to return to school.

Although this story is based on Sata's own experience as a child, Hiroko's move from secondary industry into the service industry (both food-related jobs) interestingly parallels the direction of Japanese capitalism at that period. At the same time, as depicted in Hayashi Fumiko's and many other texts of this period, working in restaurants and cafés was one of the few ways in which women could earn a living, however meager, in the rapidly growing cities.

The exploitation of laborers in the food processing industry in Kobayashi Takiji's (1903–1933) *Kani kōsen* (Crab Cannery Boat, 1929) is much more brutal and extreme than that in Sata's story. These workers are recruited from primary industries such as mining and agriculture, where they have been unable to earn even a subsistence wage or have been made redundant and thrown off the land, like "peas fried in a pan."[64] Food is frequently used in this text to depict the horrendous conditions on the crab boat.

The living quarters of the workers below decks are called *kuso tsubo* (shit pots) because of their airless and unsanitary atmosphere. It is so cold that "living creatures shiver as if they had been mistaken for salmon and trout and thrown into a refrigerator."[65] When they eat, the workers need to be careful that their running noses do not drip onto their hot rice. They eat their humble meals below decks, where they are eaten alive by fleas, lice, and bedbugs, while their superiors and their guests feast, literally, above them in the ship's saloon.

The *kuso tsubo* is a scatological melting pot of the rejected and discarded. Before working on the cannery boat, most of the men experienced abusive treatment in other industries. So they know, for example, that construction workers in the "new colony," Hokkaidō, are called "octopuses" because they "eat their own limbs in order to survive" and that miners are sliced like tuna in explosions.[66] Gruesome descriptions of the abuse, torture, and murder of workers continue, along with an analysis of the true cause of such brutality.

> When workers on the mainland became "arrogant" and could no longer be readily exploited, and when there was no more room for a new market, capitalists extended their claws to Hokkaidō and Sakhalin. There, just as in the colonies of Korea and Taiwan, they could abuse and maltreat people as they wished. They knew that no one would be able to speak out. Laborers building national roads and railways were crushed to death more easily than lice. Some just could not take any more and ran away. When those fugitives were caught, they would be tied to a post and kicked by a horse or bitten to death by a dog in a backyard. [...] At mealtimes workers might hear a scream, which would be followed by the smell of scorched human flesh.[67]

This tale of the scorched, torn, beaten, bitten, and eaten (in the last two cases not literally by the torturers themselves but by dogs, fleas, and other animal life) flesh of the workers is, to say the least, strong stuff. The horror of these descriptions has by no means waned over time: in fact it is so powerful that seven decades after its publication critic Aramata Hiroshi suggested a new reading of this canonical proletarian novel—as a "splatter horror" novel.[68] Aramata believes that the brutality depicted in the text is so extreme that it comes close to jeopardizing its political intent. Before this new reading was suggested by Aramata, Nakamura Murao, in response to the depiction of a superintendent on the factory ship as a representative of pernicious brutality, expressed the view that the novel's fatal flaw was that it "treated individual evil but not organizational evil."[69] How should we read these horrendous descriptions that are juxtaposed with the neatly outlined, almost textbook-like, explanations of the background, motivation, and structure of exploitation?

One point to note is what Suzuki Sadami calls "genre mix"—the cross-generic or transgeneric characteristics of this period.[70] From the printed view of literary history, the literature of early Shōwa (i.e., the late 1920s and early 1930s) is customarily divided into several genres and subgenres, such as shishōsetsu, proletarian literature, modernist literature, and "mass" literature (which is further divided into detective stories, samurai novels, and so on). Such categorization, however, ignores the fact that certain characteristics and motifs recur across genres. As we shall see in more detail in chapter 4, ero guro nansensu (eroticism, grotesquery, and nonsense) is the phrase associated with the popular culture of this period. However, if we can free ourselves of discourses associated with the cult of serious literature, we can find this triad even in an overtly serious and politically committed novel such as this work by Kobayashi. This is exactly what Aramata tries to show in his reading of this and other proletarian classics as detective stories, erotic novels, or science fiction.

Of course, the reader cannot ignore the fact that Kobayashi himself was tortured and killed by the police only a few years after the publication of this novel. The novel was banned soon after, and was not available again in its entirety until after the war. We may or may not accept Keene's assessment that Kobayashi's fame "may owe more to his political martyrdom than to literary excellence,"[71] but it is impossible for the postwar reader not to read the descriptions of the atrocities committed against workers in this novel, both on board the ship and elsewhere, without thinking of the brutality that culminated in the murder of the author. In other words, in overt contrast to the theories of the autonomy of art or Barthesian "death of the author," this text demands that the reader take into account the author's life (or to be more precise, his literal, historical death), regardless of his own intent.

To return to our concern with food and eating in this text, we notice that the first two-thirds of the novel are full of hideous, even nauseating, food metaphors and metonymy, examples of which appear above. When the workers start to react against their inhuman treatment by management through strikes and sabotage, however, food suddenly disappears from the text and does not surface again until the concluding chapter. The exploited workers, now united, become aware of "who their enemies are, and how those enemies are (*quite unexpectedly!*) connected to each other."[72] The enemies of the workers are, first of all, the industrialists and politicians who endlessly exploit them on the pretext of "a mission to solve the problems of overpopulation and food shortage."[73] The police and the military in turn protect the industrialists rather than the workers and in return are allowed to share in the capitalist feast. And presiding over them all is the imperial family, to whom the company makes a presentation of its product every year. While it takes no time for the workers to identify the first category of enemy, many continue to harbor illusions about the goodwill of the military, while the emperor is simply too remote a figure to stir up any antagonism among them. However, with the bitter failure of their first uprising, the workers come to realize that the imperial navy would side with the capitalists rather than those being exploited by them. The position of the emperor in this exploitation mechanism becomes evident, too, leading one worker to observe that "[the presentation cans] are made from real flesh and blood squeezed out of us. I bet they taste good. They're lucky if they don't get stomachache."[74]

We have seen in this chapter texts that are usually categorized as peasant literature, Bildungsroman, children's literature, and proletarian literature respectively. Despite the fact that they are all roughly contemporaneous, these writers and their texts, with the exception of the three proletarian writers (including Miyamoto), are rarely discussed together. The broader category of down-to-earth literature allows us to compare and contrast the diverse approaches and techniques these writers adopted, while the specific focus on food has enabled us to highlight the multiplicity of the seemingly simple and straightforward.

Chapter Three

Down-to-Earth Eating
and Writing (2)

As we saw in the previous chapter, down-to-earth representations of food and eating tend to focus on disempowered, marginalized people, although the style and form vary. This chapter begins with an examination of some women's texts that demonstrate that hunger is not simply a physical and socioeconomic issue, but has also a deep connection with gender. In the middle section of the chapter I discuss three novels that depict the hunger and appetite of various social dropouts, outcasts, and marginalized people in the prewar, wartime, and postwar periods. The final text examined in this chapter is somewhat different from the others, as it does not deal with marginalization or poverty, but with an issue that obviously concerns us all, regardless of sex, age, class, or race—namely, food safety. In the texts discussed below issues concerning the body, which played important roles in some texts discussed in the previous chapters, feature even more prominently. Important also in this chapter are the myths and the discriminations that concern "purity" and "cleanliness" that are closely linked to the body and to the production and consumption of food.

Gender-Specific Hunger in Women's Narratives

As Deborah Lupton summarizes the situation,[1] feminist critics have focused on three major issues in relation to food and gender: women's historical deprivation of food, women's responsibility for food preparation, and the links between the construction of femininity and the dietary practices of women. We have seen in the previous chapters some examples of the first two points, which are often closely related. The depiction of these issues is by no means limited to women's literature. In many cases, however, even when texts written by male writers such as Shiki and Nagatsuka clearly mark the gender division, this fact went unnoticed until feminist scholars drew attention to it. Furthermore, whereas women, understandably, have tended to imply or actually articulate criticism of the gender division with respect to food and eating, male writers seldom make an issue of it, even when they depict that division. In this section I shall discuss further representations of Lupton's first two points in women's texts (the third issue, that of femininity and diet, will be discussed in chapter 6). Most of the texts chosen here are broadly regarded as being based on the authors' own experiences. However, they are seldom discussed as *shishōsetsu*, precisely because, as Mizuta Noriko notes, in modern Japanese literary discourses female subjectivity has been nonexistent, even though women's urge to write and their methodological struggles may have drawn some attention.[2]

Starting with three writers who were involved in the Marxist/proletarian movement, we will see how each text consciously depicts not only class but also gender division. Hunger, both physical and metaphorical, is the recurring theme. "Hunger is hunger," as Gayle Rubin remarks, "but what counts as food is culturally determined and obtained."[3] We might further say that even hunger, although often metaphorical rather than physical, can be determined and obtained culturally and gender-specifically. Depicting this gender-specific hunger is a statement of protest against oppression as well as a desperate need for empowerment.[4] Sharalyn Orbaugh identifies three main strategies employed by women writing fiction against the dominant economies of power:

1. to maintain and *describe* the current configurations of power, exposing the harm done through them;
2. to maintain and describe the current configurations of power, but to *invert the hierarchy of value*, to valorize the object/passive side of the equation;
3. to maintain the current binary configurations of power, but to *reverse the gender coding* of the hierarchical power roles.[5]

These strategies are certainly dominant in the women's texts discussed here and in other chapters.

Nearly a decade after depicting the hunger of children in *Mazushiki hitobito no mure*, Miyamoto Yuriko wrote *Nobuko*.[6] *Nobuko* contains several scenes in which food marks relational disunity, mainly between the eponymous heroine and her husband. Nobuko's husband, Tsukuda, refuses to share the family meal or teatime at Nobuko's parents' home, where the young couple temporarily live.

This refusal seems partly to stem from the class difference between him and the rest of the family—Nobuko is an upper-middle-class daughter, whereas Tsukuda is from the working class. More important, it is brought about by their personal incompatibility, which in this particular case clearly relates to gender issues. When Nobuko realizes that the marriage is unworkable, the metaphor of eating is used: "to Nobuko, who was at the height of her inner growth, an artistic atmosphere was just as essential as food; the lack of this deeply tormented her."[7] It is used again a few pages later:

> His kind of happiness did not need Nobuko. Should she watch her satisfied husband eat his happiness, with a smile on her face and with nothing to eat herself? She was the sort of person who wanted to eat. She felt hunger acutely. She was someone who could not help eating. She realized that she had to find or create what she wanted by herself. If she asked him, he would give her some. Only she could never eat his; she wanted something cleaner.[8]

Unlike the narrator of *Hōrōki*, Nobuko never physically suffers from hunger; food represents the intellectual and artistic fulfillment that the heroine considers lacking in her relationship with her husband. Orbaugh's second strategy—the inversion of the hierarchy of value—is evident. For centuries women have been stigmatized as unclean in myths, religions, and sociocultural discourses. As Rebecca Copeland summarizes:

> Ancient worldviews frequently equated the female with the impure, often with evil itself. Given that her body was the site of discharges and emissions, of miraculous change and transformations, she has been suspect of harboring all that is dangerous and threatening. Her power was most apparent during her menses or at childbirth, when her body demonstrated the amazing capacity to reproduce itself. Women in these states were thus labeled unclean and defiled.[9]

Accordingly, the primal female and mother of the Japanese archipelago, Izanami, dies after giving birth and is sent to the underworld for the dead, Yomi. And once she has eaten the unclean food of Yomi, her body starts to decay. She "becomes the very embodiment of both desire and defilement."[10] The powerful myth of Izanami and its variations have been inscribed upon the female body for centuries.

In Miyamoto's novel, however, it is Nobuko who regards her husband's food and his happiness as unclean and who feels that eating what belongs to him would be unclean. Perhaps because of this inversion some (male) critics have labeled Miyamoto, and particularly this novel, masculine and even "phallic."[11] Refuting this absurd claim, Mizuta Noriko remarks:

> Many male readers find Nobuko disagreeable and even offensive because her husband Tsukuda is neither patriarchal nor tyrannical but willing to be of service to her. Had he been depicted as a husband with no sympathy for the heroine torn between her writing and her duties as wife and mother, male readers and critics would surely have accepted *Nobuko* as a typical feminist novel.[12]

One recalls that Izanami, too, offended her husband, Izanagi, during their courtship by speaking first and thus "usurping male authority."[13] While the myths suppress Izanami's voice and confine her to Yomi and transform her into the horrible, dangerous, disgusting, and foul body oozing with maggots and worms, Nobuko rejects confinement and seeks for clean and inspiring food for her mind.

The following texts by Sata Ineko and Hirabayashi Taiko are much closer to the "typical feminist novel," or at least may be easier for male critics to accept as such than *Nobuko*. Their narratives clearly show that it was more or less taken for granted that women who engaged in leftist literary and political movements would provide food and other necessities for their whole family, including their husbands and lovers, who might be imprisoned for illegal political activities. These men were regarded as martyrs to their principles, both within their circle at the time and by later generations. However, the support of their partners, who themselves were involved in similar activities, went unrecognized until much later. In Sata Ineko's novels, the protagonist, Akiko, is a writer deeply committed to the Marxist movement. Although written after the war, *Haguruma* (Cogwheels, 1958–1959) is set in the early 1930s, when "the oppressive atmosphere after the Manchurian and Shanghai incidents was lowering outside."[14] The problems Akiko faces are not simply poverty and severe political oppression, but also the conflict between her family duties and her professional and ideological principles. As a wife, she is expected to look after the family while her husband, Kōsuke, is in prison. However, as if feeding herself and her young children is not difficult enough, she is also expected to send extra food and clothes to her husband, who clearly takes her contributions more or less for granted.

In *Kurenai* (Crimson, 1936), Kōsuke is out of jail. Akiko's problem is no longer how to feed her family but how to find a balance between her wifely duties and the pursuit of her own interests. She confides thus to her close friend and comrade Kishiko, who is obviously modeled after Miyamoto Yuriko:

"I know this is a rather trivial example, but when Kōsuke is arguing with someone else, I just make tea without uttering a word. That's all I can do, make tea
silently. Otherwise it would be awkward—as if I were speaking in league with my
husband. When I'm with him, I know others just see me as his wife."[15]

The dilemma plunges her into a severe depression accompanied by a complete loss of appetite ("I cannot eat even a small teacup full of rice").[16] Anorexia
nervosa, if we accept Counihan's view of that disorder, is a rejection of "re-
ceptivity, connection, and reproduction."[17] Instead, Akiko attempts a quicker
method of rejection—suicide by gassing herself in the kitchen. Nakano Shigeharu suggests that the gas stove is a symbol of the only option left to many
women.[18]

If the gas stove is one topos, there is another, at once concrete and symbolic,
that indicates the cumulative difficulty faced by women as mothers—a charity
maternity ward. In the opening scene of *Haguruma* Akiko is giving birth in the
charity delivery ward of the Imperial University hospital. Her three-year-old
boy is waiting at home with a babysitter, and her husband is in jail. Compared to
O-Shina in *Tsuchi*, she is lucky: surrounded by a medical team, her baby daughter is safely delivered, and she herself is competently treated for massive hemor-
rhaging. What troubles Akiko is not the doctor's advice that she should never
have another baby but the fact that she is not producing milk. This is for her
"a defeat at the hands of her own body."[19] She wonders if it is a result of all the
stress caused by the recent mass arrest—of her husband, her friends, and her
comrades. Her most urgent task is to eat as much as she can afford in order to
be able to breast-feed the baby and avoid having to use expensive and less nutritious baby formula. Thus even when she does eat, it is not for herself but for her
family, to whom her body belongs.

This scene is reminiscent of a similar but much more extreme situation in
which a young mother finds herself in Hirabayashi Taiko's short story "Seryōshitsu nite" (In the Charity Ward, 1927). The first-person narrator-protagonist returns from the custody of the military police to the charity ward of a hospital in
Manchuria to have a baby. Her husband is in jail for his involvement in a labor
dispute and the bombing of a railway construction site. Regarded as an accom-
plice, the young woman is to be sent back to prison as soon as she recovers. On
top of all this, she is suffering from a severe case of beriberi, apparently caused
by long-term malnutrition and "the atmosphere of the colony with so much red
dust,"[20] which implies, as in *Tsuchi*, that the soil contains something harmful.
She delivers a baby girl, as she wanted, a "Bolshevichka" with slanting eyes, but
the young mother is in no condition to give her daughter even the most basic

care. Unlike Akiko in *Haguruma*, this young woman can produce milk. However, because it is contaminated by the mother's beriberi, it would only make the baby sick and perhaps even kill her.[21] The hospital management is devoid of any vestige of charitable spirit and refuses to give anything to its impoverished patients—even something as essential as artificial food supplements for the baby.

> Be it beriberi milk, or pus, my dear child is drinking it with pleasure. My poor peasant grandfather and my craftsman father, in fact they all worked and worked in order to feed their children, as numerous as maggots, till they died totally worn out. The strong desire to provide food for one's children is a thread of steel that runs through the age-old tradition of the poor.[22]

While the narrator-protagonist, as we have seen, thinks of her father and grandfather as nurturers, the predominant image in Hirabayashi's text is that of the incompetent male. The heroine's husband and their male comrades, here and in many other works by Hirabayashi and other women writers, are oblivious to and thus incapable of adopting any sort of responsible attitude to the necessities of survival. This is in spite of, or perhaps because of, their strong political convictions.

> I shall not hold a grudge against my husband. It was all too obvious to me that if we were to carry out such an act of terrorism this would be the consequence. My husband and our three comrades laughed at my thoughts as the cowardice of a pregnant woman. The result, however, was just as I predicted. If it is a general rule, however, that we cannot break through without facing up to this kind of difficulty, then those of us committed to the movement must face it, and I, as a wife, must follow my husband. I have no regrets.[23]

It may be surprising to find this seeming echoing of the patriarchal "good wife and wise mother" (*ryōsai kenbo*) in a revolutionary woman. However, the story makes it clear that this protagonist actually leads in her own way, despite everything. Even in their dire predicament she has this message for her "weak-willed" husband: "My dear comrade, do not look to either side, but look straight ahead."[24] And to herself and other women she urges, "Believe in the future. If your love for your children is strong, you must vow to fight for your love."[25]

Despite such courageous words, the heroine cannot rescue her baby from her inevitable death. The harshness and sinisterness of the situation and the sheer hypocrisy of the "charity" are captured in the manner in which a trainee nurse brings the news of the baby's death to the mother. "I'm really sorry," says the messenger, with a smile on her face, "but she died at exactly four o'clock."[26] The baby's body is sent to the mortuary for postmortem. The autopsy is to prove that the infant's death was caused by the milk and that a mother suffering from beriberi should not breast-feed her baby. The brutal hypocrisy of this practice is only too clear to the dead child's mother, who observes, "What they will never be able to deduce from the autopsy of my poor little baby, however, is what those who cannot afford artificial food supplements should do."[27]

If these stories present women bearing the unbearable, a story Hirabayashi wrote after the war presents a very different picture. The narrator-protagonist of "Watashi wa ikiru"[28] (I Mean to Live, 1947) is bedridden. Her husband, recently released from jail, is devotedly looking after her with the help of a carer-maid. Her illness is not specified in the story. Unlike in Shiki's diaries there is no description here of excruciating pain or oozing pus, but her condition seems to be serious. As we have seen, the invalid writer of Shiki's diaries supped on sardines, eels, and oysters, while his sister and mother ate pickles in a corner of the kitchen. In the same manner, the heroine in this story is fed real soup that comes from the butcher every day, while her husband and the maid eat the tasteless remnants of the meat used to make the soup. Illness has given this protagonist the power to claim "the right to be cured" by any means.[29] Her husband not only is in charge of cooking but also looks after her chamber pot. And she unhesitatingly commands him to close the window on a midsummer's day or to keep it open on a cold winter's night, to search every part of Tokyo for ice cream, or to fetch a hot-water bottle or check her pulse in the middle of the night. The results are highly effective: "I felt as if the illness had removed all the old leaves from the lettuce that was me and replaced them with fresh green leaves. My tired old blood was completely consumed and fresh young blood was forcing its way in instead."[30]

Although it was published in 1947, the story curiously does not mention the nationwide food shortage or the social turmoil of the times. In fact, it is not clear whether it is set in the immediate postwar years or during the war. This is presumably because the heroine, confined to her sickbed (like Shiki), has lost interest (unlike Shiki) in anything but her own illness. And yet it seems tempting to see a metaphor for the postwar recuperation and rebirth of women in the growth of new leaves and the new blood replacing the old, albeit in the confines of the sickbed. Hirabayashi here successfully employs the third strategy on Orbaugh's list—namely, "to reverse the gender coding of the hierarchical power roles."[31] The heroine's self-centeredness and obsession with her body, when contrasted with the oppression and hardship symbolized by the kitchen gas stove and the maternity ward, certainly communicates its significance to the reader, especially the woman reader.

Hunger does not disappear from postwar women's literature, and this applies not only to autobiographical texts or to writers involved in leftist political activities. Kōda Aya (1904–1990), for instance, started her writing career as a "literary daughter"—daughter of the famous writer Kōda Rohan (1867–1947; see chapter 5 for a discussion of his writing). Food, especially its preparation, permeates her memoirs, essays, and fiction. She was a pioneer in giving artistic form to the meticulous scrutiny of housework, including cooking. Both the scrutiny and the actual housework skills were originally taught by her father and were further developed by herself.[32] Aya's writing has often been criticized for its apparent submissiveness.[33] As some critics have already warned,[34] however, it is simplistic to regard it as narrow, submissively feminine, or antifeminist. While Aya's female narrators and protagonists try to maintain the domestic order, in their struggles they do express resentment of or at least dissatisfaction with the roles forced upon them. One of the most telling examples in Aya's memoirs recounts how a visitor's irresponsible words sharpened the appetite of the bedridden father and forced the daughter, already exhausted from the demanding task of looking after him in the midst of wartime food shortages, to go out in search of seafood, even though she was still feverish after a bout of pneumonia.[35] Aya also recalls how she hated New Year's feasts, which to her father meant long drinking sessions with his friends but to her were times when she had to "taste the melancholy of the kitchen."[36]

In Aya's fiction the dissent is often not directed toward the powerful father but toward other characters. The incapable and selfish husband of "Shokuyoku" (Appetite, 1956), for instance, is silently but firmly criticized when he expects his wife, Sunao, who has with great difficulty managed to borrow the money for his hospitalization, to bring him expensive tidbits during his convalescence:

> Without a single word about money, her husband clamored for food. [. . .] This dish from such and such a restaurant, that from another, eels from such and such, and smaller skewers from another, and as for tempura, chicken, beefsteak, ham, tongue stew, vegetarian dishes, pickles . . . Sunao would not protest. Silently she wrote in her mind, "I'm exhausted," and engraved on her heart, "I want to let my child eat, and I want to eat too. But we don't want to eat nice dishes like this."[37]

The situation reminds us of Masaoka Shiki's appetite and his relationship with his sister. In Aya's story the woman protagonist is given a voice, albeit merely "silently" and "in her mind." The reader recognizes the collective voice of hundreds and thousands of women in Sunao's silent declaration. We may also note that the sumptuous food demanded by her selfish husband disgusts her; though she does not use the term, it is unclean.

Another important representative of "women's literature,"[38] Enchi Fumiko (1905–1986), also wrote of a woman looking after her invalid husband. Unlike most other texts discussed in this section, this story, poignantly titled "Himojii tsukihi" (Starving Days, 1953), has no autobiographical element. Here, hunger has multiple meanings: the physical sensation caused by lack of food is much less important than the psychological and emotional hunger of the female protagonist, who looks after her paralyzed husband. That physical hunger is unimportant is evident also in the case of one of her daughters, who is happy to go without supper in order to save money for her marriage. Only when there is no such hope for the future and no affectionate memory of the past, as in the case of the mother, does having to skip meals become something deeply resented. Enchi's story concludes with the sudden death of the older woman, a death certainly brought about by decades of exhausting and stressful work and physical and emotional starvation.

In Enchi's much later short work "Hana kui uba" (The Old Woman Who Eats Flowers, 1974), eating flowers is given an erotic significance. Although this story does not really belong to the category of down-to-earth literature, it deserves mention here because its eating metaphor certainly indicates the gender issue. The narrator-protagonist meets a mysterious old woman who, although obviously her double, has no hesitation or compunction, unlike the narrator herself, about eating flowers. The old woman considers this act a natural consequence of admiration. Here is one exchange between the two women:

"There's no rule that says flowers are to be seen but not to be eaten. If we think they are beautiful, we feel like keeping them around us, and then naturally we feel like going further than just looking at them. We want to touch them, pluck them, and own them, even if it will deform them. Ultimately we want to eat them."

"You sound as if you're talking about a man falling in love with a woman."

[...]

"You're munching on red flowers like that. People may think you're either suffering from some illness or [are] simply crazy."

"Crazy . . . mad . . . Very well. But I know you yourself are dying to pluck and eat flowers. You just don't have the courage to do what you want to do."[39]

The old woman advises the narrator to eat what she likes. What we must note is that eating flowers in this story is connected not only to eroticism but also to artistic and intellectual pursuits. In this sense it reminds us of *Nobuko*, although the narrative style and structure and the personality of the protagonist in Enchi's story are very different from those of Miyamoto's novel. As if in a Noh play, the old woman leads the narrator, who herself is not very young, into another world, in this case the narrator's girlhood, a time when sexuality was repressed and concealed. On her way back from the library (where she was reading Galsworthy's *Strife*), the narrator as a young woman meets a young man, her brother's friend. While he insists that happiness cannot be found in books, she claims that it cannot be found outside books, either.

> "I studied law, so I don't understand literature. But I must say I don't like the face of a woman reading a book."
> Oh, well—I said nothing but just turned sideways. Emotionally I was too immature and inflexible to retort, for example, "You like the face of a woman chopping something in the kitchen."[40]

Even in this daydream the narrator does not feel carefree enough to "eat flowers." Miyauchi Junko regards this "flora-eating" as a rejection of connection between eating and sexuality and contrasts it with the "fauna-eating" as represented by Tanizaki literature,[41] which will be discussed in chapter 5.

From Crap to Scrap: Yasuoka Shōtarō and Kaikō Takeshi

While the totally self-centered husbands in the stories discussed above are given only minor roles, modern Japanese fiction boasts a long list of pathetically useless male protagonists. In a peacetime setting, Yasuki Kasuke, the protagonist of Yasuoka Shōtarō's novel *Tonsō* (An Escape, 1956), would merely make a mediocre antihero. In the absurdly brutal milieu of the Japanese Imperial Army, however, he is, in his own estimation, the first or second from the bottom among the lowest-ranking soldiers. Loyalty and patriotism mean nothing to him, and although at one stage he tells a fellow soldier that he is an antimilitarist, he does absolutely nothing to demonstrate this. Since he is slow and sluggish, he becomes the object of constant bullying. Among the perpetrators of this bullying, a young corporal called Hamada is particularly sadistic, reminding us of the superintendent in *Kani kōsen*. The title of the novel refers to a series of escapes by Kasuke. These include escape from Hamada, escape from being sent to Leyte and certain death, and finally escape from the *gaichi* (foreign land, colony) of Manchuria and the Imperial Army. His successes in this respect are the result of a combination of his weak condition and sheer luck. We have seen how illness curiously empowers the heroine of Hirabayashi's postwar story. Kasuke's survival owes much to his morbid appetite, his chronic diarrhea, and his pleurisy.

Obsessed with food, Kasuke wonders at the outset of the novel when it was that he became so fixated: was it when they were crossing the frontier between Korea and Manchuria, or was it much earlier? What is clear is that his obsession has more to do with the authoritarian nature of military life than with actual hunger due to the shortage of supplies. Soldiers have no privacy—even in the toilets. They must report whenever they have to leave their position, so the brutal corporal Hamada knows how often each soldier under his command visits the toilet. He even checks the toilet for any sign of diarrhea or masturbation should someone exit suspiciously. Chillingly, this bully is not yet twenty years old. Since the punishment for those with loose bowels is an enforced fast of at least twenty-four hours, Kasuke needs to be extra careful not to make any noise while in the toilet. One day, when he is unable to control the noises emitted during his bowel movement, he hears a similar sound coming from the next cubicle, which "rescue[s] Kasuke from despair."[42]

Kasuke's company is initially stationed in northern Manchuria. When it is mobilized to be sent somewhere in Southeast Asia, obviously a much more dangerous area, Kasuke's appetite becomes uncontrollable. The soldiers in the company are given unusually generous provisions, the implication being that this is a final feast, since they are surely going to be starved or killed in the south. Kasuke eats and eats until his stomach is painfully distended.

It was a feeling similar to the joy of revenge. But revenge for what? For his own stomach that emitted such a base and mean desire against his will? Maybe so. Yet he gained absolutely no pleasure from the taste of what he ate. No matter how familiar, it hardly tasted like food; it was pungent and salty, and reeked of sweat and leather. Perhaps through his eating he was trying to take revenge against the army—when this thought occurred to him, he could hardly bear his own absurdity. However hard he tried, the provisions for the entire army would be too big a load for his stomach to handle. Nevertheless was it not true that the only space left for him to act freely and of his own will under this round-the-clock surveillance was inside his skin, in his internal organs? Eating things, digesting them and turning them into excrement—was this not all that he could do without being watched?[43]

A violent attack of diarrhea at their scheduled departure time saves his life. After all the others have gone, Kasuke is left behind in the toilet. The story of Kasuke's eating and excreting does not stop here, as he is sent from one military hospital to another in Manchuria. Obviously, the scatological or coprophilous emphasis of this novel is much stronger than that of *kuso tsubo* in *Kani kōsen*. Yet while this is certainly effective in profiling the already notorious inhumanity of the Imperial Army, it does not lead to any subversion as such.[44] The comic pales before the brutality, and the absurd merges into the powerlessness that sanctions the emergence of such brutality.

Kaikō Takeshi's *Nihon sanmon opera* (The Japanese Threepenny Opera, 1959),[45] by contrast, is all about subversive power, and the power belongs to the Apaches, a ragtag bunch of social outcasts who have drifted from Korea, Okinawa, and various parts of Japan into a low-class part of Osaka in the immediate postwar period. Some were forcedly brought to Japan as laborers, while others are illegal immigrants. Many have criminal records, ranging from petty theft and illegal communist activities to murder. They make a living by selling scrap metal salvaged illegally from what they call the Sugiyama mine, the huge wreckage of an arsenal.[46] It is a dangerous and physically demanding business, as it involves conflict with the authorities as well as crossing a river full of toxic mud and fumes. The actual carrying of the heavy scrap metal is done by strong adult men, but all other members of the Apaches, including women, children, and people with severe disabilities, play some role and thus contribute something to the operation.

The protagonist of this beggar's opera is known to everyone as Fukusuke, although no one knows his real name or background, except that he is a Japanese. Like Yasuoka's Kasuke and many other male Japanese protagonists, he is a hopelessly weak, useless man. Half-starved, and with no family, friends, or possessions, he is invited to join the Apaches in exchange for a place to live and their specialty food, offal. As Yomota Inuhiko notes in his brief but insightful commentary on this novel,[47] Fukusuke's meandering journey to the Apache quarters recounted at the beginning of the novel serves as a metaphor for the digestive system. Like a substance that cannot be digested, Fukusuke goes from the stomach to the intestines, and then returns to the stomach. And while Fukusuke and his fellow Apaches are indeed the offal of society—despised and discarded—they can also be understood as powerful digestive organs that "eat" scrap metal.[48]

In order to eat steel, the Apaches need to consume nutritious food that will give them energy. The nurturing figure in this story is a Korean called Gon. He has a large, sturdy body and a grotesquely ugly face. Unlike his compatriot and the leader of the group, Kim, who is an eloquent speaker of the Osaka dialect, Gon hardly utters a word. Instead, he silently and diligently works with his bull-dozer-like muscles on the "mine" by night (i.e., he "eats" metal) and feeds his Apache comrades with offal and his special sauce by day. Thus the half-starved Japanese Fukusuke is saved by the shrewdness of Kim and the "delicacy" pro-duced by Gon.[49] Yomota notes that Gon's cooking is not authentic Korean cook-ing but a combination of Korean barbecue and the Japanese way of eating raw fish dipped in soy sauce, a combination developed of necessity by "those who had to live between the two cultures." As he adds, this kind of cooking is usually called *horumon* or *tonchan* in slang, the former deriving (contrary to popular belief) not from "hormone" but from the Osaka dialect *horu mon* (things to discard), and the latter from the Korean for "excrement + entrails."[50]

Offal, regarded as repugnant in many cultures, has been the subject of a number of sociological studies of food in the West. Vialles identifies two types of logic concerning meat: a "zoophagan" logic that acknowledges the living in meat and a "sarcophagan" logic that prefers to divorce meat from its living origins.[51] Kaikō, like many other postwar male writers with an interest in food, clearly takes the zoophagan view in his celebration of the living in offal and offal eating. This can also be regarded as a criticism of the obsession with both culinary and ethnic purity and of the prejudice closely associated with that obsession. In his advocacy of offal, Dan Kazuo, whose novels will be discussed in chapter 5, writes in his cookery book:

> In our pursuit of a neat and clean cuisine, the Japanese have been accustomed to wasteful ways of eating, discarding important and tasty parts. Partly because the taking of the life of animals was forbidden for centuries, we have forgotten the real way to eat animals and poultry. [...] Before I begin my recipes, I urge you all to abandon your prejudices.[52]

The issue of cooking offal is also related to matters of gender. Discursively, the cooking of offal belongs to men, who are supposed to be free from the pris-siness and prejudices of middle-class women. Offal is, as Mennell points out, "a good example of the changeability of objects of repugnance."[53] Although his examples are limited to Europe and North America, he illustrates the cultural variety and historical changes in feelings towards offal. Mennell also suggests the existence of "a scale of feelings about offal, with objects in ascending order of repulsiveness running from liver through kidneys, tongue, sweetbreads, brains and tripe to testicles and eyes—or something like that."[54] In Japan fish entrails (totally missing from Mennell's Western-based "scale") were already regarded as gourmet food before the war. However, animal offal was absent from the traditional Japanese diet. Since the war, its image seems to have improved somewhat in Japan. While beef and pork offal, especially the less popular parts on Mennell's scale, cannot be regarded as popular or prestigious food, chicken liver and other offal are common enough. This is the result of a rise in the popularity of cheap drinking and eating places such as yakitori bars and Korean barbecue restaurants, as well as the 1980s boom in chicken and beef offal hotpot (*nabe*).[55]

Kaikō's story of the Apaches was written long before the hotpot boom but after the Japanese had emerged from the immediate postwar struggle for food and reconstruction. Offal works as a powerful metaphor in this text simply because it *is* regarded as repugnant. The extreme example is pig's womb with fetus, complete with amniotic fluid and membrane, which is eaten fresh. In many cultures this would be regarded as too grotesque for consumption, which is why it does not appear on Mennell's scale. It is, however, every Apache's favorite because of its delicate taste as well as its supposedly powerful effect on the eater's physical and sexual powers.

The significance of the offal does not simply relate to the vitality of the outcast; it can also be regarded as a "visceral" antipathy towards middle-class complacency, which both erases the bitter memories of war, starvation, and destruction and continues to discriminate against marginalized people. Gon's offal nurtures every Apache, of all ethnic and cultural backgrounds. While it is inclusive, it also has the power to subvert both the remnants of prewar and wartime Japanese institutions, symbolized by the ruins of the imperial arsenal and the postwar equivalents of the police, the bureaucracy, and the press. Thus the offal in this story not only offers sustenance for the physical labor of digging steel; it also encourages and urges people to destroy, little by little, the Sugiyama mine—the monstrous wartime legacy—through "eating" its iron.

Food, Earth, and Discrimination: *The River with No Bridge*

If the Apaches are at the bottom of the socioeconomic ladder in postwar Japan, there is another group of people who have been the victims of institutionalized discrimination for centuries. Although ethnically no different from the rest of the *yamato* people, this group, usually called *burakumin*, has long been treated as an ethnic minority or, worse still, as subhuman. In premodern times they were completely segregated from the rest of the population, working either as vagrant performers or in "unclean" and "impure" occupations such as butchery, tanning, and grave digging. Even after they legally ceased to be *hinin* (nonhuman) and became *shinheimin* (new commoners) in 1871, they continued to be treated as social outcasts, often called by yet another highly derogatory term, *eta* (or *etta*; literally, "much filth"). The etymology of this last term is particularly significant for our discussion: it derives from the earlier term *etori*, which means collector of feed—namely, those engaged in slaughtering animals to feed the lord's falcons. The replacement of the original *e* (feed) with another *e* (filth, impurity), which seems to have taken place in the early medieval period, signifies the victimization of the nonagrarian population. Ohnuki-Tierney rightly points out that the *eta hinin*, or "special status people," to use her term, "were assigned the impurity of the dominant Japanese, who objectified their own impurity by creating 'the internal other.'"[56]

While Kaikō used a picaresque novel to present a powerful critique of the discourse of purity, Sumii Sue (1902–1997) developed her novel dealing with the discrimination against and liberation of *burakumin* into a massive *roman-fleuve*. *Hashi no nai kawa* (The River with No Bridge) began to appear in the journal *Buraku* in 1959. The first six volumes were published between 1961 and 1968, and to general amazement the ninety-year-old author completed the seventh volume in 1992, with a postscript declaring her intention to write an eighth. Some parts of the novel were made into films,[57] and Susan Wilkinson's English translation of the first volume was published in 1989.

Sumii, roughly a contemporary of Miyamoto, Hayashi, Sata, and Hirabayashi, was involved in the proletarian movement. After a relatively brief period working as a primary-school teacher and then as an editor for major publisher Kōdansha, she began writing around 1920. Although she was little known before *Hashi no nai kawa*, her writing, especially in the genre of children's stories, was an important source of income for her family from around 1930. Her work clearly shows some of the characteristics of proletarian literature as well as of the *nōmin bungaku*.[58] *Hashi no nai kawa*, like *Tsuchi*, is full of seasonal and agricultural detail, and like Nagatsuka, Sumii chose to write about the area she knew from her childhood, the outskirts of Nara, traditionally known as the province of Yamato. Sumii herself is not a *burakumin*, but she combines her own experience and observations with historical facts. Sumii's *roman-fleuve* flows well, incorporating the lyrical, symbolic, romantic, dramatic, realistic, and even melodramatic, and connecting tiny streams, major currents, and violent torrents with a powerful undercurrent of humanism. Interspersed with its descriptions of landscapes and events are dialogues and conversations (mostly in gentle and earthy Yamato dialect), letters, newspaper items, popular songs, children's stories, references to literary texts (ranging from Chuang-tzu, Tolstoy, and Walt Whitman to Tōson,

Takuboku, and Arishima Takeo), and excerpts from school textbooks, Buddhist scriptures, and legal and historical documents. If we recall Noguchi Takehiko's definition of the *shōsetsu*, quoted in the Introduction, this is an excellent example of textual and generic predation and ingestion of a very omnivorous kind. The novel also works as a Bildungsroman. The central character in the novel, a male *burakumin* named Kōji, is the same age as Sumii—six years old at the beginning of the novel and twenty-six at the end of volume 7. The period covered (i.e., from late Meiji to early Shōwa) is that depicted in *Tsuchi* as well as the slightly later period covered by *Mazushiki hitobito no mure*. As in these earlier works, both women and children play significant roles in Sumii's novel.

Like the poor peasants in Nagatsuka's and Miyamoto's texts, Kōji's family and many others in their village of Komori make their living by producing rice and vegetables. With few exceptions they are poor tenant farmers, exploited by their non-*burakumin* landlords, who exact extremely high rents. In fact rents are much higher in Yamato than in other parts of Japan. Kōji's family are tenants of a mere 2.3 *tan* (a little over twenty acres), with rent of five *hyō* (about 360 liters) of rice per *tan*. After paying the rent they have on average only three to three and a half *hyō* to themselves. This is hardly enough for a year's supply for the family of two women and two growing boys. Hence, their everyday meals consist of watery rice gruel (*kayu*) with the addition of sweet potatoes or some other cereal or vegetable. At several points in the novel rice gruel is referred to as one of the two Yamato specialties—the other being *eta*. If the crops are poorer than average (for example, in 1909, 1917, and 1923) because of drought, insect damage, severe storms, or other natural causes, even thin gruel becomes a luxury.

Like Kanji and others in *Tsuchi*, the tenant farmers and their families need to supplement their incomes—by producing secondary products such as straw sandals, by peddling, or by engaging in seasonal construction work outside the village. Sumii skillfully weaves into her descriptions of the idyllic landscape of Yamato stories of deep-rooted prejudice against the *burakumin*. Beef may have gone from being considered impure to being a delicacy in modern civilization, but the *burakumin*, engaged in butchery, are still treated like beasts. Kōji and other Komori children are subjected to persistent and systematic abuse, insults, and bullying by the non-*burakumin* children as well as by some teachers. When told that the soldiers camping in the area for military maneuvers appreciated the hot sweet potatoes offered to them by Kōji and his brother, one bully responds, to the accompaniment of malicious laughter from his entourage:

> "Those soldiers are from the Nagoya division. [. . .] They don't know these parts. D'you think they'd have eaten the potatoes if they'd known you're from

Komori? On top of losing the battle [in the maneuvers], the poor things ended up eating *eta* potatoes! Stinking *eta* potatoes!" and he held his nose, pretending to vomit.[59]

"Stinking" is perhaps a universal term of abuse, but Sumii reminds us that here it is partly related to the fact that the kinds of occupations traditionally assigned to the *burakumin* require or produce strong smells—such as the chemicals used for refining gelatin or for processing the straw used in sandal production. That such smells are inevitable and indispensable in this particular work never occurs to these child bullies and their adult counterparts. When such verbal insults lead to a fight, it is always the Komori children who are punished. And when there is a fire in Komori, the fire brigade does not even bother to try to extinguish the "stinking" fire.

Sumii's novel does not simply describe the plight of the *burakumin*; it relates individual incidents to socioeconomic and political constructs and recounts the protagonists' questioning of and revolt against these constructs. Since the introduction of rice inspection in 1910, rice, like people, is classified. Rice inspectors are generally unfair to the people of Komori. Kōji's mother, Fude, ponders: "If it was in the interests of the landowners and speculators to grade rice, [. . .] then it must be in somebody's interests for people to be graded as well."[60] Rice is not only used for exploitation at the production level but is a commodity for speculation. As Kōji's uncle explains, "[T]he rice market goes back to the time of the shogunate, and it started off in Osaka, too."[61] Kōji's brother, who starts work as a rice dealer's apprentice in Osaka halfway through volume 1, realizes that rice is a commodity that enables the rich to become richer even (or especially) in times of famine. All of this prepares the reader for later volumes that trace important historical events, including the rice riots of 1918—in which 30–40 percent of some seven hundred thousand participants were *burakumin*[62]—the *buraku* liberation movement, and the 1922 formation of the Suiheisha (Levelers' Society), in which Kōji and others from Komori are involved.

Despite its extensive descriptions of the abuse and marginalization of the *burakumin* and other minorities, the novel never loses its ultimately optimistic tone. This is reflected in the frequent communal eating scenes. The food may be humble rice gruel, rice balls in emergencies, or lunch boxes sent to the imprisoned Suiheisha activists by their supporters. Food is not simply a gift but a token, and at the same time a vehicle of solidarity among the marginalized people. By sharing food, they help and encourage one another to fight against oppression. This may seem reminiscent of the second and third readings of *Tsuchi*—namely, as false consciousness and as exemplar of the healing powers of community. Given the context of the suffering and the analysis of its causes, however, neither of these readings is applicable to Sumii's novel and its communal eating.

With this novel Sumii presents a challenge in relation to two taboo issues: the *burakumin* and the emperor system. She shows us again and again how the two are intertwined and how these constructs neglect and distort the plain fact that emperors, the *burakumin*, and everyone else are exactly the same— mortal human beings. Relating an episode in which someone finds "a specimen of imperial feces" on the mountain used for army maneuvers, Kōji's neighbor comments: "'Funny what a difference there is between people when we're all the same human beings. There they are, treating the Emperor's crap like treasure, but in our case, they think even the rice we grow is dirty and stinks.'"[63]

Kōji's grandmother was born in the same year as the Meiji emperor. Having lost her son in the Russo-Japanese War, she is determined to outlive both the emperor and General Oku (1847–1930), who was the commander of the Second Army to which her son belonged.[64] When the headmaster speaks at a school assembly about the "wicked," "sordid," "despicable" plot against His Imperial Majesty, his words serve only to spark Kōji's admiration for the leader of the alleged assassination plot, Kōtoku Shūsui (1871–1911):

> "Boys and girls, these scoundrels not only opposed the war, they had other ideas even more dreadful; ideas that would be the ruin of our society. They sought to deprive people of their wealth, to take away their money. They thought that since all men are equal, money too should be distributed equally among us."[65]

The connection between imperialism and militarism is emphasized throughout the novel, and the message is clear and simple: freedom, equality, and peace for everyone, including the *burakumin*, Koreans, and other colonial victims. The novel makes it clear that it is not the emperor as an individual who is at issue, but the system of discrimination that places the emperor at the top, even though he is merely a "decoration, a puppet who knows nothing about what's going on."[66] Towards the end of volume 7, after the death of the Taishō emperor, Kōji says to himself, "The emperor is a victim, too. A victim at the pinnacle of the structure of discrimination."[67] Notably this final volume was published only a few years after the death of the Shōwa emperor. No doubt the publication of the novel was possible only after the war, but both issues, *burakumin* and the emperor system, have remained extremely sensitive, which must surely have provided Sumii with strong motivation for writing her novel.

Compound Pollution

Culturally constructed impurities and pollution aside, the idea of contaminated earth and food (milk) harming people was evident in earlier works such as *Tsuchi* and "Seryōshitsu nite." In the second half of the century contamination of the soil, water, air, and food became a serious issue. As already mentioned, in Kaikō's novel the "Apaches" need to cross the highly toxic river in order to "eat" steel. Ariyoshi Sawako's *Fukugō osen* (Compound Pollution, 1975)[68] is one of the earliest and most direct expressions of fear and concern about the issue of compound pollution. Serialized in the morning edition of the *Asahi shinbun* for eight and a half months in the mid-1970s, it deals with the alarming spread of pollution and is full of detailed information about some of the toxic chemicals around us. It is in many respects an extraordinary text. As Karen Colligan points out, Ariyoshi's attempt to describe the "synergistic and cumulative effects of chemical pollutants" marks a clear change from the traditional "isolated problem" approach.[69] The style and form Ariyoshi chose also surprised the reader.

By the 1970s Ariyoshi was widely recognized as a popular and skillful storyteller, something that did not necessarily appeal to the male-dominated "pure" literature rearguard. The *Asahi* must have expected Ariyoshi to produce yet another best-selling novel with a well-researched historical setting that touched on controversial issues. Ariyoshi hesitates to call this text a *shōsetsu*;[70] it has, she admits, no plot and no hero or heroine. Abandoning her usual novelistic techniques, she "tried to write something easy-to-understand and interesting" so that "a wider public would be aware of the facts about which experts and pioneers had already issued warnings and made accusations."[71] It was a courageous decision, and Ariyoshi, well equipped with both research and communication techniques, pursued it with tremendous energy. Ironically, it resulted in enthusiastic praise not only from her loyal readers and concerned citizens but also from the least expected quarters, even though it is highly doubtful if this last kind of recognition had any meaning for Ariyoshi herself. In his "Kaisetsu" commentaries for the paperback edition of *Fukugō osen*, the critic Okuno Takeo emphasizes that this is a deeply moving "pure" literary text, even if it does not look like a conventional novel. Okuno then inserts this telling anecdote:

> A somewhat eccentric former chief editor of a literary journal once said to me in a deeply impressed tone, "Ariyoshi Sawako has written pure literature at last. *Compound Pollution* is what I regard as the ultimate in pure literature." This was the same editor who had stubbornly rejected Ariyoshi's novels for years.[72]

Ariyoshi mentions in the text how she came to give up her plan to write a novel about pollution a decade earlier. The story she had planned was about a mayor who devotes his life to the development of a small country town. He successfully attracts a large chemical factory, which improves the city's economy to the point of bringing its young people back from the bigger cities to work. When the media start to attack the mayor and the factory over pollution, he drinks wastewater from the factory to demonstrate both his innocence and the safety of the factory. His granddaughter, however, dies from chemical poisoning caused by the factory. Thus, the novel Ariyoshi had planned clearly shows women and children as innocent victims of the male economy and politics. After spending three years in preparation for writing this novel, Ariyoshi found it difficult to pursue her plan any further.

> As I watched the Minamata case develop, I was less and less interested in my plan for the novel. Realizing that factory managers actually did drink wastewater from their factories in front of newspaper reporters, I gave up altogether on writing this novel.
> [...] I realized that pollution could no longer be captured by fiction. The reality is far too heavy and serious for a novel to deal with.[73]

Ariyoshi, a writer of fiction, seems to have surrendered to the gravity of fact. Yet despite her skepticism about what fiction can depict, Ariyoshi—or strictly speaking, the narrator of *Fukugō osen* who is also called Ariyoshi Sawako—never for a moment ceases to be a novelist. The voluminous (five hundred pages in paperback) text is anything but an arid compilation of data. To achieve the comprehensible and interesting narrative she wants, she frequently uses dialogue—between herself and experts (almost always male) or between herself and a grumpy old man from the neighborhood. This last persona is a familiar type in the narrative convention of *rakugo*. Highly specialized knowledge is thus made digestible to the reader through questions and comments from two nonspecialist personae.

> "Well, then, could you first tell me what elements cadmium is made of?"
> The scientist staring at me turned pale for a moment. He looked down as if to control his feelings. Suddenly his face went bright red. After a while he said, looking straight at me and with resolution, "Cadmium *is* a chemical element."
> I laughed cheerfully. "Oh, I see. I thought it was a relative of aluminum."
> To this the scientist replied indignantly, "Aluminum, too, is a chemical element."

If you get embarrassed by this, you'll never be a novelist. "Asking is a moment's shame; not asking is a life-long shame"—that's my motto.[74]

The narrator courteously acknowledges the assistance of many people, as well as such pioneering works on pollution as Rachel Carson's *Silent Spring* and Ishimure Michiko's *Kugai jōdo* (Pure Land, Suffering Sea, 1969). At the same time, however, she expresses doubts and frustration in the face of the experts' jargon and their inability to arrive at definite conclusions. It is notable that both Carson and Ishimure are women. Although many other women, both high-profile and obscure, appear in the book, Ariyoshi never seems to foreground the cause of women,[75] except in the case of maternal concerns about the health of children. Neither does she emphasize the identification of women with the natural world, an emphasis that, as Orbaugh points out, has played a significant role in many women's esteem-building movements and literature.[76] One can at least say, however, that when Ariyoshi criticizes experts and scientists, their unspoken gender is male.

Scientists have *not yet concluded their studies*, and it takes too much trouble and time for them to reach their conclusions. Hence there is no other way but for me, a novelist, to speak out. In order to protect our children's happiness, we must stop the agriculture of death.[77]

A scientist specializing in pollution said to me once how disappointing it was, when giving a lecture to a consumer interest group or a group of housewives, to see many women fall asleep in the middle of the lecture. Women fall asleep not because they are stupid but because experts' lectures are boring. I cannot remember how many times I have had to stifle a yawn during a conversation with an expert.[78]

The polemical tone of the text is also evident in the way in which the narrator often addresses herself directly to her readers—sometimes asking them to believe her, at other times advising them against bothering the doctor or the organic food association she has mentioned in her text.

I have said this many times, but Jikōkai is full. They have eight hundred families with only ten farmers to support them. If you do go there, Jikōkai has nothing to offer you. If you wish to maintain your own and your children's health with healthy food, organize a local group, and try to form another group like Jikōkai with nearby farmers. If you don't do it, nobody will. Neither the Ministry of

Health nor the Ministry of Agriculture and Forestry nor the Ministry of International Trade and Industry will do it for you.[79]

Out of irritation, Ariyoshi, who earlier insisted that women are not stupid, scolds "women who have been turned into complete idiots by TV commercials": "The postwar constitution has realized equality between the sexes; but no law can make a fool clever. This detergent will, no doubt, sell well, thanks to the power of advertising."[80]

As noted above, *Fukugō osen* does not overtly treat environmental problems as gender issues. The voice of the narrator is, however, distinctly that of a woman, even when it fiercely berates women. Moreover, with Ariyoshi's reputation as a woman writer who has dealt with many issues that directly concern women (e.g., relationships within the family, the generation gap, cross-cultural experience and interracial marriage, and care for the aged), the writer's gender is never forgotten by the reader.

Since Takuboku proposed "Poems to Eat," writers have searched for styles, forms, and strategies to produce literature that is committed to issues concerning various groups and communities of people. One of the strategies is to focus on food, eating, and hunger. Inequality and deprivation surrounding food have been described, and the sociocultural constructs that have produced and supported such inequity have been exposed. Some writers have maintained a certain distance from the subject and tried to describe the situation, while many others have chosen to take an overtly engaged, sympathetic viewpoint or even address the reader directly (as Ariyoshi did) to call for action. Each of the texts discussed in these two chapters (with the exception of Ariyoshi's) has given voice to those that are, to use Mizuta's words, "discursively nonexistent," including not only women but also children, the elderly, the *burakumin*, exploited laborers, impoverished peasants, dropout soldiers, and "Apaches." The deprivation is often associated with "purity" myths, which, as Kobayashi and Sumii, in particular, articulated with graphic examples, are closely linked to the configurations of power culminating in the emperor. Ariyoshi's text, on the other hand, tries to warn the great majority of people who are unwittingly removed from nature and are deprived of safe food. She was as deeply committed as Miyazawa Kenji was to clean, natural, and genuine food as the basis of happiness for all people. While Kenji used fantasy and imagination to communicate such commitment, Ariyoshi invented a hybrid of *shōsetsu* mixed with essays and documentary and used comic and polemic elements mingled with social and scientific data explained in accessible everyday language, the kind of language that Takuboku identified as an essential part of "Poems to Eat."

Chapter Four

Cannibalism in Modern Japanese Literature

Cannibalism, or anthropophagy, appears in many mythologies and fairy tales, as well as in classical and modern literature. It is a topic that has attracted scholarly attention across a wide range of disciplines that include anthropology, psychology, semiotics, history, and literary and cultural studies, at the same time triggering heated debates as to its possible meanings, particularly over the last few decades in the West. Anthropophagy has been seen variously as a colonialist myth (William Arens, *The Man-Eating Myth*, 1979), as a means of controlling evil or illness (Jacques Attali, *L'ordre cannibale*, 1979), as a so-called concrete device for distinguishing the "cultural self" from the "natural other" (Peggy Reeves Sanday, *Divine Hunger*, 1986), as an elementary form of institutionalized aggression (Eli Sagan, *Cannibalism*, 1993), and as an important trope in the Western literary canon and in Western popular culture, particularly as a form of metaphoric incorporation that acts to dissolve opposites (Maggie Kilgour, *From Communion to Cannibalism*, 1990).

Western scholars, however, have so far paid little attention to the representations of anthropophagy that can be found in Japanese literature. This is understandable, given that Japanese literature in general still occupies a peripheral position in Western literary scholarship. What this inevitably privileges is a Western ideological polarity that sets the "civilized" West against that other "savage" and anthropophagic world that has been the object of Western fascination, fantasy, and horror. It is a polarity that leaves out Japan, Japan's Otherness being another, marginal Otherness. Even within Japan itself the representation of cannibalism is an area that conventional literary history has never touched on. This has certainly not been for want of examples to study; rather it is because

Japanese literary criticism has been preoccupied with traditional author-centered studies. As a consequence, the sorts of texts in which cannibalism appears have tended to be regarded as "minor" or "maverick" works, unworthy of serious critical examination and unrewarding as objects of study. It is also perhaps because cannibalism, as a theme, has seemed intractable within the reigning methodologies of Japanese literary studies.

It is true that recent scholarship on the subject has expanded in scope and now includes the work of Gang Yue on hunger, cannibalism, and the politics of eating in modern China.[1] Given the indisputable importance of Chinese food and literature in Japan, Yue's study of "double orality"—eating and speaking—in "Chinese" literature, from ancient to modern and up to Amy Tan, gives us an excellent aid to our reading of Japanese texts. Nevertheless, however deeply embedded or incorporated some Chinese and, for that matter, Western literary works may be in Japanese literature, texts discussed here will clearly illustrate particular sociocultural and literary situations that cannot be explained by simple adoption or adaptation of existing studies.

This chapter offers one possible way to situate these works within the broader examination of the thematic of anthropophagy in twentieth-century Japanese fiction. The texts under discussion include a variety of genres, and the representations of anthropophagy within them vary widely: cannibalism appears in most of the categories into which anthropology classifies it—ritual, mortuary, institutional, and pathological, all of both the "aggressive" and the "affectionate" varieties. Its representation in some of the texts is to be taken literally, in others metaphorically—as, for example, a feminist rebellion against social or sexual victimization. In other texts it is simply a satirical device for attacking bourgeois smugness and hypocrisy, together with bourgeois literary conventions.

What is noticeable, however, and possibly more interesting, is that all of these texts that have cannibalism as a theme involve, in one way or another, a notion of "displacement."[2] In its literal representations, anthropophagy, in these Japanese texts, does not simply pop up of its own accord, rearing its ugly head, so to speak, out of the everyday, like a long-repressed element in what is domestic and familiar. On the contrary, to encounter it, we have to move out of the everyday, and beyond any notion of the familiar. Cannibalism is not a skeleton in *our* cupboard. It is part of the Other, and for it to be represented, for us to experience it—and perhaps even to participate in it—we have to undergo a displacement, a crossing of the frontier into the Other. Some who cross the frontier will return, while others will not. The frontier is, of course, most often geographic and the displacement spatial, but it can be seen from the texts we will examine that the displacement may also be temporal, or a matter of finding oneself in extreme circumstances—in a shipwreck, for example, or in the extreme circumstances of war and defeat.

It is at least arguable surely that, for the modern Western imagination, the world of the Other is coextensive with the world that the West has, historically, colonized. It is in this colonized world that anthropophagy is imaginable and indeed, if Arens is right, that anthropophagy acts as a mythic justification for the dominance of colonizer over colonized. In the Japanese imagination, the world of the Other is more ambiguous. If, at certain moments in the nineteenth century, Japan had some reason to fear the prospect of colonization, by the beginning of the twentieth, far from being colonized, it was clearly, and notoriously, a colonizer. Yet despite this, in the national imagination, the outside world never became, and perhaps has not yet become, quite what it is for the colonizing Westerner: a place in which—in spite of its Otherness—one may walk, if not always in safety, at least with certainty.

Some Earlier Examples

Before I embark on a survey of cannibalism in twentieth-century Japanese literature, it seems helpful to mention a few earlier examples that offer certain prototypes for what was to come. The first of these is a mid-Meiji work of popular fiction, *Ukishiro monogatari* (The Story of a Floating Castle, 1890) by Yano Ryūkei (1850–1931). Nationalist ambition, such as that already detected in the writings of Shōyō and Shiki, is also prominent in this utopian tale about a group of young Japanese men trying to build a new and ideal *Japanese* nation outside Japan. The novel is set mostly in the so-called South Seas (Nan'yō), which refers here not to the South Pacific but to Southeast Asia. Although I will not go into the entire story of the novel itself here, at least one episode is relevant to the present topic. This is a scene in which the protagonist goes to an island of cannibals. Instead of being made into human steak he becomes the king of the island by marrying a young woman from the royal family, who instantly (and conveniently for him) falls in love with him. Rather than assimilating to the native culture, he declares himself to be Bunmei (Civilization) Tennō, the first emperor of the New Japan he plans to build on the island.[3] The association of the South Seas with cannibalism appears frequently in the literature under discussion, although it is mostly the Japanese in these narratives who commit or contemplate the act of eating human flesh. Notably Ryūkei's protagonist regards himself as civilized—different from the "savage natives," but also different from the European exploiters. Significant also is the role of the woman, without whose power and connections his very survival, let alone his political ambitions, would not be possible. Her contributions, however, are taken for granted. We will see these same elements formulated in this way again and again in later stories of cannibalism.

Travel—whether foreign or domestic—as the site of an encounter with the unknown is indispensable to all kinds of literature. Adventure stories such as *Ukishiro monogatari* provide foreign travel as a pretext for the encounter with the unknown, but many Japanese ghost and horror stories suggest it is possible to meet cannibals closer to home. Of particular interest here is a mid-Edo text, "Aozukin" (The Blue Hood), one of the tales in Ueda Akinari's *Ugetsu monogatari* (Tales of Rain and the Moon, 1768). In the mountains—a quasi-foreign topos—a vagrant monk meets an abbot who has turned into a man-eating monster. Demons living in mountains are common in Japanese (and Chinese) mythology and folklore, and many are given to devouring people. But this case is different from any the learned monk has ever heard of. He is acquainted with "Ma Shu-mou, minister to Yang Ti of Sui, who liked the flesh of children and secretly kidnapped youngsters in order to have them steamed and served as food."[4] But this new mountain demon has at one time been a revered priest himself, driven to cannibalistic practices by the death of his beloved disciple. The infatuation of this priest with his disciple is said to have been so deep and obsessive that "refusing to allow the body to rot and decay, he sucked the flesh and licked the bones until he utterly devoured it."[5] Now, his insatiable appetite for human flesh brings him down from the mountain to violate village graves and devour newly buried bodies, terrifying the villagers in the process. Here we have an archetype—though *Ugetsu monogatari* certainly has Japanese and Chinese origins—of pathological cannibalism beginning as affectionate and becoming aggressive. As we shall see, this type of cannibal tale set in the bewitching and bewitched mountains will reappear in some modern texts. That the monk recognizes the uniqueness of this case and its divergence from its Chinese precedents is also worthy of our attention.

While comparing this extraordinary case to other stories of cannibalism he knows, the monk also contemplates that women's turning into demons, snakes, and other things would not surprise him, as Buddhist teaching has taught him about the malice in women's nature. Indeed, the man-eating woman appears in many tales and stories. Here it is worth mentioning a typical example, one of the *yamanba* (mountain witch) stories.[6] It begins with a man marrying a woman who is beautiful, hardworking, and, most important, has no need of or desire for food. He discovers, however, that on top of her head his wife has a huge mouth, usually covered by her hair. This mouth eats anything and everything, including men. Kawai Hayao interprets this and similar stories from many other cultures as representing the positive and negative aspects of the Great Mother.[7] On the one hand she is selfless, productive, nurturing, affectionate, and embracing; on the other hand, however, she is greedy, unforgiving, and simply horrific. Interestingly, some variations depict the transformation of *yamanba* into a man-eating spider, the insect, Kawai reminds us, that is associated with the art of weaving as well as with trapping and devouring. Kawai also associates the change from not eating to devouring with the physical transformation surrounding maternity. So an ideal wife may turn into a fiend, and it is not that one is true and the other false but that they are seemingly polarities of the same being.

The following examples, arranged in chronological order from the early 1920s onwards, are written in modern Japanese and are mostly from *shōsetsu*. Many, however, differ considerably from the realistic novel that Shōyō had in mind. In fact, they present alternatives, in one way or another, to the supposedly dominant *shishōsetsu*. These alternatives often incorporate preceding texts, of both native and foreign origin, and display the influences of both. In this context it is important to mention the attraction to Dada for some Japanese writers and artists of the modern period as a way of understanding their departure from realism.

Dada and Anthropophagy

Anthropophagy, as we know from Francis Picabia's "Manifesto Cannibale Dada" (1920) and the review *Cannibale* founded by Picabia and Tristan Tzara in the same year, has a special significance in European Dadaism. In Brazilian *modernismo* (1920–1930), anthropophagy is, according to Sérgio Luiz Prado Bellei, "a metaphor for an elitist cultural strategy of identity construction based on a diagnostic of the social evils plaguing an undeveloped, colonised country desperately in need of becoming modern in terms of aesthetics, politics, and social reform."[8] Bellei argues that Oswald de Andrade, for instance, uses cannibalism in "Manifesto Antropófago" (1928) not only to deny frontiers but to produce them. This can be related to the point William Arens makes that cannibalism has been used historically for one group to "appreciate its own existence more meaningfully by conjuring up others as categorical opposites."[9] In this sense *modernismo* is neither a simple imitation of European Dadaism nor a nostalgic return to nature, but a strong resistance to being devoured by the hegemonic discourse of the colonizers by devouring it instead. Traveling plays a significant role in this resistance:

> For the travelling anthropophagus of Brazilian *modernismo* experiencing the encounter on the frontier, the significant move—and here lies perhaps the central significance of modernist cultural *antropofagia*—is the ambivalent strategy of incorporation by means of which the strength of the cultural other is used for the creation of a separate cultural identity.[10]

European Dadaism had a strong impact on young Japanese poets[11] such as Takahashi Shinkichi (1901–1987), whose "Dangen wa dadaisuto" (Declaration Is Dadaist, first published in 1922) clearly shows the devouring of the newly imported ideas: "Can anyone declare that Dadaists are inedible? Are they not lickable? All is food; and food is anarchist."[12]

Here the division between the eater and the eaten, which is used to highlight the ethical, class, and gender divisions in most other prewar texts, is questioned and denied, together with all other accepted demarcations and associations. Unlike in Brazilian modernism, cross-cultural experience through traveling is absent from Takahashi's Dadaist writing, although it is prominent in many other texts discussed in this chapter. What Takahashi does declare is a fierce and constant battle against everything: "Cursing everything to death, devouring everything, and still insatiable, Dadaist's tongue licks, like an eternal proletarian."[13]

Dadaism thus is not only edible and lickable itself but also eats up and licks up everything that is not itself. Here there is no sign of the poet targeting European or any other specific culture as the enemy. Takahashi simply seems fascinated by European Dadaism.[14] In contrast, some of the texts examined below are much more voracious in textual cannibalism.

Kaijinmaru

Nogami Yaeko's (1885–1985) novella *Kaijinmaru* (*The Neptune*, 1922) would seem to be the earliest modern canonical Japanese text that deals with the theme of anthropophagy.[15] A story of physical and ethical conflict on a schooner disabled and adrift after severe storms, it does not *quite* describe the anthropophagous act itself: two members of the ship's crew murder Sankichi, the captain's young nephew, along with the ship's cook. The intention to cannibalize the victims is there, but the captain manages to rescue the body of his nephew before it is eaten. The captain in this story clearly represents moral fortitude in the face of extreme adversity. The crewman Hachizō, who becomes obsessed with a craving to eat the slender Sankichi's supple flesh, represents the opposite ethical pole, and between these two extremes the simple Gorosuke oscillates. Initially an accessory to Hachizō's crime, Gorosuke, through his tears of terror and remorse, is finally successful in persuading Hachizō to surrender Sankichi's body to the captain. Nogami fills out this almost allegorical structure with a realistic, detailed depiction of the ship, the violent storms that beset it, and the physical and psychological suffering of the crew.[16] This is obviously a serious study of human nature under extreme duress. The subject matter, the all-male cast, and the plain and powerful style of the novel all challenge the stereotypical image of women's literature.[17]

The sea, in the novel somewhere vaguely south of Japan, is undoubtedly a dangerous zone. The threat of cannibalism, however, comes not from the region's "barbaric natives" or as the consequence of any cross-cultural contact with them, but from within the crew itself as a consequence of its displacement at sea. Their prolonged hunger causes Hachizō and Gorosuke to have vivid food dreams and hallucinations. Hachizō soon associates his persistent visions of beef with the flesh of Sankichi:

> It was hot, so Sankichi was dressed in a short coat, and his slender legs and full thighs were clearly outlined within a pair of blue trunks, like the limbs of a little girl who has not yet become slim. This could be seen from below and excited Hachizō's brutal interest. In his depravity, he was reminded of the round at the meat-shop in the back-street of the harbour. Only that one was much larger. Although bewildered somewhat by such a thought, again he perceived the thighs and legs passing above his head, the setting sun casting a crimson glow upon them. Hachizō started and devoured feverishly. But whether it was real meat or Sankichi's lacerated thigh could not be discerned distinctly. Coming to himself, Hachizō shuddered at his own terrifying thought.[18]

Hachizō's desire is obviously different from that of the abbot in "Aozukin" who is driven mad by love and grief. Hachizō desires to eat Sankichi's flesh because he is literally starving, and yet the same homoerotic element is discernible in both tales.

We are given to understand that it is the captain's devotion to Konpira, the guardian deity of seafarers,[19] that prevents his men from succumbing to the ultimate evil. His faith dissuades the murderers from eating his nephew's body, then informs the captain, by means of a dream, that help is at hand for him and his crew. Indeed, two months after the storm, the ship is rescued, and the evil that stems from extremity and displacement is checked. Further-more, the captain is able to forgive both of the murderers: Gorosuke, who dies just before the rescue ship reaches Yokohama, and Hachizō, who breaks down when he hears the captain report Sankichi's death as having been from natural causes.

The Man-Eating Woman and the Baby-Eating Mother

We have already seen a number of texts published in the late 1920s, including examples of proletarian literature, with its recurring motif of workers devoured by capitalists and its representations of women struggling for independence and financial security. Nakamoto Takako's (1903–1991) short story "Suzumushi no mesu" (Female Bell-Cricket, 1929) presents a putatively novel situation: an at-tractive young woman lives, like the "modern girl" Naomi in Tanizaki's *Chijin no ai* (A Fool's Love, 1924–1925, trans. *Naomi*), at the expense of a male admirer whom she disdains. This disdain preserves her independence. In Nakamoto's text, however, this becomes an anthropophagous, or (more precisely) andropha-gous—strictly one-sided—war of the sexes. The male-devouring behavior of the female insect of the story's title is well known.[20] Nakamoto is not a Tanizaki, however; she is not concerned with the androphagous woman as aesthetic cre-ation, nor does her (third-person) narrative invite the reader to identify with the male participant's masochism.

The central character, Tomoko, is depressed and miserable at the beginning of the story, having lost her job as well as her lover. Unlike the protagonist of *Hōrōki*, Tomoko shows no compunction about exploiting to the full her de-spised admirer. Miki responds by idolizing her and giving her everything he can, including food. This only increases her contempt for him. She mocks his hopeless romanticism and exploits her sexual attraction to gorge herself on the ever better, ever richer food Miki starves himself to provide. While the man fades away, the woman gains in power, beauty, and weight. Tomoko, unlike the leg-endary *yamanba*-wife, never pretends not to need food. Neither does she hide her sexual desire—not for Miki but for the man who has deserted her. In other words she, who was the prey—an apt expression for this would-be *kuimono* (lit-erally, "something to eat"; i.e., someone to be deceived and exploited)—of one man, becomes predator to another.

In Okamoto Kanoko's[21] "Kishimo no ai" (The Love of Kishimo,[22] 1928) the desire of the protagonist Kishimo (Hariti) is much stronger and more sensual than that of Nakamoto's protagonist. Kishimo devours children—not her own but those of others. She eats neither for survival nor for revenge, but for her "overabundance of love":

> Finally, she could not stand it any longer. Knowing her own bad habits, she did her best to keep her eyes shut as she passed. Before she could close her eyes, however, she had already caught a glimpse of that child out of the corner of her èye, the image of its skipping form rushing into her eyes like a beam of light. Even when she closed her eyes, the image of that small form did not fade. Wrapped in the luster of velvety darkness in the back of her skull, it called out to the sun and kicked up pebbles like a starfish in the ocean. Then, when she felt the fingertips of that silhouette lithe with vivacity churning in the back of her skull, passion at once boiled all over her body.
>
> She staggered into the alley. Propping the child's chin in her hand, first she sucked on his lips. The small lips were softer even than the moist petal of a flower. Then she sucked the child's eyes, whereupon the child's eyelids and eyelashes shuddered slightly and he let out a small laugh. [. . .] Children with the tips of their noses chilled like jujubes. As soon as Kishimo's lips touched that child's cheek, that delightful touch, as of ripened fruit, reverberated in her heart. Whereupon a mysterious blood rushed backward through her whole body and gathered at the roots of her teeth. In spite of herself, she bit down on the child's cheek.[23]

Although Kanoko refers briefly to Aozukin in this story, Kishimo's desire is treated not as perverse and degenerate morbidity but as excessive love, passion, and vitality. Despite the fact that it is about eating children, the story neither shocks nor disgusts the reader in the way that Sade's perverse stories shock and disgust, or in the way that some other tales of cannibalism do. This is partly because we know that it is based on a Buddhist tale and that through Buddha's guidance Kishimo not only stops eating children but also becomes the god of fertility. But the surprisingly warm and positive impression Kanoko's story creates is surely due to her handling this famous tale. The self-centeredness of Kishimo's love and the horrendous nature of its consequences are corrected by Buddha, who nevertheless recognizes the strength of her love. Instead of denying or punishing the desire of this Great Mother, he, as a "practical man" (kurōnin), advises Kishimo to eat a pomegranate next time she wants to eat children because "it tastes like human flesh."[24] Although this pomegranate episode is not Kanoko's invention but part of the Buddhist tale, the image and the taste of the fruit present a striking contrast to the grisly descriptions and imagery that appear in other cannibalism stories.

Cannibalism as Addiction

In Edogawa Ranpo's *Yami ni ugomeku* (Squirming in the Darkness, 1926), cannibalism is depicted as a pathological, transmittable, and addictive habit—features it shares, of course, with the popular notion of vampirism. Edogawa Ranpo (1894–1965), who derived his pseudonym from Edgar Allan Poe, is known as a pioneer of mystery stories characterized by a grotesque eroticism.[25] Suzuki Sadami notes the curious case of cross-generic incorporation in Ranpo's writing, in which interest in modern technology sits oddly with a garrulous narrative style. Suzuki points to a likeness in Ranpo's style to that of Uno Kōji, the leading *shishōsetsu* writer, and to the rich decadent quality of Tanizaki's[26] writing and that of Kitahara Hakushū, into which features of the narrative tradition of Western mystery stories are imported.

So even if, in the manner of Poe, the story is said to be contained in a manuscript found by accident (on a ship, one notes),[27] *Yami ni ugomeku* is a distinctly modernist horror story. The main character is a Western-style painter, and a rather decadent hedonist. The action takes place principally in a Western-style hotel in a remote mountain region. The artist visits the hotel with his girlfriend, who goes missing. With a companion, the artist sets out in search of her, and the two men find themselves trapped in a cave underneath the hotel, where they find partly eaten, decaying human remains. They are soon joined by a third man, a menacing *yakuza* (gangster) who falls from the hotel into the cave through a trapdoor in the floor, in a manner reminiscent of the Demon Barber's unfortunate clients.

We learn from the *yakuza* that the perpetrator of these terrible deeds is the hotel's owner and that his cannibalism began (as in Nogami's *Kaijinmaru*) in response to extreme circumstances—the need to survive after a shipwreck in the Mariana Sea. The *yakuza*, who happens to be another survivor of the same shipwreck, has been blackmailing the hotel owner over his pathological and habitual cannibalism. As the hunger of the three captives intensifies, the *yakuza* proves not to be averse to human flesh himself. A series of violent events ensues, narrated somewhat elliptically, but ending with the artist being the only survivor. Emaciated, white-haired, and no longer innocent of consuming his fellow man, he makes his escape, only to find himself addicted to human meat. To satisfy his craving he is reduced to digging up recent graves in the forest, where he comes upon the hotel owner engaged in the same activity. The corpse the latter is exhuming is that of the artist's missing girlfriend. In the end, the local villagers stumble across a macabre and grisly scene: the fat hotel-keeper with his throat bitten open, the girlfriend with her heart removed—in order to be eaten—and the artist hanged from a tree, his mouth dripping human blood.

The two men, like the abbot of "Aozukin," have become addicted to the taste of human flesh, and their cannibalism, like the abbot's, is connected with sexual desire. Both the hotel owner and the artist are infatuated with the girlfriend, dead or alive. While in "Aozukin" one of the two Buddhist protagonists has the power to put a stop to the other's demoniac act, in Ranpo's story the two men share the same obsession and are powerless to resist its logic. The artist even feels a kind of sexual attraction for the hotel owner. "Saburō [the artist] could not hate the man completely. On the contrary, he felt, though this may sound strange, a kind of indecent sympathy, mingled with the revulsion for a sufferer of the same disease. The sympathy turned at times into peculiar physical attraction."[28]

Thus what is repugnant may become appetizing, and an obvious Other may not be so different from the self. Such reversal and discovery are made possible through displacement.

Cannibalism in *ero guro nansensu*

Ero guro nansensu (eroticism, grotesquerie, and nonsense)—such is the expression often used to describe the popular culture of the 1920s and 1930s, and one can hardly deny that the label is appropriate to *Yami ni ugomeku*. It is even more fitting as a description for Yumeno Kyūsaku's (1889–1936) *Ningen sōsēji* (Human Sausages, 1936),[29] in which the *nansensu* is obviously as important as the other two elements. *Ningen sōsēji* belongs to the broad genre that has subsequently acquired the sobriquet "black comedy."

The narrator of this story is an aging carpenter; his audience (for he is speaking to an audience) is the couple whose house he has just finished building. Inspired perhaps by the sake his hostess brings out to mark the completion of his work, he starts to tell his listeners a story. It is the tale of an adventure that befell him as a young man, some thirty years earlier, and its most striking formal feature is its mode of narration, which shows many of the generic features of the *rakugo* monologue. More precisely it refers to the style of a monologue of a *hōkan*, a male geisha, whose profession is to entertain patrons with jokes, talk, and song and dance, and generally to amuse them. He does this by playing the bumbling clown who is nevertheless acutely attuned to the pride and egoism of his paying customers. In his use of the form *de gesu* for the normal polite *desu*—a peculiarity of old-style *rakugo* and *hōkan*—Yumeno explicitly signals this appropriation of the *rakugo* genre in his narrative. The initial setting of the story—a telling scene that precedes the narration itself—is in fact also a borrowing from *rakugo* (the device known as the *makura*).[30] The story ends, as we shall see, with the traditional "twist" that *rakugo* demands, known as the *ochi* or *sage*. Moreover, as a story being told in a particular social setting to a particular audience, rather than being directed at a silent, passive reader, the carpenter's monologue in *Ningen sōsēji* indirectly incorporates his audience's reactions, so that the narration becomes as much a dialogue as a monologue. Again this owes much to the art of *rakugo* as live performance.

Yumeno's choice of this native, traditional, familiar, and comfortingly social genre to recount a nightmarish encounter with the exotic seems significant. The *rakugo* familiarizes and naturalizes the social situation depicted by Yumeno as the milieu in which the narration takes place. There is security and reassurance in the knowledge of shared expectations, in the professional competence of the old carpenter, in the appropriateness and familiarity of the proffered sake. Yumeno juxtaposes, and opposes, two worlds—our comforting, familiar world and the exotic world of the Other—and makes the first into a frame for the latter. In providing the carpenter's nightmarish story with such a frame, Yumeno gives its macabre content an even more extreme, quasi-hallucinatory nature; but at the same time, by distancing the nightmare, Yumeno allows it to be detraumatized and to be presented as essentially comic.

The events narrated concern, essentially, the (then) young carpenter's narrow escape from being made—yes, we are not far from the world of Sweeney Todd—into sausages.[31] Sucked into the danger zone by a mysterious mantra—"the world is round"—he travels to the 1904 World's Fair in St. Louis, Missouri, to promote the tea produced in the then-Japanese colony of Formosa—note the double Otherness that this project involves. His main task is to build a Taiwanese-style teahouse, but he also acts as a barker, exhorting the crowds to visit the pavilion, shouting a line he has been given to memorize without any idea of its meaning: "Japan gabamen forumosa uuronchi wankapu tensensu. Kaminkamin"[32] (Japanese government Formosa oolong tea one cup ten cents. Come in, come in.). His ignorance of the meaning of this speech will save his life later in the story. In the meantime his deep ignorance of English gives rise to a particular style of humor, by means of which he succeeds in entertaining his middle-class hosts: he tells them, for example, that the ship's doctor on the journey to America diagnosed his depression as *ōmu shikko* (parrot pee); his amused host explains that the doctor must have said "homesick."

Stereotypes of both the foreign (the Other) and the domestic are not hard to find in this story. Chief amongst them is a gangster—American, naturally—who owns a large sausage-making machine. The gangster has a harem of Asian mistresses, and pimps for a stable of Asian prostitutes whose earnings he siphons off. In need of a skilled workman to build a secret safe for his ill-gotten gains, he employs the carpenter. The carpenter is forbidden to leave the World's Fair exhibition grounds, but one of the gangster's mistresses (thought at first to be Taiwanese, she turns out to be even more dangerous—Eurasian,[33] with Chinese and Italian parents) lures him into their quarters. Another mistress (masquerading as Chinese but in fact a Japanese from Amakusa—a well-known source of traveling prostitutes) tries to warn him of the danger he is in by writing a note, in fine Japanese and in beautiful brush and ink calligraphy—like classical poetry:

> Do not go with Chii-chan. She is Chinese, and being used by an American gangster. I am a poor Japanese woman, who, like Chii-chan, has become the gangster's mistress. Please give my regards to my parents in Japan.
>
> Nakada Fujiko
> Born in Hayaura, Amakusa[34]

This note, however, is intercepted, with fatal consequences: Fujiko is fed into the sausage machine.

Much of this may seem a crude and naive expression of racial and cultural prejudice: throughout his narrative the carpenter uses the derogative *ketō* (hairy foreigners) to refer to male Americans. The reader is constantly reminded, however, that this is the talk of a tipsy old man whose worldview, in spite of his professional skills and overseas experience, is limited, and whose language tends to be rough but lacks real hostility. That said, there can be no doubt that on another level *Ningen sōsēji* is "about" a Japan or a notion of Japanese-ness that contrasts with an Other world into which one ventures at one's own risk: this latter world being unpredictable, dangerous—ludicrously so—and the locus of cannibalism. Japanese-ness on the other hand represents what is competent and workmanlike (it is the young man's carpentry skills that define him against the American gangster's criminality), resourceful, and real.

After the girl is made into sausages, the carpenter, still in captivity, cries out for help, but because of the language barrier all he can do is shout the only "English" line he knows: "Japan gabamen forumosa . . ." As the carpenter remarks in his narrative, had he known the meaning of this line, he would have thought it useless to shout it and would have remained silent. It is only thanks to his ignorance that he calls out, with the result that he is heard and rescued, and the gangsters are arrested. So the "nonsense" rescues the protagonist-narrator from the fatal trap of *ero* and *guro*.

The story does not end there, however. There is still the *ochi* (or *sage*), the final twist in the tail of the *rakugo*-like narrative. The carpenter is on his voyage home after months of recuperation in St. Louis when he opens a tin of sausages given to him by a Japanese acquaintance in San Francisco. He finds, to his horror, some strands of black hair in among the tinned sausages, along with a piece of paper that looks rather like the note of warning written by the unfortunate woman from Amakusa. "The world is round," after all, just as the mysterious mantra at the beginning of the story said it was, and the girl returns home to Japan with the carpenter, albeit in conveniently edible form.

In *Ningen sōseji* "displacement" does not appear exclusively in the guise of *ero guro nansensu*; at least at one point in the story, it becomes a matter of something akin to social commentary. The young Japanese woman from Amakusa may be the protagonist's only ally in his nightmare (with unfortunate consequences for herself), but she also belongs to a group that is singled out for mention in an earlier episode in the story, an episode in which Yumeno appears to want to talk about displacement in a much less fanciful way.

On his first venture outside Japan the young carpenter has been assigned to Formosa (Taiwan) to build residential quarters for colonial officials. He is terrified by the idea of leaving his comfort zone, Tokyo, and confides in a Japanese fellow passenger, an engineer, who tries to raise the young man's spirits by exhorting the courage and vitality of the Amakusa women. They, says the engineer, are the real pioneers, the first to get to mines and plantations in all corners of the world, and they even blaze a trail that Western men follow, when they come to build their towns and railways. If these women—usually termed *karayuki-san*—can take the displacement so fearlessly and competently, surely, or so goes the moral of the engineer's story, a Japanese man such as our young carpenter can do the same. Before their departure these young women have no idea about the world—they don't know "whether it's round or square"—but they have no fear of going out there. They cater to men of all races and send home the money they earn. Once they learn about life and the world—how it works, how they can survive, how they can make the most of it, in short that "the world is round"—they are ready to go home and settle down and get married.[35] (We might recall the same kind of rosy tale of young women transformed into prostitutes for American officers and then back into respectable wives and daughters in *Tōkyō sebun rōzu*—only that transformation takes place in Tokyo.)

There is no doubt that the engineer's picture of the life of a *karayuki-san* is a sanguine one and ignores what must have been its darker and more cruel realities (revealed, for example, in Yamazaki Tomoko's 1972 nonfiction *Sandakan hachiban shōkan* [Sandakan Brothel No. 8]). It is as though what is of interest to Yumeno here is the often-noted—as we have already seen in *Tōkyō sebun rōzu*—resourcefulness of Japanese women, in contrast to the timidity of their male counterparts. In Yumeno's fantasy, one notes that the young woman from Amakusa speaks Chinese well enough to masquerade as Chinese and that both the Eurasian woman and—to our great surprise—her gangster pimp speak enough Japanese to communicate with the young carpenter. In contrast the hapless carpenter's only foray into a foreign language is the garbled English sentence he repeats parrot-like without any curiosity as to its meaning.

In reality the overseas prostitution of Japanese women was banned in the early 1920s, and all the *karayuki-san* were forced to return from Southeast Asia to Amakusa and elsewhere, not to settle down happily in their home villages but to suffer a lifetime of disdain and discrimination. This particular *karayuki-san* returns home, but only in the form of sausages, and is very nearly eaten by the young man she saved. All that is left of her recognizable human form is her hair, which is "woman's life" according to the common saying, and a scrap of her beautiful handwriting. The latter is handy proof of her true identity in the story, but highly unlikely in real circumstances of poor country girls sold into prostitution.

Cannibalism in postwar literature has a completely different meaning from what it exhibits in the various prewar examples discussed. The realities of wartime encouraged writers to deal with cannibalism not as a grotesque and exotic fantasy but as a fundamental issue of human existence and survival. The new focus on universal human existence has pushed class and gender divisions, if not quite into the background, certainly to the middle ground, the implication being that the physical and psychological devastation of the war affects everyone, even the most privileged. The connection between cannibalism and the discourse on Japanese-ness, however, has not disappeared.

To Eat or Not to Eat

Ōoka Shōhei's (1909–1988) *Nobi* (Fires on the Plain, 1952) is the first important work to treat cannibalism during the war as an existential problem. The novel takes the form of the journal of the narrator, Private Tamura. It begins with a scene in which Tamura is abandoned by his own squad in Leyte because he is suffering from tuberculosis. Neither the army nor the hospital can afford to feed useless soldiers like him—even though he seems to be less useless than the protagonist of Yasuoka Shōtarō's novel discussed earlier. In his solitary wandering through the Philippine plains and mountains, Tamura notices that some of the corpses by the roadside have lost the flesh on their buttocks. He realizes the cause of this peculiar phenomenon when one day the sight of a fresh corpse makes him feel like eating its flesh. Tamura, however, strongly doubts if the idea of eating human flesh occurred to him spontaneously:

> Never, I thought, would it have occurred to me to alleviate my hunger in this way had I not heard the story of how the survivors of the *Medusa*[36] ate each other on their raft, and later listened to reports of cannibalism on Guadalcanal and hints of the same practice from New Guinea. Anthropology has, of course, clearly established that in prehistoric times people did eat each other, just as that primitive societies practice incest; but for us who live in the shadow of a long history and deeply rooted custom it is impossible without an access of abhorrence to imagine fornicating with our mothers or eating human flesh.[37]

The passage clearly tells us that Tamura sees himself as belonging to a civilized society in which incest and anthropophagy are taboo. He has enjoyed the status of a highly literate and educated man in that society. On the battlefield, however, neither civilization nor knowledge can solve basic problems such as hunger. As we have already seen in the many examples from Yasuoka's novel, the military institution places the uncivilized above the civilized. Tamura's literacy means nothing, as he is forced to speak the ridiculously rigid army language. All he can do is try to understand, and reconstruct in his writing, his own thoughts during his futile wanderings. Obviously the narrator Tamura survived and is writing this some time after the war.[38] But the reader is not told until towards the end of the story where and how Tamura is and why he is writing. As for his desire to eat human flesh, the narrator records that he cannot remember exactly how he felt when it first came to him, "just as lovers forget the exact feeling that they experienced at a certain moment in their intercourse."[39] Inability to recollect occurs in a few other places in this narrative, always at a crucial moment.[40]

Tamura tries to eat the flesh of a dead officer. The officer has, in a brief, serene moment before his death, regained his sanity long enough to grant permission to Tamura, a complete stranger, to eat his left arm. Tamura first eats the leeches on the dead man's arm, but when he tries to eat the arm itself, his own left hand—as if it has a will of its own—stops his bayonet-wielding right hand. From this moment on, the left half of Tamura rejects not only eating human flesh but killing all living things, including plants: a flower tells Tamura (in feminine language) that he may eat her, but his left side stops him.[41] He feels he is constantly being observed by someone. At first he wonders if it is the spirit of a Filipino woman he killed in a Catholic church. Increasingly, however, it becomes clear that this observer is God. By the time he returns to the spot where the dead officer lies, the body has become "inedible": "God had transformed him before my arrival. He was beloved of God. And I, too, perhaps."[42]

Tamura is not a practicing Christian, although he regularly went to church during his childhood. The novel is full of Biblical references and symbolism, from its epigraph—"Even though I walk through the valley of the shadow of death"—to its last line—"Glory be to God."[43] Whether Tamura himself is "beloved of God," however, is left ambiguous. He maintains that up until now, he has killed but not eaten human flesh, but when he meets an acquaintance, another discarded soldier called Nagamatsu, he eats the cooked meat Nagamatsu offers, without at first knowing what it is:

> It had the taste of dry cardboard. When I had eaten several of the objects, however, I realized that it was meat. It was dry and hard, but with it came a taste that I had not experienced once in all the months since I had left my unit; a taste of grease permeated my mouth.[44]

He is told that it is monkey meat, but the ensuing events make it clear that it is in fact cooked human flesh. Tamura feels "an ineffable sorrow," still believing that he has just eaten animal meat, which the left half of his body has forbidden him to do. But he admits that the meat was delicious. Only when he realizes that Nagamatsu and his companion, Yasuda, have been eating human flesh and even killing people for that purpose does he refuse to join them. The only flesh he can eat without hesitation is his own torn from him by grenade shrapnel. After Nagamatsu kills Yasuda, Tamura confronts him:

> I was seized with anger: if as a result of hunger human beings were constrained to eat each other, then this world of ours was no more than the result of God's wrath. And if I at this moment could vomit forth anger, then I, who was no longer human, must be an angel of God, an instrument of God's wrath.[45]

In this climactic scene Tamura's memory fails again: "I do not remember whether I shot him at that moment. But I do know that I did not eat his flesh; this I should certainly have remembered."[46]

In the third to last chapter, which comes immediately after the above memo-ry lapse, the reader is told that Tamura is in a mental hospital in an outer suburb of Tokyo and, on his doctor's advice, is writing this journal six years after the events it describes. The reserved and analytical style of the journal betrays no obvious signs of insanity or confusion—with the exception of the memory loss. While the doctor observes that it is well written—just like a novel—Tamura in sists that it is just as he experienced it. Their conversation is recorded in the new part of Tamura's journal:

> "You may believe that you have recorded things exactly as they were, but that is precisely where some modification of the truth takes place. The same psychol-ogy is found in novelists."
>
> "Recollection is inevitably accompanied by organizing and rationalizing."
>
> "You have a highly developed consciousness, I'm sure. But you do modify the truth."
>
> "Even popular psychology books tell you that remembering is somewhat similar to imagining. What else could I do but compose my writing in accor-dance with my present thoughts and feelings?"[47]

This metafictional dialogue indicates on the one hand the impossibility of unmodified recollection and on the other the deep mistrust Tamura has of the doctor and everyone else. Even God seems to him "an existence so tenuous that it depends entirely on people's disposition to believe in it."[48] Nevertheless Tamura is eager to believe in his existence and to believe that the dying officer who offered him his own flesh was a transfiguration of Christ. In his final at-tempt to recollect the crucial moment in his memoir, he thinks that his left arm lifted his rifle not to commit any further killing but to surrender to the people surrounding him. It is not clear who they were, and it does not seem to matter. Symbolically, the imperial chrysanthemum crest on the rifle was crossed out,[49] suggesting that the crucifix of Christ had triumphed at that moment over the sign of imperialism.

Anthropophagy in the Contact Zone

While *Nobi* thus deals with the painful solitary wanderings of an intellectual through the Philippine mountains and through his consciousness, Takeda Tai-jun's (1912–1976) *Hikarigoke* (Luminous Moss, 1954) explores the significance of the contact zone. "Contact zone" is the term used in postcolonial studies in place of "frontier." While the frontier implies expansion and contraction, a contact zone indicates "the space of colonial encounters, the space in which peoples geographically and historically separated come into contact with each other and establish ongoing relations of some kind, even if these are often marked by conditions of coercion, radical inequality, and intractable conflict."[50] The contact zone in Takeda's text is Rausu in the northeastern corner of Hokkaidō, where the Japanese may encounter the Russians, the Ainu may meet the Yamato, and the local people meet visitors from the city. Furthermore, Takeda's text tempts us to expand the application of the term to include other encounters such as those of the eater with the eaten, the judge with the judged, the dead with the living, the speaker with the listener, the reader with the writer, fact with fiction, war with peace, and so on. It is also a space in which one text meets another text, one style meets another, and one genre meets another.

The story begins like a travelogue, with a first-person narrative recounting a trip to Rausu. Between descriptions of a peaceful and beautiful landscape in mid-September, there are suggestions that the scenery could be completely different in another season. The style, mostly using the polite *desu-masu*, incorporates occasional plain endings. Mixing *desu-masu* and plain styles occurs commonly in speech but is usually avoided in writing. Earlier we saw the deliberate transgression of this distinction in Hayashi Fumiko's text. Takeda too seems to challenge the norm in order to create a certain rhythm and to increase the flow and immediacy of the narrative voice. The narrator frequently interpolates his views and opinions, but he also includes other people's voices and texts. Of these, the most important is that of a school principal, a shy and calm person, who accompanies the narrator to the Makkaushi Cave, which is famous for its luminous moss. The principal tells the narrator "without a trace of exaggeration or forced enthusiasm"[51] the story of his ordeal drifting for three days among the ice floes near the Soviet border. While this episode itself contains no anthropophagy, the principal also mentions in a cheerfully naive manner a horrifying incident that took place towards the end of the war at a local promontory called Pekin Misaki: the captain of a wrecked ship on a military mission ate the flesh of his crew in this totally isolated, snowbound place. The carefree tone of the principal and his subdued personality play an important role in the second part of the story.

The principal's talk reminds the narrator of his friend, M,[52] who is an Ainu linguist with an indigenous background. He remembers particularly M's rage over a Japanese scholar's thoughtless asides at a scholarly meeting to the effect that cannibalism was practiced by some Ainu tribes in the distant past. Had M known of the Pekin Misaki incident, muses the narrator, he could have launched

a counterattack, pointing out that there was clear evidence of cannibalism practiced not by some vague ancient Ainu tribe but "among the unmistakably 'pure'
Japanese, in fact, 'among the people under the glorious reign of the Emperor
when their war spirit was at high tide!'"[53] Thus the introductory section of the
work clearly shows how discourses on cannibalism reflect the colonial myth,
which influences even supposedly unprejudiced and well-meaning scholars.

The narrator further points to the absurdity of the nationalist discourse. He
learns from the *Local History of Rausu Village*, compiled by a young man called
S, that when the captain was rescued and taken to Rausu in early February 1945,
two months after the shipwreck, he was enthusiastically admired by the locals as
the courageous hero of a "beautiful wartime drama" until the discovery in May
of a box containing human remains. Overnight, a hero devoted to the national
cause turns into a criminal. As for the legal consequences, which are omitted in
the *History*, the narrator has this to say:

> [S]upposing that the sentence had been imposed before August 15, 1945, that is,
> before the end of the war, in which killing the enemy was the one and only de-
> sire of our nation, I wonder if the punishment would not have been lighter than
> had it been given after the war when "democracy" is everybody's motto. Had the
> victims been Americans or British, on the other hand—American or English
> "white beasts" as they were customarily referred to—the "human flesh-eater"
> might have been found not guilty.[54]

As he reads S's writing, the narrator often comments that some parts are like
a well-written novel. This reading, together with the reading of other texts such
as *Kaijinmaru* and *Nobi*, is incorporated into his thoughts about "what kind of
novelistic dish he should put this incident into."[55] One of the major points he
makes is that while murders and even genocide are common in the twentieth
century, cannibalism is treated somehow as less civilized.

> "Civilized men" can commit murder, but they cannot eat human flesh without
> bringing disgrace on themselves. "Our nation, our race, may murder," they in-
> sist, "but we can never commit cannibalism." They are smug in their conviction
> of the excellence of their nation, an advanced race, one worthy of the blessings
> of God.[56]

Not surprisingly, the protagonist-narrator of *Nobi* is cited as an exemplar of
such "smug civilization." To conclude this metafictional introduction, the narrator explains his decision to use the form of a *Lesedrama* (or "closet drama," a

play that is intended to be read) in order to avoid the restrictions of realism and to encourage readers to produce the play in their own way, as a melodrama, a comedy, a religious fantasy, or whatever they prefer.

The dramatic part of *Hikarigoke* consists of two short acts, the first set in the Makkausu Cave and the second in a courtroom.[57] The first act has four characters, obviously created with Nogami's *Kaijinmaru* in mind: the captain, a handsome young man called Nishikawa (a counterpart to the captain's nephew Sankichi in Nogami's text), Hachizō, and Gosuke (Gorosuke in Nogami's text). Like Nogami's characters, they speak in heavy dialect. The actions of these characters, however, differ radically from those in Nogami's text. The captain, instead of preventing cannibalism, tries to persuade Nishikawa and Hachizō to eat the flesh of Gosuke, who has died of starvation. The captain uses the imperialist discourse for this purpose: for the sake of emperor and country they should overcome their personal fears and antipathy to eating human flesh and try to survive rather than die meaninglessly. While the patriotic Nishikawa reluctantly follows the captain, Hachizō refuses to break his promise to Gosuke not to eat him. The nationalist discourse has no effect on Hachizō, who points out that "the Emperor's takin' it easy in the Imperial Palace"[58] and hence would not even be able to imagine hunger. Hachizō soon succumbs to the same fate as his friend. He dies of starvation and is eaten by the two survivors. The actual eating scenes are not included in the play but only suggested. The dramatic and symbolic device used to distinguish those who have eaten human flesh from those who have not is a ring of light like the halo behind a statue of Buddha. Only those who have not eaten human flesh—like Hachizō—can see the "halo" attached to those who have.

Act 1 ends with Nishikawa trying to commit suicide by jumping into the sea, followed by the captain, who will not let his food escape.[59] The stage directions for this final scene specify two important effects. First, the music: it is to be based on the chanting used in the Ainu bear festival, a thanksgiving ceremony with the offering of a bear as a gift to the god who has given meat to the people. The other relates to the faint light of a luminous moss that transforms into a ring behind the captain's neck. These effects prepare the audience for the transformation of the captain in the next act.

While the captain in act 1 is described as "the most sinister-looking man," in act 2 Takeda asks that he be played by another actor to emphasize the difference in him. The captain now has "a peaceful face like that of Christ," closely resembling that of the school principal who appeared in the first half of the text. The language is standard Japanese, polite *desu-masu* spoken by the captain, and plain style spoken by the prosecutor. The imperialist discourse is presented by the prosecutor rather than by the captain, who quietly repeats that he is "bearing up" (*gaman shite iru*). This key word, *gaman*, first appears towards the end of act 1, when the captain tells Nishikawa, "I ain't got no one else t'take care a me. I gotta bear anythin' and everthin' all by myself. When I say I'm bearin' up, I mean I'm bearin' up under every single thing. To bear up ain't so clear and easy as seein' a watermelon split clean in two."[60]

In act 2, the captain tells the prosecutor, who accuses him of offending against the dignity of the nation and the emperor, that the emperor, like everyone else, seems to be merely "bearing up." Despite the scathing criticism of the nationalist discourse and the imperialist institutions, the emperor is treated here as a human being, no different from any other (and hence the implication is that we must forgive him).

In the final scene the captain insists that those who have not eaten human flesh must be able to see a ring of light behind his neck. No one present in the courtroom can see it, but the audience of the *Lesedrama* can see not just one ring attached to the captain but a multitude of rings behind the crowd, who are likened to those gathered around Christ on his way to Golgotha. To a Christian reader, it may not be easy to accept the image of Christ used in this way, but Takeda, unlike Ōoka, does not pursue the Christian theme. Rather, he combines Buddhist religious imagery (the halo), the Ainu bear festival, and the "bearing up" of Christ to show what is invisible. The moral seems to be Let him who is without sin cast the first stone. Every human being, including the emperor, has to "bear up" in order to live, and this may involve aggression towards others. The discursive distinctions between good and evil, innocent and guilty, and civilized and primitive are unreliable.

Nakano Miyoko, a scholar of Chinese literature and one of the leading commentators on cannibalism in literature, sees strong echoes of Lu Xun (1881–1936) in the final transformation of the captain in Takeda's text.[61] Lu Xun uses cannibalism in "Diary of a Madman" (1918, translated as "Kyōjin nikki" in Japanese) as a metaphor for the vicious circle of exploitation in his country, where people have enslaved, exploited, and devoured each other for four thousand years. Like those on the raft of the *Medusa*, they continue to devour their countrymen. Those who have eaten others will be eaten in their turn by others still. The only hope is for children who have not yet eaten human flesh.[62] The greatest paradox, however, is that the children to be saved are also on the raft called China. How can they survive without eating others? In *Hikarigoke* there is no such message that we should try to stop the cannibalistic circle; human beings are simply "bearing up." Nevertheless, Nakano is right in connecting the two texts through their transformation of cannibalism from fact or physical reality to image or metaphor. Moreover, both texts treat cannibalism not as an exotic or pathological custom of the Other but as something prevalent within their own culture and society. Takeda does not mention Lu Xun in *Hikarigoke* as he does *Kaijinmaru* and *Nobi*.[63] But given Takeda's background in Chinese literature and his involvement in Marxism in his earlier days, it seems appropriate to see *Hikarigoke* as his response to "Diary of a Madman."

Cannibalism in the Anti-Novel

Cultural contact, metafiction, intertextuality, and existential questions are even more thoroughly explored in Kurahashi Yumiko's (1935–2005) full-length novel *Sumiyakisuto Q no bōken* (The Adventures of Sumiyakist Q, 1969). Kurahashi's early works are known for their anti-roman qualities and their strong affinity to Kafka, Sartre, and Camus. Kurahashi is also known for her outspoken criticism of the *shizen shugi–shishōsetsu* literary codes and practices.[64] Like many other Kurahashi texts written in the 1960s, *Sumiyakisuto Q no bōken* fits neatly with her manifested ideal of the novel: "[a]t an uncertain time, in a place that is nowhere, somebody who is no one, for no reason, is about to do something—and in the end does nothing."[65] The nowhere (i.e., utopia) in this case is a reformatory on a remote island and the no one protagonist is Q, who arrives at the reformatory on a Sumiyakist mission, but achieves nothing. Sumiyakism (the term is coined by Kurahashi as a calque on Carbonari, i.e., *sumiyaki*) is an obvious parody of Marxism, although the author rejects the kind of reading that sees this merely as a satire of any existing organization.

Cannibalism plays a crucial role in this anti-novel about nowhere. It is presented as an institutionalized practice of the staff of the reformatory. The most enthusiastic participant is the grotesquely obese Rector. To him, eating—like knowing—is a means of incorporating the external world and expanding his existence. The consequence is "an obese mind in a corpulent body."[66] While his gross obesity is by no means regarded as a problem by the Rector himself, his twitching suggests that there is something deeply unhealthy: "This surface earthquake indicated the accumulation of some as yet unknown energy advancing in the deep recesses of his being, surface twitchings reflecting structural faulting somewhere within him, which might give birth at some time to weird ideologies, or to death."[67]

The food supply of the reformatory consists of students who, on reaching a certain age, are processed as food unless their guardians request their return. This systematic eating of human corpses, we are told, was first proposed by the

Doktor, who regards anthropophagy as merely one of many taboos that should be challenged. Although the Doktor is just as greedy and free of prejudice or conscience as the Rector, he seems to be selective, choosing what pleases him. His room is littered with piles of books on subjects ranging from sexual postures in classical literature, through artificial sexual organs, sodomy, scatology, spiritualism, and phenomenology, to the art of meat cookery. These "remnants of that food which the soul of the room's owner fed upon"[68] are closely connected to the physical means of his existential incorporation, namely eating and sex.

Not every member of the staff shares the insatiable appetites of the Rector and the Doktor. The Overseer, for example, is a vegetarian. In Q's case, both ideology and instinct cause him to refuse to participate in the institution's eating practice or even to admit the possibility that such a system is at work. In other words, he rejects both the food and the knowledge that the institution offers him. He feels nauseous when he swallows pieces of unidentified meat served to him by the Rector. Indeed, just as "bearing up" is the key word in *Hikarigoke*, "nausea"—a very Sartrian topos—is the key word in *Sumiyakist Q*. From his arrival on the island until his departure at the end of the novel, Q often suffers from nausea and throws up what he has eaten. Subconscious rejection also occurs on a verbal level: Q refuses to accept or understand words that refer to or suggest the ongoing cannibalism. When the Doktor tells him that the smoked meat Q has just tasted is human flesh, Q laughs, believing it is a joke. Similarly, when he hears that in the war that has recently broken out the so-called savages are slaughtering their former oppressors and eating their flesh, Q believes this is a nasty rumor put about by the oppressors. He explains this to the Doktor:

By that I mean that what the oppressors want the war to look like is just a revolt of savages against civilized values which they are out to destroy, so they give out propaganda like that, because if they can fix the barbarous act of cannibalism upon the oppressed, then they can smear them with the name of inhuman savages, and at the same time give themselves as oppressors the prettier sounding name of guardians of civilization.[69]

Although this may vaguely remind us of William Arens' view of cannibalism as a colonial myth, as a Sumiyakist, Q is simply programmed to interpret everything, cannibalism included, as a product of class conflict. Elaborating on the above, he insists that even if a tribe does practice cannibalism it must have been driven to do so by starvation caused by oppression. Naturally Q's materialist view never convinces the Doktor.

The reader knows that Q's thoughts and observations are extremely limited and is also left in no doubt that cannibalism is being practiced in the reformatory; but beyond that nothing seems definite. This ambiguity, despite detailed descriptions of Q's actions and his lengthy dialogues with other characters, accords with the anti-roman theory, which is elaborated through the voice of another character—the language instructor with a monomaniacal passion for literature. The novel, according to this "literary man," should have no clear story, as it is the reader rather than the writer who creates the story. In his view, the writer "ceases to be God," and "must bestow no deterministic character upon any of his characters." "The world is to be rendered meaningless," and "[t]he novel is not to be made to comply with external time." Nor is it to describe the writer's personal life or to express his opinion.[70]

However, the literary man's elucidation merely bores Q. Neither does the literary man's incomplete experimental novel "Doktor's Notebook" find a creative reader in Q, who merely confuses fiction with fact. The "Notebook" includes the narrator Doktor's recollections of his earliest experiment in cannibalism: when he was working in a university hospital, he attempted to eat the flesh of a dead fetus. He purposely avoided cooking it, as the aim of the experiment was to challenge his own hypothesis that human beings do not eat each other because they perceive a fragment of "god" in one another. The experiment failed as the fictional Doktor was overcome by a violent nausea. Q automatically identifies the Doktor of the literary man's novel with the Doktor he has met on the island, which is precisely the kind of reading the literary man rejects.

Nausea and its existential meaning are analyzed in the second part of "Doktor's Notebook." The narrator Doktor muses on his being:

> The equilibrium I have is that of a drowned corpse drifting half floating and half sinking in yellow vomit. Its flesh has almost all rotted, and one cannot recognize the face of this drowned man. Still, it is undoubtedly me. This nausea I perpetually feel is because of the stench of death which comes from this form of drowned corpse being of mine. Also I have swallowed down too many alien things into my stomach. For me the meat of other men is the most alien thing of all.[71]

This second part of the literary man's manuscript also exploits the ambiguous relationship between textual truth and historical truth. Despite his rejection of literature determined by external reality, his writing seems to refer to or even to reveal that external reality, including as it does an account of the death of one of the instructors and a description of how systematic cannibalism was introduced at the reformatory. It also includes a commentary on Q, as if to instruct Q as the intended reader: "Of course Q has already eaten human beings, but it is so hard to make him realize the fact that one despairs of doing so. For Q the fact of man-eating does not exist because he does not wish to believe in it."[72]

Just as nothing can make Q realize the facts presented in the literary man's text, Q, as the reader of the text, simply becomes annoyed with what he believes to be an unfounded personal attack. "There's a limit to everything" is his response, and he never takes any notice of things that go beyond the limits he draws.

Ironically, the Doktor himself tells Q that the account of cannibalism in the "Notebook" is accurate. However, it is not through reading this "Notebook" that Q is finally convinced of the awful truth. It is only when he overhears the Rector and the Doktor discussing the urgent problem of a "food" shortage at the reformatory that it finally dawns on Q what "food" they are talking about. Even then Q's response is governed by the Sumiyakist discourse: he decides it is now time to persuade the oppressed masses to achieve a revolution against the cannibalist establishment. Unlike protagonists in other texts who have eaten human flesh, Q does not seem to be particularly concerned about the fact that he himself has participated in this act; he can still deceive himself with the pathetic excuse that his cannibalism has been unintentional. His nausea continues, but as the Doktor points out—echoing the fictional Doktor's words quoted above—vomiting does not help to purge one of the elements of the others that one has consumed; Q has already eaten so much of the flesh of others that he is no longer himself but somebody else.[73]

Just as Q's nausea is regarded as useless and meaningless as a defensive mechanism against complicity, his materialist interpretation of cannibalism is written off by the Doktor as nonsense. While Q still tries to explain the changes in the diet of the "menials"—from seaweed and fish to dogs, and then finally to people—in terms of food shortage and exploitation, the Doktor claims that they eat human flesh simply because it tastes better. The higher up the evolutionary chain one's food source is, according to this theory, the sweeter its meat. Moreover, he relates degrees of civilization to cooking methods, and presents a culinary quadrangle: raw, boiled, grilled or roasted, and fermented. This is obviously based on Lévi-Strauss' "culinary triangle" of raw, cooked, and rotten, and its extension, the "triangle of recipes."[74] The raw, according to the Doktor, indicates a "precivilized stage," while sharing food "boiled" in a pot is a closed-in "communal digestive process using shared saliva." The "menials" eat only raw or boiled food. The grilled or roasted, on the other hand, "reflects an open form of social relationships," which allows individual eaters, including outsiders, to join in the meal.[75]

This final dialogue between Q and the Doktor, however, has absolutely no effect on either party. The Doktor's knowledge and intellect do not change Q's perception or actions, let alone stop the destruction that goes on both within and outside the reformatory. As we saw, *Hikarigoke* suggests that it is not the so-called savages but those who regard themselves as civilized who practice cannibalism. In Kurahashi's novel cannibalism spreads from the supposedly civilized staff members to the menials and the totally deprived students. Needless to say this is not the revolution Q had in mind. Q as "no one" "does nothing in the end"; his understanding of the world is no better than it was at the beginning; he cannot change the social structure or save the children, and the world is "rendered meaningless."

In a series of more recent and much shorter works, Kurahashi has dealt with cannibalism generally in a much lighter, at times almost frivolous, vein. These recent works can take the form of a witty short story about a cannibalist couple making fun of (and actually devouring) people involved in the popular media, or of a sophisticated parody of Swift.[76] There are some familiar elements in these stories: a reversal of hierarchy (e.g., between the savage and the civilized), cannibalism as the ultimate pursuit of eroticism or gastronomy or both, and ridicule of anthropology and other studies. The power of subversion, which was evident in *Sumiyakist Q*, however, seems to have waned in these later cannibalism stories.

Misreading Letters from Sagawa

Kurahashi is by no means the only contemporary writer who has exploited the theme of cannibalism. Tsutsui Yasutaka (b. 1934) and Atōda Takashi (b. 1935), for example, have written a number of stories that are usually categorized as works of mystery or of black humor. *Sagawa-kun kara no tegami* (Letters from Sagawa, 1983) by Kara Jūrō (b. 1940), on the other hand, does not belong to any existing subgenre or form; it is a kind of metafictional fantasy about a 1981 incident in which a Japanese student in Paris killed and ate his Dutch girlfriend. Despite using this incident and the letters written to him by Sagawa, Kara makes it clear that it is not his intention to pursue the actual truth or to join the media in speculating about Sagawa's particular sexual fantasy or his purported inferiority complex. Neither is he interested in Sagawa's own dramatic or fictional account of the incident. In the Author's Note attached to the novel Kara writes that he found in Sagawa's letters an infantilist self-concluded, closed-in scenario. His own writing, then, was an attempt to "step into [Sagawa's] experience and yet to misread it."[77]

In his deliberate misreading Kara introduces a number of texts, including letters to and from Sagawa and a German Expressionist poem[78] that the victim Renée is said to have read to Sagawa. He also invents a character called K. Ohara, a young Japanese woman who lives in Paris and has some contact with Sagawa. She has a few odd jobs, some of which seem to be dubious—reminding us, in fact, of the *karayuki-san.* Her background is ambiguous. The narrator meets her during his stay in Paris and tries to gather information for his book on Sagawa. As one would expect, given the talent of Kara as a leading avant-garde dramatist, some breathtakingly acrobatic dialogues take place between Ohara and the narrator.

Another important character in this novel is the narrator's late grandmother. Like Ohara, she has been exposed to cross-cultural contacts in her earlier life, while working as a housemaid in a foreigner's house in Yokohama. The narrator remembers one of the horror stories she told him when he was a child. It was about a drinking place in Nagasaki (another famous contact zone) where customers drank in the presence of human corpses. The narrator assumes that the customers were probably Japanese and the corpses belonged to people from neighboring countries. The narrator's imagination places his grandmother in this seedy drinking place as a barmaid. So there are interesting elements—contacts between the living and the dead, between different cultures, and between a man and a woman. Equally interesting is the conscious exploitation of transtextuality, to borrow Genette's term, and its subcategories such as intertextuality, paratextuality, and hypertextuality.[79]

Despite this intriguing structure and textuality, and despite the fact that the novel was awarded the Akutagawa Prize, one must say that Kara's misread fantasy is hardly convincing.[80] In one of his letters to Sagawa the narrator suggests that the flesh Sagawa ate probably had no taste, since his act of cannibalism was nothing but a criticism of those around him who considered such an act taboo.[81] There is no evidence that this limitation has been overcome in the misread version. The narrator tells Ohara that Renée's flesh has never become Sagawa's blood or flesh but has merely become his regrets and tears. To this Ohara responds, "'But it seems to me that Renée was no more than a flower. It wasn't like a wolf invading another wolf's territory and devouring a female in there, or like slaying a natural enemy and eating his guts. Eating because of love is something you do to a flower.'"[82]

Needless to say, this is a very different kind of "flower eating" from that in Enchi's 1974 story. Even though the old woman insists that flowers are not just to be seen but to be touched, plucked, and owned, "even if it will deform them," and ultimately eaten (quoted in chapter 3), there is no suggestion of sexual violation or subjugation. One might also "rub" the "flower" in the above passage against the flower in *Nobi* that speaks to Tamura in feminine language, granting him permission to eat her.[83] Tamura's left half would not allow this. In Kara's novel, although the "affectionate" flower eating is contrasted with the overtly violent act of a male wolf devouring a female wolf outside his own territory, the gendering of the eater and the victim is the same. Furthermore, in this novel Ohara, who herself is a kind of flower in a foreign land, compares the human victim Renée to a flower eaten "because of love."

At the same time as Sagawa's letters present a closed-in scenario of infantile identification, it might be said that Kara's text, too, is enclosed in a nostalgia for childhood fantasy. The finale of the novel contains a surprise, which impressed Ōe Kenzaburō and Niwa Fumio, who were members of the Akutagawa Prize selection committee. In his final letter to the narrator Sagawa denies having any acquaintance with a person called K. Ohara. Then, before the eyes of the puzzled narrator appears K. Ohara herself, who tells him that the K stands for Kiku, which was his grandmother's name. One may be tempted to read, or misread and interread, a symbolic meaning into the name: chrysanthemum—the imperial emblem used effectively in *Nobi* and the name of Pierre Loti's exoticized, flower-like heroine. Such misreading and interreading would take us further towards the notions of displacement and a man eating a flower/woman. In Kara's novel, however, all is left "in the fog," so to speak, just like the title of Sagawa's fictional work, the manuscript of which is mentioned a number of times but is never delivered to the novel's narrator.[84]

Memories of Wartime Cannibalism

If World War II made us conscious that anthropophagy is not a grotesque and erotic fantasy but a reality, the affluence of the last quarter of a century in Japan has resulted in a certain forgetfulness about what is real. The tendency in this period has been to indulge in the production, distribution, and consumption of cannibalism stories as sophisticated or bizarre commodities. At the same time the topic of anthropophagy has been used as a site for attacking postmodern complacency. Kaikō Takeshi, for example, concludes his collection of essays on food and eating, *Saigo no bansan* (The Last Supper, 1979), with two essays, the first on the 1972 incident of cannibalism by survivors of a plane crash in the Andes and the second on cannibalism in Chinese history. While Kaikō focuses on eating human flesh as the result of extreme conditions, Nakano Miyoko, in her studies of the cultural history of cannibalism, warns against the pitfalls of approaching the topic from a commonsense or literal point of view. In an essay originally published in 1972 she insists that both cannibalism and war are "the erotic desires that human beings have made taboo, yet have not been able to avoid completely." Nakano suggests that the only way to understand the true horror of cannibalism or war is to scrutinize both phenomena closely.[85] While memories of the war have been fading in recent times, and while the shock value of cannibalism has weakened, there are some writers who insist on refreshing these memories and revitalizing the power of cannibalism to disturb by finding new ways to incorporate forgotten texts and voices into their own texts.

The journalist-novelist Henmi Yō (b. 1944) includes a chapter on his visit to Mindanao in his 1994 collection of essays on food and people he has encountered in his travels around the world. One of the characters he meets on the island is a seventy-four-year-old Filipino man. This man, who was once a captain in the Philippine army, shows the Japanese visitor (the narrator) around the mountain region where the Japanese soldiers hid during and after the war. The narrator is reminded of a record of a 1949 war crimes tribunal he has read, in which Japanese soldiers confess to having eaten human flesh. At that moment the old Filipino man starts to talk about his own experience of eating stewed human flesh by mistake. Believing it to be made from dog meat, he ate some stew left by Japanese soldiers who had remained in the area in early 1947. The man remembered that it was just before dawn. Only when he had eaten several pieces of the meat did he realize that he was eating human flesh, he tells the narrator:

As the sun started to shine, he recognized the shapes of human ears and fingers. Under a tree he also found a human skull.

"I tried to vomit," said the old man, "but it was too late."[86]

The quiet demeanor of this old man reminds us of the school principal and the captain in act 2 of *Hikarigoke* rather than of the tormented narrator in *Nobi*. It is no surprise that the narrator-visitor in Henmi's text tries to see the ring of light around the old man's neck. Naturally, he cannot see anything: "I was terribly tired. I silently apologized to the old man's back for my disrespect."[87]

This disrespect may be interpreted as the same kind of irresponsible curiosity the spectators gathered around the captain display in the final scene of Takeda's *Lesedrama*. It may also imply some kind of arrogance or frivolity in Henmi's narrator trying to understand a fact—the old man's experience—through his reading of a fictional text. The narrative goes on to include the voices of villagers at the foot of the mountain whose mothers, sisters, grandfathers, and so on had been eaten by Japanese soldiers.

> None of the villagers was shouting or crying. Their voices were calm and controlled and held no hint of rage. And yet my notebook was quickly filled with repetitions of the disturbing word "eaten." It was strange. The old man was wordlessly staring at my bewilderment.[88]

If the principal and the captain in Takeda's text are the antithesis of the introspective and ultimately self-centered Tamura of *Nobi*, the old man in Henmi's text suggests yet another alternative. Through him we glimpse a perspective that is lacking in Ōoka's text—the other side of the story of the contact zone. Henmi reminds us that while many Japanese today are either totally unaware of this history of "eating" or are eager to forget about it, there are people still living whose family members were "eaten." While being actively involved in demanding compensation from the Japanese government, the old man has kept in personal contact with former Japanese officers and soldiers. Henmi concludes his journey into the past living in the present with his alternative to Takeda's rings of light:

> The rain stopped.
> As I turned back, golden rays of sun shone between the clouds upon Mount Kitanrado.
> The dreadful mountain now looked godlike.[89]

Yapoo as Food

As we have seen, metafiction and intertextuality are significant in almost all postwar texts that deal with cannibalism. As the memory of the war fades, some writers and critics have tried to revisit the past by examining and incorporating earlier texts. Others have sought to overcome the shortcomings of these earlier texts and discourses. Some have purposely avoided realistic representations, while others have incorporated historical facts into their writing. Before leaving this topic I should like to consider one other text, which is arguably the most controversial of all of the works discussed in this chapter.

It was in 1956 that the first chapter of what would become a novel in forty-nine chapters (five paperback volumes), *Kachikujin yapū* (Yapoo, the Human Cattle, 1970–1999),[90] was published in a magazine specializing in writing on the subject of sadomasochism and other "sexual deviations." The author, "Numa Shōzō" (b. 1926), has insisted on using this pseudonym, apparently based on the name of a German specialist in S and M studies, Ernst Sumpf (*Sumpf* means bog or marsh, hence *numa*).[91] Some in the media have tried over time to discover his true identity, but in vain. Such secrecy is not unknown in literature, and the nature of Numa's work doubtless caused him to want to keep the mask of anonymity firmly on. The novel contains not only an extraordinary masochist manifesto but an array of taboo topics, some of which, the reader should be warned, are deeply disturbing and offensive.

The novel is about a young Japanese man and his German fiancée traveling from 1960s Germany to fortieth- (no, this is not a mistake) century EHS (pronounced "iisu"), the Empire of [a] Hundred Suns, aka the British Universal Empire. The central themes of this time/space odyssey are discrimination and deprivation. The caste system of EHS consists of "white" aristocracy, "white" plebeians, and "black" slaves. Among the whites, women have been placed above men since the "Feminal Revolution" of AD 2617. Women in trousers dominate this powerful empire, while "manly" (meaning quiet, meek, and patient) men in skirts are meant to stay at home. The Yapoos, who are the distant descendants of the Japanese and the only survivors of the "yellows" after World War III, are regarded not as *Homo sapiens* but as intelligent apes, *Simius sapiens*. They are treated as pet animals, livestock, living furniture, vehicles, and so on and are given all sorts of totally inhuman—as they are not regarded as "womankind"—and unthinkable roles and tasks. Neither the black slaves nor the yellow cattle would dream of revolting against the whites, who are to them divinity, the deities of "albinism," the religion that has replaced all others. If there is any sign of disobedience or political incorrectness, androids are there to deal with its perpetrators.

In this world, then, eating the Yapoos is not regarded as anthropophagy or "woman eating." Like Kōbe beef cattle, some Yapoos are raised specially to become gourmet food. "The more educated, the more patriotic, the more loyal, and the more resilient, the better they taste,"[92] as one EHS aristocrat explains. Indeed, the Yapoos are quite the opposite of Swift's Yahoos, who are "the most restive and indocible, mischievous and malicious," and more, with their loyalty and intelligence, like the "wonderful Yahoo," Gulliver.[93]

In a conversation between the EHS elites over a delicious dish of Kreap (pronounced not like "creep" but as "ku-re-a-pu," a kind of Yapoo for eating) steak, the topic of the "prehistoric" Sagawa incident comes up:

"So it seems that the cannibal Yapoo worshipped the body of the white woman so much that he ate it. He wanted to be one with the object of his love through predation and incorporation."

"But then he should have become food himself like the Kreaps. By being consumed and digested, they can be part of the body, the object of their *agape* (sacred love). That's logical. But he ate her, which is simply crazy."[94]

Equally horrendous and even more politically offensive than the above is the "tricolor food chain system," which is explained as follows: "In sum, the whites' urine becomes the wine for the blacks, and the whites' feces become medicine for Yapoos, while the blacks' urine is used as feed for the Yapoos."[95]

This food chain, much more elaborate and horrifying than the institutionalized cannibalism of *Sumiyakist Q*, has been completely accepted by all involved in the EHS. While the white deities keep their bodies intact and unchanged by the superadvanced techniques of EHS science and technology, the Yapoos are surgically, dermatologically, biochemically, and genetically modified to suit the system. Just as some Yapoos are happy to be eaten, others regard themselves as the beloved of the gods, as they are made into toilets and given "nectar and ambrosia."[96] Only those with a high IQ and proper education can enjoy this honor.

The author Numa insists that this is not a dystopian story but a story of a masochist utopia, and dedicates it "to the happy few."[97] However disturbing their degradation may seem to the nonmasochist reader, it is bliss, he insists, to the Yapoos. The Japanese protagonist chooses in the end not to return to the twentieth century but to remain in EHS as a pet Yapoo dog of his former girl-friend, who is now an EHS goddess. This is not because he knows that Japan is doomed to disappear from the earth and be reborn as Jaban (*ja* for evil and *ban* for savage) in the twenty-first century. Rather, it is "unconditional surrender"[98] and total submission to his goddess, who will continue to bless him with pain and humiliation. In other words, this is, as Maeda Muneo suggests,[99] a masochist Bildungsroman.

In the process of his transformation from elite Japanese Ph.D. student Sebe Rin'ichirō to the humble Yapoo dog Rin, the protagonist learns not only the outline of what happens to Japan and the world (or universe) between the late twentieth century and the fortieth century, but also the astonishing "true" history of earlier times. The sun goddess Amaterasu, for example, turns out to be an EHS woman, Lady Anna O'Hillman. As Governor of the Earth and its leading explorer, she has time-traveled extensively and is widely known as Anna Terras. As would be expected, the Yapoos have had difficulty in catching the correct pronunciation and have mispronounced her name as Amaterasu. Throughout the novel similar instances of EHS words, people, and ideas being transmitted to the ancient world either deliberately by the EHS rulers or by illegal time/space travelers are explained, with ample reference to the fortieth-century edition of the OED and many other sources. The entry on Swift in the EHS edition of *Britannica* notes that he must have had some contact with an EHS time traveler and used information obtained through that contact in his work.[100] Particularly insistent are the references to Japanese mythology: Izanami and Izanagi, according to EHS history books, were in fact the "raw" (i.e., surgically and otherwise unmodified) thoroughbred Yapoos, Sanamy and Sanagy, who were sent to ancient Japan by the EHS queen. Thus the very core of the Japanese cultural and religious construct is turned into a farcical travesty.

In his 1991 afterword Numa writes that the idea of EHS, the empire of discrimination, was inspired by his personal relationship with a British woman in the immediate postwar period. Rin's "unconditional surrender" to his goddess, and the persistent attempt in the novel to decompose Japanese mythology, culture, and the emperor system, clearly originated in the author's private shame and disgrace during the Occupation. It is also evident that his view of Japan in later periods is equally dark and critical. The story of the Yapoos is at once a unique masochist fantasy and a savage attack on the cultural, political, and social condition of twentieth-century Japan. No other writer, not even Tanizaki, the champion "masochist," has created a world in which one aspires literally to be eaten by white goddesses and gods. Mythology, classical literature, scholarly works, pornography, and all kinds of texts are devoured and incorporated into this monstrous work.

As one can readily imagine, *Kachikujin yapū* has created both furor and fury among critics since its appearance in 1956. Before the final complete version was published in 1999, there were long intervals between volumes and a series of last-minute cancellations of publication, obviously caused by attacks from the left, the right, and every other direction. Early supporters included Mishima Yukio, Shibusawa Tatsuhiko, and Okuno Takeo. As the novel increasingly came by the late 1960s to desecrate the nationalist institution of the emperor, violating the strong taboo that surrounds that subject in Japan, Mishima understandably became less enthusiastic. Okuno, too, admits in his 1970 commentary that he now finds the novel's emphatic treatment of the Japanese inferiority complex quite offensive, whereas it did not bother him ten years earlier. He believes that this has to do with the socioeconomic changes seen during that decade. The position of the Yapoos was more acceptable, or at least less politically offensive, in the 1950s than in the 1960s and 1970s, when Japan was in the midst of its economic miracle and when the Japanese were described unbecomingly as "economic *animals*."[101]

To younger critics such as Aramata Hiroshi (b. 1947), Takahashi Gen'ichirō (b. 1951), and Tatsumi Takayuki (b. 1955) the historical "unconditional surrender" evokes no personal feelings. Aramata suggests a reading of *Yapū* as a "philosophical novel."[102] Takahashi, on the other hand, uses Freud's *Totem and Taboo* to explain the uniqueness of *Kachikujin yapū*,[103] whereas Tatsumi attempts to deconstruct Numa's deconstruction of the Japanese myth and finds a never ending cycle, an aporia, within it.[104] Tatsumi also points to a kind of Japanese snobbery based on a superiority complex based on racial measures of intelligence: the Yapoos are not simply the only survivors among the yellows but are, despite their cattle status, highly intelligent, and diligent and competitive in their work. As Tatsumi notes, these are all familiar elements in the discourse of "Japan bashing." Thus Numa's text, which cannibalizes other texts and incorporates the sociocultural changes that have taken place over four decades in Japan, has itself become a subject of ever changing readings and consumption.

Anthropophagy has been a deeply disturbing and at the same time fascinating subject for many readers and writers. Its nauseating nature provides perfect fodder for horror stories as well as for serious studies of the human condition. It can also be used as an effective device for revealing the follies and shortcomings of various sociocultural and political constructs. The fear it creates may be the fear of being eaten or the fear of eating, which often coexist in one person. Religion may be able to help one to fight against the fear and temptation the subject gives rise to, or to come to terms with its existence as the most unpalatable possible fact of life, or to surrender oneself to the will and mercy of whatever god is on hand.

Anthropophagy, as we have seen, by no means belongs to the everyday. War and traveling take one out of the safe and mundane world into an extraordinary world, where unforeseen dangers await. Traveling includes not only spatial transfer but also movement backward or forward in time. Through encounters with the unknown, one may discover the alien in oneself (in some cases as the Other's human flesh incorporated into one's own), although there is always the possibility that, despite everything, one never changes or learns—as was the case with Sumiyakist Q.

Stories of cannibalism can often consist of the flesh and blood of other texts. Some texts aim at sublimation through eating, while others gnaw and grind until the original shape and taste of the textual food become unrecognizable. Still others vomit up what they have eaten. The devouring text, in turn, is there to be consumed or rejected by the reader. One may misread it, either unknowingly—as Q does with the novel within the novel—or deliberately—as Kara's narrator claims to do with letters from Sagawa. The reader does not necessarily resemble the intended audience, which can usually be surmised from the genre and period of the publication and is occasionally explained by the author either within or outside the text.

Texts such as those of Ranpo and Yumeno, for example, have traditionally been categorized as "mystery," a clearly separate genre from serious fiction. Even after the decline in the initial popularity of Ranpo-style stories, they have continued to be read by a devoted minority. The main attraction of the work for these readers may have to do with their *ero guro nansensu* content, or it may be in the narrative structure and techniques of these texts. As has already been noted, in more recent times critics such as Suzuki Sadami and Aramata Hiroshi have pointed out common elements across various genres and subgenres that make the barriers between them less significant.

Needless to say, changes in readership and reception also apply to postwar literature. This is most obvious in the case of *Kachikujin yapū*. It is certainly an exceptional case in that its composition took most of the second half of the century. As the volume expanded, its audience grew, from the initially intended "happy few" to a larger and less homogeneous group. As we have seen, the changing readership and the changing external conditions are reflected in the novel's writing and in its reception. It is therefore not the case that one reading—for example, the reading that focuses on the impact of the 1945 surrender—is correct and definite, or even more appropriate than the others. The text invites multiple readings. The second half of *Hikarigoke* also does this within the text. If *Sumiyakisuto Q no bōken* teases with predictable misreadings, *Sagawa-kun kara no tegami* tries to justify its own misreading and at the same time encourages the reader to produce and direct the written scenario it presents, as does *Hikarigoke*.

Different audiences will find different meanings in the same text. While the meaning of *Kaijinmaru* seems to be least affected by the sociocultural background and gender of the reader, it can easily be imagined that most other texts mentioned above have the potential to evoke a variety of responses, some of which might be contradictory. The gender, ethnicity, and race of those who eat and those who are eaten will have varying degrees of significance depending on the reader's background, experience, and awareness of issues of discrimination. We are certainly not obliged to swallow the text or to be devoured by it. What we are obliged to acknowledge, however, is that the journey into the dangerous contact zone can provide us with opportunities for the discovery of new pleasures or greater wisdom.

Chapter Five

The Gastronomic Novel

In traditional Japanese culture, eating enjoyed a status far lower than that of drinking. To talk about food, to desire food, or to be at all interested in food was generally regarded as vulgar, especially in adult men. The uninhibited eating and food writing of contemporary Japan seems to have received its impetus from a reaction to the repression and oppression of appetite during the war—expressed in the slogan *Hoshigari masen katsu made wa* (Desire nothing till victory)—and to the understandable preoccupation, during and immediately after the war, with food simply as a means for survival. By the mid-1950s eating and cooking for pleasure had begun to attract public attention, and this interest continued and developed into the gourmet boom of the 1980s. Delicacies were no longer only for the rich and the elite but were available to ordinary people, who consumed not only food itself but information about food and eating. Numerous popular cultural products emerged in response to this new appetite for food-related infotainment, among them television programs such as *Ryōri tengoku* (Cooking Paradise, 1975–1992) and *Ryōri no tetsujin* (Iron Chef, 1993–1999) and *manga* series such as *Oishinbo* (The Gourmet, 1983–) and *Kukkingu papa* (Cooking Papa, 1984–), both of which were subsequently made into other forms and genres such as animation, television dramas, and computer games. Even at the beginning of this gourmet boom, however, the pursuit of edible delicacies occupied a very limited place in literature. "Serious" literature—notoriously—interests itself more in misery than in happiness. As already noted in previous chapters, there are few examples of happiness associated with food to be found in serious literature, whereas hunger, starvation, conflict, marginalization, and other kinds of food-related problems are prominent literary themes.

The pursuit of culinary or gastronomic pleasure, however, is not entirely absent from Japanese literature and is not necessarily confined to the period of the gourmet boom. It can be found, though one has to look for it, throughout the twentieth century. This chapter will examine literature, in particular fiction, that depicts or advocates some sort of gastronomic quest.[1] Gastronomic fiction may be comic, serious, satirical, witty, romantic, melodramatic, pornographic, aesthetic, lyrical, decadent, or didactic, or several of these at once. Some texts are intended for a small, select audience, while others have sought, and gained, immense popularity. However popular they may have been, or however enthusiastically they may have been admired by a small group of readers, though, until Kaikō started his campaign in support of them, gastronomic novels had never attracted serious critical attention.

There are some points to note before embarking on a discussion of the relevant texts. First, these stories of gastronomic quests are not necessarily about *gourmandise* in Brillat-Savarin's sense of the term. Indeed, many of the protagonists encountered in these Japanese works would be totally excluded from Brillat-Savarin's world of *gourmandise*, wherein there is a distinction made between gourmet eating, which is of benefit not only to the economy and to one's health but also to one's romantic relationships, and mere gluttony or voracity. The gastronomic novel may advocate the pleasure of eating and cooking, but it may also take a cynical or ambiguous stance towards such pursuits. Moreover, while *gourmandise*, like *coquetterie*, was held by Brillat-Savarin to be a uniquely French concept and therefore untranslatable,[2] the Japanese literary examples examined here neither advocate nor represent any uniquely Japanese taste or cultural preference, and are therefore not an expression of cultural pride. On the contrary, they often express dissatisfaction with the all too familiar Japanese cuisine[3] and show a strong attraction for foreign cultures, be they European, Chinese, or American. The admiration they express for foreign cuisine is almost always accompanied by an admiration for other cultural products of the society in question, including its literature.

In an earlier brief discussion of the history of the *shōsetsu*, and then again in the survey of the thematic of cannibalism that followed, there was mention of the significance of cross-cultural incorporation to literary texts. The thematic of gastronomy seems to offer an obvious parallel to this cross-cultural transference with its enthusiasm to consume, adopt, and explore imported forms, techniques, and themes. In each case, cross-cultural incorporation and affiliation reflect certain historical and socioeconomic conditions. This raises a series of questions. Can taste (in food and in literature) be learned or acquired through training? If both food and literature are culture specific and ingredient or language specific, do they have any universal elements? Or is what might seem universal merely an illusion or a construct of hegemonic culture? Can food be egalitarian? Or is it by nature discriminatory and hierarchical? Can taste be reexpressed in language? Then there is the question of authenticity: Is French or Chinese cooking in Japan necessarily no more than imitation? And does that apply to imported language (e.g., loan words and characters) and to imported literary forms and texts? Finally, is the gastronomic novel really about food and taste?

The Gastro-Enlightenment Novel: Murai Gensai

Murai Gensai's (1863–1927) *Kuidōraku* (Gourmandism, 1903)[4] is one of the earliest examples of what we have chosen to call the gastronomic novel. Unlike Kanagaki Robun's *Agura nabe* (see chapter 1), which places more emphasis on how people from all walks of life react to the new taste of "civilization" (namely beef) than on the food itself, *Kuidōraku* treats food unambiguously as its primary subject. Gensai's novel also differs from many other prewar fictional texts discussed in this chapter in that it was intended not for a small elite audience but for the general reading public. It was initially serialized in the *Hōchi shinbun* every day from January 2 to December 27, 1903, and was then published in four volumes—"Spring," "Summer," "Autumn," and "Winter"—which sold over a hundred thousand copies.[5] When it was adapted for the theater in 1905, the actual cooking scenes were included, and the audience was invited to taste the results.[6] Thus at the very beginning of the century the gastronomic novel was closely tied to the media and to popular culture; if Gensai had been born several decades later, he might well have chosen film, television, or *manga* as his form, instead of the novel.

Like *Agura nabe*, Gensai's novel welcomes Western civilization and Western food, but Gensai is not satisfied with Japanese versions (or reinventions) of this food in dishes such as sukiyaki. Gensai presents in his novel "authentic" Western recipes, learned during his stay in San Francisco (1884–1887) and later during the writing of *Kuidōraku*, from professional Western-trained chefs. Evident throughout the novel is his intention to introduce his audience to real Western cooking, which he holds to be more nutritious, hygienic, practical, modern, and democratic than traditional Japanese fare. This is done through his two mouthpieces, the young and aspiring writer Nakagawa and his sister, O-Towa, as they discuss with their friends and patrons not only the menus for dinner parties but various other topics related to food and cooking. Their aim is to "civilize" Meiji Japan through food.

The key to the commercial success of the novel seems to be the combination of the new recipes with the familiar (age-old) story of love triumphing over obstacles. In this instance, the couple is O-Towa and Nakagawa's best friend, Ōhara, who is being pressured by his family and relatives to marry his cousin, O-Dai. While O-Towa is not only beautiful but also, like her brother, highly knowledgeable and articulate in culinary matters, O-Dai is presented as an ugly, fat, ignorant, uncouth woman with a heavy country accent and appalling taste in food and everything else. The contrast between the two young women is graphically and emphatically depicted in both the novel and its illustrations (figures 1, 2, and 3). What should be noted here is that O-Towa's beauty is only of secondary importance in the story; the most important quality of this heroine is her ability as a cook. While O-Towa does not quite accord with the image of a romantic heroine, neither is she its antithesis. Ōhara, on the other hand, is depicted as a short, fat glutton with a huge paunch (figure 4). He is not very bright (he failed twice before graduating from university), but he has a heart of gold. In fact, his surname, Ōhara, is an obvious pun on "big stomach," and his

FIGURE 1: O-Towa gives a cooking lesson to Lady Tamai (by Mizuno Toshikata; from *Kuidōraku* 1976, Shibata Shoten).

FIGURE 2: (top) O-Towa shows Koyama how to bake Western cakes. FIGURE 3: (bottom) O-Dai attempts to cook. (By Mizuno Toshikata; from *Kuidōraku* 1976, Shibata Shoten.)

Figure 4: O-Dai demands an explanation from her fiancé, Ōhara Mitsuru (by Mizuno Toshikata; from *Kuidōraku* 1976, Shibata Shoten).

personal name, Mitsuru, means "full." Similarly, "O-Dai" implies the "price" or the "cost" of the financial support Ōhara has received from his wealthy uncle (O-Dai's father) to study at Tokyo Imperial University. Ōhara's attraction to O-Towa begins even before they meet, when he hears about her extraordinary cooking skills. At first O-Towa is not interested in him, but her brother and his other close friend, Koyama, and his wife all enthusiastically commend Ōhara's honesty and sincerity to her with the result that she—rather suddenly—changes her mind. Just at the moment she decides Ōhara is the man she wants to marry and with whom she wants to build a happy family, his uncouth country cousin appears.

This romance—though the modern reader may well hesitate to use the term—is clearly inseparable from the modernizing message of the novel, which rejects irrational and inferior conventions such as arranged marriage between cousins in favor of pragmatic and democratic alternatives. Education plays a vital part in the novel's construction of modernity. O-Towa is from Nagasaki and has spent time in Kobe and Osaka before joining her brother in Tokyo. All three regions have contributed to her extensive culinary education. O-Dai, on the other hand, comes from the "deep North" of Tōhoku, where everything tends to be "too salty and chewy." (Interestingly, in this novel it is Tōhoku that is chosen as the home of the stereotypical country bumpkin—the object of undisguised disdain—which may reflect the dominance of southern provinces such as Satsuma and Chōshū in the emerging Meiji nation.)

Selective discrimination is evident not only in regional differences but also in issues of gender. Whereas Ōhara's obesity and gluttony may be corrected in future by a better diet (provided naturally by his new wife), there seems to be no hope for O-Dai. Moreover, Nakagawa's attitude shows various layers of gender division. While emphasizing the importance of education, he insists that men should study practical matters such as cooking. He criticizes men who happily spend a considerable amount of money on hats and shoes or on eating out with their male companions in expensive restaurants but make their wives live on pickles and rice. In his opinion domestic cooking is the source of health and happiness, and men should contribute to it as much as women do—in terms of knowledge, technology, and economics at least, if not in terms of actual, practical food preparation. This might sound surprisingly liberated for a Meiji man, but when it comes to choosing a partner, Nakagawa seems to have little confidence in young women, who in his opinion tend to be too emotional for such a role.

Nakagawa argues that in order to advance the nation's civilization one should civilize one's own home, and that in order to civilize one's home one should civilize oneself. Moreover, civilizing oneself involves improving one's daily diet.[7] O-Towa shares this doctrine, which strongly echoes Brillat-Savarin. She knows that a balance of intellectual, physical, and moral education is just as important as the balance of protein, fat, and carbohydrate, believing in fact that the study of food is even more important than these three aspects of education. Given that this work was written on the eve of the Russo-Japanese War, Nakagawa's critique of culinary nationalism is interesting.

> It would be sour grapes to say that Japanese cooking contains the essence of the
> nation and that therefore there is no reason for us to learn Western cooking.
> It would, of course, be imprudent to follow blindly everything Western and to
> abandon even the good things about Japanese ways. Doubtless our duty is to
> observe and judge things fair-mindedly. We writers should never be entrapped
> by sentiments; we must lead the public according to reason. [. . .] Observed
> fairly, physiological studies of food are more advanced in the West than in Ja-
> pan. Also, within what we call Western cuisine there is a wide range of styles and
> variations. [. . .] Western food in Japan combines all the merits of various types

of cooking. In future, too, we must endeavor to gather the culinary essence from cuisines all over the world and to develop Japanese-style Western dishes.[8]

This frank admission of Japan's backwardness in science and technology, accompanied by the author's optimistic faith in a bright future for the nation based on eclectic adaptation of foreign elements, reminds one of Shōyō's hope for the *shōsetsu* (quoted in the Introduction). *Kuidōraku*, which contains actual recipes for dishes that range from sweetbreads and roast lamb to rice pudding and blancmange, along with heated discussions about what constitutes "civilization," may be far from the kind of *shōsetsu* Shōyō had in mind; yet it does seem to have achieved something similar to the triple function proposed by a certain Victorian professor of English literature: to delight, instruct, and "above all, to save our souls and heal the State."[9]

Between cooking lessons and culinary discussions, Nakagawa and his friends try to extricate Ōhara from his unwanted engagement. Their argument against endogamy, based on Western eugenics, however, has no effect on O-Dai and her parents. When Ōhara himself has nearly given up hope, enter the deus ex machina in the form of Viscount Hiroumi (i.e., "wide ocean"), who is not only happy to send Ōhara to Europe to study domestic education, but is also eager to marry his own daughter (and O-Towa's cooking student) Tamae to Nakagawa. Nakagawa accepts this offer on one condition—that he and Lady Tamae exchange health certificates instead of traditional engagement gifts. Hiroumi is also eager to send O-Towa to Europe for a few years as he considers it would be even more beneficial to the nation for an able woman like O-Towa to acquire advanced knowledge of the technology of feeding and nurturing a healthy population. So the future of Japan seems bright, both in culinary terms and in domestic education, and there remains plenty of material for sequels to the novel.[10]

The Gastro-Comic Novel: Kōda Rohan

Despite its didacticism, or perhaps because of it, not every contemporary reader and gourmand was impressed by *Kuidōraku*. Kōda Rohan's short story "Chinsenkai" (The Delicacy Competition, 1904) is a comic-satirical riposte to Gensai's notion of popular gastronomic enlightenment. Rohan, Gensai's junior by four years, may nowadays be better known as the father of Kōda Aya (see chapter 3), but at the beginning of the century he was one of Japan's most celebrated writers, respected not only for his literary talent but also for his erudition in the

Chinese and Japanese classics. "Chinsenkai" is by no means representative of Rohan's work, but it does exemplify his use of his gastronomic knowledge in fiction. The entire story consists of dialogues, monologues, and the conversations of characters who are given comic and demonstrative (*nomen omen*) names such as Chokosai (pert), Muteki (invincible), Gaman (endurance), and so on. This is a device clearly borrowed from the comic tradition of Edo scribblers and performing artists,[11] a tradition dismissed as frivolous and worthless by Shōyō and others eager to develop a culture befitting a modern nation. At the beginning of the story Chokosai explains how he has decided to organize a gourmet competition with five other gentlemen:

> "It all started like this. You know there's a popular novel called *Kuishinbō* [meaning a glutton, obviously intended as a parody of *Kuidōraku*], don't you? Some ignorant bumpkin gave me a copy of this as an end-of-year gift. Having nothing much to do, I read it and then it dawned on me. The book itself is rather serious and not much fun. For seasoned debaters like us it's like drinking plain boiled water. So I thought of this little rebellion: wouldn't it be nice if five or six of us got together for a New Year entertainment, bringing all sorts of truly rare delicacies—the kinds of delicacies you can't find in the book?"[12]

So the delicacies competition is to be a rebellion against the serious, pragmatic, modern, and democratic gastronomy of *Kuidōraku*. Once this is established, however, Rohan's story shifts its focus to caricaturing the self-proclaimed gourmands, each of whom is evidently mainly interested in surpassing the others in his display of gastronomic connoisseurship. So preoccupied are they with their gastronomic rivalry that it never occurs to them, although it is obvious to the people around them and to the reader, that their pursuit is ludicrous. Mrs. Gamandō, for instance, advises her husband not to attend the planned gourmet gathering as it is not only silly but possibly life threatening. If he insists on going, she says, he should cover himself with a hefty life insurance policy. The secretary of another of the gentlemen is assigned the task of collecting snails for the competition and decides the whole exercise is ridiculous. Based on the common belief that a craving for fried tofu is a sign of possession by a fox spirit, the secretary suspects that his master has been possessed by some strange sprite from Europe.

Mrs. Gamandō's fears are realized: on the day of the competition the contestants bring along "truly rare delicacies" from the East and West, including python wine, monkey lips, escargots, steamed toads, and the legendary Cantonese delicacy of live honey-fed baby mice. The participants not only have to eat and drink what the others have brought, but must display the depth and breadth of their knowledge by guessing the ingredients and their exact sources. Those who fail to do so, or who fail to present an impressive delicacy, will be sentenced to drink ten glasses of cold water and will be fined two large casks (126 liters) of sake. As the party continues, it becomes more and more like a competition in fearlessness and endurance than in *gourmandise*. The motives of the participants and the authenticity of their knowledge and the food itself are made to seem dubious to say the least. The supposedly authentic French dish of "escargots" consists only of a few local snails that the secretary has managed to find, along with some slugs that have been fraudulently inserted into their dead cousins' shells. The baby mouse, which Chokosai forces himself to eat because he cannot bear the idea of losing to Gaman, turns out to be an innocuous imitation made of rice flour.

Whereas *Kuidōraku* advocates rational and modern gastronomy and aims to transmit knowledge and technology in the form of a *shōsetsu*, "Chinsenkai" makes fun of *gourmandise* and questions its worth as a subject for writing. It does include some esoteric culinary details, but it does not aim to teach the reader how to cook or enjoy eating. In fact no reader would be tempted to try any of the "delicacies" that appear in this story. So the seemingly gastronomic quest of these leisured gentlemen is a game made up of practical and verbal jokes, tricks, and lies. This playfulness is expressed in the style, language, and form of the novel. A ludicrous story of a ludicrous circle of gourmands, "Chinsenkai" seems to suggest two important aspects of the gastronomic pursuit. First, as Shibusawa Tatsuhiko points out, there is a strong connection between *gourmandise* and the play element of *Homo ludens*.[13] Chokosai finds the popular novel *Kuishinbō* too serious and "not much fun." The idea of "Chinsenkai" is to introduce and explore the play element that Gensai's novel lacks. Second, quite unlike the *gourmandise* of Brillat-Savarin and Murai Gensai, its essence lies in excess, eccentricity, and transgression.

Play, according to Huizinga, is "a free activity standing quite consciously outside 'ordinary' life as being 'not serious', but at the same time absorbing the player intensely and utterly."[14] The members of the Chinsenkai are certainly deeply absorbed in their play, the characteristics of which are reminiscent of those identified by Huizinga as central to the notion of play itself. These are that the activity has a superfluous and leisurely nature, a lack of material interest (the penalty involving the casks of sake has nothing to do with economic gain but is simply part of the game), temporal and spatial boundaries (the competition is held on a set day at an agreed place), and the promotion of "the formation of social groupings which tend to surround themselves with secrecy and to stress their difference from the common world by disguise or other means."[15] Furthermore, their competition clearly involves the "basic factors of play"—"to wit, contests, performances, exhibitions, challenges, preenings, struttings and showings-off, pretences, and binding rules."[16] These characteristics are evident in many other literary representations of a gastronomic quest. It is interesting to note, however, that in Huizinga's thesis, play is not confused with laughter or the comic, the comic being regarded as occupying a subsidiary position to play.

The second element of the gastronomic novel is closely related to some of the characteristics of play, such as its freedom and intensity, but sometimes breaches or transgresses the boundaries and rules of play. As the gastronomic competition or quest in "Chinsenkai" intensifies, the original search for delicious food becomes distorted or transformed into a search for more and more extraordinary food, and even for the unsavory, the unappetizing, and the inedible. Whereas this transformation offers perfect material for the comedy and satire in this particular story, it becomes an effective device in many other genres, from thriller to serious fiction, as we shall see below.

The Gourmet Mystery, or the Aesthetic of the Slime/Sublime: Tanizaki Jun'ichirō

Like Rohan's "Chinsenkai," Tanizaki Jun'ichirō's short story "Bishoku kurabu" (The Gourmet Club, 1919),[17] clearly incorporates play elements at the same times as it displays a tendency to extremity and transgression. As in "Chinsenkai," the search for delicacies in this story has no pragmatic motive, nor does the story offer practical cooking instruction or preach the importance of dietary knowledge and practice. However, whereas Rohan's story has an essentially comic-satirical intent, "Bishoku kurabu" combines detective story–like suspense with a detailed analysis of sense impressions.

The club, like the Chinsenkai, consists of five gentlemen of leisure, for whom eating is not a matter of life-sustaining necessity but a quest for unknown delicacies. Like the Chinsenkai members, they seek stronger and stronger stimuli and pit themselves against one another in their search for new and better tastes. What makes this story different from Rohan's is that the club members are too serious and sincere about their gastronomic pursuit to try to trick each other or make fun of each other. Although the members of the club are all lazy in other matters, they are so determined to pursue their consuming passions that they travel assiduously all over the country in search of the most unimaginably delicious food.

Tanizaki, a noted gourmand (and glutton) himself, often names actual restaurants (such as Hyōtei) in his fiction. Readers can visit these restaurants and try the various delicacies consumed by Misako's father, the Makioka sisters, the "mad old man," and so on. "Bishoku kurabu," however, does not serve as a restaurant guide. Having long since tired of the delicacies offered by famous restaurants, the members of the club are desperate to discover something new.

> They were naturally tired of Japanese food; there was nothing new in Western cuisine, unless one actually went to Europe; even the last fortress, Chinese food—renowned as the best developed, and the most diversified in the world— began to taste to them as disappointing and insipid as plain water.[18]

This provides the perfect framework for an adventure story or mystery. Indeed, with its descriptions of Tokyo's dark alleys and secret opium dens and its attention to an encounter with a group of mysterious Chinese, the story is reminiscent of a Victorian detective novel.

Mystery is an essential part of the ultimate gastronomy in this story. In order to taste something one needs to use not just the mouth and the tongue but the eyes, ears, nose, skin, and in fact the whole body. The appreciation of food entails judgment and inference based on multiple sensations. Herein lies a paradox, though. The gastronomic mystery, once solved, is no longer a mystery and immediately loses its charm and significance.

How do the club members and the mysterious Chinese gourmands solve this problem? They create and maintain mystery by careful preparation and calculation as well as by means of various unspoken rules. The diners are kept literally in the dark for a long time before they are served the mystery food. The reader is told that this is not simply for theatrical effect but because in this way the diners can sharpen their appetites and senses. The food is never clearly identifiable even after it is tasted. It may taste like one thing at first, but when belched it may produce an exquisite and completely different taste. Various borders such as those between food and its receptacle, between the edible and the inedible, between the eater and the eaten, are rendered porous. Barthes' remarks on his reading of Brillat-Savarin are not inappropriate to such a reading of "Bishoku kurabu":

> Added to the good food, the convivium produces what Fourier (whom we always find close to B.-S.) called a *composite* pleasure. The vigilant hedonism of the two brothers-in-law inspired them with this thought, that pleasure must be *overdetermined*, that it must have several simultaneous causes, among which

there is no way of distinguishing which one causes delight; for the composite pleasure does not derive from a simple bookkeeping of excitations: it figures a complex space in which the subject no longer knows where he comes from and what he wants—except to have his voluptuous pleasure—*jouir*.[19]

In other words, long before his later essays on the beauty of shadow and the significance of "pregnant ambiguity" (*ganchiku*), Tanizaki utilized similar aesthetic ideas in this story. Interestingly, the shadow and the ambiguity that lend the story its mystery are not yet identified as belonging specifically to Japan, as they subsequently were in Tanizaki's *In'ei raisan* (In Praise of Shadows, 1933–1934) and *Bunshō dokuhon* (A Guide to Writing, 1934). That "Bishoku kurabu" is a story about aestheticism is clear from the beginning. Cooking, we are to believe, is a kind of art that can afford those who appreciate it sublime pleasure. This level of pleasure can never be gained from the natural ingredients alone; they require a transformation through art to become a site for the sublime. The antinaturalist implications of this are clear. Tanizaki's gourmands eat not for life's sake but for art's sake, and they fear none of the possible consequences to them, such as obesity or gastric illness or mental affliction. Even death, which lurks beneath their dining table, so to speak, hasn't the power to change their devotion to their art. It is all too easy to discern a form of masochism in this seemingly fearless and tireless quest.

"Bishoku kurabu" seems much less artificial and less contrary to nature, though, than that cult book of the fin de siècle aesthetes, *À Rebours* (Against Nature), by Huysmans.[20] Despite the effort to render it unusual or mysterious, and however elaborately prepared it seems, the food described in Tanizaki's story looks natural compared to what Des Esseintes considers the "ultimate deviation from the norm," a nourishing peptone enema. Huysmans perversely describes this ultimate delicacy as "an absolute release from the boredom that invariably results from the necessarily limited choice of dishes," "a vigorous protest against the vile sin of gluttony," and "a slap in the face for old Mother Nature," thus pushing *gourmandise* even further into the territory of the masochistic.[21]

In "Bishoku kurabu" Tanizaki has no interest in pursuing an ultimate deviance such as Huysmans' enema, which literally goes "against nature." Tanizaki's story instead pursues the aesthetic of the slimy, which, as many commentators have pointed out, is another of his specialties,[22] one closely connected with the aesthetic of ambiguity. Tanizaki's fascination—which finds its expression in a rich battery of onomatopoetic expressions—with the slimy, the sticky, the thick, the murky, the ripe, and the stringy presents a striking antithesis to the aesthetic of the pure, fresh, clear, and serene that so often appears in Japanese nationalist discourse, just as the elaborately verbose style he adopts seems to challenge deliberately the simple laconic style championed by Shiga Naoya. The language he invents to describe his fascination with this most ambiguous of textures is, moreover, a challenge to the premise that words cannot express taste and other sensations. As in other Tanizaki stories, ranging from the earlier "Shōnen" (The Children, 1911) to *Fūten rōjin nikki* (Diary of a Mad Old Man, 1961–1962), the aesthetic of the slimy in "Bishoku kurabu" combines with a patent masochism in order to seek, or seek to create, a (quasi-)erotic paradise in the vicinity of death.

Its verbosity notwithstanding, the story maintains a sense of mystery; or rather, Tanizaki's elaborate descriptions of murkiness and stickiness create and deepen its sense of mystery, blurring the division between the eater and the eaten and rendering the inedible edible and the edible inedible. One of the dishes that make up the members' sumptuous feast cannot be eaten before the faces of the diners have been thoroughly massaged, inside and out, by mysterious female hands. This gastronomic foreplay is followed by Chinese ham and cabbage—but as Member A notices, the taste of the ham seems to come from his own saliva, which has been stimulated by the massage, and the taste of the cabbage seems rather like a cross between Chinese cabbage and female human fingers. The concluding paragraph of "Bishoku kurabu" suggests that the gastronomic experiments of the mysterious club led by Count G are inexhaustible and complex and not just about cooking. Quite symbolically, this is done by listing the names of the most unusual dishes, without their descriptions. Each name, comprising three or four Chinese characters, looks like that of a Chinese dish but is a product of the imagination, inspired only in part by actual Chinese cuisine.

There is no doubt, then, that "Bishoku kurabu" is an antinaturalist manifesto, albeit one that entertains the reader with its detective story disguise and its comic-satirical portrayal of gastronomic aestheticism. While *Kuidōraku*, after a brief popularity, was soon to be forgotten,[23] and "Chinsenkai" was never treated as anything more than a playful bagatelle, "Bishoku kurabu" was to become an exemplar for the gastronomic novel. At the time of its publication it inspired not only writers such as Edogawa Ranpo (see chapter 4) but also gourmands such as Kitaōji Rosanjin (1883–1959), who named his gourmet circle after the story's title. Rosanjin insists that he "borrowed, without permission, only the name of the club" pointing out that his specialty is Japanese rather than Chinese cooking.[24] His emphasis on the freshness and the natural quality of ingredients certainly contrasts with Tanizaki's attraction to the slime/sublime. Nevertheless, we see echoes of Tanizaki's story in Rosanjin's belief that the best food is a complete mystery[25] and in his observation that whether or not something tastes good depends not just on the gustatory but on other senses such as hearing and touch.[26] Nevertheless, despite Rosanjin's homage to the story, it should be noted that "Bishoku kurabu" was never the object of the same kind of intense admiration as the story of Des Esseintes was for Wilde's Dorian Gray or as the aestheticism of Wilde was for the young Tanizaki. It is worth pointing out that, despite Tanizaki's later fame as a writer and gourmet, this early story was neglected by critics for nearly six decades and was only rediscovered during the gourmet boom of the 1980s.[27]

Before this section on Tanizaki concludes, one further point needs some elaboration. In the previous chapter we saw how displacement plays a significant role in texts concerning cannibalism. Now we see that crossing geocultural and other kinds of boundaries, as an act of displacement, is important in gastronomic stories as well. Emphasis may be placed on the cultural divide between Japan and the West. China may be treated in a variety of ways—as a hegemonic and classical culture as in "Chinsenkai," as a substitute for the West, or, as in another Tanizaki story, "Tomoda to Matsunaga no hanashi" (The Story of Tomoda and Matsunaga, 1926), as part of the West. This story cannot be classed as gastronomic fiction, but it is worth mentioning its extraordinary presentation of the divide between Japan and "China as West," as it involves food, eating, and taste. The protagonist leads a double life, his identity alternating every few years between that of a Japanese country gentleman, Matsunaga, and that of a decadent cosmopolite, Tomoda, alias "Tom." Shanghai, Tientsin, and Hong Kong are, like the cosmopolitan Yokohama and Kōbe, Tomoda's territory, while Matsunaga lives in the old, archetypically Japanese province of Yamato (although this "Japanese-ness" is problematic, as was made clear in the discussion of *Hashi no nai kawa* in chapter 3). As the doubled protagonist switches identities and his tastes and lifestyles change from one extreme to the other, his weight also oscillates dramatically, between 41 kilos (while he is Matsunaga) and 75 kilos (as Tomoda). In place of his well-known dichotomy of light (West) and shadow (Japan),[28] Tanizaki suggests in this text a connected but separate analogy: a hedonistic and voracious West/China and an ascetic and anorexic Japan.

As Kawamoto Saburō points out, there was a renewed "China boom" among Taishō writers.[29] Tanizaki's preoccupation with the slime/sublime and his related proposition that China belongs in a hedonistic construction of the West/China may have owed something to this boom, which, according to Kawamoto, was the expression of a modernist amalgamation of nostalgia for the past and yearning for the new.[30] Nevertheless, within the context of Japanese modernism, Tanizaki's gastro-aesthetics, whatever their origin, still seem to stand out for the qualities they bring to that writer's literary output during the period.

Men's Art and Women's Criticism: Okamoto Kanoko

If "Bishoku kurabu" is essential to any anthology of modern Japanese gastronomic fiction, so are the stories of Okamoto Kanoko. "Shokuma" (The Gourmand, cir. 1937),[31] in particular, deserves detailed examination in this chapter for a number of reasons. First, it is one of the very few examples of prewar gastronomic fiction written by women. More important, even though its central gourmand character is a young man, accounts of his ferocious and infinitely painstaking pursuit of the culinary art are juxtaposed with disparaging commentaries on the same, delivered mostly by the story's female characters. Indeed, the story does more than simply present the viewpoints of its female characters; it suggests the vital importance of women to a true understanding of the culinary art and the workings of human and cosmic nature.

The story opens with a scene in which the protagonist Besshirō (thought to be modeled after Kitaōji Rosanjin)[32] is giving a cooking lesson to two young sisters, the daughters of his patron. The elder sister, Chiyo, is afraid of the fierce and arrogant teacher; the younger, Kinu, fears neither Besshirō nor the unfamiliar dishes he prepares. Kinu observes her teacher and is amused by his contradictory behavior: while his movements in the preparation of food look deliberately rough, uncalculated, and arrogant, at certain moments they betray nervousness and an almost mean cleverness. Besshirō himself remains absorbed in his activity and preoccupied with his art and his pride in it; cooking lessons to him are the means of demonstrating his culinary brilliance. After tasting his endive salad, even Kinu admits, if reluctantly, that he is a genius:

> O-Kinu carefully chewed a piece of endive. The moment she swallowed the fresh vinegary juice, its exquisite delicate flavor entranced her. Furthermore, there was a touch of bitter aftertaste, which was just as faint as the crescent moon. This faint bitterness swept away the obstinate aftertaste of the meat she had eaten for lunch and reduced it to a pleasant memory. Having created this effect, the endive salad disappeared softly in the mouth without asserting itself and without leaving any discernible sediment.[33]

In thus describing Besshirō's culinary genius, Kanoko's writing poignantly captures the multiple sensations involved in the enjoyment of it, refuting indirectly but firmly the myth that women cannot understand or describe taste.[34]

Besshirō triumphantly accompanies his cooking with aphorisms such as "salad, like women's makeup, should not be overdone" and "cooking, like music, can be a supreme art because of the momentariness of taste."[35] As if to prove the strength of his belief in this latter ideal, when Kinu asks him to keep the salad for supper, he indignantly throws it out. Kinu, however, continues to observe and analyze him: in her view he is "a deformed genius, destined to contribute to human culture solely through his appetite," although she also recognizes in him a "certain beauty that comes with stupidity."[36]

It is after the cooking lesson that the reader becomes aware of Besshirō's secret admiration for Kinu. He is on the doorstep of his home. His wife and small son await him inside the house. At that moment he has a vision of the young woman, imagining her as "a mysterious being who makes him dream of a youthful poem, an exquisite, supple, sad, and sonorous poem that can never be written with words."[37] He knows that his longing for Kinu is one-sided, and his seduction of her never oversteps the boundaries of their cooking lessons together.

Kinu is not the only woman to play a significant role in this story. Besshirō's passion for food is, we learn, inherited from his mother. As a child, he lived with his mother in a Buddhist temple in Kyoto. Living in a temple, mother and son were expected to be vegetarian, but Besshirō's mother could not suppress her desire for animal protein. To satisfy this desire, she would send her young son to the river to catch fish. Even after tasting all sorts of delicacies in later life, Besshirō believes that the illicit dish that his mother made from these river fish tasted better than anything he has since experienced. Women certainly play a crucial role in his life and art. It was the aunt of his best friend who persuaded him to move from Kyoto to Tokyo, and to marry her daughter. This friend, the only friend in fact Besshirō has ever had, was a flamboyant restaurateur in Kyoto, but died of cancer, "giving" his aunt to Besshirō as his "legacy."[38] The aunt is no stranger to the culinary profession; she herself teaches cooking to young women. Using her connections, Besshirō manages to find patrons and students in Tokyo so that he can pursue his gastronomic ambitions.

Compared to these other women, Besshirō's wife, Itsuko, seems passive and characterless, exactly the impression Besshirō had of her at their first meeting. Completely excluded from his culinary and other artistic performances, she is left at home to look after their young child. While Besshirō extravagantly uses and discards rare and expensive ingredients in his lessons and performances, Itsuko is under strict instructions to economize on the domestic food expenditure, so she cooks cheap sweet potatoes for her son and herself. When Besshirō comes home, she is sent to buy bottles of beer, which she carries under one arm while carrying the child in the other. This portrait of an arrogant and tyrannical artist-husband and his subservient wife is a familiar one indeed in modern Japanese fiction, especially in *shishōsetsu*. Kanoko's story suggests, however, that even this overtly passive woman possesses culinary and critical abilities sufficiently developed for her gourmet husband to notice occasionally. She finds it funny, and somewhat pitiful, that her husband, insolent though he is, becomes like an innocent child when he is dealing with food. He is disarmed when, while waiting for his beer to arrive, he tastes the sweet potatoes she has prepared and discovers that they taste good—much to his surprise.

One other female character plays an important role in the story. She is a poet and a scholar of Buddhism, obviously based on Kanoko herself, or at least on a characteristically narcissistic version of herself. While still in Kyoto, Besshirō is introduced to this poet and her painter husband by his restaurateur friend. He shows her some examples of his calligraphic art, which is another of his aesthetic pursuits. "Madame" finds his art work pretty but nothing more than *aji*, which literally means "taste" but is used here in the sense of "witty," implying dilettantism and frivolity. Deeply wounded by this assessment, Besshirō plans his revenge with his other, stronger art—cooking:

> This woman so casually wrote off his work as *aji* [frivolous]; but, he wondered, how much connoisseurship did she really have in matters concerning *aji* [taste]? The quickest way to test her would be with food. She must have hardly tried any true delicacies—beyond, at best, the home cooking of some leisured ladies and a few form-obsessed restaurant dishes. If she turned out to have no connoisseurship, he could simply disregard her remarks about his work. If she was a real connoisseur, then she would surely bow her head before his culinary art, which would mean that he had conquered her and made her concede to him.[39]

This totally egocentric motivation disappears, however, as he prepares the feast. In an effort to impress the poet, Besshirō has observed—spied on in fact— her food and other preferences. As he tries to find what would please her most and plans and prepares the food, he gradually abandons his ego and ambition to a deeper purpose.

> If that woman, who was like a little girl in an adult body, marveled at his dishes, and innocently enjoyed a pleasure deeper than that which one could gain in this world through the five senses, that would be to the credit of the cooking itself. His own existence would not matter any more.[40]

In other words, Besshirō's recognition of a childlike innocence in this woman brings out a selflessness in him. We find a hint of romance here, in fact a stronger hint than that expressed in his relations with Kinu. He comes to realize that the essence of cooking is *itawari* (consideration), although he knows at the same time that he can show such consideration only for "idiots and children." His efforts are rewarded: "Madame" gratefully savors each dish and praises his cooking as a true art with *makoto* (truth) and *magokoro* (sincerity), qualities she confesses she failed to find in an immaculately prepared full-course dinner she once ate at a famous restaurant in Paris. Pleased though he is, Besshirō also feels a faint disappointment in being recognized for his culinary art rather than for his calligraphy, for he secretly accords greater importance to calligraphy and the various other arts he pursues than he does to cooking.

Thus the women not only know the shortcomings of the cooking genius but contribute to the development of his art with their criticism, childlike innocence, and motherly love and protection. Maternal love is an important trope in Kanoko's writing, and its significance is particularly noteworthy in her stories about food. We have already discussed "Kishimo no ai." The mother in another highly acclaimed short story, "Sushi" (1939), prepares sushi for her anorexic son. While all other attempts to feed him have failed, for which the father and the son's teachers all blame his mother, the sushi works miraculously. In preparation for the meal, the mother places brand-new utensils on a new mat on the verandah. Then she presents him with her rosy palms, extending them to him and turning them inside and out like a magician to reassure him that everything is clean and safe. Helped by the play element—the magician-like gestures, the fresh outdoor air, toy-like utensils—the child ventures to eat a piece of sushi with omelette and proceeds to try things he has never had before such as squid and fish. For the first time in his life the child experiences the ecstatic joy of eating—the various sensations of chewing, biting, tasting, and swallowing. As in the earlier passage describing Kinu's sensations on eating the endive salad, Kanoko's writing here poignantly captures the multiple sensations, again disproving the myth that women cannot understand or describe taste.

In "Shokuma," Besshirō begins to understand a deeper truth than that which, in his pride, he previously claimed to know. This deeper truth has evaded the gourmands in the other stories:

> The night wore silently on into its depth. The thick moist darkness, with its
> infinite appetite, would never cease to devour the falling hail. Or seen from
> another point of view, it seemed as if it was spitting the hail forever from above.
> In other words the darkness tirelessly continued to devour and spit, devour and
> spit. Never in his life had Besshirō known such a robust appetite. Perhaps this
> resembled the one that continuously devours death and spits life?[41]

The thick moist darkness and the spitting and devouring of life all strongly suggest maternity and female sexuality.[42] The above passage seems to suggest the cosmic strength of the mother/woman, or Great Mother, the strength with which the child/man can never compete but from which he can benefit greatly.

Wartime Gourmet Fantasies: Aoki Masaru and Hisao Jūran

That the wartime and immediate postwar years were the darkest time for gourmands in Japan hardly needs explanation. As briefly mentioned in our discussion of "food diaries," extreme food shortages in this period produced frustrated gourmet texts such as glutton comedian Furukawa Roppa's record of his pathetic and obsessive hunts for food and Uchida Hyakken's long list of the food he was dying to eat but couldn't. The two stories chosen for the discussion that follows may be regarded as gourmet fantasies of the dark age, and were written shortly after Japan's defeat.

Aoki Masaru's (1887–1964) "Tōzentei" (literally, "The Entrancing House," first published in the October 1946 and May 1947 issues of *Chie*) is a vignette about the eponymous drinking house where one can be "entranced" with good sake. Eating is given only secondary importance, serving merely to enhance the joy of drinking. Nevertheless, as we shall see, "Tōzentei" may well be regarded as a concise study of the drinking man's gastronomy. Like Rohan's story, it is full of allusions to classical literature and history. Indeed, Rohan, Aoki, and many other writers discussed in this chapter are all noted for both their general erudition and their specialized scholarly knowledge—in Aoki's case in the field of Chinese literature.[43] Besides the elements of drinking and scholarship, the play elements discussed earlier are also evident in their stories. Another common and notable characteristic of almost all the writers discussed in this chapter is the masterfulness of their writing. To write a gastronomic story the writer needs to be able to assure the reader that he or she is equipped with genuine knowledge, taste, and connoisseurship not only in gastronomy but in literature, art, and culture. The reader does not have to share the enthusiasm or inclination displayed or advocated in the text; for a gastronomic story to work at all, however, it is essential for it to be written in a form, style, and structure suited to the particular kind of gastronomy with which it deals.

Aoki's story has no comic exaggeration or exploration of eroticism. Neither does it concern a sincere search for self or truth. Instead it offers the reader an ideal space for drinking and eating that is calm (but never boring), accessible (but never vulgar), orderly (but never rigid), and simple while being deeply pleasurable. All of these qualities are perfectly expressed by the style and structure of the piece. It begins in a nostalgic tone, with an introduction to the drinking place:

> Many readers probably know this house. In fact some may have been regular customers and know it much better than I do. Even in those days, when things were much cheaper than they are now, there weren't too many places like it, where one could drink so cheaply and comfortably. Having been for some time a drifter in China [*shina rōnin*], the owner of the house was quite literate; he was a connoisseur, a dilettante, easy-going, generous, disinterested, and most important of all, he had a perfect understanding of the taste of sake and the feelings of drinkers.[44]

This is followed by a sketch of the house, Tōzentei—its location, its plan, its exterior and interior. The descriptions are so realistic and the nostalgia so genuine that Nanjō Takenori, the contemporary gourmet novelist-scholar and editor of an anthology of gastronomic literature, confesses that when he first read this story he did not realize it was fiction.[45] Aoki elaborates further on the various procedures followed at Tōzentei and presents its entire menu, which goes on for several pages. The rest of the story consists of detailed commentaries on this menu—its uniqueness, its ingenuity, the history and philosophy behind it, and so on—all of which amply display the narrator's knowledge of classical literature and history.

Compared to the imaginary and slimy dishes that appear in Tanizaki's story or the ludicrous "delicacies" in Rohan's piece, the food in this story is quite ordinary. What is extraordinary about it is its structuralist emphasis. Menus in general, as Brillat-Savarin, Lévi-Strauss, Barthes, and many others have pointed out, have neat structures. What is evident in Tōzentei's menu, however, is that it displays no simple observance of conventions, relying instead on careful and creative planning. The food on the menu is divided into four categories: dry, fresh, pasty, and warm. Each of these categories represents different kinds of sensations for the palate, the teeth, the ear, and so on. The selection of individual items is based not only on gastronomic qualities but also on economic and hygienic concerns. While each item is simple and ordinary enough, the customer can also enjoy combinations and assortments that are suggested on the menu or that they themselves choose. These combinations are given elegant and playful names such as "dialogue between a fisherman and a woodman" for shrimp, fish, and nuts and "nine-transformation elixir" for a customer's free choice.[46] In this way, the neatly structured menu encourages freedom and flexibility and suggests infinite possibilities for play.

The naming of the food on the menu in this story is noteworthy. It is based on a predilection for describing dishes by means of traditional rhetoric, rather than for their literal ingredients, a custom that Maruya Saiichi tells us is disappearing. Maruya noticed this change on encountering a dish listed on a menu as *shiratama kuriimu anmitsu*,[47] an entirely literal description. This sweet dish consists of *shiratama* (small white dumplings made of glutinous rice flour), ice cream, and *anmitsu* (red beans and diced gelatin cubes in syrup) and would have traditionally been called something evocative and culturally rich like *natsu no tsuki* (summer moon). It was shocking for Maruya (and his informant, the critic Maeda Ai) to discover that this kind of tradition is dead in modern Japan, that elegant names such as summer moon have commonly been replaced by prosaic and realistic names based on a dish's ingredients. It is, Maruya comments, like calling Peach Melba "gooseberry jam, peach slices, vanilla ice cream, and almonds in caramel sauce." The names of the fictitious Chinese dishes in Tanizaki's "Bishoku kurabu" are evidence of that writer's resistance to this departure from tradition, while Aoki's "Tōzentei" is clearly a manifesto for maintaining this means of cultural expression.

The final paragraph of Aoki's story reveals the true significance of his preceding descriptions of the "entrancing" drinking house. In a style completely different from that of the rest of the story, Aoki's narrator makes the statement that Tōzentei "evaporated in the great world turbulence."[48] The passage, like Rohan's "Chinsenkai," is full of allusions, puns, and other kinds of playful language, much in the tradition of Edo comic "scribbling." While Rohan's comic intent is evident from the beginning of his story, Aoki's sudden shift to a comic tone in his concluding paragraph enhances the impression of the destructiveness of historical change. The final line—"I would not be the only one who visits the old dream of enchantment with an empty barrel in his arms"[49]—suggests that the utopian drinking and eating site, where everything was in harmony, is irretrievably lost to change. At the same time it recognizes an age-old irony: that what seems real (and is presented in a realistic manner) is in fact but a dream, and what is told in a comical style is indeed tragic. Furthermore, whereas Rohan's playfulness was a tool for criticizing modern gastronomic and nationalist discourses, Aoki's may be regarded as a requiem for "good old" cultural literacy, of which many of his readers were, as the first line of the text suggests, "regular customers."

Whereas Tōzentei is the site for Eastern utopian drinking and eating, "Hana-awase" (Flower Matching)[50] by Hisao Jūran (1902–1957) can be regarded as a witty fantasy with a French flavor. The story depicts in four brief chapters the protagonist Fukui's encounter in Tokyo in the final months of the war with the beautiful widow Senko, whom he had met twelve years earlier in Cannes. The story has a hint of an elegant romance, but it remains only a hint. The title directly refers to the artificial pollination of female flowers—in this case, pumpkins. Fukui has been back in Japan for five years.[51] In France he studied how to produce imitations of French porcelain. On his return he brought with him exotic European flower seeds, which are now flowering, somewhat wildly, in his garden. This draws the attention of the police and the neighbors. At this time of "national emergency," growing inedible flowers in one's backyard is regarded as unpatriotic. When those flowers come from an enemy country, and when some are recognized symbols of resistance or revolution, the grower, in this case Fukui, has good reason to fear for his safety. Fukui never really intends to demonstrate real resistance to the prevailing fanaticism, but is merely amusing himself with the thought of a little personal rebellion against "the general tendency to make Japan as miserable as possible."[52] So he has no compunction about abandoning his little protest and growing pumpkins[53] instead of useless and potentially dangerous foreign flowers.

It is clear from the beginning that Fukui is no grand hero. Although he does appreciate beautiful things, the best he can do to express this admiration is to appropriate European natural and cultural products. Rather than confronting the authorities and persisting with his cultivation of useless flowers, he capitulates and chooses the safer crop of pumpkins. Senko, on the other hand, seems to have no fear or doubt about her provocative way of life, describing it as "a life that follows natural human laws."[54] Unlike Fukui, she resists conforming to, or pretending to conform to, the pressure to "renounce all the beautiful things human beings have created over centuries."[55] In the summer of 1933, as a red-haired, freckled fifteen-year-old girl she played Ravel on the piano and read French comic books. When Fukui meets her again a decade later, she has been transformed, as in a fairy tale, into a beautiful, sexy, and firmly individualistic woman. As in Okamoto Kanoko's story, the man in this story is at best a dilettante, and perhaps even a charlatan, while the woman is brave and genuine. In "Hana-awase" Senko plies Fukui with glass after glass of Pernod to accompany an unthinkably rich feast of anchovies, foie gras, eel soup, crayfish, and so on, none of which would have been available to ordinary people even in peacetime. She explains to a stunned and almost indignant Fukui that all this and much more is courtesy of her late husband, Kaneda,[56] who brought 300,000 yen worth of preserved delicacies back from France when he returned to Japan seven years earlier (i.e., in 1938).

Senko is no bashful flower: she confesses a girlish attraction to Fukui on first meeting him in 1933. When the pumpkins that he advised her to plant in her garden flower in late July 1945, she invites him for a *hana-awase* meeting—between her pumpkins and his. Looking out at her pumpkin garden, Fukui notices that her flowers look much healthier and more promising than his do. It must, he deduces, be the combination of rich nutrients and superior seedlings, both of which she can afford and he cannot. When he suggests canceling the incongruous flower matching between peasant and aristocratic pumpkins, Senko interprets this as a comment on the inevitable, the demise of her social class, regardless of the outcome of the war.

We have already seen that food has often been used in literature as a marker of class division. However, in this story, unlike in the examples of proletarian literature discussed previously, there is no intention to attack or change such social divisions. There is nostalgia for the good old civilized world, but there is also a bitter realization by Fukui that the human desire for pleasure associated with that world has been "crippled" by the "horrendous multilayered traps that the militants set in order to enslave people."[57] The story ends with another transformation. In this case, it is not a commoner turning into a fairy-tale prince, though. What Fukui has believed to be pumpkins growing in his garden turn out at the end of the war to be inedible gourds, suggesting that Fukui exemplifies the comic-pathetic shortcomings of a male intellectual in practical matters.

Survivors of the Prewar Gourmet Class: Yoshida Ken'ichi

Senko's prediction about the aristocracy was realized in postwar Japan. In a satirical short story with the same title as Gensai's novel, "Kuidōraku" (The Gourmet, 1950),[58] Mishima Yukio depicts the fall of the privileged prewar gourmand class and the rise of new money in the immediate postwar period. Utako, who once enjoyed many bourgeois pleasures and privileges such as extended stays in up-market resorts like Karuizawa, has lost almost everything: her husband, her financial security, and her social status. Using her connections, she sells high-class black-market goods to her less unfortunate friends. A new customer, Miyajima, however, seems a lucky exception to the rules, having succeeded in business in the lean years after the war. Utako is impressed, not only by his money but also by his knowledge of, and taste for, good food. Together they lament how difficult it has become to maintain their former standards in this rapidly Americanizing society. Here Europe represents the glory of prewar privilege, while America (with its insipid food) is a symbol of the rise of the hoi polloi. The irony is that Miyajima has misled Utako about his origins. He is not from a good family background. He was a chef before the war, at a resort hotel where Utako and her late husband often stayed. Nevertheless, Utako accepts Miyajima's marriage proposal—perhaps out of pity, but also because of the seductive charm of his sexual and financial power.

Mishima himself claimed in an essay published in 1956 that as someone who spent his youth in an age of malnutrition he was far more interested in grand literary feasts such as that produced by L'Isle-Adam than he was in actual food. As the food situation gradually improved after the war, Mishima's taste for literature changed from the gorgeous and brilliant to "literature like pure water."[59] At the same time his gustatory tastes began to develop after he traveled abroad. That Mishima's gastronomic interest was acquired rather than natural seems to be reflected in the story of Utako and Miyajima, which does not advocate or romanticize *gourmandise*; Miyajima is ultimately depicted as a common and vulgar man, although he may suit Utako's needs. In this sense, despite its title, the story does not really fall into the category that we term gastronomic fiction, being less interested in food itself, and more concerned with the collapse of a particular social class whose privileges extended to gourmet food.

Despite the general decline of Japan's prewar elite and its erudite gourmet class, there were a few survivors. Yoshida Ken'ichi (1912–1977) called himself the "prime minister's son in poverty," the "pauper prince," and the "three-penny gentleman."[60] As the child of a diplomat, he spent extended periods overseas, including periods in China, Paris, and London. From 1935 he published numerous translations of literary works ranging from Poe and Valéry to Wilde, Chesterton, Orwell, Waugh, T. S. Eliot, Isherwood, and many others.[61] He also wrote a number of books, many of which were essays on various topics, from food and drink to literature. The text discussed here, however, is not an essay but a novel with the typically ironic title *Hontō no yō na hanashi* (A Story like Reality, 1973).

This is another gourmet fantasy. Like Hisao Jūran's Senko, the heroine of this novel is a rich and beautiful widow, Tamiko, who has a good stock of fine wines, an efficient housekeeper, and a reliable cook in her house in Tokyo. The novel is set in a period when the memories of the war and defeat were starting to fade somewhat in the minds of many people. Therefore food shortage is no longer an issue here. Neither, of course, are there watchful neighbors ready to report any suspicious conduct to the authorities. Nevertheless, the kinds of dishes and drinks the heroine and her friends consume in this story would have been just as inaccessible to ordinary people in this period as those that Senko supplies to Fukui in the period immediately after the war. Tamiko's general knowledge and sensitivity, which she sometimes shares with her friends, is equally extraordinary. This goes much further than being able to tell the name of a particular wine when it is served. In her solitary thoughts about her late husband, Tamiko thinks of a few lines of Baudelaire (not in Japanese translation but in French). In her conversation with a stranger at a dinner party she immediately recognizes that what he has just said ("J'ai roulé, roulé") is a variation on a line from Laforgue's *Hamlet*.[62] This stranger, incidentally, is a Japanese man named Nakagawa. He claims to have spent some years in Siberia as a war criminal rather than as a POW, and he later has what might be called a romantic affair with Tamiko.

Is this meant to be "a story like reality"? Certainly. It is a fable, a fabrication of reality, a reality that no *shishōsetsu* could possibly, or would bother to, fabricate. The narrative may refer briefly to another, and more common, kind of reality that could well be material for *shishōsetsu* or realistic fiction, but such material is immediately pushed aside as unworthy of our attention. For example, when touching on the trouble with scheming relatives that Tamiko has had to deal with after her husband's death the narrator remarks:

> It was a common enough story, but more precisely an absurd one that could not even be a story as such. Tamiko, as if she were regarding something strange, realized that such things do exist, but that talking about a truly contemptible deed, even when it is somebody else's deed, could harm the dignity of the speaker. Besides, as a story it is of little interest.[63]

Thus, instead of being presented with a story of miserable and mundane treachery, we are told a fable about subtle and gentle pleasures, each of which is momentary but at the same time laden with memories of the past and of other texts. The novel closes with a full-course dinner at Tamiko's house, with Nakagawa and Tamiko's lawyer and old family friend, Uchida, as the guests. The highlight of this dinner is not the foie gras, the fish, the duck, or any other item on the carefully selected menu, but a special snack that goes with the after-dinner cognac.

> Tamiko did not know exactly how it was prepared. She knew it was placed on thin slices of bread cut into diamond shapes and baked in the oven, and the topping had cheese and cinnamon. The rest of the ingredients she could only guess at from its taste. Neither she nor anyone else asked the cook how it was made. Once cooked, it no longer tasted like cheese or cinnamon or boiled egg white, but with each of these flavors replacing one another in turn, its taste resembled snow.[64]

Nakagawa observes that the mysterious, nameless food may not be the most splendid of the delicacies they have tasted during the evening, but it is certainly unique. Uchida, on the other hand, draws the analogy of one thing (the snack) leading to or inviting another (a glass of cognac), and one present moment flowing into another.

This is another example of boundaries—be they spatial, temporal, or gastronomic—temporarily disappearing. The merging and crossing of boundaries, however, has nothing to do with the kind of slimy aesthetics in Tanizaki's stories. Sometimes, as we have just seen, these moments are marked as special; but in most cases, they are part of the characters' everyday lives. For example, before an ordinary lunch at home, Tamiko muses:

> Surely she used to have such a lunch in her childhood. It was the kind of lunch
> that did not stand out; there was no need to hurry or to pay more attention to
> people surrounding her than to what she was eating; but it was in the flux of
> the day, and nothing began or ended because of it, but simply what came before
> eating was connected to what came after eating through the act of eating. Hence
> one might be conscious not only of what one was eating but of the place, and
> the sounds, if any. In Tamiko's childhood it could have been a carpenter ham-
> mering nails at a building site or the sound of a train passing in the distance.[65]

Here again we see one thing—thoughts about the day's lunch—leading to or evoking another (lunch in general), and yet another (childhood memories). Time is neither fragmented nor fissured but continuous. And it is not stagnant but constantly moving. This kind of time in Yoshida's novels, "a pregnant time," as Shimizu Tōru calls it, in which "the eye (that is, sense and sensibility) works accurately" and "the mind appreciates repose," is what the novelist proffered as an alternative to the ennui of modernity.[66] Yoshida's unique style effectively captures this flow of consciousness, in lengthy sentences that move fluidly from one point to another. This is by no means an imitation of European "stream of consciousness" literature. To Yoshida and his protagonists, Europe and its languages, food, literature, and art are part of their lived experience, but at the same time they have Japanese language, food, and literature embedded in their consciousness. Tamiko's consciousness is certainly the focal point of the novel, but at times the narrative also delves into the thoughts of other characters such as Uchida and Nakagawa. These characters belong to the elite eating (and reading) class; their inferiors—Tamiko's housekeeper and cook, and the waiters and chefs at the restaurants she and the others visit—are described only superficially. In this sense the novel reflects the prewar social order and its values, even though they have been affected by waves of personal, national, and international turbulence.

Gastronomic Fiction in Autobiographical Mode: Dan Kazuo

The above examples of gastronomic fiction represent either the disappearance or the vestigial survival of prewar elitist *gourmandise* in postwar Japan. Outside of this concentration on elites, a number of male writers have popularized gastronomic pursuits in postwar Japanese literature. The Taiwanese writer-businessman Kyū Eikan (Qin Yonghan, b. 1924), for example, pioneered the genre of the gourmet essay with a series of best-selling books such as *Shoku wa Kōshū ni ari* (The Best Food Is in Canton, first serialized in a gourmet magazine from late 1954 and published in book form in 1957).[67] This work introduced the postwar Japanese reader to the subtleties of Cantonese cooking. The popular writer Ikenami Shōtarō (1923–1990), on the other hand, explored nostalgia for the tastes of the olden days in his gourmet essays such as "Mukashi no aji" (The Taste of the Old Days, 1974), as well as in his "sword novels." These writers and many others both prepared the ground for and directly contributed to the gourmet boom of the 1980s. As far as gastronomic fiction (rather than essays) is concerned, however, the two most important writers in the second half of the Shōwa period would have to be Dan Kazuo (1912–1976) and Kaikō Takeshi (1930–1989). The two have little in common in terms of background, literary forms, styles, and themes, but their gastronomic fiction has many common elements—masculinity, global wandering, eroticism, and solitude.

Dan started writing in the 1930s, while he was still a student, his strongest influence being that of the Nihon Rōman-ha, or Japanese Romantic school. Wider literary recognition came only after the war, when he was awarded the Naoki Prize in 1950. Because of his close association with writers such as Dazai Osamu (1909–1948) and Sakaguchi Ango (1906–1955), and because of his colorful personal life, he is often labeled a member of the "libertine" school (Burai-ha). He is best remembered now as a writer of autobiographical fiction and for a series of food essays and cookbooks, and perhaps also as the father of actress Dan Fumi.

Cooking and eating are accorded prominent roles in Dan's autobiographical fiction. In works such as the two-part novel *Ritsuko sono ai* (Ritsuko, Her Love, 1950) and *Ritsuko sono shi* (Ritsuko, Her Death, 1950) he focuses on the difficulties of finding food and feeding his family during and immediately after the war. In his later novel *Kataku no hito* (The Man of the Burning House, 1975), gastronomic pleasure is an essential element. The narrator-protagonist Katsura

Kazuo[68] is, like those of most other *shishōsetsu*, a writer; but unlike many other *shishōsetsu* protagonists, Katsura does not neglect eating in preference to drugs, alcohol, and women. Indeed, he is a great enthusiast of cooking and eating, as well as of life's other pleasures.

Cooking is presented in Dan's writing, regardless of its genre, as a masculine activity. Dan emphasizes its dynamic and muscular aspects and rejects domestication and formality, an emphasis that would be handed down to the popularized cooking-man's discourse of the late 1970s and 1980s. What has traditionally been regarded as women's business such as shopping and cooking is turned into a robust and adventurous pursuit, partly by increasing the quantities involved. Katsura, like other cooking men, prefers, almost obsessively, to cook a whole fish, a whole animal carcass, or at least a large chunk of meat, rather than to deal with already cleaned, filleted, and sliced portions. Equally notable are the self-reliance and intuitiveness of the cooking man. He despises cooking instructions that talk of "half a tablespoonful of such and such" and "simmering for so many minutes." He does not need such instructions, preferring to teach himself how best to select ingredients and choose cooking methods by observation, experience, and instinct. Dan/Katsura's long experience as a cook began at the age of nine, when his mother left her husband and children.[69] His father, a schoolteacher, was ignorant of cooking, and to hide the "family disgrace" from his colleagues and neighbors he refused to employ a housekeeper or maid. This presents an interesting contrast to Kyū Eikan's father, who, according to his son, took enthusiastically to eating, drinking, and cooking.[70] Without such a role model, and literally fed up with the takeaway meals available in a small town in Kyūshū in the early 1920s, the young Katsura had to learn to cook if he was to improve the family meals. This kind of men's cooking, therefore, can be interpreted as a critique not only of what is seen as women's domestic cooking but also of traditional Japanese masculinity as interpreted by the father's generation.

This muscularization/masculinization of cooking is also closely connected to global wandering, in which open-mindedness and adaptability are essential. While there are certain hints in his writing of the cultural hegemony of the West, Katsura by no means aspires to "civilize" himself or his compatriots with more advanced culinary science and technology; he simply drifts around both Japan and the outside world in pursuit of food bought from local markets, which he cooks according to methods learned from the local people or those he has developed over decades of cooking experience.

Katsura cooked for his family every day only in the early years of his life it seems, and then for a few years from mid-1945 in extraordinary circumstances.

He recalls the time when he lived in a small Buddhist temple on a mountain in Kyūshū with his three-year-old son. "Not that I wanted seclusion," says the narrator; "the country was devastated and my wife was dead. The whole of Japan was in chaos. No one, not even relatives, would take me in."[71] His income at that time was extremely limited; translations of Tu Fu's (Du Fu's) poems and a few stories brought him just enough to avoid starvation. Every day he cooked for himself and his son—mostly vegetables and tofu, but once a week he went down the mountain to buy six sardines, which he cooked, guts and all, as their treat for the next two days. Just as Katsura had taught himself to cook in his boyhood, he read and deciphered the classic Chinese poems without the aid of a dictionary. All he had was his own intelligence and judgment. This kind of self-reliance is an important characteristic of the postwar cooking man. It is connected, on the one hand, to resourcefulness and resilience in the face of chaos and destitution, and on the other to the cult of solitude, which is yet another element of the Romantic construction of Japanese masculinity.

Katsura may cook for his family, for his lovers and friends, and even for strangers in a strange place, but ultimately he cooks for himself. At one point he prepares a feast, with a big plate of oysters, a salad of endive and carrot, stewed tongue, and wine—all for himself. He has left his family (his second wife and several children) years since, and his lover has just left him.

> Could it possibly be that I have been too deeply accustomed since my boyhood to cooking and eating on my own? [...] This long-term habit may have separated me from any lasting intimacy with any one woman. Memories of a certain period seem to me nothing but a secret history of my various solitary cookings, drinkings, and eatings, somewhere on the earth, all alone. This strange history of solitary eating may have always precluded me somehow from domestic union and the atmosphere of home. It is not that the family rejects me but that I reject them. In other words, I seem to continue to drift aimlessly, in pursuit of singular eating.[72]

Solitude, travel, and drinking are important ingredients in many literatures, including classical Japanese and Chinese poetry and the *shishōsetsu*. In Dan's texts solitude is punctuated with a series of love affairs; in these pursuits of women, however, the reader senses a kind of misogyny—another familiar element in many modern novels. Despite the emphasis on the self-reliance and resourcefulness of the cooking man, he is aware that his wandering, drinking, and womanizing are not acceptable in respectable society. In the novel, drunk and depressed in a cheap New York hotel room, Katsura attempts, or pretends, to kill himself. Suicide, of course, is yet another familiar topos in modern Japanese literature; Dan's friend Dazai and several other major male writers having ended their own lives. Towards the end of the novel this cooking man reveals that a serious stomach ulcer suffered ten years earlier has left him with ongoing and worsening symptoms. He confesses that thoughts of cancer have recently begun to haunt him. Illness and confession are, again, important elements in Romantic literature and in the *shishōsetsu*. In this way then, as in many others, the seemingly carefree, robust, unconventional, roaming chef is connected to the literary tradition.

The Impasse in Gourmet Eating/Writing: Kaikō Takeshi

We have seen in previous chapters some of Kaikō's commentaries on food and literature and a sample of his own down-to-earth eating and writing. The two texts discussed in this section, however, do not concern the age of postwar hunger; they were written on the eve of the gourmet boom, when Kaikō was already a celebrity, famous for his literary output as well as for his gourmet and fishing pursuits. As in Dan's novels, each of these texts has a male protagonist who resembles the author and who pursues eating, drinking, and other physical pleasures in all corners of the world. Unlike Dan's cooking man, Kaikō's protagonists do not cook food but consume it in the same voracious way that they pursue knowledge. While the masculinity in Dan's texts is colored by loneliness, Kaikō's later work is characterized by a paradoxical combination of nihilism and passion, instincts that together form the core of his gastronomic fiction.

The first of the two novels is entitled *Natsu no yami* (1971, trans. *Darkness in Summer*, 1973). At the beginning of the novel the middle-aged narrator-protagonist meets his former lover in Europe for the first time in ten years. Eating is given only secondary priority in the first thirty pages or so of the novel since, in the protagonist's view, "good food and sex are not compatible."[73] The main part of the novel, however, is full of eating and talk about food. These are shared activities—eating, talking about food, sex—but they are not shared equally by the man and the woman. The man—as expected—has extensive knowledge and experience of eating, while the woman, though evidently intelligent, independent, articulate, resilient, and resourceful, is almost always seen as a student or learner, eating things like innards only at his suggestion and under his tutelage. He lectures her, for example, that "kidneys should have a little smell of urine, a trace of it," and when she wonders about testicles in this respect, he replies:

"You don't understand! You must learn more about the facts of life. The testicles have nothing to do with urine. But they're not bad. They're spongy, rubbery, and very subtle. I ate some fried calf's testicles in a Madrid slum bar, with sangria. It was a truly refined and pure taste, soft and round; without being told I wouldn't have known what it was, but even after I knew I couldn't believe it. They had the texture of the steamed white fish served at an elegant tea ceremony dinner. In general, intestine dishes are not to be slighted. Fish, animals, anything, if they kill an enemy, they will eat the intestines before anything else."[74]

This love of offal is shared by many other masculine gourmets, who all despise those who are too weak-stomached or prejudiced to try these most nutritious, subtle, and usually inexpensive ingredients. The woman in *Natsu no yami* is willing to try anything her lover recommends, and is often more than satisfied by what, together, they eat and drink. This voracious eating, drinking, and talking, however, are tenuous in their cheerfulness. In truth the protagonist fears and detests domestication and for this reason insists on maintaining a play element in their relationship. His lover, for her part, occasionally reveals various grudges—against him, against men, and against her compatriots. "You have eaten it and you know all about it, but you gave me all sorts of excuses why I should not."[75] She is talking here about pike (he has just caught one in the lake and intends to release it, as he has done with the other fish they have caught), and her tone is jolly rather than serious. She is not so jolly on a later occasion, however, when she describes herself as, after all, "a station restaurant, a pizza snack" for him:

"You are incapable of loving—not just a woman; you can't even love yourself. So you go looking for danger. You are a hollow explorer. You will do anything or go anywhere to fill the vacuum. [. . .] I've heard that tapirs eat bad dreams, but you set out to eat other people's passion, and you'd do anything for it."[76]

What has triggered her rage is his decision to leave her in Europe and go back to Vietnam, where a third wave of the Tet offensive is predicted. Her comments seem much more caustic than the critical views expressed by women in Okamoto Kanoko's "Shokuma." In Kanoko's story women both criticize and also support and contribute to the "art" of the male protagonists. But in *Natsu no yami* the woman—Kaikō names neither of the two protagonists—can only be resigned in the end to her enforced solitude and humility. The couple's last supper together in Europe is at a Chinese restaurant. The man is disgusted with the "fried hodgepodge of all the leftover vegetables, goulash à la student," whereas she remarks, "'I know, I know, I understand. Please don't speak so loudly. I'm quite satisfied with it. Even this is a great treat for me. I said all sorts of unpleasant things to you, but you have treated me royally. I want to apologize.'"[77]

About the summer she has spent with him she concludes "men must work and women must weep," as the old song goes, and that "the more things change, the more they stay the same."[78] The man, fully aware of the futility of his passion for eating and talking, can only struggle to find an escape from his own inertia.

In 1972, shortly after the publication of *Natsu no yami*, another novel of Kaikō's was serialized in a weekly magazine. The title of this novel, *Atarashii tentai* (The New Celestial Bodies), comes from the ninth aphorism of Brillat-Savarin: "La découverte d'un mets nouveau fait plus pour le bonheur du genre humain que la découverte d'une étoile." (The discovery of a new dish does more for human happiness than the discovery of a star.)[79] The man, who is on a mission to discover new "stars," here is a middle-aged, middle-class, middle-ranking bureaucrat in the Ministry of Finance. His mission, however, does not derive from his own gastronomic enthusiasm. Instead he is officially instructed to examine the state of the national economy by observing the food industry. If a dark shadow is cast on a piece of *takoyaki*, the boss tells him, it is his task to see whether that shadow comes from the White House or from Tiananmen.[80] This ludicrous order, however, is simply intended to use up, literally eat up, the ministry's budget surplus before the next budget meeting. Its absurd premise clearly separates this work from the *shishōsetsu* tradition; from the beginning the reader would assume this to be a comic-satirical story about the workings of bureaucracy or a backstage look at the Japanese "economic animal." Although the protagonist remains the nameless bureaucrat *kare* (he) throughout the novel, this "he" becomes increasingly like the author, and the novel becomes more and more like a gourmet travelogue or documentary that includes gastronomic and literary aphorisms.

The reader may not regard this work highly as a novel, but it includes some interesting metafictional aspects—namely Kaikō's way of eating preceding texts and cooking his own. As if to trace Kaikō's literary trajectory, the protagonist's research begins with cheap down-to-earth working-class food such as *takoyaki* and offal stew. Observing the food and the people in stalls and small bars and listening to the lively conversation and monologues, he concludes that these eating places on the bottom stratum are the most reliable in the restaurant industry. This is because their patrons pay for the food themselves, out of their own stretched pockets—quite unlike bureaucrats and company employees, who invariably eat on the company account. While he finds a mixture of innocence, irrelevance, and sharp observation in their talk about food, he also realizes that the patrons of these places add "essential nutrients" of human communication to their meals in the form of their, often dirty, jokes.[81] Having examined this area, the protagonist goes on to the next stage of his research, trying better food in more expensive restaurants, right across the country, from Hokkaidō to Kyūshū. The boss encourages him to eat more and spend more.

> "No need to thank me. All for one, one for all. Work hard. Don't go looking for ways to spare the research expenditure. That would impoverish your mind. The reason why contemporary Japanese novels are so boring is that the writers don't dare to be extravagant."[82]

So the protagonist eats at Maruume in Yotsuya, Wadakin in Matsusaka, and numerous other renowned restaurants. Although he tries to stimulate his appetite by thinking of the famous banquet scenes in *Quo Vadis* and *Satyricon*, he soon reaches the point of satiation: the inevitable feeling of "nothingness after a banquet."[83] In each place he visits for this research he meets an impressive devotee of gastronomy, but there is in these meetings none of the warm, inclusive, and comic interaction he experienced at the poorer establishments. His boss begins to remonstrate with him about his lack of enthusiasm for his research and tries to spur his satiated subordinate to greater efforts by showing him the legendary list of what Balzac was said to have consumed at one dinner. The great man started, apparently, with no fewer than one hundred oysters and ended with a dozen pears, a whole duck and many other things having been devoured in between.[84]

As the dessert is being served at an expensive restaurant in Akasaka, the protagonist's satiation overwhelms him: "In a moment of aberration, everything fell down. Everything collapsed, crumbled, was crushed, and shattered. Pleasure, excitement, and intoxication, gone. 'It's over,' he felt."[85]

What he now longs for is water—pure, plain water. As we saw in the stories by Rohan and Tanizaki, plain water is often regarded as the opposite of rare, exquisite delicacies. So is this a fable about the futility of (in this case assigned and almost forced) gastronomic quests? Or is it yet another example of a return to the uncomplicated and the pure? Kaikō being far from a simple storyteller, this plain water references another story—a French joke about a wine connoisseur who could tell the details of any wine he tasted when blindfolded, but was completely at a loss as to how to describe a glass of water. The intertextual "plain water" becomes a palimpsest for the protagonist's wanderings in the mountains. There he drinks pure water, and then disgorges and jet-propels "just like water" everything he has consumed, from *takoyaki* to crêpe suzette, from steak tartare to *suppon* (turtle), from cognac to mountain water. And then, the final, playful line of the novel turns everything, including things that are obviously based on the writer's own research and experience, into a story: "*to iu ohanashi deshita*" (so the story goes).[86]

So the "new celestial bodies" are indeed a new arrangement of old ingredients or a familiar arrangement of new ingredients. While a quest for the ultimate delicacy is at the core of many of the stories we have looked at, in this story it is neither intuitive nor voluntary, but forced upon the protagonist. Futility and satiation, or nihilism and loneliness, are by no means new in modern literature; but the comic and the ludicrous in this novel—including jokes, enumeration, scatology, and many other devices—may be regarded as a revival of qualities that serious fiction had tended for some time to suppress.

Postmodern Gourmet Fantasies

Kaikō's novels testify that fiction is often ahead of its time; while the nationwide gourmet boom was still to come, his novels had already identified both the insatiability of man's quest for the unknown and the futility of affluence and materialistic pursuits. In this final section we shall examine how, in a later period and now, contemporary writers have tackled the genre of the gastronomic novel in the midst of, and after, the mediatized gourmet boom.

Of great interest here is a collection of gourmet short stories by Murakami Ryū (b. 1952), *Murakami Ryū ryōri shōsetsu shū* (first serialized in *Subaru* from 1986 to 1988, published in book form in 1988). This serialization coincided with the release of numerous literary and other cultural products relating to food, such as Yoshimoto Banana's *Kitchen*, Tawara Machi's collection of tanka poems *Sarada kinenbi* (both of which are discussed in chapter 6), and Itami Jūzō's film *Tanpopo*. Murakami was already widely recognized as the author of the Akutagawa Prize winner *Kagiri naku tōmei ni chikai burū* (1976, trans. *Almost Transparent Blue*, 1977) and other novels. The eponymous title of this story collection is indicative of Murakami's celebrity status as a writer and filmmaker: unlike the still unknown Tawara and Yoshimoto, Murakami's name by the 1980s had value as a "brand name." The book consists of thirty-two more or less independent stories, each about five pages long. These are called "subjects," using the English word, and all except "The Last Subject" are allocated subject numbers instead of proper titles. The matter-of-fact flatness this affects matches the general tone of the narrative. There is no beginning, middle, or end except within each subject. The only common thread running through the collection is the narrator-protagonist, who is, like Murakami himself, a writer-filmmaker in his late thirties. Almost all of the other characters appear only once. Each subject has at least one central food, usually some delicacy the protagonist eats or remembers eating in some corner of the world, and each delicacy is closely associated with a sexual encounter.

This format obviously takes into account certain patterns of consumption in contemporary society. The reader of one subject does not have to know the import of the previous or ensuing ones. Neither is the reader required to spend a long time reading one subject or pondering it, even though it may involve something that would normally be regarded as shocking or disturbing or morally complex, such as drug abuse or child prostitution. Uninflected consumption, in fact, is taken for granted within the stories: the narrator (or someone he knows) consumes food, be it turtle, fugu, oysters, caviar, truffles, or whatever, without there seeming to be any apparent moral point or purpose to each subject. Women are treated like food; just as some food tastes better than others, some women impress with their physical charms, naivety, or stylishness.

There are no witty conversations or arresting moments, although there are many attempted metaphors and aphorisms, either from the narrator himself or from his friends: turtle and fungi taste like "life itself"; the duck served at Tour d'Argen is like "one's own organ taken out, forgotten, and finally returned to one's body"; the goat-brain curry of a famous restaurant in Delhi "symbolizes exciting but vain attempts"; and truffle is "the lack itself, lack that resembles fear and can never be appeased by anything but truffle."[87] Clearly, "X is Y itself" seems to be the favorite equation here. This is often extended to the protagonist's involvement with women: the raw reindeer liver in Lapland smells like "meat itself, life itself," and this special smell is shared by "the very best kind of women" who are "without exception beautiful, clever, and good-natured, because the smell can only belong to those who are full of animal confidence and at the same time sophisticated."[88] This observation is made by the narrator's friend, G, who is a rich and well-known commercial film director, a fashion leader within consumer culture. He makes this remark to the narrator in a stylish four-star hotel restaurant in Rome, while they watch G's girlfriend return carrying her shopping bags. Like all of G's other girlfriends, she is tall, slender, and beautiful. She is neither stupid nor demanding, and of course she looks absolutely gorgeous in her Armani blouse and skirt and low-heeled Polini shoes. G claims to recognize instinctively the "very best of women" by their special aroma, which is, according to him, only faintly discernible during lovemaking. He then "educates" them to keep a certain distance from him, especially in his relationships with other people. Conforming beautifully to type, the gorgeous girlfriend makes only a brief remark about the superior quality of the expensive items she has bought, then happily retreats to their hotel room, leaving G and the narrator to enjoy their conversation in the restaurant. There is no suggestion of rebellion or irony in her behavior, or indeed in the entire narrative.

Arguably the whole collection is about this kind of distinction and inequality—among commodities and among commodified human beings. G's girlfriend is considered to be among the most prestigious of women, matched only by superior male counterparts such as G. The young woman in "Subject 18" is depicted as more or less the opposite. After working in a nightclub in Kyūshū, this woman has recently moved to Tokyo and found a new job as a party "companion," the kind of job where women are subject to hierarchical classification based on age and physical appearance. She lives in her sister's flat surrounded by cheap furniture and sentimental bric-à-brac, all expressive of her low status. The food in this subject is caviar—the genuine, expensive kind. How she obtained this luxury foodstuff and the way she explains the event to the narrator both suggest she is compliant with the notion of categorizing women and classing them hierarchically. After asking the narrator a few blunt and awkward questions about how men feel during sex, she tells him about her former lover, a married man.

> "It's a bit embarrassing, but we were making love when I was having a period, and I gave him oral sex without wiping him. He was really thrilled. He said nobody else ever did such a thing, and gave me some caviar. It's real caviar. He said it's hard to get. He bought it in New York for me."[89]

The woman opens the jar, which she has kept unopened in the fridge for five years. When asked why, she answers, "'Because you're the first person I have met who knows the taste of real caviar.'" She and the narrator then eat the whole four ounces of caviar in five minutes flat, and she washes the jar and puts it on a plywood shelf next to a cheap souvenir doll.

In his Afterword to the volume that includes this *ryōri shōsetsu*, Murakami writes that his short stories are *gūwa* (allegory, fable, parable), which are "based on the greatest common divisor," and hence a kind of means for him to "approach the world."[90] The greatest common divisor may not be the same as the lowest common denominator, but one certainly feels the poverty of imagination in the "allegory" of the fabulous people and fashionable food.[91] Only when dealing with the least fabulous people—such as the caviar girl or the middle-aged sisters desperately seeking the missing daughter of the older sister ("Subject 26")—does the "allegory" seem slightly more interesting. In any case the world approached in this method is no doubt characterized by inequality, and the "allegory" seems more likely to be consumed by that world than to tell us something new about the larger world beyond it.

Murakami's *ryōri shōsetsu* with its emphasis on masculinity and global wandering has much in common with other postwar gastronomic novels. The stories of Nanjō Takenori (b. 1958), in contrast, clearly show a close connection to the earlier gastronomic tradition of Rohan, Aoki, and their Chinese predecessors. Like many of the writers of these earlier gastronomic novels, Nanjō is a scholar—of English literature—with an extraordinary passion for Chinese food, drink, and writing. In his work we see familiar elements and devices such as erudite references and allusions, humor, and playfulness. His is a return to the playful gastronomic quest that excludes sex or romantic love. At the same time, however, there is no doubting that Nanjō's gastronomic fiction is the product of a postindustrialized society in which eating and writing are affected in one way or another by the media and consumerism.

The first of Nanjō's works of gastronomic fiction, *Shusen* (The Wine Hermit, 1993), places more emphasis on drinking than on eating. It is a fantasy about the victory of blissful, divine, genuine, forgiving, inclusive drinking over evil, miserable, greedy, mercenary, scheming drinking. Parody, allusion, and quotation play a vital role in this fantasy, which takes the form of a quest for the holy grail and the holy *tokkuri* (sake bottle, an allusion to *Pantagruel*). The tale ends with a scene in which poetic justice is seen, literally, to be done: the good (represented by a drunken hermit) and the evil (represented by a brewing tycoon) compete against each other by reciting drinking poems by Li Po, Pai Lo-tien, Omar Khayyám, and others. *Shusen* is a highly entertaining and erudite novel, which seems to confirm Kaikō Takeshi's remark about the supremacy of drinking in literary tradition and the much lower status of eating as a literary theme.

Nevertheless, the novel includes some detailed descriptions of the elaborate dishes that accompany and enhance the drinking.[92] There is, for instance, a dish inspired by Petronius' *Satyricon*. While the original dish in Trimalchio's banquet consists of a thrush inside a boar, the version in the novel is much more complex and intriguing. Not only does it comprise multiple layers of animals, but the flesh of the larger animal is wrapped in that of the smaller one, the innermost meat being elephant mince. Thus the food has rich intertextuality highlighted and exaggerated by reversal and modification. Another dish is a culinary representation of the underwater world, consisting of numerous sea creatures gathering around the dragon king. This miniature world made of tempura is so elaborate that the protagonist's spirit is transformed into a fish and swims around inside it, as sometimes happened in Chinese legends.

Shusen placed second in the fifth competition for the Japan Fantasy Novel Prize, and the prize money was used for an extravagant all-day banquet in Hangzhou with top-class local chefs cooking 124 dishes for forty people. We know this from "Tōei no kyaku" (Visitors from the Eastern Sea), which is included in Nanjō's collection of short stories *Mankan zenseki* (The Chinese Banquet, 1995). The narrator-protagonist of the story is called Defu, derived from Nandefu, which is Nanjō written in the old kana orthography, and also perhaps a play on *debu*, being a derogatory term for an overweight person. He decides to abandon his quiet scholarly activities and try to earn some prize money with a novel he has written on the side. To the surprise of his drinking friends, his novel, "a chimerical, absurd, and incoherent nonsense, which only a complete fool or a genius could write,"[93] is a place winner in the Fantasy Prize, although it misses out on the first prize and thus reaps only half the coveted five million yen.

The first half of the story deals with how Defu plans the subsequent banquet, with the help of revered gourmet literati such as Aoki Masaru and Yuanmei (1716–1797) and of his friends and acquaintances. The event is also meant as a token of gratitude on Defu's part to those whose features, personalities, and actions he has borrowed for use in his fiction. The second half of "Tōei no kyaku" is an account of the banquet and includes detailed descriptions of the dishes consumed. Like "Chinsenkai" and "Bishoku kurabu," the story abounds in Huizinga's play element. Defu and his company, consisting mainly of academics, editors, and owners or employees of restaurants and bars, are deeply absorbed in their play, just as those in the gourmet groups discussed earlier were in theirs. Their obsession with food unites them and separates them from the mundane ordinary world, if only momentarily. At the same time there are those basic factors of play that we saw earlier in our discussion of "Chinsenkai"—contests, performances, exhibitions, challenges, and so on. The comic intent is as obvious here as it was in "Chinsenkai," but instead of generating comedy from bogus *gourmandise* and fake delicacies, Nanjō's text emphasizes the authenticity of the dishes, which include stewed camel hoofs, fried venison tendons, tortoise soup, venison tails, and duck tongues in soy sauce, amongst many others. Ironically enough, though, the banquet as a whole is a summarized imitation of Empress Dowager Xi Taihou's[94] more famous three-day extravaganza, and so its authenticity, in that sense, is compromised.

The story closes with a faint touch of sadness, expressed by Defu: "Human pleasure comes to an end in a moment, while hermits *[sennin]* never know sorrow. How I wish I could become a *sennin!*"[95] So the fantasy about the drunken hermit enables its creator to enjoy the exquisite delicacies he has dreamed of; but the pleasure is fleeting. Even so, there is neither the bitter aftertaste of satiation nor the explosive realization of futility that we saw in Kaikō's later fiction. Instead, the momentary pleasure of eating is recalled, masticated, and made into another story. Eating and writing in Nanjō's case certainly seem to be closely related, not only in spirit but also in a practical sense. In 1996, three years after the banquet in Hangzhou, the royalties earned from *Mankan zenseki* were used for another, though smaller, banquet in Shenyang. In 2000, with the royalties from another book, Defu and company returned to Hangzhou for a special party to celebrate his old teacher's 77th birthday, which is the subject of another book,[96] the profits from which will surely lead to yet another banquet and another book.

In gastronomic fiction taste is not egalitarian. To some extent it may be learned or improved by training or experience, but that can only happen under the right circumstances and if one is willing to learn. Some texts aim to improve, in the sense of educating, the reader's taste. Others assume, or in some cases ensure, that the reader shares, or at least understands, highly particular tastes. Not everyone would share a liking, for instance, for the slime/sublime of "Bishoku kurabu"; and yet when it is presented within a mystery-like structure and in a style perfectly expressive of its special pleasure, one cannot but "taste" it. The taste of sincerity or truth may sound like sentimentality, but in Okamoto Kanoko's story this taste has the power to move the reader, as it does the arrogant chef in the text itself. The taste that evokes memories and unites the past with the present and future in Yoshida Ken'ichi's novel similarly appeals to those living a much less privileged life than that of the story's protagonists. Aoki's piece on the ideal drinking house, too, has a nostalgic charm even for those younger readers, like Nanjō, who did not experience the war that destroyed this utopia. All of the above may be regarded as successful examples of specific tastes represented in literary language.

While some of the narrative elements appearing in the texts so far discussed do seem to transcend class and cultural barriers and to remain relevant despite radical social change, others are very much the product of the specific constructs of their time. *Kuidōraku* may have had much to offer the reader at the beginning of the twentieth century with its advocacy of cooking and eating as a driver for modernization; a century later, however, what it offers the reader is more or less limited to its value as a historical document detailing tastes that were then considered to be modern and civilized. Some of the actual recipes included in the text may still be useful; but the language (including the names of imported ingredients and dishes) and the discourse are so dated that the contemporary reader, surrounded by thousands of contemporary recipes in the print, broadcast, or electronic media, would not read the novel for any practical purpose. This is also true of the romance that accompanies the cooking: it is hard, for instance, to imagine that this novel could be made into a credible film or a television drama series for a modern audience without major changes to the characters and to the plot.

That certain texts and certain styles of cooking have a "use by" date seems undeniable. The masculine cooking of *Kataku no hito* may have already reached its expiration date, and the hard-boiled gourmet consumption stories of Murakami Ryū may be coming close to reaching theirs. Kaikō and Nanjō have made significant contributions to the contemporary gastronomic novel by unearthing obscure or esoteric gastronomic stories from the past. It is possible that their own gastronomic fiction may, in turn, need to await future conservationists to rediscover it and interpret its relevance to future generations of readers.

Chapter Six

Food and Gender in Contemporary Women's Literature

I n recent years the connection between food and gender has been the subject of numerous and diverse studies.[1] Certain kinds of food and certain ways of eating are generally regarded as either feminine or masculine. While meat and offal tend to be categorized as masculine food in many cultures, sweets are usually considered feminine food. More important, the production, preparation, and consumption of food may be regarded exclusively as the preserve of either men or women. In Japan, as in many other countries, men's cooking was confined to the professional sphere until relatively recently, while women were, and to a large extent still are, expected to take charge of the much less glamorous, unpaid work of everyday domestic cooking. This has meant that the celebrated chefs of Japan have all been men. It is interesting to investigate why this is so. Ishige Naomichi, a leading scholar of the cultural history of food and eating, sees it as simply the result of the historical dominance of most professions by men.[2] But art historian Miyashita Kikurō believes public expectations have also been a factor in excluding women from the ranks of elite chefs, as well as from the elite level in other artistic professions, and that "male chefs rejected allowing women positions of authority in the culinary world."[3] In addition to these historical factors, the religious and sociocultural myths of purity (as discussed in chapter 3) have worked against women's becoming successful in the culinary world; women have traditionally been considered unclean in Japan—not unclean enough to prevent them from cooking dinner, but too unclean to handle food at the elite level.

The preparation of food is not the only aspect of our relationship with food that is heavily gender oriented; eating and talking (or writing) about food are also clearly influenced by gender. There are gender-based differences in "entitlements" to food.[4] We may recall Shiki's mother and sister eating pickles in the kitchen while he was given eels, sardines, and many other dishes, on top of which he demanded sweet dumplings. Barthes remarks that "[m]ythologically, food is men's business; woman takes part in it only as a cook or as a servant; she is the one who prepares or serves but does not eat."[5] This corresponds to Miyashita's explanation of representations of women in traditional European art:

[I]f women were present at banquet scenes, their roles were only secondary. More often they were shown inside the kitchen cooking. In Renoir's paintings women are prominent. However, these women, all young and beautiful, are treated merely as motifs to add gorgeousness—like the fruits and flowers on the dining table.[6]

Alongside this exclusion of women from the sphere of food sits another commonly held, but seemingly contradictory, perception that everyday food is a "feminine" subject, which is how sociologists such as Beardsworth and Keil explain the traditional lack of scholarly interest in the subject.[7] No doubt many women would empathize with Luce Giard when she writes that as a child she "refused to surrender to [her] mother's suggestions to come and learn how to cook by her side" and that she "refused this women's work because no one ever offered it [to her] brother."[8] Another important area of study related to eating and gender is that concerned with eating disorders, which have recently been recognized, particularly in North America, as "intimately linked to gendered notions of identity and subjectivity, and to conceptions of the body and health."[9]

As we saw in chapter 3, depictions of women's historical deprivation of food and their responsibility for food preparation (i.e., the first two of the three issues Lupton identified as the focus of feminist critics) are found not only in texts written by women but also in men's texts. Generally speaking, however, there seems to be a clear difference in the attitudes of male and female writers to these issues. We have seen, for instance, many examples of how women's bodies are used to bring food to their families. From the prewar *karayuki-san* to the postwar *panpan* girls, female bodies are inscribed (and even devoured) by the discourse of economic, militaristic, and cultural nationalism. In texts dealing with postindustrial conditions such as Murakami Ryū's *ryōri shōsetsu*, women are not actually deprived of food, but they themselves are compared to the series of expensive gourmet dishes the male protagonist-narrator consumes. Despite evidence of a pervasive gender imbalance in relation to food, we cannot find any sign of dissent among the women in these texts written by male writers.[10] In contrast, Hayashi Fumiko, Hirabayashi Taiko, Sata Ineko, and many other women writers allow their female narrators and characters to describe gender inequality and to express their dissent against it.

The Contemporary Situation

Gender, as it relates to food, is one of the major determinants, if not the only one, of the construction of values at different stages of production, distribution, and reception of the text. It is not that all texts relating to food implicitly or explicitly deal with the gender issue; but even when gender appears to be absent, it is present, either deliberately or unconsciously, as subtext. The aim of this final chapter[11] is to clarify how gender is reflected and represented in the treatment of food, eating, and cooking in contemporary Japanese texts. Three questions would appear to be especially relevant here. Are the issues and strategies identified by Lupton and Orbaugh (quoted in chapter 3) still prominent in more recent works? Which genres, forms, and styles are chosen by writers interested in the contemporary connection between gender and food? What innovations are evident in the most recent work in this area?

To begin our discussion, let us consider the following two scenarios:

Scenario One: A high-school girl enjoys cooking with her artist father for the first time in the six months since he left his wife and daughter. The girl is quite good at cooking—even though her mother, a lecturer in art, can barely cook—because she used to watch him cooking. The divorced couple are on friendly terms and respect each other and have (hetero)sexual relationships with their respective new partners. Under the guidance of her father and a maverick boy from her school, the girl learns many things about life (and food), at the same time confronting various social issues such as domestic violence, mental illness, and physical and mental disability for the first time. The daughter tries to cheer up each of her parents by cooking: for her mother when she is suffering from depression after a failed relationship, for her father when he is falsely accused of plagiarism.

Scenario Two: A young woman enters a university in Tokyo and moves into her aunt's flat. Her parents have been divorced for several years as a result of her father's homosexuality. Her mother runs a Japanese-style inn in her hometown, while her father is a hotel manager in Tokyo. He has been living with a middle-aged male "flower artist,"[12] but appears to be having an affair with a younger man. The protagonist appreciates neither her mother's professionally familial and local cooking nor her father's snobbish sophistication in food, wine, and fashion. Rather, it is with her closest friend (who is a young woman like the heroine but looks like a schoolboy), her aunt (an unmarried novelist), and her other friends (including gay men) that she enjoys sharing food, drink, and good conversation.

These synopses are drawn from novels published in 1988 and 1989 respectively. They share many common elements. Each has a young female protagonist whose parents are divorced. Both strongly question the stereotypical view that a stable marriage is essential for the happiness and well-being of the children. In each story men and women have equal access to food, drink, education, and a career. Food abounds in both scenarios and does not cause any major conflict or struggle between the characters. Cooking is not forced on women and is an activity practiced by both sexes.

To ask the reader to guess from the above the sex of the writer of each novel would be inappropriate and unfair because my brief descriptions of the novels reflect my own interpretation of them in the context of this chapter's theme, and also because such a question presumes that the writer's sex determines the representation of gender in his or her work. Nevertheless, when one knows that the first was written by a man and the second by a woman, some "obvious" signs begin to emerge even in these brief summaries of the novels. In the first story the protagonist's father and her male school friend teach and guide her, reminding us more of the cooking man discussed in chapter 5 than of the fierce cooking lessons provided by father figures in Kōda Aya's texts.[13] In the second novel, however, neither the father nor the mother has power or influence over their daughter. Sexual relationships among the adults in the first novel are all heterosexual, whereas the second story includes male homosexuality and gender/sex ambiguity, which have both been extremely popular and common themes in girls' comics since the 1970s. In other words, the girl in the first text is depicted primarily as the *musume* (daughter), though free from the kind of restrictions the daughters of the house were subjected to in previous eras. The protagonist of the second novel, in contrast, represents the *shōjo* (girl, young woman), whose characteristics are often said to express liminality, ambivalence, and "freedom and arrogance."[14] This *musume-shōjo* contrast will be discussed in more detail below.

The novels summarized above are Haitani Kenjirō's *Shōjo no utsuwa* (The Vessel of a Girl, 1989) and Kanai Mieko's *Indian samā* (Indian Summer, 1988).[15] Haitani (1934–2006) is known as a writer of children's stories with a strong commitment to the humanization of education, especially for disabled and marginalized children, hence his target audience includes adolescents and their parents, and those interested in the development and education of young people. Kanai (b. 1947), on the other hand, writes what might be broadly termed postmodern (meta)fiction. *Indian Summer* is no exception; it is a kind of parody of *shōjo shōsetsu* (girls' fiction). This is not, by any means, to suggest that Haitani and Kanai respectively represent male and female views generally or male and female writing as a whole. The point is simply that the two novels represent different levels of gender awareness.

While there does seem to be a connection between gender awareness in these stories and the sex of their authors, it might be more meaningful to turn our attention to the question of how these two writers are received. Even though Haitani's works are classified as children's literature, many of his most devoted readers are adult men and women. Also, many of the "Kaisetsu" commentaries on the paperback editions of his stories are written by women, who unanimously express their admiration for Haitani's views, writing, and cooking. Children's story writer Satō Takako, for instance, concludes her commentary on *Shōjo no utsuwa* thus:

> The dishes Kasuri [the girl protagonist] cooks in the story seem terribly delicious. I wonder, since I have heard about the wonderful dishes Mr. Haitani cooks with homegrown ingredients, whether they are part of his own repertoire, or appear on his favorite menu. In the novel Kasuri learns Japanese-style cooking from her father, who himself learned to cook by observing and copying his mother. [. . .] So a high-school girl can prepare fine Japanese dishes, the intricacies of which she learns at her father's side. I cannot help feeling a bit envious of Mizoguchi Kasuri.[16]

Kasuri is essentially a *musume* rather than a *shōjo*, despite the title of the novel. This is reflected in Haitani's postscript to the novel. Here he confesses to taking the greatest pleasure from the words of a friend (male) who, speaking of the novelist's fictional creation Kasuri, remarks, "I wish I had a daughter like her!"[17] Of course not every commentator reads Haitani's work or writes about it in such an overtly naive manner. Some do not thoroughly endorse the gender implications presented in Haitani's texts, even though they generally admire his work. Singer Katō Tokiko points to certain gender stereotypes in Haitani's stories: while his male protagonists can be awkward, uncool, and stubborn, she remarks, their female counterparts tend to be young, cute, and gentle. Even so, Katō happily declares that the Haitani collection in her family library will sooner or later come to be treasured by her own daughters.[18]

Kanai's *Indian Summer*, on the other hand, can be read as a story of a *shōjo* who detests daughterly duties and restrictions and expresses her "freedom and arrogance" through her unrestrained enjoyment of eating, drinking, reading, watching (films), and talking. So while we hesitate to come to the essentialist conclusion that male writers (and readers) are less aware of gender issues than female writers (and readers), in the above two texts, just as in earlier texts, a clear difference of approach is discernible. To some extent it is up to the reader to be aware of this difference and either to collude with the gender subtext of the writing or to resist it. Kanai's novel will be revisited below, but in the meantime some common characteristics of food and gender in contemporary women's texts are worth investigating. There are four key words to take note of in this context: critical, jubilant, parodic, and disturbed. The trope of *shōjo* is important here as it plays a central role in connecting these characteristics.

Women Criticizing Men's Cooking and Writing

The "gourmet boom" has produced and consumed thousands of books relating to food, including fiction, poetry, essays, and recipes. Most of these texts, like the gourmet food they describe, are no longer the exclusive preserve of certain socioeconomic or gender groups but are supposedly accessible to everyone. At the same time, as noted in chapter 5, men's cooking has become fashionable, and many male writers including Dan Kazuo, Kaikō Takeshi, Ikenami Shōtarō, Mizukami Tsutomu, and Shimada Masahiko have published food essays and recipes. In response to this trend women have expressed their reservations about men and cooking. The poet Maki Yōko (1923–2001), who was married to Kaikō, sarcastically comments thus on the difference between women's and men's cooking:

> When men's cooking attracted attention I thought this was a very welcome change. It was, however, accompanied by such grand manifestos and declarations that men's cooking is a hobby requiring extraordinary imagination and creativity. I listened to these declarations with a smile, as I felt, in their exalted language, the conviction and the desire to convince us that men's cooking is not just different from, but far and fundamentally superior to, women's.[19]

Maki believes that men's cooking aims at absolute gastronomic values, while women seek a balance between absolute and relative values, the latter including the question of who is going to eat the food and the particular state of health of that person. She also argues that men's cooking may make money while women's cannot, even though men, too, depend on women's cooking in order to live and work. We may recall the case of the arrogant chef in Okamoto Kanoko's story. The significance of relative values, particularly in interpersonal relationships, is clearly seen in Kōda Aya's stories, and even in more recent women's texts. It is significant that Maki coats her criticism in humor and irony, which may be regarded as an example of the second strategy on Orbaugh's list, "to invert the hierarchy of value." This tolerant and intelligent humor, however, has the potential—if not in this particular essay but elsewhere—to turn into something provocative and threatening.[20]

Women's cooking, though traditionally regarded as private and non-profit-making, experienced a breakthrough with the best-selling book by Kirishima Yōko, *Sōmei na onna wa ryōri ga umai* (Bright Women Cook Well, 1976). Kirishima believes that cooking requires attributes such as courage, judgment, an active imagination, intelligence, agility, and energy, all of which are usually considered "masculine" qualities. In her highly polemic style she warns that many women are becoming just as incompetent at housework as men, and insists that women should enjoy cooking just as they should enjoy other activities.

> Men cannot do what women can do, but women have been achieving more and more in the realm of men's work. Instead of women catching up with incompetent men, men should catch up with competent "androgynous" women: this would produce a desirable equity between sexes.[21]

Indeed, Kirishima's recipes are laden with descriptions of other means of enjoying life, such as communication with friends and lovers, and traveling. Although she uses the term "androgynous" in the above passage, it is clearly heterosexual love that underwrites the book's message, albeit heterosexual love enjoyed outside, rather than inside, the institution of marriage. The book also advocates cosmopolitanism. The message, in short, is that intelligent women are not only good cooks but also excellent workers and fantastic lovers, as well as well-traveled, cosmopolitan, and everything else that is desirable.

Jubilant Cooking by Senior "Girls"

Confidence and jubilation are also evident in older women writers' recipes. Uno Chiyo (1897–1996), Kirishima's senior by forty years, passionately persuades the reader to try her "secret" recipes. She guarantees the taste as well as the plea-sure in life that comes with these dishes.[22] Mori Mari (1903–1987) also boasted of her individualistic taste and cooking—about a decade before Kirishima pub-lished her best-seller. Just as Kōda Aya was always treated in literary journalism as the daughter of Kōda Rohan, Mori Mari was known as the daughter of the celebrated literary figure Mori Ōgai. But while Aya tended to be seen in me-dia as the paragon of the loyal daughter and master of domestic skills, includ-ing cooking, Mari was seen as, in a sense, an ageless *shōjo*, full of "freedom and arrogance."[23] The writer-translator Yagawa Sumiko, a close friend of Mari, has pointed out the great gap between the exquisite food in Mari's texts and the simple diet she actually followed.[24] Whether Mari's tastes were acceptable to others never affected her confidence. Unlike many other women of her genera-tion, Mari never had to cook in order to please or nurture her family; her cook-ing was first and foremost for her own pleasure.

> I love cooking and eating what I have prepared; I do not find it pleasurable just
> to provide food to someone, be it my husband, sons, or anyone else, even when
> they enjoy my cooking. My love of cooking is nonmaternalistic and based on
> Western individualism. If my friends love and admire my food, I will cook for
> them, but on condition that I eat with them. Whenever I visit a friend in hospi-
> tal, I take food for two.[25]

Although she mentions her husband and sons in this passage published in 1965, she had actually left her first husband and their sons almost forty years before this, and her second marriage in 1930 lasted only several months. Just as she was confident of her taste and her cooking skills, Mari's writing is generally free of painful self-dissection and avoids dwelling on life's struggles.

> I simply find great pleasure in cooking.
>   In a silver saucepan clear hot water is bubbling and swirling and a pure
> white egg is swimming. This gives me pleasure.
>   With a frying pan in my left hand, I drop some butter with my right hand
> and then break eggs into the pan. After a moment I stir the eggs lightly with
> chopsticks and give them form. In no time the eggs turn into a beautiful fluffy
> omelet. This gives me pleasure.[26]

Indeed, Mari is one of the few writers to have written about happiness rather than misery. This is despite the failure of two marriages and numerous financial and other difficulties. It is noteworthy too that, even though the above excerpts do not make it clear, Mori Mari demonstrates freedom and arrogance in her writing style, which can be simple, funny, and caustic, but also complex, mature, elaborate, and meditative. Although there is no overt reversal or criticism of gender constructions in Uno's or Mori Mari's recipes, their cheerfulness and individuality clearly stand outside the code for the *ryōsai kenbo* and the respectable daughter of the house, and this individuality has attracted a new generation of readers.

The Celebration of Food: *Kitchen* and *Salad Anniversary*

This literary celebration of food and cooking culminated in the two best-selling books of the late 1980s—Yoshimoto Banana's novel *Kitchin* (1988, trans. *Kitchen*, 1993) and Tawara Machi's collection of tanka titled *Sarada kinenbi* (1987, trans. *Salad Anniversary*, 1988). *Kitchen* has widely been recognized as representative of the *shōjo* culture, though its reception has varied from adoration to derision. *Sarada kinenbi*, on the other hand, retains some daughterly characteristics.

Yoshimoto's story begins with the line "The place I like best in the world is the kitchen."[27] Indeed the kitchen is the only place where the narrator-protagonist Mikage can sleep after the death of her grandmother, the only surviving member of her family. (An orphan protagonist is, needless to say, one of the most popular motifs in classical *shōjo shōsetsu* and *manga*.) It is also a kitchen that she "[falls] in love with [. . .] at first sight"[28] when she is invited to live with another family. None of her "dream kitchens"[29] oppress or repress her with reminders of the old *ie* system and its patriarch, or what Ueno Chizuko calls "the transvestite patriarch"—the mother acting as the substitute for the absent patriarch.[30] Mikage has a passion for food—food that is neither expensive nor rare, just simple ordinary vegetables and dishes like *katsudon*. She cooks not out of duty or obligation, but for her own pleasure and the pleasure of her surrogate family: Yūichi and his transsexual "mother" Eriko.

Traditional or stereotypical gender roles and images seem to be either reversed or denied in this story. Mikage learns to cook not from her mother but from books, television, and her professional Sensei (female), whose gentle demeanor presents a striking contrast to the rigor of the male chefs and connoisseurs discussed earlier. Yoshimoto does not treat Mikage's cooking as overtly gendered. Mikage distances herself from the "young ladies of good family" at the cooking school,[31] but there is neither antagonism nor pity on either side. Similarly, Yūichi is "neither cold nor oppressively kind" but a vulnerable young person with "natural" tenderness.[32] The idea of "manliness" is turned into a tension-relieving joke between Mikage and Yūichi.[33] Moreover, Eriko has managed to transform her(him)self, thanks to plastic and other forms of surgery, from Yūichi's biological father into his mother, and is stunningly beautiful. With amazement and some concern, Mikage observes Yūichi and Eriko going on shopping sprees, a pastime that is commonly associated with women.[34] The extent of Eriko's transformation is evident in his/her final notes before being murdered by a male admirer:

> Just this once I wanted to write using men's language, and I've really tried. But it's funny—I get embarrassed and the pen won't go. I guess I thought that even though I've lived all these years as a woman, somewhere inside me was my male self, that I've been playing a role all these years. But I find that I'm body and soul a woman. A mother in name and in fact. I have to laugh.[35]

It is misleading, though, to overemphasize the gender-bender aspect, or Orbaugh's second and third strategies, in the story. It is equally pointless to attack the novel as antifeminist on the grounds that it is always Mikage, the woman, who cooks and that it is men who eat her food. There is, however, something slightly disturbing here (although perhaps we are supposed to feel that "[we] have to laugh"). In his/her will Eriko expresses a strange resignation about his/her fate: "But I have cheerfully chosen to make my body my fortune. I am *beautiful*! I am *dazzling*! If people I don't care for are attracted to me, I accept it as the wages of beauty. So, if I should be killed, it will be an accident."[36]

When that "accident" does occur, Eriko, in self-defense, manages to beat the attacker to death, but this does not save his/her own life. What we have here is the familiar picture of a beautiful woman using her body for a living then resigning herself to death at the hands of a man, as "the wages of beauty," the only unusual element here being that the woman was once a man. Without her past as a man and without the artificial devices used to gain her beauty and femininity, such apparently passive acceptance of her fate by a woman would surely have been unacceptable to Yoshimoto's readership, which consists predominantly of women. Thus, while celebrating food that is shared by ultimately lonely individuals and encouraging the reader not to be afraid to be different or alone, the novel devolves into the old story of a slain beauty. It may be far-fetched to regard Eriko as a postmodern version of the "transvestite patriarch"; nevertheless, with all her cheerfulness, she, as the mother, does replace the absent father and ultimately sacrifice herself.

John Treat remarks that *Kitchen* "reeks with nostalgia for family and its old-fashioned comforts" and that "at the same time it is the material product of a postmodern Japanese consumerism that has generated aesthetics as well as profits."[37] Examining published reviews of the novel, Saitō Minako concludes that the key to the commercial success of *Kitchen* is, just as in the case of *Sarada kinenbi*, old wine (content) in a new bottle (style).[38] Kawasaki Kenko believes, however, that Yoshimoto's literature is far from simplistic, for it deals with the kind of anxiety that does not originate in the conventional *family*-based hetero-sexual desire.[39] Kawasaki also points out:

> The girl in the Banana world—even in *Kitchen*—would rather cook than eat; and rather than eat she will wash up, take the rubbish out, and clean the sink and the floor. She would also rather sleep than eat. If you ask her why, she would probably say it is because she is exhausted.[40]

Furthermore, the critic notes, almost poignantly, the way the body in the "Banana world" "equalizes sleeping and awaking," and the way "the body that moves back and forth between anorexia and bulimia, [gains] no comfort from eating or not eating."[41] I will return to the theme of tired, disturbing, and futile eating later in the chapter, but for the present it is important to note that the seemingly fresh and bright novel of Yoshimoto Banana incorporates some dark elements, which may not be noticed by every reader.

Tawara Machi's *Sarada kinenbi* also has food, loneliness, and love as its major elements. As in Yoshimoto's text, the language is colloquial and the food ordinary. In fact, the huge commercial success of this collection and its impact not only upon the tanka genre but even upon newspaper sports pages and the sales of *kanchūhai*[42] may be explained by the marked ordinariness and accessibility of its language and themes. In tanka this ordinariness and accessibility, this celebration of the quotidian, had hitherto been unthinkable:

> "*Kono aji ga ii ne*" *to kimi ga itta kara shichigatsu muika wa sarada kinenbi*
> ("This tastes good" you said and so/ the sixth of July—/ our salad anniversary)[43]

Salad—fresh, light, healthy, and nonthreatening[44]—is prepared by a young woman and admired by her boyfriend. Again, the woman cooks and the man eats, which may remind some older readers of the television commercial for instant noodles from the 1970s in which a young woman says, "I cook," and a young man, "I eat."[45] In Tawara's tanka the woman is eager to know what sort of food the man likes and to cook it for him,[46] while the man's expression of loe takes the imperative form (*meireikei*) of verbs (e.g., "do this" and "do that").[47] Traditional gender roles seem to be reaffirmed in lines such as

> *Gogo yoji ni yaoya no mae de kondate o kangaete iru yō na shiawase*
> (Happiness of standing before a grocer's/ at four in the afternoon/ planning the supper menu)[48]

Unlike those hungry women in earlier periods, there is no resentment here about cooking. The waiting woman is another recurring motif in the collection, a different kind of hunger being referred to:

> *Kimi o matsu doyōbi nari ki matsu to iu jikan o tabete onna wa ikiru*
> (Another Saturday of waiting for you/ Time spent waiting—/ food a woman
>   lives on)[49]
> *Tamanegi o itamete matō kimi kara no denwa hodo yoku amami deru made*
> (I'll wait for your telephone call,/ frying some onion/ till it gets nice and
>   sweet)[50]

This is by no means a helpless woman waiting for a Prince Charming; she has her own space as well as a job as a schoolteacher and a loving family in her hometown. She is possessed of wit, social respectability, and sociability, none of which directly challenges or confronts the social norm. At the same time, however, there are poems such as the following that are contrary to the image of a meek, pretty young woman:

> *Hanbāgā shoppu no seki o tachiagaru yō ni otoko o sutete shimaō*
> (Like getting up to leave a hamburger place—/ that's how I'll leave/ that man)[51]

She may appear to be listening to what the man says, be it a tipsy marriage proposal[52] or a piece of advice to "be an ordinary woman,"[53] but she may also be laughing at or at least questioning the validity of his opinions, if not directly to him, then certainly in the tanka itself. The writing, in this way, reverses or modifies the power relationship between the lovers. The salad anniversary may be celebrated each year, but not necessarily with the man, as the final tanka in the collection suggests:

> *Aisareta kioku wa doko ka tōmei de itsu demo hitori itsu datte hitori*
> (Memories of being loved,/ somehow transparent—/ always alone, forever
>   alone)[54]

Parodying Food and Eating in Men's Texts

One of the most prominent strategies in women's fiction in the last part of the twentieth century has been the use of parody. Parody, of course, is limited neither to feminist writing nor to postmodern writing. We have already seen some examples, including the extraordinary "textual cannibalism" of *Yapoo* in chapter 4 and the playful gastronomic parodies in chapter 5. Various theorists have defined parody[55] as a combination of imitation (similarity) and transformation (difference), often accompanied and enhanced by humor, irony, and criticism. The texts discussed previously all evidence these qualities. The parodic texts selected for the discussion to follow, however, differ from these earlier texts in that they lay bare the hidden gender issues in the works that they parody.[56]

As we saw in chapter 2, Shiga Naoya's "Kozō no kamisama" depicts food that is only permitted to certain classes—represented by the upper-class A—and denied to others such as Senkichi, the errand boy. While the class division here is obvious, no attention was paid to the subtle indication of gender division in the story until Ogino Anna (b. 1956) referred to it in her parody of canonical modern fiction *Watashi no aidokusho* (My Love-Hate Affair with Books, 1991).[57] The protagonist A's wife, who appears only twice in Shiga's original story, expresses on both occasions a wish to have some sushi home-delivered. Her husband, though loving and considerate, is apparently too absorbed in his own thoughts to take any notice of this repeated request. Upper-class men may try lower-class food on a street corner; their wives may not try it, even in the safe and clean environment of their own home. Thus, A's wife is, as Ogino calls her, a *kakure kozō* (closet errand boy).[58]

"Kozō no kamisama" does not consciously address the gender issue, and A's wife plays only a minor role in Shiga's story. Only an observant reader such as Ogino could have uncovered the representation of this less obvious inequity underneath the social inequality with which the original novel is more concerned. That Ogino chose parody instead of the conventional critical essay to expose the earlier novel's underbelly is worth noting. Parody, like food, became extremely popular in Japan (and in many other countries) in the final part of the twentieth century. Ogino and many other women writers use it, often in combination with food themes, as a means of revealing neglected issues and hidden social and sexual discrimination.

Ogino's love-hate reading does not miss the discrimination permeating Kawabata Yasunari's *Izu no odoriko* (1926, trans. *The Izu Dancer*, 1963).[59] Like Shiga's story, it involves the encounter of a privileged male with marginalized people. The novel has been widely described as a pure and beautiful love story between a student and a young itinerant dancer. Food is not as important here as in "Kozō no kamisama." When it appears, however, it always plays a specific role. There are several scenes in which the middle-class male protagonist accepts food or drink humbly offered by lower-class people. Most of these scenes mark class or gender divisions and are expressive of the student's longing to break the shell of his solitude. Traveling entertainers are regarded as outcasts and denied entry to some villages. Women are ranked lowest in the troupe; hence the older woman (the mother-in-law of the eponymous dancer's brother) apologizes twice to the student that he has to share food and drink with "unclean" women. To the modern reader the mother-in-law's words may seem merely a formality, but in the context of the novel that formality is absolutely necessary to these doubly marginalized women in all their relations with the society that rejects them.

The narrator-protagonist of Ogino's parody "Yukiguni no odoriko" (The Dancer in Snow Country) is the Izu dancer several decades later. Looking back on her past, she shares this insight with a fellow passenger on a train to the snow country: "Come to think of it, I was in a really disadvantaged position. An illiterate traveling entertainer, and female. Well, I can tell you how miserable it was in those days to be a woman."[60]

Needless to say, the position of women in the early 1990s, when Ogino was writing her parody, was considerably different from their situation in the 1920s. By foregrounding the class and gender divisions implied in these earlier texts, Ogino shows how gender permeates even the least likely narratives. Ogino also shows that the gender discrimination these narratives take for granted is by no means irrelevant to contemporary gender relations. To make this point she often introduces some contemporary elements into her parody (in "The Dancer in Snow Country" the narrator transforms herself briefly into a contemporary Filipino entertainer). Furthermore, Ogino includes in her text a critique of conventional readings (by male critics) of these canonical works. For instance, quoting some lines from Mishima's commentary on *The Izu Dancer*, Ogino's old (or mysteriously ageless) dancer-narrator suspects that "maybe men of letters just can't handle real women."[61] The pomposity, even stupidity, of Mishima's comments become clear when they are removed from their original safe and conservative context. In Ogino's parody Mishima's commentary on a major literary work in a mainstream publisher's paperback is placed beside an apparently uneducated and unprivileged woman's comments on his views. Through the voice of the female outcast, Ogino thus deconstructs the mythology and the aura surrounding canonical texts and their male authors and critics.

Ogino often combines this kind of subversive intertextual strategy with food and eating motifs—both as metaphor and as theme. In fact she is one of the most publicly "food-conscious" of contemporary writers. Food, dieting,[62] pica,[63] binge eating,[64] food as an object of fear, food as an object of disgust, and even—curiously—food as an antidote to intellectual pretentiousness all feature prominently in her writing. This last use of food deserves more elaboration. "Kobayashi Hideo (de gozaimasu)" ([I Am] Kobayashi Hideo) is, like the pieces on Shiga and Kawabata, a short story that uses parody, pastiche, and travesty for comic and critical purposes. As the title shows, the subject of this piece is Kobayashi Hideo (1902–1983), one of the most revered literary critics of the Shōwa era, who authored works such as "Mōtsaruto" (Mozart, 1946) and "Mujō to iu koto" (The Fact of Evanescence, 1946). In Ogino's parody the title, including the parenthesized part, is supposed to be the name of the author of a critical essay entitled "Minami Haruo to iu koto" (The Fact of Minami Haruo). Minami Haruo is a popular *enka* singer, who always announces his appearance on stage with the humble *de gozaimasu*. Whereas the real Kobayashi Hideo without "(de gozaimasu)" was absorbed in Mozart's music, KH (de gozaimasu) is captivated by the music of Minami Haruo ("low" culture). Kobayashi's "Mozart" includes the following passage:

> I have forgotten what I was thinking about at the time. Probably I was wandering around aimlessly as a dog, my head filled with useless words, the meaning of which I myself did not know—life, literature, despair, isolation, and the like. . . . As I walked through the crowded street, I could distinctly hear in the absolute silence of my head somebody playing the music.[65]

The music referred to here is the theme of the first movement of Mozart's Symphony No. 40. In KH (de gozaimasu)'s essay the music is Minami Haruo's "Chanchiki Okesa" and the same passage becomes

> I have forgotten what I was thinking about at the time. Probably I was wandering around aimlessly as a dog, my head filled with high-calorie words, which my stomach did not know how to handle—*tetchiri, dote-yaki, tako-yaki, okonomi-yaki*, and the like.[66]

Thus Ogino replaces the abstract nouns in Kobayashi's text with food. This particular parody does not overtly deal with gender as such. However, when the reader juxtaposes it with Kobayashi's essay "Women Writers,"[67] for instance, the underlying critical intent becomes clear. This is a woman writer subverting a canonical male writer. A similar, and yet much simpler, example of food as anti-dote to pretentious language is found in another work, in which Ogino mocks a male academic's essay on Sakaguchi Ango by changing the critic's favorite term *sai* (difference), an extremely fashionable term in critical discourse in the 1980s, to plain old "banana" (no reference to Yoshimoto).

> "What shall we call this? A bananified banana? Or perhaps a pure and refined banana. In other words, it is an excessive banana space where nothing moves and yet winds are roaring."
>
> Well, it seems much more difficult than you would think for a human being to speak in his or her own words.[68]

Ogino is not an outsider; she is an academic and critic herself as well as a novelist. Yet in all of the genres she works in she clearly indicates her critical position vis-à-vis dominant (male) discourse. The criticism can be caustic, but it can also be hilariously nonsensical or farcical. While she makes light of the self-importance and seriousness of some writers and critics, she does recognize some good qualities in them. Even in praising them, however, she refuses to use the sort of language used in conventional (and purportedly postmodern) criti-cal discourse. The thematic dominance of food in Ogino's writing can also be seen as an attempt to reconcile the tradition of male writing, which she regards as "a self-*ex*pression that involves the self *ex*tending, *ex*truding, *ex*panding into the outside"[69]—as represented by Rabelais (the subject of her doctoral thesis)— with the inward-directedness of contemporary women's writing, which I shall discuss in more detail below.

Gustatory Fear and Disgust

Another prominent element in contemporary women's texts is fear of food and eating. Here, food is regarded as something superfluous, addictive, deeply dis-turbing, even toxic, rather than as something pleasurable and nutritious. This fear of food acts as a warning against complacency in reading the "gourmet boom" as an uncomplicated outcome of increased prosperity and ignoring its implications in terms of the market economy, environmental destruction, disin-tegration of the family, and gender bias. Despite the apparent distance between fear/disgust and jubilation/celebration, the former, as some of the texts we have discussed illustrate, is often a gradual or sudden transformation of the latter. In Yoshimoto's text, for example, a seemingly light and cheerful style and mood can conceal something inherently disturbing. This relates to the third issue on Lupton's list—the link between the construction of femininity and the dietary practices of women. Also notable is the strong connection between this fear and the critical reading of texts produced by men. Just as eating can distort or destroy the body, the discourse of food can, according to these critical texts, be manipulative and unreliable. The discourse deconstructed ranges from media reports and restaurant guides to canonical literary texts involving eating, all essentially produced by men. The following comments by Ogino explain the gender implications of such fear and disgust for food and eating:

> As opposed to the gustatory gusto of the male writers, the women writers are depicting gustatory disgust, or gastronomic unhappiness—the unhappiness, we might say, of alienated people who are using the act of eating as their final avenue of self-expression. In contrast to the active, male subject/consumer who eats up the world, we have the female subject, who has lost her sense of self, being eaten or consumed by the world as she becomes at once both subject and object, and the relationship between subject and object dissolves.[70]

Fear and disgust about eating, of course, are neither new nor limited to women. In Akutagawa Ryūnosuke's "Imogayu" (Yam Gruel, 1916), for example, the protagonist feels not satiation but total disillusionment when he is offered his eponymous dream food. As mentioned in chapter 5, Okamoto Kanoko's short story "Sushi" (1939) depicts a young boy's fear of food:

> Indeed the child found meals painful. He felt that digesting a solid lump of matter that had color, smell, and taste would make his body impure. He wondered if there was some food like the air. He did feel hungry when his stomach was empty but this did not make him feel like eating just any food.[71]

"Gustatory disgust" is evident in the bulimic antihero of Yasuoka Shōtarō's *Tonsō* (discussed in chapter 3) and in the Dazai Osamu texts discussed below.

Fear and disgust may also be connected to issues of food safety and environmental concerns, as we saw in Ariyoshi Sawako's *Fukugō osen* (chapter 3. Shortly after Ariyoshi published her novel, Kaikō Takeshi began to write a series of essays under the title *Saigo no bansan* (The Last Supper, serialized in *Shokun!* January 1977–January 1979). He explains that the title comes partly from "vague, everyday fears" about predictions of large-scale earthquakes, overpopulation, food crises, industrial pollution, environmental degradation, and abnormal weather.[72] Unlike Ariyoshi's text, however, *Saigo no bansan* treats these

more or less as assumed background rather than as issues that need our urgent
action and attention. He focuses instead, at least in the first half of the book,
on two concerns. The first is that food and drink and the discourse on them
have been a last resort for people resisting oppression, as exemplified in texts by
Lu Xun, Lao She, Solzhenitsyn, and Yasuoka Shōtarō. All of the writers he cites
are men—as if women had never written about resistance through food.[73] The
second but equally important issue treated in the book is, as I have already mentioned a few times, how food, unlike drink, has been neglected in mainstream
Japanese literature. Kaikō cites some exceptional texts by Tanizaki, Satō Haruo,
and Takamura Kōtarō, again without mentioning any of the women writers who
have written about food, such as Okamoto Kanoko and Hayashi Fumiko. The
second half of Kaikō's book seems to be more concerned with simply describing ultimate experiences of gourmet cooking and eating. It is only towards the
end of the novel, after he has described many extraordinary banquets (in which
women, including Kaikō's wife, none other than Maki Yōko, do appear and eat,
though merely as accompanying guests), that the author's fear in relation to
food becomes apparent. The real ambivalence of *Saigo no bansan* emerges when
the reader learns that the narrator is suffering from some serious but undefined
gastric problem.

> There's no pain. Nothing is swollen or stiff. And yet there is always this feeling
> that something is squatting there. [. . .] I cannot help feeling that the inevitable
> is on its way. Besides, with no gallbladder, all my drinking and eating needs to
> be for quality rather than for quantity. Gone are the days of Balzac. The age of
> expansion, in wealth and arms, ended three years ago.[74]

We have already seen a similar passage in Dan Kazuo's *Kataku no hito* (chapter 5). We may also recall the pains and even life-threatening dangers associated
with eating depicted in Masaoka Shiki's diary and Tanizaki's fiction. Like his
predecessors, Kaikō pursues "absolute" values, which Maki Yōko considers to
be the aim of male cooking. At the center of this literary and culinary pursuit is
the male subject, who eats, cooks, travels, reads, and writes until he dies.

The Women's Gourmet Club

Hayashi Mariko's short story "Bishoku kurabu" (The Gourmet Club, 1986) tells
us how impossible it is for women to pursue absolute values. The title is borrowed from Tanizaki's 1919 story, examined in chapter 5. In Hayashi's version

the club members are all women with higher than average disposable incomes. Their gastronomic obsession seems just as powerful as that of the men in Tanizaki's story. The conventional gender roles may seem to have been reversed, but this is hardly a triumphant story. One of the club members, the director of a modeling agency, takes a young man out to expensive restaurants. It is she who pays for the blowfish, foie gras, and caviar, and she who teaches him to be a gourmet. Eating is, as in Tanizaki's and Murakami Ryū's stories and in Itami Jūzō's film *Tanpopo*, closely connected to eroticism and sexuality; but in contrast to these male narratives, Hayashi's text presents gastronomic bliss as being in direct conflict with sexual pleasure. When the protagonist discovers that her weight has reached sixty kilos, she is too shocked to have sex with her boyfriend. When, after a failed attempt to diet, her weight exceeds sixty-five kilos, she decides to leave him for good. While the men in Tanizaki's story would pursue their gastronomic pleasure to the extremity of insanity or death,[75] the women in Hayashi's story tell each other that "here and now is paradise as long as one does not want too much."[76] In Tanizaki's story, and in his writing generally, fear enhances desire. In contrast, in Hayashi's almost antigastronomic story the futility of eating overrides the happiness it brings.

The author of this short story, Hayashi, became a media celebrity in the early 1980s for her work as a copywriter and essayist. Her essays dealt with her own ambition and her desire for sex, fame, and wealth, all of which, Saitō Minako points out, have long been regarded as masculine desires permissible only in men.[77] Hayashi's desire extended to gourmet food, it being at once a symbol of fame and wealth and of literacy in media and fashion. Her image as an outspoken and successful woman, however, has made Hayashi the target of jealousy and antagonism—something none of Japan's male celebrity gourmands such as Tanizaki, Kaikō, Dan, and Itami has had to suffer. The media antagonism towards her, dubbed "Mariko bashing" at the time, often manifested itself in derogatory remarks about her personal life and her character. Of particular interest were her sexual history and her physical attributes, public criticism about which was enthusiastic "almost to the extent of libel and sexual harassment."[78] This, Saitō believes, "proves how many people sensed [in Hayashi] a threat against male-dominated society."[79] Furthermore, Saitō observes that even though there is a clear dissimilarity between Hayashi and women who are activists for feminism, the media have been equally hostile to both. What feminist activists and Hayashi share, according to their critics, is their abnormality when it comes to sexual desire. Hayashi has successfully overcome this bashing by changing genres and themes: instead of continuing to write novels and stories about young women with various desires and appetites, Hayashi started to write biographies and historical novels in the 1990s, and this won her literary respectability and awards. This new respectability, however, seems to have been accompanied by an increasingly conservative and misogynistic tone in her writing.[80]

Hayashi's "Bishoku kurabu" may seem at least superficially to "maintain the current binary configurations of power, but to *reverse the gender coding* of the hierarchical power roles," thereby applying a strategy identified by Orbaugh (cited in chapter 3). However, the reversal does not work; it does not bring happiness to the women in the narrative, and hence what it ultimately does is only "to maintain and *describe* the current configurations of power, exposing the harm done through them."

Megalo-Eating Heroines

With a few exceptions,[81] recent texts dealing with eating disorders have all been written by women. Moreover, these texts include an awareness on the part of women of the external manipulation associated with eating, which indicates the shift towards the third focus mentioned by Lupton—the links between the construction of femininity and dietary practices. There are many such texts, ranging from polemical essays such as Nakajima Azusa's "Daietto shōkōgun" (The Diet Syndrome, 1991) to girls' comics like Ōshima Yumiko's "Daietto" (Diet, 1989). For the purposes of this discussion I have chosen two novels that are, like *Kitchen* and *Sarada kinenbi*, rather like twin sisters.

Matsumoto Yūko's *Kyoshokushō no akenai yoake* (The Dawn That Hasn't Seen the End of Megalo-Eating,[82] 1988) and Ogawa Yōko's *Shugā taimu* (Sugar Time, 1991) are both by young women (Matsumoto, b. 1963; Ogawa, b. 1962), and are both first-person narratives of young female university students with bulimia. The two heroines have problematic relationships with their boyfriends. In Matsumoto's text Tokiko, her boyfriend, and her new lover all have other ties. In Ogawa's text Kaoru and her boyfriend often sleep together but never have sex. He eventually leaves Kaoru for a much older woman whom he met through a counselor he visited with Kaoru to discuss their relationship. Tokiko, too, visits a counselor about her eating disorder. As well, each of the heroines has a close girlfriend who is willing to listen to her.

As mentioned earlier, none of the girl protagonists of *Shōjo no utsuwa*, *Indian Summer*, and *Kitchen* lives with a stereotypical middle-class family. The same applies to Tokiko and Kaoru. We are told (though this narrative of Tokiko's turns out later in the novel to be unreliable) that when Tokiko was a baby, her mother left her and her alcoholic father. Kaoru's mother died when Kaoru was very young, and her brother—or strictly speaking, her stepmother's son—suffers from a disease that stunts his growth. Her father hardly appears in the text. Kaoru identifies two incidents that may have triggered her overeating: one is eating leftover wedding desserts at the hotel where she works part-time, and the other is her brother's moving out of their apartment into a kind of neoshintoist church run by their landlord. Although in Okamoto Kanoko's "Sushi" the boy's mother successfully cures his anorexia, no one in Tokiko's or Kaoru's family can offer a solution to their bulimia. In Ōshima Yumiko's *manga*, too, the family of the protagonist is depicted as one of the causes, if an indirect one, of the girl's eating disorder, rather than as the potential source of a cure. There is no hint of nostalgia for traditional family values in these stories. On the contrary, everything seems to indicate a rejection of such values.[83]

Both *Kyoshokushō no akenai yoake* and *Sugar Time* contain scenes depicting food shopping that resemble, but aren't, acts of celebration. Tokiko goes to the food department of a department store, and Kaoru goes to a supermarket called Sunshine Market. Tokiko calls the department store a paradise, "an edible art gallery."[84] The Western cake section is likened to a jewelry exhibition, while Japanese sweets are compared to woodblock prints. Lunch boxes are miniature gardens, and sushi is colorful *nishikie* prints. European dishes are watercolors, and Chinese dishes are medieval paintings. Fresh vegetables are pop art, and fish are etchings. Kaoru admires the sophisticated beauty of the Sunshine Market: in its well-designed, orderly, and quiet space she can appreciate numerous kinds of food. It also gives her the security and privacy she seeks to read her boyfriend's letter of farewell. This is public and yet private: Kaoru can read her letter without being bothered by anyone.

There is no doubt that these women are situated in the midst of a world driven by consumer capitalism. While appreciating what this world can offer, neither protagonist is content. Tokiko, for instance, reflects:

> I know nothing of starvation, and to me food is an ornament, a toy, and of course a commodity, but it is also entertainment, fashion, a hobby or study, a favorite theme in television and books; it is necessary but at the same time unnecessary.
>
> [...]
>
> We have had this "gourmet boom" for quite some time. But our interest is not in food safety or food itself but in its added values such as sophistication, coordination, and presentation.

I studied the theory of proper eating and nutrition at school and memo-
rized the textbook so thoroughly that I can still remember all of the photographs in it. And yet I do not know how to put that theory into practice.[85]

Food and eating are, in this consumer-driven world, very far removed
from the kinds of down-to-earth ideas discussed earlier. The last part of the
quotation presents a striking contrast to the cooking lessons that Kōda Aya
and her protagonists experienced,[86] or to the happy training sessions that
absorbed *Kitchen*'s Mikage. Like food, knowledge and information appear
to be readily available to Tokiko and Kaoru; neither, however, finds them
convincing or adequate. They are aware that specialist knowledge and its
mediatization may do more harm than good. While Ariyoshi's criticism in
Compound Pollution was focused on the inaccessibility and incomprehensi-
bility of information, Matsumoto and Ogawa reveal the bias and limitations
of male-centered knowledge. Tokiko finds her psychiatrist Sasaki irritating
because he judges people in his own terms: "I was totally amazed. When I'm
with Sasaki, my overeating becomes an act of desperation caused by being
rejected by a lover. His one-sided, leading questions reduce it to this simple
problem."[87]

Moreover, a mumbled comment from Sasaki about another of his bulimia
patients gives Tokiko the idea to try vomiting after eating, something that it has
never occurred to her to try before. Reading Freud, which the psychiatrist has
recommended she should, does not help Tokiko but only accelerates her binge
eating. She rejects accepted medical terms such as anorexia nervosa and bulimia
and instead coins the term *kyoshokushō*—a pun on anorexia (*kyoshokushō*) but
using the character for "gigantic" rather than that for "refusal" for *kyo*. She wonders if the feeling of emptiness in her stomach is connected to her empty vagina,
an organ not shown in—literally absented from—the human anatomy pages of
the encyclopedia she consulted as a child. On the other hand, when it comes to
an adjacent organ, she and her feminist friend are cautious about the popular
discourse of woman as womb:

> "But what's the womb feeling? It's far too simplistic to explain everything like
> female physical senses and voices with this word 'womb.' Besides, I never think
> of how my womb feels. If anything, I think I'm more aware of how my liver
> feels."[88]

Just as Tokiko used to consult the encyclopedia, Kaoru has "always liked to
read *Home Doctor*, ever since her childhood."[89] When she tries to find informa-

tion about bulimia in the same book, however, there is hardly anything there. It is not even listed in the index. The entry on abnormal appetite places much more importance on anorexia nervosa than on overeating. The questioning of knowledge and authority by these protagonists extends to literary texts and education. Tokiko feels a kind of sentimental self-pity when she reads a passage from Dazai Osamu's *Ningen shikkaku* (1948, trans. *No Longer Human*, 1957) in which the protagonist claims that he has never felt or understood hunger. She parodies the famous line from the novel to express her own feeling: "never in my life have I felt full."[90] Indeed, it seems possible to interpret Matsumoto's text as a critique of the stories we often find in modern Japanese literature, of anorexic male protagonists who are usually addicted to alcohol, drugs, or both. Tokiko's father, alcoholic and absent, reminds us of the drunken fathers in many of the stories of Dazai and his fellow writers.

In *Sugar Time* the questioning of canonical literature is less obvious than it is in Matsumoto's text. Kaoru and her girlfriend study *The Charterhouse of Parma* for a French examination. The canonical literary text is no longer read as "food for thought"; the two students highlight certain lines in the French text and memorize (or swallow, if you like) their Japanese translation in order to do well on the examination. Just as the studies of food and diet have no direct impact upon Tokiko's life, literature, which was once supposed "to delight and instruct us, [...] and above all, to save our souls and heal the State,"[91] has become mere examination fodder.[92]

In her essay on what she terms "the diet syndrome" Nakajima Azusa emphasizes that the pressure of competition is much greater for girls than for boys:

> [F]or girls, selection had started long before competitiveness came to dominate society; women had always been selected, as long as they existed as women, throughout history. For girls, the emergence of a highly competitive society meant additional competition with boys. But long before this, girls had been forced to accept that they would be subject to selection regardless of whether they resisted or complied.[93]

Naomi Wolf, too, writes in *The Beauty Myth*: "Young women have been doubly weakened: Raised to compete like men in rigid male-model institutions, they must also maintain to the last detail an impeccable femininity."[94]

These comments, however, do not seem to be immediately applicable to Tokiko or Kaoru; both are so used to competition that they do not appear to be stressed by it. Tokiko, who is writing an essay assignment on starvation in the Third World, tells her girlfriend:

"We always knew very well that school study had no direct relevance to our life. Still, we have been doing it since primary school. Studying for the university entrance exam, especially, was nothing but a game of getting better marks, though I actually found it kind of fun."[95]

The irony of writing an essay on starvation while suffering from an overeating disorder redoubles the doubt expressed here about the validity of education and writing. Nevertheless, both women write. Kaoru keeps a food diary, in which she lists all of the food she consumes. This diary is completely different from any of the diaries we saw in chapter 1. Hunger and appetite in these earlier texts signify the strength of the desire for life. Kaoru's, however, is a "strange diary," as she herself remarks:[96] in it she records everything she has eaten, and by reading it she retastes the food it lists. Here the actual eating produces writing, which then functions like food when the writer-eater reads it. As Ogino Anna argues,[97] this whole process is an inward-looking act.

While the "megalo-eating" Tokiko goes from forty-seven kilos to sixty-five kilos, Kaoru in *Sugar Time* does not gain any weight despite her eating habit, and at the end of the story she shreds her food diary and burns all the food in the house to mark the end of her "sugar time." It is a quasi-religious ceremony, which accords with Kim Chernin's interpretation of bulimia as a religious rite of passage.[98] The shredded diary becomes confetti that is used to celebrate the victory of her university team in a baseball game. Tokiko's writing, too, goes through a dramatic change in the final chapter of Matsumoto's novel. Abandoning the first-person narrative, this chapter is narrated in the third person.[99] The third-person narrator reveals that all of the previous chapters are fiction and not a real diary. Tokiko's mother, who we have been misled into believing deserted Tokiko as a baby, reads the manuscript, believing that it is a diary. Consequently Tokiko violently attacks her mother, who avoids further confrontation by leaving the house.[100] Abandoning her unfinished novel, Tokiko heads for the local convenience store to get some more food.

Thus, whether within the context of a bittersweet story of passing adolescence or a story of mother-daughter conflict, each heroine ultimately abandons her writing. Their writing does not give them *jouissance*. One seems to have given up her bulimic eating, while the other concludes that there is no end to her fiction or to her eating. One finds allies in her girlfriend and stepbrother, while the other drives herself into total isolation, with food her only companion.

Towards Subversive Jubilation

Somewhere on the continuum between happy eating or cooking stories and un-
happy ones there exists a third possibility, which not only incorporates the two
opposite extremes of eating but presents an alternative that is at once subversive
and jubilant. To illustrate this, let us return to Kanai Mieko's *Indian Summer*,
which was introduced earlier in this chapter. Published shortly after Yoshimoto's
Kitchen,[101] Kanai's text seems intended to make fun of both the light and fresh
touch that Yoshimoto champions and its obvious naivety. Momoko, the narrator-protagonist of Kanai's novel is, like *Kitchen*'s Mikage, a young university
student. In fact, the two women belong to exactly the same generation, although
their style and their linguistic and aesthetic sensitivities diverge radically. Momoko, for instance, has reservations about what exactly the word "kitchin" refers to: "Some people use the word *kitchin* instead of *daidokoro* or *okatte*, but—
unless it's as part of words such as *shisutemu kitchin*—I don't fancy calling an
ordinary kitchen anything other than *daidokoro*."[102]

The above remark is made in Momoko's narrative about preparing a ham
and cucumber sandwich for herself after having a bath to cure a hangover. This
takes place in the kitchen of her aunt's flat, where she lives. This *daidokoro* is
different from that in Momoko's mother's house, where, as we will see, Momoko often experiences minor conflicts with her mother. In the aunt's kitchen,
however, there is no such friction. The kind of fierce battles between father and
daughter or husband and wife depicted by Kōda Aya[103] are unimaginable here.
In Momoko's world the aunt's kitchen is not a shelter from the hostile world,
for there is no apparent hostility there anyway. Neither is she confined to the
kitchen; she is free to go in and out of that space, and other people may come in
to cook with her or for her.

As is noted in the earlier synopsis of *Indian Summer*, Momoko rejects the
kinds of cooking and eating represented by her parents, who are both in the
hotel business. The mother's cooking is traditional Japanese style, with fresh
local ingredients and the "motherly" touch as its main selling points. Even for
a private breakfast for herself, her sister, and her daughter, she cannot help producing exactly what she would offer the guests at her inn for dinner. There are
eleven items in all, including grilled beef marinated in miso with peppers,
mushrooms, and sliced onions; scallops; sea urchin; and grated yam with egg,
the entire menu forming part of Momoko's narrative of the meal. As Yoshikawa Yasuhisa notes in his detailed thematic study of Kanai's work, menus and
shopping lists appear frequently in her fiction.[104] Though superficially they describe food as physical objects, these lists always imply or lead to some kind

of questioning or criticism of certain assumptions and actions associated with the items on them. In the above case, for instance, all of the elaboration and quantifying made apparent by the menu is in preparation for the supposedly physically demanding work associated with Momoko's move into her aunt's flat. Such a full and rich breakfast might have appealed to Masaoka Shiki, but neither Momoko nor her aunt finds it appetizing. It is evident that the text contains criticism of the age of consumption and satiation to which the hospitality industry ostensibly contributes. It is not that Kanai is committed to the improvement of the actual world. What she is doing is questioning the heretofore unquestioned, retrieving fiction and writing from the confines of uninflected representation without completely rejecting the representational aspect of literature and language. Or to quote Yoshikawa, "[W]hile generously incorporating food and eating into her fiction, Kanai Mieko juxtaposes surfeit next to appetite."[105] And as the agent of this juxtaposition in Kanai's texts, we often see the figure of a *shōjo*.

Momoko's mother conforms to a type that Ueno has called the "transvestite patriarch," mentioned above in our discussion of *Kitchen*. Although she works full time at her inn and is therefore not always with her children, she is obviously trying hard to maintain the traditional gender roles in her family despite the absence of her husband. Momoko firmly rejects the quasi-patriarchal values her mother tries to impose on the family. The daughter remembers with great bitterness a time when she was still studying at home for her university entrance exam. She was making a tasty sandwich for herself—with a *menchi katsu* (deep-fried ground meat in bread crumbs), shredded cabbage, and some pickled cucumber. Her younger brother came home and wanted the same, but Momoko told him to make it himself. Their mother, who had just popped in during a break in her work at the inn, remonstrated with her daughter about her meanness and pushed the tray containing the sandwich, complete with a cup of tea, towards her son. Momoko would not give in. She retrieved the tray, and to a further scolding from her mother made the following retort:

> "You *are* joking, aren't you?" I said. "Maybe you haven't noticed but he's not a baby. He has no difficulty masturbating so I'm sure he can deep fry a hamburger patty by himself! I don't see any need to run after him."[106]

Unlike the *katsudon* episode in *Kitchen*, the *menchi katsu* scene in Kanai's novel points to lingering gender expectations and the protagonist's resistance to them. Momoko's refusal to concede to her mother reminds us of Luce Giard's rejection of "this women's work" called cooking, referred to earlier, because it was never forced on her brother. Momoko rejects not the cooking itself but the gender-based discrimination associated with cooking and eating.

Momoko's father's food, in stark contrast to that of her mother, is urbane, trendy nouvelle cuisine. As the manager of a hotel in Tokyo, he has the knowledge (or rather the information), contacts, and money to take Momoko to the best restaurants and offer her not only the best food but also the benefit of his knowledge about it. Momoko does not refuse the food (and other expensive gifts), but she sees her father's efforts to keep up with the latest and the best merely as snobbish affectation. After one of their shopping excursions in Ginza she comments:

> He was stupid enough to be acting like the father in *Bonjour tristesse*. In other words, he was being insufferably pretentious. There's a father like that in *The Goddess*, a popular novel by Mishima Yukio. I remember reading it when I was a child. [. . .] This father was thrilled when he trained the daughter he adored to choose a cocktail to match the color of her outfit. Later that night, when we were back home in Mejiro, my aunt and I had a good laugh at all three—my father, the father in the novel, and any man who could write such melodramatic nonsense.[107]

Momoko's father, tall, well groomed, generous, and absent, is given only a comic role in the novel. His homosexuality, too, is given an almost farcical twist, which marks a change from male homosexuality as the romantic and aesthetic trope seen in some of Mori Mari's stories and in typical *shōjo manga*. In the first half of the novel Momoko is unaware of her father's sexuality. It comes as a shock to find that the person he is living with is not a woman but a man. After her initial shock, however, she becomes sympathetic to her father's partner, a middle-aged flower artist "with a face like an earthenware pot,"[108] when it becomes apparent he is being betrayed by her father and his young boyfriend.

If Momoko's mother is repressive and her father shallow and unreliable, her best friend Hanako's heterosexual father is even worse; he is notorious for using his position as editor of a magazine to harass women. Not as objectionable as Hanako's father, but pathetic in his own way, is Momoko's admirer. This young man, heir to a successful family seafood-processing business in Momoko's hometown, has the wherewithal to take her out and wine and dine her in expensive, trendy places in Roppongi. He has carefully drawn up a future plan for himself and Momoko—to build a "new-age enterprise for food production, distribution, and service industries by directly connecting [his father's] seafood-processing business and restaurants with [Momoko's mother's] hotel."[109] Momoko responds to this with a clear "No," accompanied by an audible burp, which is the result of the *menchi katsu* she ate earlier. Behind the young man's back she calls him a most unromantic nickname, *kani kamaboko* (seafood sticks), for she finds him as phony and pathetic as the fake crab sticks that his father's company produces. She has no illusions about food, marriage, or any other enticements he or any other eligible young man can offer, and consequently, she never surrenders her subjectivity, unlike the women in Murakami Ryū's gourmet stories.

Sexuality, whether hetero or homo, is not the source of *jouissance* or longing in this novel. The characters' truly blissful moments seem to come from their "freedom and arrogance" and from friendship (rather than sex or romance), for the opportunities it affords to share this sense of freedom and pride. There are numerous scenes in which the protagonists enjoy food, drink, and conversation in this novel and in many other novels by Kanai. As in some of the gastronomic novels we saw in chapter 5, the play element of *Homo ludens* permeates Kanai's texts and their eating scenes. These scenes are characterized by play's superfluity and leisureliness, its lack of material interest, its temporal and spatial boundaries, and its promotion of the formation of social groupings. While there is no secrecy or competition attached to this kind of play, the emphasis on its distinctiveness from the common world (represented by Momoko's parents, her would-be boyfriend, and Hanako's father) is obvious. Interestingly, the play element in this novel is markedly different from that in the earlier gastronomic novels discussed because, within it, the subjectivity of the women characters remains central.

The regular members of the convivial, playful gatherings are Momoko, her aunt, and Hanako. They are all single, intelligent, and highly critical of the philistines with whom they are surrounded and of their conventions. Hanako has chosen her name herself, in preference to her real given name, Arisa, which her sexist father chose for her from Gide's *La porte étroite*. Her refusal to conform is obvious from her appearance and language: she looks like a schoolboy (with extremely short hair) and behaves like one, usually referring to herself by the plain male first pronoun—not even the cute and young *boku* but the rough and tough *ore*. Momoko's aunt refuses to cooperate with her innkeeper sister, who obviously wants her to guide and oversee Momoko—in other words, to meddle in her business. While enjoying each other's company, Momoko, her aunt, and Hanako maintain a respect for one another's privacy.

Added occasionally to this trio are Momoko's father's partner, who speaks quaint feminine language, and the aunt's old male friends, one of whom, a middle-aged tax accountant called Ken-chan, also speaks like a woman. Hanako's mother is also sometimes present. The food they cook and share is inclusive and appetizing to the reader—in great contrast to the rare delicacies of "Chinsenkai" and Tanizaki's "Bishoku kurabu." Ken-chan, for example, produces wonderful dishes for his companions, starting with a lovely endive salad with fried onion and chestnut oil, followed by marinated mushrooms, seafood paella, and another green salad with bacon. He is willing and efficient not only at food shopping and cooking but at cleaning up afterwards! What's more, he never tries to preach to or teach his companions or to seduce any of them by doing so. What brings Hanako's mother into this convivial cooking and eating circle is the new business she is launching now that she is divorced—a shop specializing in terrines and pies. The choice of specializing in terrines and pies seems to suggest a certain playful girlishness in Hanako's mother—this is not a plain butcher's or greengrocer's or a yakitori bar. The two girls help her in this new food venture. As it is a business for Hanako's mother and a part-time job for Hanako and Momoko, there is certainly a material interest here; nonetheless, their plans to explore new products and customers do have strong elements of play—quite unlike Momoko's admirer's plans to combine marriage and business expansion—and do not involve any sexual seduction or attraction.

The play element is also obvious in the structure of the novel. Inserted into Momoko's narrative are eight short pieces—essays and short stories written by her aunt for literary magazines and other publications. These pieces are themselves entertaining and often subversive, but when they are juxtaposed with the primary narrative, the intratextual writer (the aunt), her immediate readers (Momoko and Hanako), and extratextual readers can share the added pleasure of identifying and musing about the various connections between what is written and what has happened or has been talked about (often while eating and drinking together) in the primary narrative.

While celebrating the joy of convivial and playful—but at the same time subversive—eating, reading, and writing, the novel also seems to suggest that this jubilation, too, can be, and probably needs to be, subverted. Momoko's aunt concludes the essay on Barthes that she writes for the monthly bulletin of the respectable *Iwanami kōza tetsugaku* (Iwanami Lecture Series: Philosophy) with these words: "Am I a reader, and a writer too, who, despicable in my bourgeois complacency, reads in books only those things she can understand?"[110]

Momoko, Hanako, and the aunt are free to read and eat. There is no "gustatory disgust" or "gastronomic unhappiness," to use Ogino's terms, here. The act of eating is by no means "their final avenue of self-expression." Rather than being "eaten or consumed by the world," they firmly maintain their individual subjectivity and develop it further by constantly examining what they read and

eat and at the same time being wary of their own complacency. Despite this jubilant and convivial, if critical, mood, Momoko's world is not without some dark
and dull moments. While her aunt is away in Europe, for example, Momoko,
alone in the apartment, falls into an alarmingly inert state:

> Since in the ten days or so in question I clearly hadn't felt like doing anything
> but sleeping, I'd spent the whole time in the track suit I used as pajamas. This
> outfit was off-white to start with, but it had now turned a sort of dirty gray, a bit
> like a cat that'd been rolling around in the dirt under a verandah. I'd just pulled
> a raincoat on over the top to go to the supermarket. All I ate was frozen Chinese
> buns. I only had a bath once and didn't bother washing my face. Neither had
> I tidied my room. The television was broken, but I didn't feel like watching
> anything anyway. Nor did I even feel like listening to music. Apart from sleeping,
> I did absolutely nothing at all.[111]

Momoko's strange fatigue, sleepiness, and lethargy remind us of Mikage
in *Kitchen* and even of the "megalo-eating" Tokiko.[112] They also remind us of
the fact that Kanai's earlier works are full of much more disturbing scenes and
images surrounding food and eating.[113] It is not the case that Kanai has mellowed
or that complacency has overtaken her; on the contrary, this work demonstrates
her unwillingness to stagnate, to repeat the same style and devices. The trope
of the girl seems to have been useful in exploring diverse possibilities and in
inventing a gastronomic novel that is both woman-centered and, on the whole,
celebratory.

Brave Women Keep on Fighting

As we have seen, women have chosen various genres and have developed their
own styles and strategies for writing about the celebration and the fear of food.
Some, like Ariyoshi (chapter 3), find fiction unsuitable for expressing their concerns about food and writing, while others seek new types of fiction to incorporate their dissent from the socioliterary conventions of gastronomic narratives. In this chapter we have identified four prominent elements: jubilation,
criticism, parody, and fear. We have also noted the frequent appearance of the
girl in these texts, who, in contrast to the daughter confined to the house (and
kitchen), possesses the freedom and arrogance to consume, criticize, reject, and
transform or parody both food and texts. In fiction, poetry, essays, and even in
recipes, women have voiced both their concerns and their desire and pleasure.

Both their jubilation and their fear motivate and feed the desire to write, and through writing they have uncovered the gender bias that is either passed over in silence by, or reinforced in, men's texts. These writers question male-centered knowledge, and highlight the significance of relative values.

Writers such as Kanai and Ogino effectively use food and eating in their writing for the purposes of gender criticism and constantly explore innovative techniques and strategies to investigate the gender implications of food. Whereas food and eating in Kanai's texts have changed from something violent and disturbing to the comic and convivial, Ogino's focus seems to have moved from parodic and intertextual to intergenerational and interpersonal. In *Kenage* (2002, Brave Women), for instance, we see brave and resilient women feeding their families. This sounds familiar, and indeed some of these contemporary women remind us of the farmer women, factory girls, communist women, prostitutes, or wives and daughters in the older texts discussed in previous chapters. Moreover, the first-person narrative seems to invite the reader to read this as Ogino's own story, a series of struggles to juggle her work as a writer and academic with her family commitments. Conflict and discord within the family, illnesses and injuries, particularly those associated with aging—none of this is new in modern Japanese literature. Despite some comic moments and some poetic expressions, the narrative is much less playful here than in Ogino's earlier works. Is this indicative of her conversion to the *shishōsetsu*, the genre that she mocked in her parody? Two things suggest that it is not—at least not of a conversion to the conventional, male-centered *shishōsetsu*. Scattered throughout the book are comments such as the following on the gender imbalance in contemporary Japan: "Work for a man means providing for the family. For a woman it is regarded as a hobby. Even when her whole family depends on her work, she takes leave to work outside the home."[114]

Second, Ogino's narrative is not confined to the immediate surroundings of the narrator; it extends to other women, other families, and other temporal and geographical spaces. What connects these various times, spaces, persons, and their experiences is the theme of "brave women" who are not only resilient but also willing to develop their own personal networks and to help one another. By writing about these personal networks, Ogino attempts to extend these networks to other women, including those who are more isolated. In this sense Ogino's later work can be seen as a return to what we called down-to-earth literature.

What we have seen here is only a small sample of food and gender in contemporary women's literature. As the works of Kanai and Ogino indicate, even the same writer can employ and develop diverse ways of dealing with gender issues through writing about food and eating or using them as metaphors for social or sexual concerns. Despite the fact that many of the texts discussed above have met with critical acclaim and commercial success, their particular achievement in expanding the repertoire of contemporary literature that is acutely attuned to issues of gender has hardly been recognized. It is hoped that this chapter helps both to counter this neglect and to inspire further studies in this area, for there are certainly many other texts and issues that deserve our attention. To quote Ogino's last line in *Kenage*: "My journey continues."[115]

Conclusion
Confessions of an Obsessive
Textual Food Eater

There are things in it that will ruin their appetites. But in the end this is
a book about the pleasures of eating, the kinds of pleasure that are only
deepened by knowing.
—Pollan, *The Omnivore's Dilemma*, p. 11

I started this book with a series of question about reading food in literature:
what, how, why, and how far do we or can we or should we read? My questions
arose out of a decade of reading food in literary texts driven by an omnivorous
desire to know. Not that this desire has had a significant effect on my actual
eating habits. Neither has my cooking repertoire been extended significantly,
though I did try some of the recipes that appear in the writings of Uno Chiyo,
Dan Kazuo, Kanai Mieko, and a few others. The reading experience has, however, certainly changed many of my previously held views and prejudices about
literature and other things. I never realized before I embarked on this project
how biased and limited my knowledge of modern Japanese literature had been.
Nor had I understood how my biases and limitations had arisen from presump-
tions that I had always treated with skepticism, but had nevertheless failed to
challenge—the dichotomy, for instance, between serious (or "pure") literature
and popular (or "mass") literature. On a simple level, I have read—in some
cases forced myself to read—a number of texts that I had avoided or had had
no chance (or appetite or guts) to read before. In so doing I have certainly filled
many gaps, but only with the result that I now know even better how little I
know. Even with the books I thought I knew well, my rereading of them with

a focus on food, and the process of textual and contextual mastication that has been involved, have brought me many new discoveries.

Reading is such a never ending pursuit that it is simply impossible to write a comprehensive book on food in modern Japanese literature. We have seen again and again how the same text—be it Shiki's diary (chapter 1), Nagatsuka's *The Soil* (chapter 2), the extraordinary story of *Yapoo* (chapter 4), or *Kitchen* (chapter 6)—can be, and is, read in different, even conflicting, ways, each reflective of the reader's personal background as well as of social, historical, and cultural differences, changes, and variations. Reading with a focus on food enables, encourages, and demands multiple interpretations, many of which destabilize our understanding of how literary work depends on and creates its conventions. From our very first text, *Some Prefer Nettles*, we have seen numerous instances where a clear-cut or even stereotypical binary distinction turned ambiguous and unstable. This is not to suggest that we simply need to disregard and discard binaries and stereotypes; they are useful, even essential, for understanding what is assumed, reinforced, transgressed, or transformed in the text or its reception. Some texts are very transparent in this regard. The introductory part of Takeda Taijun's *Luminous Moss* (chapter 4), for instance, outlines the key binaries and dichotomies such as center/peripheral, savage/civilized, and ethical/unethical and in this way prepares us to understand the blurrings and transgressions that are caused by, symbolized by, or demonstrated by the act of cannibalism.

Food is so essential to everyday life that it can be used in literature to highlight the significance of the everyday, the ordinary, and the basic. In many cases a focus on food in literature becomes a focus on the disruption of its connection to the ordinary, exposing the links between food shortages, dietary problems, and unequal distribution of food to class, gender, ideological, and other issues. Stories of the war—not only WWII and other historical wars but also the fictive ones we found in *Sumiyakist Q* and *Yapoo*—deal with the brutal invasion of the everyday and the impossibility of the ordinary. War's invasiveness of private space extends even to toilets and digestive organs, as Yasuoka, among others, has effectively depicted. Perpetual hunger in peacetime is not always caused by poverty; hunger in affluent society is often associated with intellectual, sexual, or emotional dissatisfaction, although some of the texts examined here resist a mechanical and formulaic linking between, for instance, food and sex. Many texts examined illustrate how one food item leads to, reminds one of, or is associated with all sorts of other foods, memories, associations, discrimination, and even distant time and space. Food, then, is seen to indicate or symbolize all sorts of relationships both within and outside the text. Interpretations of those relationships are commonly neither fixed nor homogeneous. Something insipid now may taste exquisite later; what looks completely useless may turn out to be invaluable, and vice versa.

The subject of food keeps popping up not only in gastronomic novels, down-to-earth writing, and food-obsessed diaries but also in poetry, detective novels, science fiction, horror stories, action-picaresque tales, war literature, and even in literary criticism. Of necessity I have been highly selective in my choice of works to discuss here, with the result that many obvious texts have been left out. The reader may have gained the impression that I have purposely avoided canonical texts and authors, which to a certain degree I have in order to include neglected texts and authors. But my selection was primarily governed by whether a particular work was relevant to the issues and themes discussed in each of my six chapters. Hence there is no discussion on Sōseki except for the brief mention of *The Miner* and his comments on *The Soil*. This has inevitably entailed some sacrifices. It is a great pity, for instance, that, having left out Sōseki, I could not mention Tachimachi Rōbai, one of the minor characters in *Wagahai wa neko de aru* (I Am a Cat, 1905–1906). Before he is taken away to a mental hospital, Rōbai's gluttony combines with a kind of perverse Zen derangement to have him utter some stunning lines referring to cutlets flying to a pine tree and digging *kinton* (mashed and sugared sweet potatoes) in a ditch.[1] In a discussion of nervous breakdown among Meiji intellectuals this seemingly nonsensical episode would surely have thrown up some interesting insights.[2] Another canonical author, Kawabata, is also underrepresented in this book, with only a brief discussion of food as a division marker in *The Izu Dancer*. This is not to suggest that Kawabata neglected food and eating in his novels. *Yama no oto* (1952, trans. *The Sound of the Mountain*, 1964), for example, more or less begins with three *sazae* (top shells, turbos; in Seidensticker's translation, whelks) shared by a family of four adults and ends with three *ayu* (sweetfish, changed to trout in the translation, as in the case of *Some Prefer Nettles*) shared by the same family, which has now grown to include five adults and two children. The particular foods selected, as well as the spinach that appears in between, tell us much about the subtle and complex relationships within the family. In each case the seafood that is referred to is also associated with sexuality and reproduction. Mishima, Dazai, Ōe Kenzaburō, Abe Kōbō, Nakagami Kenji, and Murakami Haruki have also been either left out of this discussion or mentioned only briefly in it. Moreover, writers such as Tanizaki, Okamoto Kanoko, Kaikō, Inoue Hisashi, Kurahashi, Kanai, and Ogino, whose works have been included in our discussion, have produced numerous other interesting and intriguing works in which food and eating appear prominently or play an interesting role. These, too, I have had to leave out.

Despite an effort to pay more attention to women's texts than has been the case in conventional literary studies, omissions have also been inevitable in this area. It would have been interesting, for instance, to compare the portrayal of food (and experimental cultivation) in Osaki Midori's modernist stories with that of her contemporary, Miyazawa Kenji. The eating disorders that appear in Yi (or Lee) Yangji's stories are obviously different from those discussed in chapter 6, since the former are related to *zainichi* Korean issues. For the young heroine of Kanehara Hitomi's *Hebi ni piasu* (2004, trans. *Snakes and Earrings*, 2005), anorexia nervosa represents only a small part of her obsession with modifying, manipulating, and even transgressing her body and body image. Whereas the bulimic heroines of Ogawa's and Matsumoto's novels are obsessed—despite their concerns and awareness—with the consumption of food as well as of knowledge, the girl in Kanehara's story rejects both. The significance of the girl figure is evident in these works, too. Kawakami Hiromi's *Sensei no kaban* (Sensei's Briefcase, 2001), on the other hand, may be regarded as representing a new type of jubilant eating. A woman in her late thirties shares food, drink, and tender love and respect with Sensei, her former high-school teacher, mostly at a local drinking place—reminiscent of the civilized Tōzentei in chapter 5. The relationship between the first-person narrator, Tsukiko, and her Sensei, who is more than thirty years her senior, does not involve any conflict. There is no hint of patriarchal oppression or the law of the father in this relationship. Still, the relationship does accord with the age-old tradition of quasi–father-daughter love.

Kawakami's gentle love story reminds us of one issue associated with food and eating that has been mentioned but not discussed in any depth in this book, namely aging. As we saw in chapter 2, Nagatsuka's novel deals with this to some extent in some down-to-earth yet skillfully organized episodes surrounding food. It was also mentioned very briefly that Ogino's *Brave Women* (chapter 6) makes reference to various difficulties contemporary women face, including caring for their aging parents. Given that food "looks like an object but is actually a relationship" (Eagleton, quoted in the Introduction), and given the vital link between food and body, it is hardly surprising that food and eating play important roles in many other novels that deal with the theme of old age.[3] While most of these texts are written from the perspective of the carers (or in some cases non- or un-carers) of elderly people, Tanizaki's *Fūten rōjin nikki* (Diary of a Mad Old Man, 1961–1962) is unique in its exploration of an old man's desires, which tend to cause problems within his family and for his health. Unlike the characters in Tanizaki's earlier story "The Gourmet Club" (chapter 5), who all have the choice to favor the desire for food over that for sex or health, the "mad old man" seems to find it easier to control his appetite than his sexual desire.[4] While Tanizaki's *Fūten rōjin* ignored the view (and desire) of the aging protagonist's wife, in the decades that followed, older women's voices have been heard in novels and essays by Uno Chiyo, Mori Mari, Satō Aiko, Tanabe Seiko, and many others. There are many other issues aside from aging that have not, for reasons of space, received enough attention in this book—environmental degradation, climate change, famine and food crises brought about by natural disasters and human error, genetically modified food, BSE ("mad cow" disease), and other food safety issues, and globalization.[5] The wide significance of food and its popularity as an important theme in diasporic film and literature makes it highly deserving of further study, especially within the context of gender and postcolonial studies.[6]

While I have been writing this book, a number of new publications on food in literature have come out.[7] Of particular interest is Saitō Minako's *Bunga-kuteki shōhingaku* (A Study of Commodities in Literature, 2004). In her introduction Saitō states that the aim of her book is "not to extract things (*mono*) but to examine how things are depicted" and that its interest is "not in an apple itself but in the touch of a pencil drawing an apple."[8] This is similar to my approach, though Saitō's book includes only one chapter on food—"Hōshoku no jidai no fūdo shōsetsu" (Food Fiction in the Age of Satiation)—and only three of the ten texts discussed in it overlap with my discussion here. What Saitō's book does demonstrate is that the approach I have taken to analyzing food in literature can be applied, at least partially, to other "commodities," such as fashion and music, as they appear in literary (and other) texts. I must reiterate, however, that it is not "an apple itself" or the commodities themselves that we are interested to find in books, but rather their complex significance for both writer and reader. In this sense, for me at least, the discovery of a new textual food "does more for human happiness than the discovery of a new star,"[9] and even than the discovery of a new dish, though Brillat-Savarin, Kaikō, and some readers may disagree.

As we saw in Noguchi Takehiko's definition (quoted in the Introduction), *shōsetsu* has ingested a wide range of other genres through predation. In fact *shōsetsu* is omnivorous and much more varied than *shishōsetsu*. Even in the heyday of naturalism, Mori Ōgai's protagonist asserted that *shōsetsu* should not be confined by the shackles of certain styles and subjects but could be written in any fashion and about any subject.[10] Although historically this liberal view of the genre has not been shared by everyone, this selection of texts is testimony to its power to inspire both writers and readers alike. Many writers consciously explore the "ingesting" and predatory nature of *shōsetsu*. Kanai Mieko, in celebration of this exploration, often quotes Gotō Meisei's answer to the question Why write?: "Because I read" (*yonda kara*).[11]

The readings here have also included what I have called down-to-earth food and literature. For with all the charm and disillusion of the notion of self-reflexive texts, there are always extratextual elements that determine and influence the production and consumption of a text. One may cook because one is hungry or because there happens to be an ingredient that invites, needs, or demands cooking. As we saw, down-to-earth writing may be prompted by existing gender, class, ethnic, and other inequalities or by the fact that earth is contaminated or hidden beneath concrete. We have seen many cases in which the desire and passion for freedom, equality, and other human rights, or a love of nature, however naive that may seem, have produced texts that have the power to move the reader. This, however, does not make these seemingly organic, down-to-earth texts exempt from deconstruction, or ingestion by the critical reader.

This book is not intended to be a reader's guide to gourmet "written food"—for although some types of food may be more popular than others, taste, as we have seen, is relative and shifting. We have sampled both ordinary and extraordinary textual food, some skillfully cooked and some presented more or less raw. Some depictions of food and eating are based closely on actual food or events, while others are totally or partly imagined. The most simple-looking food, moreover, may have a complex and delicate taste, and what is supposed to be a delicacy may in fact be tasteless, unsavory, or even inedible. What this book does intend to be is a refutation of the long-held belief that Japanese literature is lacking in an interest in the food and appetites that abound in some other literatures such as those of France and China.[12] My hope is that the reader finds something interesting and amusing in the menu I have written, and that this menu will be of some use to his or her future reading of food in Japanese writing.

Notes

Introduction

1. Tanizaki Jun'ichirō, *Some Prefer Nettles*, trans. Edward G. Seidensticker, pp. 191–192.

2. Gaye Poole, *Reel Meals, Set Meals: Food in Film and Theatre*, p. 2.

3. Terry Eagleton, "Edible Écriture," pp. 204–205.

4. James L. Watson and Melissa L. Caldwell, eds., *The Cultural Politics of Food and Eating: A Reader*, p. 1.

5. Kilgour, *From Communion to Cannibalism: An Anatomy of Metaphors of Incorporation*, p. 3.

6. Poole, *Reel Meals, Set Meals: Food in Film and Theatre*, p. 4. As the subtitle indicates, Poole's subject is food in film and theater rather than in fiction.

7. The Shinchō Bunko paperback edition (revised edition published in 1969) includes a note about this restaurant, which indicates that not every reader of the Japanese text would be familiar with the Hyōtei.

8. Tanizaki, *Tade kuu mushi*, p. 193; *Some Prefer Nettles*, p. 196.

9. In the Japanese text the first of the three dishes (given as "deep-fried salmon eggs" in translation, which, as a dish seems very odd) is deep-fried *amago*, which carries a note in the Shinchō Bunko edition: "a term used in Lake Biwa district for the *yamame*, a freshwater fish of the salmon family" (annotation by Miyoshi Yukio, in Tanizaki, *Tade kuu mushi*, p. 208). The second item, "baked trout," is a replacement for the young *ayu* (sweetfish) grilled with salt (i.e., *shioyaki*). Similarly, "salad" is for the root vegetable *gobō* (edible burdock) served with a white dressing (*shira-ae*) made of tofu, white miso, sesame seeds, sugar, and vinegar. It is understandable therefore that the translator replaces all three quite simple but nice dishes with what he regards as functionally equivalent—although fried salmon roe does seem a poor choice. A much more convincing example of functional equivalence is the "nettle" in the title of the novel for *tade*, "a polygonum; a jointweed; a smartweed; a knotweed," according to *Kenkyusha's New Japanese-English Dictionary*. Seidensticker chose another plant, the nettle, which functions well in an

equivalent proverb of the Japanese *tade kuu mushi mo sukizuki,* "Every worm to his taste; some prefer to eat nettles" (p. v).

10. *Bunshō dokuhon* (A Guide to Writing, 1934) is included in *Tanizaki Jun'ichirō zenshū,* vol. 21.

11. David Pollack, *Reading against Culture: Ideology and Narrative in the Japanese Novel,* pp. 71–72.

12. Tanizaki, *Some Prefer Nettles,* pp. 31–32; for the Japanese text, *Tade kuu mushi,* p. 34. I have modified "O-hisa" in the translation to "O-Hisa," which is the method I adopt in this book for women's names with the honorific/familiar prefix "o."

13. Similarly, culture-specific food terms such as *norimaki* rolls, Japanese-style omelet (*tamago-yaki*), and the *makunouchi* (literally, "between acts") lunch boxes are omitted, and the names of specific fish and vegetables such as *anago* (conger eel), *tsukushi* (field horsetail), *zenmai* (flowering fern, osmund), and *warabi* (bracken) are either omitted or simplified (e.g., as "spring greens"). See *Some Prefer Nettles,* pp. 21, 114, 127, 129, 139; *Tade kuu mushi,* pp. 24, 117, 127, 130, 138.

14. Tanizaki, *Tade kuu mushi,* pp. 91–93; *Some Prefer Nettles,* pp. 86–88. Part of this section is quoted in Ken Ito, *Visions of Desire: Tanizaki's Fictional Worlds,* p. 144.

15. For instance, Noguchi Takehiko, *Tanizaki Jun'ichirō ron,* pp. 156–164; and Ito, *Visions of Desire,* pp. 140–141.

16. Kōno Taeko has always emphasized what she terms *yokaku* (presentiment) in Tanizaki's works, particularly this work (see Kōno, *Tanizaki bungaku to kōtei no yokubō,* pp. 62–84, and *Tanizaki bungaku no tanoshimi,* pp. 106–120). In English, Kōno Taeko, "Presentiments," is included in Adriana Boscaro and Anthony Hood Chambers, *A Tanizaki Feast: The International Symposium in Venice,* pp. 117–124. This is an example of the conventional biographical approach that I discuss in this introduction. Kōno, like many other critics, finds in the text "presentiments" of Tanizaki's shift of interest from modernist Kanto to classical Kansai and his divorce and remarriage.

17. Tanizaki, *Tade kuu mushi,* p. 117; *Some Prefer Nettles,* p. 114.

18. Carole M. Counihan, *The Anthropology of Food and Body: Gender, Meaning, and Power,* p. 63. The last part of the quotation reminds us of the motif of longing for the "mater nutrix" that Noguchi Takehiko identifies in Tanizaki's texts (see Noguchi, *Tanizaki Jun'ichirō ron,* p. 278).

19. This lover never appears in the primary narrative; he is only alluded to or talked about. Biographical readings of the novel identify this man as Satō Haruo and Misako as Tanizaki's first wife, Chiyoko. Aso lives in Suma, which is not included in Pollack's topographical diagram. Situated west of Kobe, Suma has a strong classical association, particularly with the *Tale of Genji.*

20. Tanizaki, *Tade kuu mushi,* pp. 92–93; *Some Prefer Nettles,* pp. 87–89.

21. Kaname and Misako live in Toyonaka, which is, symbolically, in the middle of the triangle linking Kyoto, Osaka, and Kobe. Misako's father's house, or to be precise, his retirement villa, is in the eastern suburb of Kyoto called Shishigatani. Both these names

(Toyonaka and Shishigatani) and several others such as Umeda, Dōtonbori, Kuramae, and Kobikichō are omitted in the translation.

22. Stephen Mennell, Anne Murcott, and Anneke van Otterloo, *The Sociology of Food: Eating, Diet and Culture*, pp. 1, 118.

23. Deborah Lupton, *Food, the Body and the Self*, pp. 2–3.

24. Alan Beardsworth and Teresa Keil, for example, note that "[t]he purchasing, preparation and presentation of food (and indeed, the disposal of leftover food and the more menial tasks of the kitchen) are strongly associated with the mundane, unglamourous [*sic*] labour of housework, the traditional domain of women, and hold little intellectual appeal to the male researchers and theorists who have historically dominated the profession" (*Sociology on the Menu: An Invitation to the Study of Food and Society*, p. 2).

25. The editors of *Food in Russian History and Culture*, for example, while acknowledging a recent surge in scholarly interest in food, point to the fact that their book is the first to focus on Russian food culture (Musya Glants and Joyce Toomre, *Food in Russian History and Culture*, pp. xii–xiii).

26. Kilgour, *From Communion to Cannibalism*, p. ix.

27. Gang Yue, *The Mouth That Begs: Hunger, Cannibalism, and the Politics of Eating in Modern China*, p. 372.

28. Poole, *Reel Meals, Set Meals*, p. 4.

29. Ibid., p. 14.

30. Kaikō Takeshi, *Saigo no bansan*, p. 139.

31. See, for example, the comments by film and food critic Ogi Masahiro ("Kaisetsu" in Dan Kazuo, *Danryū kukkingu*, pp. 230–231) and writer Maruya Saiichi ("Kaisetsu" in Kyū Eikan, *Shoku wa Kōshū ni ari*, pp. 223–226).

32. Donald Keene explains this term as "[t]he 'literary world,' which consists of influential writers and critics who establish reputations by their praise or condemnation" (*Dawn to the West: Japanese Literature of the Modern Era*, vol. 1, p. 1239). I follow Keene's translations of most literary terms.

33. This cross-cultural incorporation is obvious in Shōyō's use of the written scripts. In a diagram illustrating the classification of fiction, Shōyō places *noberu* (novel, from the English word) in small font katakana next to *shōsetsu*, which is in normal font kanji. This kind of juxtaposition of small font (ruby) kana next to kanji is normally intended to help the reader to read the kanji, but it can also be used, as in the above case, to indicate the source of translated terms. It can also present an alternative word or phrase, usually in colloquial native Japanese, sometimes offering a kind of parodic palimpsest. In Shōyō's diagram the katakana *noberu* and the kanji *shōsetsu* are juxtaposed with a phrase consisting of Sino- and native Japanese for "ordinary stories/tales": *jinjō* (in kanji, with *yo no tsune* in hiragana) *no tan* (in kanji, with *monogatari* in hiragana). *Shōsetsu shinzui* is included in *Tsubouchi Shōyō shū*, Meiji bungaku zenshū, vol. 16, and the diagram is found on p. 21.

34. Noguchi Takehiko, *Ichigo no jiten: Shōsetsu*, p. 104. Emphasis added.

35. Cited by Sérgio Luiz Prado Bellei (p. 100) and Peter Hulme (p. 28) in Francis Barker, Peter Hulme, and Margaret Iversen, eds., *Cannibalism and the Colonial World*. The context was a discussion of the Brazilian modernist movement and their Anthropophagic Manifesto (1928) (which offers an interesting comparison with the anthropophagic motif in Japanese texts of the late 1920s and early 1930s).

36. Jameson, *Postmodernism, or, the Cultural Logic of Late Capitalism*, p. 96.

37. "Pastiche" derives from the Italian word *pasticcio*, which means a pasty or pie dish containing several different ingredients. See Margaret Rose, *Parody: Ancient, Modern, and Post-Modern*, p. 73.

38. Gérard Genette, *Palimpsests: Literature in the Second Degree*.

39. In the puppet theater scene of *Tade kuu mushi*, for instance, Kaname thinks, "[T]here [is] much to be said for seeing a puppet play with a bottle of saké at one's side and a mistress to wait on one" (*Some Prefer Nettles*, p. 22; *Tade kuu mushi*, p. 25). The play they are watching is Chikamatsu's *Shinjū Ten no Amijima* (The Love Suicides at Amijima, first performed 1720), which adds complexity not only to the already complicated relationships of the four viewers but also to the two male viewers' aestheticism. The same applies to the later chapters (chapters 9–11) when they (without Misako) go to Awaji to see the local production of *Shō utsushi asagao nikki* (Morning-Glory Diary, first performed in 1832). Kaname's comments on the lacquerware boxes full of colorful food that the audience bring to the theater remind us very much of Tanizaki's collection of essays *In'ei raisan* (In Praise of Shadows, 1933).

40. Cited and translated by Donald Keene, *Dawn to the West*, vol. 1, p. 102.

41. Noguchi, *Ichigo no jiten*, p. 61. Noguchi uses Wayne C. Booth's notion of "implied author" (from *The Rhetoric of Fiction*). As Noguchi notes, this applies to the *shishōsetsu* of the Taishō period. Later texts with some *shishōsetsu* features are not included.

42. Kume Masao, "'Watakushi' shōsetsu to 'shinkyō' shōsetsu," originally published in *Bunshō kōza* (May 1925), included in Miyoshi Yukio and Sobue Shōji, eds., *Kindai bungaku hyōron taikei*, vol. 6, p. 53.

43. Kurahashi Yumiko, an outspoken antinaturalist writer, for example, uses the metaphor of fish "cooked on a boat by a fisherman with a dirty chopping board." Kurahashi Yumiko, *Atarimae no koto*, p. 139.

44. Arashiyama Kōzaburō, *Bunjin akujiki*, pp. 50–52. The "wizened apples" refer to Tōson's essay "Mi no mawari no koto" (Things around Me).

45. This poem was first published in the October 1896 issue of *Bungakukai* and was included in Tōson's first collection of poetry, *Wakanashū* (Seedlings, or Young Herbs, 1897). See Shimazaki, *Tōson zenshū*, vol. 1, p. 54. Donald Keene translates this poem in *Dawn to the West*, vol. 2, p. 210. The poem is also included in James Kirkup's anthology *Modern Japanese Poetry*, p. 1.

46. Keene, *Dawn to the West*, vol. 2, p. 210.

47. In his chapter on Tōson, for example, Arashiyama proposes an interpretation of the reference to grapes in some of the poems in the same collection as "First Love," whereby the fruit to be picked was Tōson's niece, and the wine made from the fruit was

the sexual relationship between uncle and niece, which was to become the subject of Tōson's autobiographical novel *Shinsei* (A New Life, 1918–1919). Arashiyama, *Bunjin akujiki*, pp. 57–60.

48. Louis Marin, *Food for Thought*, p. xx.

49. We may note that even Tanizaki's story "Bishoku kurabu" (The Gourmet Club), which is discussed in Kaikō's essay and Arashiyama's book, as well as in chapter 5 of this volume, had to wait more than eighty years before its English translation was published.

Chapter 1. Food in the Diary

1. Seafood, seaweed, or vegetables cooked in thick soy sauce. Tsukuda is a small island in the mouth of the Sumida River in Edo (Tokyo). Like pickles, *tsukudani* is salty and is regarded as an aid to eating plain rice.

2. *Masaoka Shiki, Itō Sachio, Nagatsuka Takashi shū*, p. 16.

3. As with Sōseki and Shōyō, I use the *gagō* (elegant sobriquet) Shiki rather than his surname, Masaoka, to refer to this poet. For a detailed study of Shiki, see Janine Beichman, *Masaoka Shiki*. In the following I cite Beichman's translation of Shiki's diary titles. Translations of extracts are mine.

4. There is another slightly earlier text, *Bokujū itteki* (A Drop of Ink, 1901), which is not included in this discussion.

5. Donald Keene, *Modern Japanese Diaries: The Japanese at Home and Abroad as Revealed through Their Diaries*, p. 4.

6. This is the prevalent view, although Joshua Mostow tells us that there were earlier examples. See Joshua S. Mostow, "Mother Tongue and Father Script: The Relationship of Sei Shōnagon and Murasaki Shikibu to Their Fathers and Chinese Letters," in Rebecca L. Copeland and Esperanza Ramirez-Christensen, eds., *The Father-Daughter Plot: Japanese Literary Women and the Law of the Father*, pp. 118–120.

7. Donald Keene, *Travelers of a Hundred Ages*, pp. 6–7.

8. Janice Brown's "De-siring the Center: Hayashi Fumiko's Hungry Heroines and the Male Literary Canon," in Copeland and Ramirez-Christensen, eds., *The Father-Daughter Plot*, p. 161. It is common to refer to this author by her personal name, Fumiko (see Brown's note 1, "De-siring the Center," p. 164). In this book, however, I use her surname as I do with other women writers of her generation such as Sata (Ineko), Hirabayashi (Taiko), and Enchi (Fumiko).

9. Fowler, *The Rhetoric of Confession: Shishōsetsu in Early Twentieth-Century Japanese Fiction*, p. 27. Emphasis added. For the relationship between diaries and *shishōsetsu*, see Irmela Hijiya-Kirschnereit, *Rituals of Self-Revelation: Shishosetsu as Literary Genre and Socio-cultural Phenomenon*, pp. 297–300.

10. While in principle Japanese names are cited in Japanese order in this book, in quoting published translations names may be cited in reverse order (i.e., personal name

followed by family name), as in this instance, which is from John Bester's translation of Ibuse Masuji's *Kuroi ame* (*Black Rain*).

11. Quoted and translated in Keene, *Travelers of a Hundred Ages*, p. 3.

12. Ibid.

13. Another interesting example of diaries intended as communication is the schoolgirls' *kōkan nikki* (diary for exchange). See Honda Masuko's study, *Kōkan nikki: Shōjotachi no himitsu no purei rando*.

14. Tanizaki effectively uses this combination in his two postwar novels in diary form, *Kagi* (The Key) and *Fūten rōjin nikki* (Diary of a Mad Old Man) to indicate the age, gender, education, and even personality of the diarists.

15. The term *shasei* (literally, "copying life") is used in Japanese Western-style painting (*yōga*) for *dessin* (sketch). Shiki's point is that the *dessin* is essential in any painting, even when depicting gods, monsters, and nonexistent things. The painting may be based on a sketch of the whole scene or may consist of a number of sketches of details. Likewise, *shasei* is a crucial basis for the modern tanka and haiku. This idea was further applied to prose writing and had an important influence on a number of writers, including Sōseki.

16. The annual rice consumption per capita at the beginning of the twentieth century was 147.2 kg; by 1989 it had declined to 70.1 kg (see tables 24 and 25 appended to Inoue Hisashi, *Dō shite mo kome no hanashi*). This has decreased further to about 60 kg.

17. Yamada Yūsaku, "Fetisshu na nikki: shoku, yume, sei," p. 23.

18. Beichman, for example, finds "tremendous fascination" in this diary and writes that she doubts "that there has been anything like it in Japanese literature before or since" (*Masaoka Shiki*, p. 129).

19. Saitō Mokichi, "Masaoka Shiki," in *Masaoka Shiki, Itō Sachio, Nagatsuka Takashi shū*, p. 400.

20. Ibid., p. 399. *Bokujū itteki* (see note 4 above) is a collection of essays and sketches serialized in the *Nihon shinbun* from January to July 1901.

21. Arashiyama, *Bunjin akujiki*, p. 125, citing Mokichi's essay "Iro to yoku to."

22. See ibid., pp. 115–127. See also Satomi Shinzō, *Kenja no shokuyoku*, pp. 117–128.

23. Arashiyama, *Bunjin akujiki*, p. 46.

24. Arashiyama adds (ibid., p. 48) an interesting personal experience that taught him that eating does need willpower: he, who could not control his appetite, became anorexic after reading *Gyōga manroku*.

25. Kanai Keiko, *Mayonaka no kanojo-tachi: kaku onna no kindai*, pp. 4–14.

26. *Masaoka Shiki, Itō Sachio, Nagatsuka Takashi shū*, p. 25. Beichman cites and translates excerpts from this entry (*Masaoka Shiki*, pp. 133–135).

27. *Masaoka Shiki, Itō Sachio, Nagatsuka Takashi shū*, p. 26.

28. Kanai Keiko, *Mayonaka no kanojo-tachi*, pp. 18–20.

29. Ibid., p. 14. Kanai notes the multiple meanings of the Japanese verb *miru*,

which include not only seeing, observing, watching, perceiving, checking, and judging, but experiencing, trying, meeting, having an intimate relationship with, and looking after.

30. On September 26, for example, frustrated by his calls not being heard by his family, who were talking outside, he "devoured milk and rice cakes" and brought on a stomach upset (*Masaoka Shiki, Itō Sachio, Nagatsuka Takashi shū*, p. 29).

31. Ibid., p. 40.

32. Ibid., pp. 82–83.

33. Excerpts of *Hōrōki* have been translated as "Vagabond's Song" by Elizabeth Hanson (included in Tanaka Yukiko, ed., *To Live and to Write: Selections by Japanese Women Writers 1913–1938*). Joan E. Ericson's complete translation of the first part as *Diary of a Vagabond* is included in Ericson, *Be a Woman: Hayashi Fumiko and Modern Japanese Women's Literature*. Apart from Ericson's book and Janice Brown's aforementioned "De-siring the Center," there are a few other detailed studies available in English, including Susanna Fessler's *Wandering Heart: The Work and Method of Hayashi Fumiko* and chapter 4 of Seiji M. Lippit's *Topographies of Japanese Modernism*. Translations of the excerpts quoted in this chapter are mine, and the text used is the revised Shinchō Bunko edition, which includes all three parts.

34. See Tanaka's commentary in *To Live and to Write*, p. 99.

35. As Seiji Lippit notes (*Topographies of Japanese Modernism*, p. 169), the chronological order of events was adopted not in the original installments in *Nyonin geijutsu* but from the 1930 Kaizōsha edition.

36. Keene, *Travelers of a Hundred Ages*, pp. 7–8.

37. Kanai Keiko, *Mayonaka no kanojo-tachi*, p. 107.

38. Some of these have been translated by Janice Brown and included in Hayashi, *I Saw a Pale Horse and Selected Poems from Diary of a Vagabond*. Brown also includes an insightful discussion of intertextuality from the gender studies perspective in "De-siring the Center."

39. Hayashi, *Hōrōki*, p. 291.

40. Joan E. Ericson, "The Origins of the Concept of 'Women's Literature,'" in Paul Gordon Schalow and Janet A. Walker, eds., *The Woman's Hand: Gender and Theory in Japanese Women's Writing*, p. 98.

41. Noguchi Takehiko, *Sakka no hōhō*, p. 307, citing Akutagawa's *Zoku bungeiteki na amari ni bungeiteki na* (Literary, All too Literary, II, 1927). The first Japanese translation of Hamsun's text appeared in 1921. For more detailed comparison between Hamsun and Hayashi, see Brown, "De-siring the Center," pp. 151–156.

42. In Colette's *The Vagabond*, p. 26, the narrator muses: "You can get used to not eating, to having toothache or a pain in your stomach, you can even get used to the absence of a beloved person; but you cannot get used to jealousy."

43. Ibid., p. 62.

44. Although *Hōrōki* does not go into detail about this factory job, the reader can easily imagine that it must have been just as hard and exploitative as that of the young

factory girl depicted in Sata Ineko's short story "Kyarameru kōjō kara" (From the Caramel Factory, 1928, discussed in chapter 2 of this volume).

45. Hayashi, *Hōrōki*, p. 383. The English words strongly suggest the kind of modern and bourgeois culture shared by middle-class young women in Taishō Japan.

46. Ibid., pp. 96–97.

47. Ibid., p. 46.

48. Ibid., p. 47.

49. Ibid.

50. Ibid., p. 51.

51. Takamura, *Takamura Kōtarō zenshū*, vol. 1, p. 332.

52. Kaikō Takeshi, *Saigo no bansan*, p. 131.

53. The young Fukuzawa Yukichi (1834–1901) was one of the few Japanese who started eating beef in the late 1850s. See Kosuge Keiko, *Guruman Fukuzawa Yukichi no shokutaku*, p. 172.

54. An excerpt from this text is translated as "The Beef Eater" in Donald Keene, ed., *Modern Japanese Literature*, pp. 31–33.

55. Sukiyaki restaurants today tend to be more selective. As Ōtsuka Shigeru notes (*Tabemono bunmei kō*, p. 204), beef was initially consumed by ordinary people but gradually became an expensive and prestigious ingredient. Fighting for the few pieces of meat in a family sukiyaki pan is a common scene that is depicted or commented on in many later stories and essays.

56. Hayashi, *Hōrōki*, p. 53.

57. Ibid., p. 51.

58. Ibid., pp. 116, 122, 130, 131.

59. Ibid., p. 290.

60. Akutagawa, for example, uses *desu-masu* in "To Shishun" (Tu Tze-chun, 1920) and "Shūzanzu" (Autumn Mountain, 1920), while "Kumo no ito" (Spider's Thread, 1918) and "Jigokuhen" (Hell Screen, 1918) are written in *de gozaimasu* style. "Yabu no naka" (In a Grove, 1922) combines all three styles: *de gozaimasu* spoken by the first four witnesses, *desu-masu* by the accused and the victim's wife, and finally plain style spoken by the spirit of the dead man through the mouth of a medium.

61. Hayashi, *Hōrōki*, pp. 295–296. The first line of this quoted passage reminds us of the opening of Yoshimoto Banana's popular novel, which will be discussed in chapter 6.

62. Ibid., pp. 309, 312, 440.

63. Ibid., p. 305.

64. Ibid., p. 311. This poem (?) is included in Janice Brown's translation, *I Saw a Pale Horse*, p. 101.

65. Many believe her death was caused by years of overwork. Arashiyama Kōzaburō further suggests that the cause might have been heart failure brought on by being overweight, and notes that before her death she ate eel, one of the dishes described superbly in her unfinished novel (Arashiyama, *Bunjin akujiki*, p. 321).

66. Janice Brown points out, "In *Meals*, food is written about not only as bland and

commonplace but also as particularly unsatisfying, as the female protagonist rebels against the new postwar world where men go out to work and women stay home to cook" ("De-siring the Center," p. 162).

67. The reversal of surname and personal name is mentioned in Kaneko Hiroshi, "*Kuroi ame* (Ibuse Masuji)," p. 81, and John Whittier Treat, *Pools of Water, Pillar of Fire: The Literature of Ibuse Masuji*, p. 206. When writing the first draft of this chapter, I was not aware of Inose Naoki's allegation that Ibuse abused Shigematsu Shizuma's trust and that the novelist neither returned Shigematsu's diary nor properly acknowledged the extent of his dependence on it. While it has been generally believed that the novel *Kuroi ame* was a work of fiction based on a number of texts written by others, the extent of Ibuse's borrowing, especially from Shigematsu's diary, had never been clarified until the publication of *Shigematsu nikki* in 2001, more than twenty years after the death of the original diarist and eight years after Ibuse's death. Inose believes that this delay was the result of Ibuse's suppression of the diary, which was aided by his power and authority (see Inose's "*Kuroi ame* to Ibuse Masuji no shinsō"). Like many other readers, I was shocked by this revelation, but after some consideration I have realized that this actually gives us even more material for considering the "fictionality" of *Kuroi ame* and the complex issue of originality.

68. Even with the above allegation of plagiarism in mind, one can still appreciate this "quintessentially Ibuse" style. About comic elements in Ibuse's writing (and Inoue Hisashi's, too), see Joel R. Cohn, *Studies in the Comic Spirit in Modern Japanese Fiction*.

69. Sakaki Atsuko, *Recontextualizing Texts: Narrative Performance in Modern Japanese Fiction*, pp. 57–58.

70. Ibid., pp. 94–95. Both *Kōi to shite noshōsetsu* and *Recontextualizing Texts* were published before *Shigematsu nikki* and Inose's claims. It is worth noting, however, that the plagiarism controversy does not affect Sakaki's argument.

71. The 1944 diary of the popular comedian Furukawa Roppa, published after the war as *Hishokuki* (A Record of Sad Eating), graphically shows how he coped with his gigantic appetite and his obsession with food. Hyakken wrote in June 1944, in the midst of a food shortage, a list of all the food he would love to eat (included in *Gochisōchō*, pp. 230–237).

72. The first critic to note this "ordinariness" seems to have been Etō Jun (see Shimada Akio, "*Kuroi ame*," p. 86). See John Whittier Treat, *Writing Ground Zero*, pp. 265–270 for a summary of the reception and evaluation of this work.

73. The historical Shigematsu Shizuma's wife was also called Shizuko, and she did keep a food record. The "Diary of the Illness of Yasuko Takamura," also attributed to Shizuko in the novel, is fictional. *Shigematsu nikki* includes the urtext for Iwatake's notes (pp. 219–252) and a series of letters from Ibuse to Shigematsu (pp. 255–271), one of which (dated February 2, 1965) includes a request for detailed information about the wartime diet in Hiroshima (p. 262).

74. Shigematsu uses the katakana word *hisutorii* in his declaration that his diary is his personal history that is to be submitted to the library (Ibuse, *Kuroi ame*, p. 33). A brief

note appears at the beginning of Shigematsu's "Journal of the Atomic Bomb": although its dated entries cover from August 6 to 15, it was written in September 1945. Given the extraordinary immediacy of the descriptions, however, it is easy for the reader to forget this one small line. Not surprisingly, Inose Naoki finds a kind of irony in this "copying" within the primary narrative of the novel, "for it was Ibuse himself who was copying" (*"Kuroi ame* to Ibuse Masuji no shinsō," p. 10).

75. Sakaki, *Recontextualizing Texts*, p. 69.

76. Ibuse, *Black Rain*, trans. John Bester, p. 63.

77. Ibid., p. 62.

78. See note 68 above. The episodes cited here are not strikingly original—most people will have read or heard similar stories elsewhere—which fits well with the intended ordinariness of this text and its writer.

79. Four *gō* is approximately 720 cc. The poem is commonly known as "Ame ni mo makezu" (Unyielding to Rain). Saitō Minako notes that the change from four to three *gō* was made in the immediate postwar period (*Senka no reshipi: Taiheiyō sensōka no shoku o shiru*, p. 66).

80. Ibuse, *Black Rain*, trans. John Bester, p. 66.

81. Ibid., p. 71.

82. Ibid., p. 49. A similar but simpler description can be found in the historical Shigematsu Shizuma's *Shigematsu nikki*, p. 17.

83. Ibuse, *Black Rain*, trans. John Bester, p. 50. This is not in *Shigematsu nikki*.

84. Ibuse, *Black Rain*, trans. John Bester, p. 122. This is not in *Shigematsu nikki*.

85. As noted earlier, the *ur*text by Iwatake Hiroshi is included in *Shigematsu nikki*, pp. 219–252.

86. Ibuse, *Black Rain*, trans. John Bester, p. 266. Blood transfusions, vitamin C, and peaches are very briefly mentioned in Iwatake's *ur*text (*Shigematsu nikki*, p. 250).

87. "Obsessed with Inscription" is the main part of Sakaki's title for her chapter on *Kuroi ame* in *Recontextualizing Texts*.

88. In Japanese, the English plural "s" is often omitted (e.g., Sebun Sutā for the cigarette name Seven Stars). Although some of the characters in the novel use *sebun rōzezu*, this would sound pedantic. The omission of "s" is surely also based on the fact that it sounds closer to Tōkyō Rōzu, which is the nickname for the group of women involved in the Japanese propaganda radio broadcasts addressed to American soldiers during the war.

89. In the mid-1970s Inoue acquired, at a secondhand bookshop, various private diaries written around 1945. Among them was the diary of a fan maker. While the story of *Tōkyō sebun rōzu* has no relation to this private diary, Inoue did incorporate details such as the prices of black-market goods and the weather in the particular Tokyo suburb, Nezu, where both the historical and the fictional fan maker diarists lived. See "Chosha ni kiku: Inoue Hisashi san" in the March 28, 1999, issue of the *Sankei shinbun*, available on the Internet: http://www.sankei.co.jp/databox/paper/9903/28/paper/today/book/28boo001.htm.

90. Although Inoue does not spell it out within the novel for his general audience, the original of this "Hall" is USNR Lt. Comdr. Robert King Hall Jr. (b. 1912), the author of *Education for a New Japan* (1949). According to its Preface (p. iii), Hall was "Chief of the Education Sub-Section, Educational Reorganization Officer, and Language Simplification Officer, of CI&E, GHQ, SCAP in the military occupation of Japan until the latter part of 1946." Marshall Unger states that "denunciations of Hall are a stock feature of Occupation reminiscences in the Japanese press" and emphasizes that "what really happened between 1945 and 1951 was anything but a simple black-and-white story of arrogant Americans versus powerless Japanese" (*Literacy and Script Reform in Occupation Japan: Reading between the Lines*, p. 7). Inoue's characterization of Hall in this novel certainly reflects the "black-and-white" view of the popular press in Japan. In my discussion I treat Inoue's "Hall" as a fictional character. For the historical Hall and his involvement in the script reform, see Unger's book.

91. According to Unger (*Literacy and Script Reform in Occupation Japan*, p. 76), in reality Hall's successor, Abraham Halpern, was "better schooled in linguistics."

92. Inoue Hisashi, *Tōkyō sebun rōzu*, p. 380.

93. Ibid., p. 75.

94. Ibid., pp. 347–348.

95. Ibid., p. 246.

96. Ibid., p. 259.

97. Ibid., p. 765.

98. Ohnuki-Tierney, *Rice as Self: Japanese Identities through Time*, p. 110.

99. Inoue Hisashi, *Tōkyō sebun rōzu*, p. 750.

100. Inoue Hisashi, "Suki de kirai de suki na Amerika," in *Kome no hanashi*, pp. 215–220.

101. Inoue Hisashi, *Tōkyō sebun rōzu*, p. 742.

Chapter 2. Down-to-Earth Eating and Writing (1)

1. Ishikawa Takuboku, *Takuboku zenshū*, vol. 4, pp. 211–212. This essay was first published in seven installments in the *Tōkyō mainichi shinbun* in late 1909. Its original title was "Yumichō yori" (From Yumichō), but it is usually referred to by its subtitle, "Kurau beki shi," partly to distinguish it from other essays titled "Yumichō yori." While the first word is usually read as *kuu*, the text (ibid., p. 211) indicates that it should be read here as *kurau*, which sounds even more vulgar than the plain *kuu* (to eat). It seems curiously postmodern that the title of this polemic essay was chosen under the influence of advertising copy. The choice of subtitle betrays the traditional importance given to drinking, for even though Takuboku claims that his interest is in "eating," his title actually derives from the "drinking" of beer. We may also note that "poems to eat" are likened here not to the national staple food—rice—but to humble pickles.

2. Carl Sesar's acclaimed translation of selected poems by Takuboku is titled

Takuboku: Poems to Eat. Sesar's Introduction includes translations of excerpts from the essay. As Sesar rightly points out, the most striking quality of Takuboku's poems is "their overwhelming personalism"; that is, "Takuboku is the subject of every poem he writes" (p. 17). While Takuboku may sincerely focus on what he somewhat hesitantly called "man's emotional life," he somehow fails to extend this focus to the community or society around him.

3. *Takuboku zenshū*, vol. 4, p. 215.

4. Ibid. Emphasis in original.

5. Quoted in the Introduction.

6. *Takuboku zenshū*, vol. 4, p. 215.

7. Ann Waswo, Acknowledgments, in Nagatsuka Takashi, *The Soil: A Portrait of Rural Life in Meiji Japan*, p. vi.

8. Ibid., Translator's Introduction, p. xv.

9. Ibid., pp. xvi–xvii. On the film adaptation of the novel, see also Keiko McDonald, *From Book to Screen: Modern Japanese Literature in Film*, pp. 40–45.

10. Waswo, Translator's Introduction, in Nagatsuka, *The Soil*, p. xviii.

11. Natsume Sōseki, "*Tsuchi* ni tsuite," *Sōseki zenshū*, vol. 9, pp. 1126–1127. My translation. Excerpts before and after the quoted passage are cited by Waswo Translator's Introduction, in Nagatsuka, *The Soil*, pp. xv–xvi.

12. See, for example, Usui Yoshimi's "Kaisetsu" in *Masaoka Shiki, Itō Sachio, Nagatsuka Takashi shū*, pp. 424–426. Usui regards Sōseki's lack of knowledge of farmers' life and his physical and mental condition as the two main causes of his limitations.

13. Kosugi Tengai et al., *Kosugi Tengai, Okamoto Kidō, Oguri Fūyō, Mayama Seika shū*, p. 297.

14. Yoshida Seiichi, "Kaisetsu," ibid., p. 411.

15. See, for example, Iwasa Sōshirō's chapter on *Tsuchi* in his *Seikimatsu no shizen shugi: Meiji yonjūnendai bungaku kō*, pp. 106–138. It is interesting that Komori Yōichi presents his reading of Sōseki's *Kōfu* as shaseibun (*Dekigoto to shite no yomu koto*, pp. 211–272).

16. *The Soil*, p. 180. Waswo's translation is considerably shorter than Nagatsuka's original (*Masaoka Shiki, Itō Sachio, Nagatsuka Takashi shū*, pp. 348–349), with both omissions and modifications. While this makes the translation much easier to read than the original, my point about the combination of the lyric and the scientific may not be as obvious as it is in the original. I have modified Waswo's romanization method of female names with the prefix "O" (e.g., Oshina and Otsugi) to conform to the method I use in the book (e.g., O-Shina, O-Tsugi).

17. See Iwasa, *Seikimatsu no shizen shugi*, p. 115.

18. *The Soil*, p. 28.

19. Ibid., p. 47.

20. Yasu-san is a character who appears in Sōseki's *Kōfu*. He is depicted as an exceptionally kind and educated miner who plays the role of mentor/protector of the young narrator-protagonist.

21. That eggs were a luxury and were given only to the sick is also evident in Mayama's *Minamikoizumi-mura*. While Kanji genuinely cares for O-Shina, Mayama's "beastly" peasant would rather let his wife die than feed her their eggs and reduce their income (*Kosugi Tengai, Okamoto Kidō, Oguri Fūyō, Mayama Seika shū*, p. 303). See also ibid., p. 308, where another farmer emphatically tells the doctor-narrator that he gave his sick child two large eggs.

22. Nakayama Kazuko, "Jendaa to kaikyū," in Nakayama Kazuko, Egusa Mitsuko, and Fujimori Kiyoshi, eds., *Jendaa no Nihon bungaku*, pp. 84–85.

23. The legend of "Obasute" (or Ubasute, Dumping the Old Woman) is found in *Yamato monogatari, Konjaku monogatari*, as well as in the Noh play and Fukazawa Shichirō's *Narayamabushi kō* (The Ballad of Narayama, 1966).

24. Frequently cited examples include Niwa Fumio's "Iyagarase no nenrei" (The Hateful Age, 1947), Tanizaki's *Fūten rōjin nikki* (Diary of a Mad Old Man, 1961–1962), and Ariyoshi Sawako's *Kōkotsu no hito* (Twilight Years, 1972), although some earlier texts such as Tayama Katai's *Sei* (Life, 1908) do include detailed depiction of old people.

25. Waswo, Translator's Introduction, in Nagatsuka, *The Soil*, p. xiii.

26. See *Masaoka Shiki, Itō Sachio, Nagatsuka Takashi shū*, p. 279, or *The Soil*, p. 80.

27. Nakayama, Egusa, and Fujimori, eds., *Jendaa no Nihon bungaku*, p. 86. See also ibid., pp. 88–89.

28. *Masaoka Shiki, Itō Sachio, Nagatsuka Takashi shū*, p. 346. Waswo translates this as "Uhei had never been a troublemaker" (*The Soil*, p. 177), which is both correct and appropriate in terms of his relationships with other villagers and his reputation, but in the particular context of our discussion the literal translation "wicked" seems more suitable.

29. For a concise summary of opposing views on this issue, see Iwasa, *Seikimatsu no shizen shugi*, pp. 124–129.

30. *Masaoka Shiki, Itō Sachio, Nagatsuka Takashi shū*, p. 314.

31. Iwasa, *Seikimatsu no shizen shugi*, pp. 125–126. The "intentional fallacy," from the title of an essay by W. K. Wimsatt and Monroe C. Beardsley, is explained in J. A. Cuddon's *Dictionary of Literary Terms* (p. 330) as "the error of criticizing and judging a work of literature by attempting to assess what the writer's intention was and whether or not he has fulfilled it rather than concentrating on the work itself."

32. Nakayama, Egusa, and Fujimori, eds., *Jendaa no Nihon bungaku*, pp. 86–87.

33. Karatani Kōjin, *Nihon kindai bungaku no kigen*, pp. 155–187.

34. Waswo, Translator's Introduction, in Nagatsuka, *The Soil*, p. xiii.

35. Or we might use Maeda Ai's key term, *de aru* (to be), to describe this representation of childhood as it (supposedly) is, in contrast to the *naru* (to become; i.e., childhood as a period of preparation for achieving success and prosperity) or the nostalgic *kaeru* (to return). See Maeda, "Kodomotachi no hen'yō: Kindai bungakushi no naka de."

36. Miyamoto Yuriko, *Miyamoto Yuriko shū*, p. 5.

37. Ibid., p. 7.

38. See Ogi Masahiro's *Rekishi wa gurume*, pp. 194–196.

39. Ibid., p. 196.

40. Shiga Naoya, *Shiga Naoya shū*, p. 367.

41. Ibid., p. 370.

42. *Miyamoto Yuriko shū*, pp. 41–42.

43. See, for example, the essays by Sakai Toshihiko and Itō Noe in Honda Shūgo, ed., *Miyamoto Yuriko kenkyū*.

44. *Miyamoto Yuriko shū*, p. 10.

45. Ibid., p. 17.

46. Ibid., p. 22.

47. See Miyoshi Jūrō, "Burujoa kishitsu no sayoku sakka," in Honda Shūgo, ed., *Miyamoto Yuriko kenkyū*, pp. 144–168.

48. An earlier (and much shorter) version of parts of this section and the next section on food in proletarian literature is to be found in my chapter "The Divided Appetite: 'Eating' in the Literature of the 1920s," in Elise K. Tipton and John Clark, eds., *Being Modern in Japan: Culture and Society from the 1910s to the 1930s*, pp. 156–157, 163–164.

49. *Miyazawa Kenji zenshū*, vol. 12, p. 10. Kenji, like many other poets of Meiji and Taishō, is often referred to by his personal name rather than by his surname.

50. *Miyazawa Kenji zenshū*, vol. 8, p. 346. As Oikawa Hitoshi notes ("Kenji dōwa no naka no kaze: *Chūmon no ōi ryōriten* kō," in Kusano, ed., *Miyazawa Kenji kenkyū*, p. 182), from a stylistic perspective it is doubtful whether this advertisement was written by Kenji himself.

51. *Miyazawa Kenji zenshū*, vol. 8, p. 244.

52. This was not published during Kenji's lifetime. It is included in *Miyazawa Kenji zenshū*, vol. 9, together with an unfinished draft of "1931-nendo kyokutō bijiterian taikai kenbunroku" (A Record of the 1931 Far East Vegetarian Convention). This latter manuscript is set at a hot-spring resort in Kenji's hometown Hanamaki instead of Newfoundland Island.

53. Saitō Bun'ichi, *Miyazawa Kenji to sono tenkai*, p. 70.

54. *Miyazawa Kenji zenshū*, vol. 9, p. 193.

55. Ibid., pp. 274–275. In these "production exercises" Takahashi Seori recognizes a strong element of *biomekhanika*, the Russian modernist theory of acting, which combines the "bio[logical]" with "mecha[nical, nism]." See Takahashi, "Biomehanika to Kenji engeki," in Andō Kyōko, ed., *Miyazawa Kenji*, pp. 142–146.

56. *Miyazawa Kenji zenshū*, vol. 8, p. 219.

57. Ibid.

58. Ibid., p. 220.

59. Amazawa Taijirō, "Sugame yomi *Chūmon no ōi ryōriten* ron: *Chūmon no ōi ryōriten* no naka no 'Chūmon no ōi ryōriten' no naka no 'Chūmon no ōi ryōriten'," in *Gengo bunka*, no. 21, p. 50. This issue (March 2004) of *Gengo bunka* (Language Culture, a journal of Meiji Gakuin University) features many other interesting essays on food, culture, and language.

60. This, in modern terms, is twelve years old.

61. Sata Ineko and Tsuboi Sakae, *Sata Ineko, Tsuboi Sakae shū*, p. 207.

62. G. T. Shea calls this father "an unsympathetic and indolent step-father" (G. T. Shea, *Leftwing Literature in Japan: A Brief History of the Proletarian Literary Movement*, pp. 298–299), but nowhere in the story is it suggested that the father is her stepfather; it is her mother who died, and her father's second marriage broke up. Shea's description of a letter from Hiroko's teacher is also misleading: it does not say "that trying to get money for school expenses is unimportant, that it is good enough if one has only finished elementary school" (ibid., p. 299); rather, it urges her to finish at least primary school and find someone to pay for her school expenses, which, in the teacher's opinion, should not be too difficult.

63. Sata and Tsuboi, *Sata Ineko, Tsuboi Sakae shū*, p. 207.

64. Hayama Yoshiki, Kobayashi Takiji, and Nakano Shigeharu, *Hayama Yoshiki, Kobayashi Takiji, Nakano Shigeharu shū*, p. 147.

65. Ibid., p. 150.

66. Ibid., p. 163. The metaphor of an octopus eating its own limbs also appears in nonproletarian literature such as Hagiwara Sakutarō's prose poem "Shinanai tako" (Itō Shinkichi et al., eds., *Nihon no shiika*, vol. 14, pp. 352–353).

67. *Hayama Yoshiki, Kobayashi Takiji, Nakano Shigeharu shū*, p. 162.

68. Aramata, *Puroretaria bungaku wa monosugoi*, pp. 30–39. Aramata also compares the horror elements in Japanese proletarian literature with late-nineteenth- to early-twentieth-century European socialist avant-garde theater and film.

69. Cited by Keene, *Dawn to the West*, vol. 1, p. 618.

70. Suzuki Sadami, *Nihon no "bungaku" o kangaeru*, pp. 213–218.

71. Keene, *Dawn to the West*, vol. 1, p. 616.

72. *Hayama Yoshiki, Kobayashi Takiji, Nakano Shigeharu shū*, p. 182. Emphasis in original.

73. Ibid., p. 148.

74. Ibid., p. 182.

Chapter 3. Down-to-Earth Eating and Writing (2)

1. Lupton, *Food, the Body and the Self*, p. 11.

2. Mizuta Noriko, *Nijusseiki no josei hyōgen: Jendā bunka no gaibu e*, p. 91.

3. Gayle Rubin, "The Traffic in Women: Notes on the 'Political Economy' of Sex," in Rayana Reiter, ed., *Toward an Anthropology of Women*, p. 165.

4. Janice Brown "prefer[s] to read Fumiko's writing of hunger primarily as literary strategy" ("De-siring the Center," p. 155).

5. Sharalyn Orbaugh, "The Body in Contemporary Japanese Women's Fiction," in Schalow and Walker, eds., *The Woman's Hand*, p. 123. Emphasis in original.

6. It was initially serialized in *Kaizō* from 1924, and was then published in book form

in 1928, the year, incidentally, that also saw the publication of Sata's "Kyarameru kōjō kara," Hayashi's *Hōrōki*, and Tanizaki's *Tade kuu mushi*.

7. Miyamoto Yuriko, *Miyamoto Yuriko shū*, p. 157.

8. Ibid., p. 165.

9. Rebecca Copeland, "Mythical Bad Girls: The Corpse, the Crone, and the Snake," in Laura Miller and Jan Bardsley, eds., *Bad Girls of Japan*, pp. 17–18.

10. Ibid., p. 16.

11. Ericson cites Nakamura Mitsuo's 1953 remark that writers such as Miyamoto are "closer to men or [. . .] give the reader the feeling of outdoing men, rather than being women" (Ericson, "The Origins of the Concept of 'Women's Literature,'" p. 96). Mizuta (*Nijusseiki no josei hyōgen*, pp. 74–94) carefully refutes Chida Hiroyuki's more recent (1998) claim that feminist critics have failed to understand the "phallic" text *Nobuko*.

12. Mizuta, *Nijusseiki no josei hyōgen*, p. 86.

13. Copeland, "Mythical Bad Girls," p. 16.

14. Sata and Tsuboi, *Sata Ineko, Tsuboi Sakae shū*, p. 8.

15. Ibid., p. 151.

16. Ibid., p. 191.

17. Counihan, *The Anthropology of Food and Body*, p. 75.

18. Nakano Shigeharu, "*Kurenai* no sakusha ni yosete," in Hirabayashi Takiko et al., *Hirabayashi Takiko, Sata Ineko, Amino Kiku, Tsuboi Sakae shū*, p. 404.

19. Sata and Tsuboi, *Sata Ineko, Tsuboi Sakae shū*, p. 10.

20. Hirabayashi et al., *Hirabayashi Takiko, Sata Ineko, Amino Kiku, Tsuboi Sakae shū*, p. 18.

21. In both this story and Sata's, there is absolutely no eroticism associated with the *mater nutrix* that we find in Tanizaki's literature.

22. Hirabayashi et al., *Hirabayashi Takiko, Sata Ineko, Amino Kiku, Tsuboi Sakae shū*, p. 24.

23. Ibid., p. 19.

24. Ibid., p. 20.

25. Ibid., p. 24.

26. Ibid., p. 26.

27. Ibid.

28. I thank Dr. Rebecca Copeland for directing my attention to this story.

29. Hirabayashi et al., *Hirabayashi Takiko, Sata Ineko, Amino Kiku, Tsuboi Sakae shū*, p. 55.

30. Ibid., p. 58.

31. Nakamura Mitsuo seems to believe that Hirabayashi, like Miyamoto, is a masculine-type writer (cited by Ericson, "The Origins of the Concept of 'Women's Literature,'" p. 96).

32. An earlier version of the following discussion is included in Aoyama, "Literary Daughters' Recipes: Food and Female Subjectivity in the Writings of Mori Mari and

Kōda Aya." I refer to this author by her given name, Aya, in order to distinguish her from her father, Kōda Rohan.

33. One recent caustic remark is found in Shōno Yoriko's *Yūkai Mori musume ibun*. Shōno criticizes the correctness and righteousness demonstrated by the heroine of Aya's *Nagareru* (Flowing). She even compares Aya's upbringing by Rohan to that of the Yapoo (from Numa Shōzō's novel discussed in chapter 4) for its "servile mode which makes her useful to others and at the same time makes her find aesthetic value in it" (p. 203).

34. For example, Alan M. Tansman, *The Writings of Kōda Aya: A Japanese Literary Daughter*, p. 8; and Ann Sherif, *Mirror: The Fiction and Essays of Kōda Aya*, pp. 131–135, 148–152, 159.

35. *Kōda Aya zenshū*, vol. 1, pp. 53–54. Aya's daughter Aoki Tama writes about this episode in more detail in Aoki, *Koishikawa no uchi*, pp. 161–170.

36. *Kōda Aya zenshū*, vol. 1, pp. 203–204.

37. Ibid., vol. 6, pp. 386–387.

38. Enchi was awarded the Joryū Bungakukai shō (Association of Women Writers Award) for the story discussed here and the fifth Joryū Bungaku shō (Women's Literature Award; 1965) as well as the Noma Literature Prize (1957), the Tanizaki Prize (1969), and the Order of Culture (1985).

39. Enchi Fumiko, *Yō, Hanakui uba*, pp. 145–146.

40. Ibid., p. 154.

41. Miyauchi Junko, "Hamo to satōgashi: Kindai bungaku no naka no 'hitokui' to 'hanakui.'"

42. Yasuoka Shōtarō, *Yasuoka Shōtarō shū*, p. 293. Perhaps it should be mentioned here that there is an earlier text containing scatological details. Hino Ashihei's *Funnyō tan* (A Tale of Excrement), the winner of the 1937 Akutagawa Prize, skillfully depicts the day-to-day lives of ordinary people from the perspective of a night-soil collector.

43. *Yasuoka Shōtarō shū*, pp. 315–316.

44. Kaikō Takeshi, however, rates this story and the futility it depicts as "by far the best of Yasuoka's works in terms of clarity and power" (*Saigo no bansan*, p. 22).

45. The title is modeled on Brecht's *Dreigroschenoper*. Kaikō's novel bears no relation to Takeda Rintarō's 1932 novel of the same title (see Sasaki Kiichi's "Kaisetsu" in the Shinchō Bunko edition of Kaikō, *Nihon sanmon opera*, pp. 289–290; and in Tatsumi Takayuki, *Nihon henryū bungaku*, p. 259). The discussion of this work overlaps part of my chapter "The Cooking Man in Japanese Literature," in Kam Louie and Morris Low, eds., *Asian Masculinities: The Meaning and Practice of Manhood in China and Japan*, pp. 165–167.

46. The Apaches did actually exist in postwar Osaka. Kaikō heard about them from a friend in Tokyo in September 1958 and spent a few weeks during October in his hometown of Osaka researching this novel. See Tanizawa Eiichi, *Kaisō Kaikō Takeshi*, pp. 181–182.

47. Yomota, *Bungakuteki kioku*, p. 181.

48. "Eating steel" is Apache slang for stealing scrap metal. Tatsumi Takayuki exam-

ines the theme of "iron-eating man" in a series of literary and *manga* texts (*Nihon henryū bungaku*, pp. 33–62).

49. Kaikō actually uses the word *derikashii* to describe Gon's highly developed sensibilities (*Kaikō Takeshi zenshū*, vol. 2, p. 373).

50. Yomota, *Bungakuteki kioku*, pp. 182–183.

51. *Animal to Edible*, pp. 127–128, cited in Lupton, *Food, the Body and the Self*, p. 120.

52. Dan, *Danryū kukkingu*, p. 24.

53. Stephen Mennell, *All Manners of Food: Eating and Tasting in England and France from the Middle Ages to the Present*, pp. 310–316.

54. Ibid., p. 311.

55. In the West (or at least in Britain), too, there seems to have been "something of an offal boom in recent years" (Bob Ashley, Joanne Hollows, Steve Jones, and Ben Taylor, *Food and Cultural Studies*, p. 1).

56. Ohnuki-Tierney, *Rice as Self*, p. 98.

57. See chapter 8 of McDonald, *From Book to Screen*, for a brief summary of the novel and an analysis of its film adaptations by Imai Tadashi (1968) and Higashi Yōichi (1992).

58. Sumii's husband, Inuta Shigeru (1891–1957), was a leader of the *nōmin bungaku*. The biographical information I give about Sumii is mainly based on her son's memoirs: Inuta Akira, *Haha, Sumii Sue no yokogao*.

59. Sumii, *The River with No Bridge*, p. 31 (*Hashi no nai kawa*, vol. 1, p. 50).

60. Sumii, *The River with No Bridge*, p. 231 (*Hashi no nai kawa*, vol. 1, p. 373).

61. Sumii, *The River with No Bridge*, pp. 209–210 (*Hashi no nai kawa*, vol. 1, pp. 339–340).

62. See Ohnuki-Tierney, *Rice as Self*, p. 38.

63. Sumii, *The River with No Bridge*, p. 38 (*Hashi no nai kawa*, vol. 1, p. 61). As Wilkinson notes in her Translator's Introduction (Sumii, *The River with No Bridge*, p. xiii), Sumii herself heard of this episode as a child. See also Sumii's Afterword in *Hashi no nai kawa*, vol. 1, p. 573.

64. It is interesting to compare Sumii's treatment of the Russo-Japanese War with the positive representation of the war in Shiba Ryōtarō's popular historical novel *Saka no ue no kumo* (Cloud above the Hill), which began its serialization in 1968, the year in which vol. 6 of *Hashi no nai kawa* was published.

65. Sumii, *The River with No Bridge*, p. 189 (*Hashi no nai kawa*, vol. 1, p. 308).

66. Sumii, *Hashi no nai kawa*, vol. 2, p. 60. The emperor referred to here is the Taishō emperor.

67. Ibid., vol. 7, p. 356.

68. The text used in this chapter is the Shinchō Bunko edition. Although the novel has not been translated into English in its entirety, Karen Colligan's "The Emergence of Environmental Literature in Japan" devotes one chapter to a discussion of it and appends translated excerpts. An earlier version of the discussion of this text was includ-

ed in my article "Food and Gender in Contemporary Japanese Women's Literature," pp. 119–122.

69. Colligan, "The Emergence of Environmental Literature," p. 242.

70. Ariyoshi Sawako, *Fukugō osen*, pp. 110, 228, 503.

71. Ibid., pp. 503–504.

72. Ibid., p. 508.

73. Ibid., pp. 84–85. Those in power still often attempt to reassure the public of their safety through demonstrations of drinking or eating: they are regularly to be seen on the television news eating vegetables suspected of dioxin or O-157 contamination. On the NHK news on February 19, 1999, for example, Prime Minister Obuchi ate spinach suspected of dioxin contamination, pronouncing it "Oishii!"

74. Ariyoshi, *Fukugō osen*, pp. 142–143.

75. When the *Asahi shinbun* commissioned Ariyoshi to write, she initially planned to write about the women's movement in Japan. This plan, however, altered completely when she realized that Ichikawa Fusae, who was to be one of the key figures in her serial, had suddenly made a "comeback" to the political arena from retirement. See Colligan, "The Emergence of Environmental Literature," pp. 244–245. Colligan (p. 248) also cites Ariyoshi's reply to a male science critic who suggested that she chose food as her topic because she is a woman: "Actually, I've never touched kitchen work. If you are trying to explain my selection of this theme as a female interest, you should see it as an expression of my basic responsibility toward children. This sense of responsibility is much greater in women than in men."

76. Orbaugh, "The Body in Contemporary Japanese Women's Fiction," pp. 157–158.

77. Ariyoshi, *Fukugō osen*, p. 251; emphasis in original.

78. Ibid., p. 327.

79. Ibid., p. 265; see also pp. 250, 252, 264.

80. Ibid., p. 368.

Chapter 4. Cannibalism in Modern Japanese Literature

1. This is the subtitle of Gang Yue, *The Mouth That Begs.*

2. I do not use this term in a Freudian or other theoretical sense, although Metz's notion of the text as a "'non-finalized' perpetual displacement" (cited in Robert Stam, Robert Burgoyne, and Sandy Flitterman-Lewis, *New Vocabularies in Film Semiotics: Structuralism, Post-Structuralism, and Beyond*, pp. 51–52) is a very interesting one, especially in relation to the notion of textual cannibalism.

3. Yano, *Yano Ryūkei shū*, p. 125.

4. Ueda, *Ugetsu Monogatari: Tales of Moonlight and Rain*, p. 189.

5. Ibid., p. 188.

6. For a more thorough study of the *yamanba* (or *yamauba*), see Mizuta Noriko and Kitada Sachie, eds., *Yamauba-tachi no monogatari: Josei no genkei to katarinaoshi.*

See also Meera Viswanathan's chapter "In Pursuit of the Yamanba: The Question of Female Resistance," in Schalow and Walker, *The Woman's Hand*, pp. 239–261; Rebecca Copeland's "Mythical Bad Girls"; and S. Yumiko Hulvey's "Man-Eaters: Women Writers and the Appropriation of the *Yamauba* Motif," in Eiji Sekine, ed., *Love and Sexuality in Japanese Literature*, pp. 240–249. Honda Masuko's *Kowakare no fōkuroa* also includes an insightful discussion of *yamauba* (pp. 67–120) although her prime focus is *yamauba* as mother.

7. Kawai, *Mukashi-banashi to Nihonjin no kokoro*, pp. 41–69.

8. Sérgio Luiz Prado Bellei, "Brazilian Anthropophagy Revisited," in Barker, Hulme, and Iversen, eds., *Cannibalism and the Colonial World*, p. 92.

9. Ibid., pp. 96–97, citing William Arens, *The Man-Eating Myth: Anthropology and Anthropophagy*, p. 145.

10. Bellei, "Brazilian Anthropophagy Revisited," p. 99.

11. Hayashi Fumiko, too, was influenced by Dadaism. See Brown, "De-siring the Center," pp. 145–151, about a comparison between Hayashi and male Japanese Dadaists such as Hagiwara Kyōjirō.

12. Itō Shinkichi et al., eds., *Nihon no shiika*, vol. 20, p. 197.

13. Ibid., p. 200.

14. This fascination is reported to have been aroused by an article on the movement in the *Yorozu chōhō* newspaper in August 1920. See Iijima Kōichi's notes and commentaries ibid., pp. 195–213. After that he produced Dadaist prose and poetry for several years, until he found a new interest, in Zen. But just in case one might think that Takahashi's Dadaism was merely a passing, imitative phase, as late as 1966 he wrote, "Is Dada dead? The Dadaist movement is over, but Dadaists are still alive. [. . .] After half a century Dada is not yet dead. [. . .] No one can predict what will bud in future" (quoted ibid., p. 277).

15. Murayama Kaita's 1915 cannibalism horror story (see note 25 below) cannot be regarded as a canonical text, even though it had a great impact, as mentioned later, upon writers such as Edogawa Ranpo.

16. The events depicted here were actually based on the story Nogami's brother heard from a family friend who was the captain of the sixty-ton schooner *Takayoshimaru*, which was rescued in February 1917. See Nogami's essay "*Kaijinmaru* gojitsu monogatari" (The Later Story of *Kaijinmaru*, first published in 1968, included in the revised Iwanami Bunko edition of *Kaijinmaru*, pp. 77–97), which also includes the fascinating real stories of the captain and the model for Hachizō, as well as an interesting meeting between Nogami and a retired seaman who rescued the *Takayoshimaru*.

17. Rebecca Copeland, ed., *Woman Critiqued: Translated Essays on Japanese Women's Writing*, has a good sample of texts that conform to the stereotypical image of women's literature. See also Ericson's "The Origins of the Concept of 'Women's Literature,'" pp. 74–115. See *Subaru*, January 2002, for an interesting roundtable discussion (*zadankai*) between Tsushima Yūko, Inoue Hisashi, and Komori Yōichi ("Josei sakka: Nogami Yaeko, Sata Ineko, Enchi Fumiko o chūshin ni") in which the significance of *Kaijinmaru* is men-

tioned. At one point in the discussion, however, it is erroneously stated that Hachizō eats Sankichi (p. 284).

18. Nogami Yaeko (shown as Yae-ko Nogami in this publication), *The Neptune, The Foxes*, trans. Ryōzo Matsumoto, pp. 53–54. In the Iwanami Bunko edition of *Kaijinmaru* this appears on pp. 40–41.

19. Konpira, or Kumbhira, is to be found in Shinto shrines, but the deity comes from India and is one of the twelve divine generals guarding Yakushi (Bhéchadjaguru). Kaijinmaru, the title of the story and the name of the boat, suggests the symbolic power of this imported and naturalized deity.

20. We may also remember the female black widow spider that appears as the tattoo design in Tanizaki's short story "Shisei" (The Tattoo, 1910; trans. *The Tattooer*). As Suzuki Sadami points out, female black widow spiders are said to eat the ugly and much smaller males after mating ("Eroticism, Grotesquerie, and Nonsense in Taishō Japan: Tanizaki's Responses to Modern and Contemporary Culture," in Boscaro and Chambers, eds., *A Tanizaki Feast*, p. 45).

21. In the following I shall refer to the author as Kanoko rather than Okamoto, both to distinguish her from her husband, Ippei, and her son, Tarō, both of whom will be referred to in chapter 5, and to conform to the convention.

22. English translation is included in Charlotte Eubanks, "Re-Writing the Myth of Motherhood: Short Stories by Okamoto Kanoko and Hirabayashi Taiko," pp. 289–294.

23. Ibid., p. 289.

24. Ibid., p. 294.

25. Ranpo is by far the best-known writer of horror stories with the theme of cannibalism. There were many other stories of this sort published in the late 1920s and 1930s. The earliest example, however, seems to be "Akuma no shita" (The Satanic Tongue, 1915) by Murayama Kaita (1896–1919), which is included in Nanakita Kazuto, ed., *Jinniku shishoku*, and also in the Aozora Bunko (http://www.aozora.gr.jp/). The story, which takes the form of a discovered manuscript, involves a murder, in fact a fratricide, for the purpose of anthropophagy. Murayama died of Spanish flu only a few years after this publication. Ranpo admired the work of this meteoric artist-poet. For more about Murayama, see Jeffrey Angles, "The Heritage of Symbolism: The 'Aesthetic' style of Kitahara Hakushu and Murayama Kaita."

26. In *Yami ni ugomeku* Ranpo alludes to Tanizaki's foot fetishism (*Ankokusei, Yami ni ugomeku*, p. 161).

27. As noted above, Murayama's "Akuma no shita" also takes this form, although the manuscript is hidden by the murderous poet near his house in Tokyo before his suicide so that his friend (narrator) can secretly retrieve it.

28. *Ankokusei, Yami ni ugomeku*, p. 302.

29. The second half of the title is written in the Chinese characters for sausages (*chōzume*) with the reading *sōsēji* indicated in hiragana rather than katakana.

30. *Makura* is an introductory part, usually short but in some cases quite extensive, placed before the main part of the *rakugo* narrative. Beginning with seasonal greetings

and thanks to the audience, it introduces the main topic, usually by relating it to familiar events or scenes. In recent years *makura* has often been used to familiarize the younger audience with terms, events, or old customs that play a crucial role in the main part of the narrative.

31. There is another text, slightly earlier than Yumeno's, that deals with a historical demon butcher. Maki Itsuma's nonfiction "Nikuya ni baketa hitooni" (A Human Devil in the Disguise of a Butcher, included in Nanakita, ed., *Jinniku shishoku*) recounts the story of Fritz Haarmann, who raped and killed at least twenty-eight boys, mostly teenagers, between 1918 and 1924, and sold their flesh in his shop in Hanover.

32. Yumeno, *Yumeno Kyūsaku*, p. 372.

33. We have seen another dangerously sexy Eurasian (Korean-Russian) prostitute, Louise, in Tanizaki's *Tade kuu mushi*.

34. Yumeno, *Yumeno Kyūsaku*, pp. 396–397.

35. Ibid., pp. 364–366.

36. The 1816 incident inspired not only Géricault's *Raft of the Medusa* but also works of fiction and nonfiction. See Nakano Miyoko, *Kanibarizumu ron*, pp. 15–18. In Japan, Hisao Jūran, for example, wrote both the nonfiction *Kainanki* (1952) and a novel *Noa* (1950), which adapts the historical incident to a Japanese military ship in the Philippine Sea. The protagonist of *Noa* presents an interesting contrast to that of *Nobi*. He is a Japanese American who is repatriated to Japan after two years of internment in America. His humanitarian mission as a member of the International Red Cross and his Christian beliefs make him reject both suicide and cannibalism, the latter occurring on a huge raft like the *Medusa*. In the final part of the novel the protagonist, the only survivor on the raft, chooses to feed his flesh to a starving bird rather than to eat the bird to prolong his life. After three days the bird recovers and flies away, while the hero calmly dies (*Hisao Jūran zenshū*, vol. 3, p. 229).

37. Ōoka Shōhei, translated by Ivan Morris, *Fires on the Plain*, pp. 177–178. For the Japanese text see *Ōoka Shōhei zenshū*, vol. 3, p. 95. Hereafter the page numbers in the Japanese text are indicated in parentheses unless otherwise noted.

38. In the earlier version of the novel Tamura's narrative followed an introduction by another narrator who encouraged Tamura to write. This introduction, which is completely omitted in the revised version, also mentions the deterioration of Tamura's mental and physical condition and his subsequent death. The omitted part is included in *Ōoka Shōhei zenshū*, vol. 3, pp. 137–143. For a discussion of the revision, see Tabata, "Kaisō to genzai: Ōoka Shōhei *Nobi*," in Kitaoka Seiji and Mino Hiroshi, eds., *Shōsetsu no naratorojī: Shudai to hensō*.

39. *Fires on the Plain*, p. 178 (p. 96).

40. Dennis Washburn carefully analyzes the significance of amnesia in "Toward a View from Nowhere: Perspective and Ethical Judgment in *Fires on the Plain*."

41. *Fires on the Plain*, p. 190 (p. 103).

42. Ibid., p. 193 (p. 104).

43. As Erik Lofgren points out ("Christianity Excised: Ichikawa Kon's 'Fires on the

Plain'"), in the 1959 film adaptation of the novel by Ichikawa Kon, the Christian element and much of the cannibalism are excised.

44. *Fires on the Plain*, p. 199 (pp. 107–108).

45. Ibid., p. 223 (p. 123).

46. Ibid., p. 224 (p. 124).

47. *Ōoka Shōhei zenshū*, vol. 3, p. 129. This conversation, which goes on to discuss the diagnosis of the "Messiah complex," is omitted in Morris' translation. Morris also omits the epigraph of the novel.

48. *Fires on the Plain*, p. 238 (p. 131).

49. In an earlier chapter the word *batten* (the X mark, symbol of negation and erasure) is used for the mark on the crest, whereas in the final chapter it is replaced by another word, *jūji* (a mark in the shape of the character for ten—i.e., shaped like +—a strong reminder of the crucifix, *jūjika*). *Fires on the Plain*, pp. 118, 244 (pp. 65, 134).

50. Peter Hulme, "Introduction: The Cannibal Scene," in Barker, Hulme, and Iversen, eds., *Cannibalism and the Colonial World*, p. 20, in reference to Mary Louise Pratt's *Imperial Eyes*.

51. Takeda Taijun, *This Outcast Generation, Luminous Moss*, trans. Yusaburo Shibuya and Sanford Goldstein, p. 102. For the Japanese text see Takeda, *Hikarigoke*, p. 175. Hereafter the page numbers of the Japanese text are indicated in parentheses unless otherwise noted.

52. In the English translation M is changed to Mori and S to Sato.

53. Takeda, *This Outcast Generation, Luminous Moss*, p. 105 (p. 178).

54. Ibid., p. 112 (p. 184). The last remark reminds us of Endō Shūsaku's novel *Umi to dokuyaku* (The Sea and Poison, 1957), the main theme of which is the vivisection of American prisoners of war, although eating the liver of the victims is also mentioned.

55. Takeda, *Hikarigoke*, p. 185—my translation, to highlight the cooking metaphor (*shōsetsu no sara ni moriageru*). In *This Outcast Generation, Luminous Moss*, p. 112, it is translated as "the best way to turn this incident into a novel."

56. Takeda, *This Outcast Generation, Luminous Moss*, p. 114 (p. 187).

57. No explanation is given as to why Takeda changed the Makkaushi of the first half of the story to Makkausu. The only hint in Takeda's text seems to be that Rausu comes from the Ainu word Raushi (Takeda, *Hikarigoke*, p. 166). The Ainu meaning of Makkaushi is given as "a place abundant with butterburs" (ibid., p. 170). Perhaps the reader as the "director" is expected to take special note that Makkausu is different from the actual place and that the play is not confined to the historical facts. As mentioned earlier, the actual incident took place in Pekin Misaki rather than in Makkausu or Makkaushi.

58. Takeda, *This Outcast Generation, Luminous Moss*, p. 125 (p. 202).

59. Nakano Miyoko sees a suggestion of homosexual desire in the captain (Nakano, *Kanibarizumu ron*, p. 25).

60. Takeda, *This Outcast Generation, Luminous Moss*, p. 131 (p. 210).

61. Nakano, *Kanibarizumu ron*, pp. 28–37.

62. In Takeuchi Yoshimi's Japanese translation the famous last line of the story is

more suggestive than "Save the children": "Are there any children who have not eaten human beings? At least those children should ..." (Lu Xun, *Rojin bunshū,* vol. 1, p. 28).

63. It should also be noted that "Kyōjin nikki" is used as a chapter title in *Nobi.*

64. See Aoyama, "The Love That Poisons," pp. 38–39, and Atsuko Sakaki's Introduction in Kurahashi, *The Woman with the Flying Head and Other Stories by Kurahashi Yumiko,* pp. xiv–xv.

65. Sakaki (in Kurahashi, *The Woman with the Flying Head and Other Stories by Kurahashi Yumiko,* p. xv), citing Kurahashi's "Shōsetsu no meiro to hiteisei," translated by Dennis Keene.

66. Kurahashi, *The Adventures of Sumiyakist Q,* p. 47 (*Sumiyakisuto Q no bōken,* p. 64). Hereafter the page numbers of the Japanese text are indicated in parentheses.

67. Ibid., p. 51 (p. 68).

68. Ibid., p. 183 (p. 223).

69. Ibid., p. 194 (p. 237).

70. Ibid., pp. 176–177 (pp. 215–217).

71. Ibid., p. 236 (p. 289). Here we see clear traces of Sartre. See Michel Onfray's *Le ventre de philosophes* (trans. *Tetsugakusha no shokutaku,* pp. 167–190) for an interesting analysis of food in Sartre's life and works.

72. Kurahashi, *The Adventures of Sumiyakist Q,* p. 243 (pp. 299–300).

73. Ibid., p. 353 (p. 430).

74. Claude Lévi-Strauss, *The Raw and the Cooked.*

75. Kurahashi, *The Adventures of Sumiyakist Q,* pp. 361–362 (*Sumiyakisuto Q no bōken,* pp. 440–441). The Doktor seems too tired in this scene to elaborate on the "fermented."

76. The first story is "Kanibarisuto fusai" and the second "Ōgurukoku kōkaiki," both in *Kurahashi Yumiko no kaiki shōhen.*

77. Kara, *Sagawa-kun kara no tegami,* p. 175. It would be difficult, if not impossible, to connect Kara's use of the term "misreading" to that of Harold Bloom in *A Map of Misreading;* in Kara's text we cannot find the oedipal fear of the "influence" of the preceding texts.

78. The poem is Johannes R. Becher's "Abend," part of which is included in the Appendix of Kara, *Sagawa-kun kara no tegami,* pp. 152–153.

79. For a concise explanation of these terms from Genette's *Palimpsestes,* see Stam, Burgoyne, and Flitterman-Lewis, *New Vocabularies in Film Semiotics,* pp. 206–209.

80. About half the Akutagawa Prize selection committee members rejected this novel as "completely unintelligible" (Maruya Saiichi), an "uninteresting treatment of an interesting incident" (Nakamura Mitsuo), and "not much more than research memos" (Kaikō Takeshi). The other half, particularly Ōe Kenzaburō and Niwa Fumio, praised the dramatic or performative devices in the novel. See "Akutagawa-shō senpyō," *Bungei shunjū,* March 1983, pp. 394–398.

81. Kara, *Sagawa-kun kara no tegami,* p. 30.

82. Ibid., p. 123.

83. *Ōoka Shōhei zenshū*, vol. 3, p. 103. "Rubbing," like "misreading" and "interreading," is a term used in intertexuality theory by Jonathan Culler and others. See Tsuchida Tomonori, *Kantekusutosei no senryaku*, pp. 70–87.

84. In real life Sagawa did publish *Kiri no naka* and a series of other books.

85. Nakano, *Kanibarizumu ron*, pp. 64–65.

86. Henmi, *Mono kuu hitobito*, p. 49.

87. Ibid., 50.

88. Ibid., pp. 50–51.

89. Ibid., p. 53.

90. The English title is the one chosen by the author and shown on the cover of the Gentōsha paperback edition. Most of the English terms cited below were coined by Numa. The publication dates refer to various book-form editions (1970, 72, 83, 91, 93, 99) rather than to the serialization in magazines. The Gentōsha edition not only has the complete version of the novel but also includes a series of the author's afterwords attached to previous editions and commentaries by five critics.

91. Numa, *Kachikujin yapū*, vol. 5, p. 336.

92. Ibid., p. 166.

93. Jonathan Swift, *Gulliver's Travels*, pp. 204–205.

94. Numa, *Kachikujin yapū*, vol. 5, p. 215. The term *agape*, "a 'love feast' held by the early Christians in connection with the Lord's Supper" (*The Shorter Oxford Dictionary*), is deliberately distorted here to indicate the pious love of the Yapoos for their white goddesses.

95. Ibid., vol. 1, p. 120.

96. Ibid., p. 119.

97. See Numa's 1970 "Atogaki," ibid., vol. 5, p. 340. Numa uses the English (as Stendhal did).

98. Ibid., p. 317.

99. Maeda, "Kaisetsu," first published in 1984, included ibid., vol. 2, pp. 313–342.

100. Ibid., vol. 1, pp. 214–215.

101. Okuno, "Kaisetsu," included ibid., pp. 350–358.

102. Aramata, "Kaisetsu," ibid., vol. 4, pp. 334–354.

103. Takahashi, "Kaisetsu," ibid., vol. 5, p. 380.

104. Tatsumi, "Kaisetsu," ibid., vol. 3, p. 401.

Chapter 5. The Gastronomic Novel

1. An earlier version of the discussion of four prewar texts (*Kuidōraku*, "Chinsenkai," "Bishoku kurabu," and "Shokuma") was published as "Romancing Food: The Gastronomic Quest in Early Twentieth Century Japanese Literature," *Japanese Studies* 23, no. 3 (December 2003): 251–264.

2. Brillat-Savarin, *Physiologie du goût avec une lecture de Roland Barthes*, pp. 103–104. In Japanese translation (by Sekine Hideo and Tobe Matsumi) *Bimi raisan*, vol. 1, pp. 206–207.

3. The Kyoto cuisine praised by Misako's father in *Tade kuu mushi* (discussed in the Introduction) is exceptional. Even this, however, can be interpreted as the Tokyoite's admiration for a foreign culture.

4. The reading of the title in the original newspaper serialization is *kuidōraku*, but its book-form publication adopts the reading *shokudōraku*, which Gensai himself seems to have favored in his later years. See his daughter Murai Yoneko's notes in *Fukkokuban Kuidōraku kaisetsuhen* (the Appendix to the boxed set of *Kuidōraku*, reprint of the 1903 publication of the complete novel in four volumes), p. 38. See also Kuroiwa Hisako's *"Kuidōraku" no hito Murai Gensai*, p. 181, for an interesting comment by Miyatake Gaikotsu about the change of reading from *kui* to *shoku*. As for the text, the more accessible *Kuidōraku no reshipi* includes an abridged and annotated version of volume 3 of the novel. Shibata Shoten made the complete edition available on the Internet: http://www.yumyumtown.com/lib/shokudoraku/ (accessed May 2006). The text is now also available in Iwanami Bunko edition (2 vols.).

5. For more detailed estimation, see Kuroiwa, *"Kuidōraku" no hito Murai Gensai*, p. 169.

6. According to Murai Yoneko (Appendix to *Kuidōraku*, p. 37), the kabuki actor Onoe Baikō VI played the part of O-Towa and cooked *chou à la crème* for the audience in the Kabukiza theater. Kuroiwa reveals, however, that the production was not regarded as a success financially or artistically (*"Kuidōraku" no hito Murai Gensai*, pp. 174–175).

7. *Kuidōraku*, vol. 3, p. 115. Also found in *Kuidōraku no reshipi*, p. 40.

8. *Kuidōraku*, vol. 3, pp. 273–274. An abridged version is found in *Kuidōraku no reshipi*, p. 96.

9. Terry Eagleton, *Literary Theory: An Introduction*, p. 23, quoting George Gordon's inaugural lecture at Oxford.

10. Besides sequels to *Kuidōraku* and a number of other popular novels and didactic books, Gensai published a novel in English (translated by his friend Kawai Unkichi). Entitled *Hana, a Daughter of Japan*, the eponymous heroine, again a young, beautiful woman talented in cooking, is involved in an international love triangle with a Russian spy and a young American man; the latter, predictably at the time of the Russo-Japanese War, wins Hana's heart. Gensai's interest gradually moved from food to fasting and alternative medicine. For more about this fascinating figure see Kuroiwa's biography, *"Kuidōraku" no hito Murai Gensai*.

11. As noted above, *Kuidōraku*, too, adopts some demonstrative names. It also begins with a comic dialogue, very much in the Edo tradition, between the personified Stomach and Intestines of Ōhara, which are complaining about their host's monstrous eating. Such comic elements, however, are limited to this scene and a few others.

12. Kōda Rohan, "Chinsenkai," in Nanjō Takenori, ed., *Bishoku*, pp. 53–54. Given the popularity of *Kuidōraku*, it is not surprising to find numerous other parodies, includ-

ing Miyatake Gaikotsu's "Kuchi[mouth, linguistic]dōraku," which takes the form of an interview with O-Towa, cleverly imitating her enthusiastic speech style in Gensai's novel. See Kuroiwa, *"Kuidōraku" no hito Murai Gensai*, pp. 179–180.

13. Shibusawa Tatsuhiko, *Hanayakana shokumotsushi*, p. 73.

14. Johan Huizinga, *Homo Ludens: A Study of the Play Element in Culture*, p. 32.

15. Ibid., pp. 26–32.

16. Ibid., p. 67.

17. The English translation of this story is included in *The Gourmet Club: A Sextet*. In Tanizaki's text, "Gastronomer Club" is given as the English version of the club name. Tanizaki Jun'ichirō, *Tanizaki Jun'ichirō zenshū*, vol. 6, p. 167.

18. *Tanizaki Jun'ichirō zenshū*, vol. 6, pp. 144–145.

19. Roland Barthes, *The Rustle of Language*, pp. 267–268.

20. In his younger days Tanizaki was keenly interested in Western aesthetic writers, particularly Oscar Wilde, whose Dorian Gray, in turn, was famously fascinated by *À Rebours*.

21. Joris-Karl Huysmans, *Against Nature*, trans. Robert Baldick, pp. 208–209. Shibusawa Tatsuhiko discusses the peptone enema and a few other examples of extraordinary "eating" from Huysmans' book as a paragon of the play element in *gourmandise* (*Hanayakana shokumotsushi*, pp. 74–78).

22. Arashiyama, *Bunjin akujiki*, pp. 186–196; Kaikō, *Saigo no bansan*, p. 152.

23. In recent years, however, there seems to be a move to examine Gensai and his work, as indicated by Kuroiwa's biography and the addition of *Kuidōraku* to the Iwanami Bunko.

24. Kitaōji Rosanjin, *Rosanjin midō*, p. 382.

25. Ibid., p. 37.

26. Ibid., pp. 14–15. It is also notable that in the course of these two pages fifteen different onomatopoeic terms are used.

27. Kaikō Takeshi, for example, writes that this text is "neither a very famous work nor a widely known short story" (*Saigo no bansan*, p. 144). For discussions of the story, see Arashiyama, *Bunjin akujiki*, pp. 186–196; Takahashi Gen'ichirō, *Bungakuō*, pp. 55–59.

28. The best-known and most elaborate manifesto is his collection of essays *In'ei raisan* (In Praise of Shadows, 1933–1934).

29. The writers Kawamoto cites include Tanizaki, Akutagawa, Kinoshita Mokutarō, and Satō Haruo. See Kawamoto, *Taishō gen'ei*, pp. 165–201.

30. Ibid., p. 182.

31. The date of first publication is unknown. It was included in the collection of short stories *Sushi* (1941).

32. In her dialogue with Kanoko's son, Okamoto Tarō (entitled "'Haha' naru Kanoko"), Ariyoshi Sawako mentions "Shokuma" as a story about the young Rosanjin. Okamoto Kanoko, *Okamoto Kanoko zenshū*, Bekkan 2, p. 268.

33. *Okamoto Kanoko zenshū*, vol. 5, p. 288. The story is also included in Okamoto Kanoko, *Rōgishō*.

34. When men's cooking was popularized in the 1970s and 1980s, this kind of discourse also gained currency. See, for example, the dialogue between writers Yoshiyuki Junnosuke and Dan Kazuo, both noted gourmands, in Yamamoto Yōrō, ed., *Seihin no shokutaku*, p. 252.

35. *Okamoto Kanoko zenshū*, vol. 5, pp. 286–287, 289. Ironically, Kanoko is well known for her thick makeup. Besshirō's frequent use of simile may be a typical rhetoric in gourmet aphorism. We will see similar examples in Murakami Ryū's stories.

36. Ibid., p. 290.

37. Ibid., p. 294.

38. This inevitably calls to mind Gayle Rubin's account of the notion of a "gift of women" and "the traffic in women." As Rubin notes, "The result of a gift of women is more profound than the result of other gift transactions, because the relationship thus established is not just one of reciprocity, but one of kinship" (Rubin, "The Traffic in Women," in Reiter, ed., *Toward an Anthropology of Women*, p. 173).

39. *Okamoto Kanoko zenshū*, vol. 5, p. 314.

40. Ibid., p. 315.

41. Ibid., p. 211.

42. One must note that Kanoko's "motherly love" is just as complex and problematic as the equally prominent trope of "eternal mother" in Tanizaki literature. While it is outside the scope of this book to discuss either trope in detail, it is relevant to point out that they are both literary and fictional tropes. In Kanoko's case, her son Okamoto Tarō and writer Ariyoshi Sawako agree that in real life Kanoko did not possess any maternal instinct. See ibid., Bekkan 2, p. 265. A similar fictionality can be found in her treatment of *gourmandise;* unlike Tanizaki, she was never regarded as a gourmet. This is also discussed by Ariyoshi, ibid., p. 271.

43. While studying at Kyoto University, Aoki was taught by Rohan.

44. Aoki Masaru, "Tōzentei," in Nanjō Takenori, ed., *Bishoku*, p. 22. The story is also included in Aoki Masaru, *Kakoku fūmi*, Iwanami Bunko.

45. See Nanjō's "Kaidai," in *Bishoku*, p. 232. That this story was included in Aoki's collection of essays must be another reason for this misunderstanding. Like Nanjō, poet Takahashi Mutsuo thought at first that the restaurant actually existed; see Takahashi, *Shijin no shokutaku*, pp. 197–199.

46. Nanjō, ed., *Bishoku*, pp. 25, 27.

47. Maruya Saiichi, *Shikō no ressun*, pp. 53–54.

48. Nanjō, ed., *Bishoku*, p. 37.

49. Ibid., p. 38.

50. This story is included not in the 1969 collection of his works, *Hisao Jūran zenshū*, but in Hisao Jūran, *Pari no ame* (pp. 53–66), one of the volumes published in the series Collection Juranesque. According to the editorial note in *Pari no ame*, p. 66, "Hanaawase" was first published in the May 1946 issue of *Fujin bunko*. In the following discussion I use the text in Nanjō's anthology *Bishoku*.

51. Hisao, whose real name was Abe Masao, went to Paris in late 1929 and remained

in France until early 1933. The purpose of this stay is not clear: he is said to have studied optics and drama. For more information on this interesting but mysterious writer, see Eguchi Yūsuke's *Hisao Jūran.*

52. Hisao Jūran, "Hana-awase," in Nanjō, ed., *Bishoku,* p. 157.

53. This brings to mind one of the wartime slogans, "Nani ga nan demo kabocha o ueyō" (Plant pumpkins at every opportunity), which is mentioned in Shigeko's record in *Black Rain* (Ibuse, *Kuroi ame,* p. 67).

54. Nanjō, ed., *Bishoku,* p. 164.

55. Ibid., p. 161.

56. This name, like those in Rohan's story, is comic and demonstrative (*kane* means "money" or "gold"). The *maro* in his given name Katsumaro, on the other hand, suggests his aristocratic status (as in Konoe Fumi*maro*). It is mentioned in the story that Kaneda died of stomach cancer in 1942, only one year after his marriage to Senko.

57. Nanjō, ed., *Bishoku,* p. 165.

58. The story was first published in the October 25, 1950, issue of *Sandē mainichi.* It was not published as part of a collection during Mishima's lifetime, but is included in *Mishima Yukio zenshū,* vol. 7, pp. 107–130.

59. Ibid., vol. 27, p. 270. It is doubtful that his readers would agree with him.

60. All of these were used as the titles of his books: *Saishō onzōshi hinkyū su* (1954); *Kojiki ōji* (1956); and *Sanmon shinshi* (1956), which is a parody of the derogatory term *sanmon bunshi* (penny-a-liner).

61. Yoshida also translated Hisao Jūran's "Boshizō" as "Mother and Son," which won the first prize in the second series of World Prize Stories in 1955.

62. Yoshida Ken'ichi, *Hontō no yō na hanashi,* pp. 35–36. Yoshida's translation of Laforgue's *Hamlet* (as *Hamuretto ibun*) was published in 1947.

63. Yoshida, *Hontō no yō na hanashi,* p. 20.

64. Ibid., p. 218.

65. Ibid., p. 62. In this translation of the passage I have purposely tried to maintain the length of each sentence in the original.

66. Shimizu Tōru, *Kagami to erosu to: dōjidai bungaku ron,* pp. 47–48.

67. On this book and the theme of men's cooking, see Aoyama, "The Cooking Man in Modern Japanese Literature," pp. 155–176. The following discussion of Dan's novel overlaps part of this earlier essay (ibid., pp. 160–162).

68. The name is an easily recognizable modification of Dan Kazuo. Kazuo is written in different characters here, but Katsura and Dan are both names of trees. Such transparent modification is a convention of *shishōsetsu.*

69. Dan Kazuo, *Kataku no hito,* vol. 1, p. 111; vol. 2, p. 246.

70. Kyū Eikan, *Shoku wa Kōshū ni ari,* p. 17. Although Kyū's father was not a professional chef like the father in the Taiwanese film *Eat, Drink, Man, Woman,* his culinary knowledge and passion seem just as advanced.

71. Dan, *Kataku no hito,* vol. 1, p. 36. "The country was devastated" is an allusion to Tu Fu's famous line.

72. Ibid., vol. 2, p. 248. A similar passage can be found earlier in the novel, vol. 1, p. 138.

73. Kaikō, trans. Cecilia Seigle, *Darkness in Summer*, p. 20. (For the Japanese text see *Kaikō Takeshi zenshū*, vol. 7, p. 328.) Hereafter page numbers of Seigle's translation are placed first, followed by corresponding pages in *Kaikō Takeshi zenshū*, vol. 7, in parentheses.

74. *Darkness in Summer*, pp. 39–40 (p. 348).

75. Ibid., p. 143 (p. 452).

76. Ibid., p. 190 (p. 499).

77. Ibid., p. 205 (p. 514).

78. Ibid., p. 206 (p. 515).

79. Brillat-Savarin, *Physiologie du goût*, p. 37. The English translation is M. F. K. Fisher's in *The Physiology of Taste*, p. 4. In the Japanese translation of this aphorism (see *Bimi raisan*, trans. Sekine and Tobe, vol. 1, p. 23) that Kaikō uses as an epigraph to the novel, *étoile* is translated as *tentai*.

80. *Kaikō Takeshi zenshū*, vol. 6, p. 276. *Takoyaki* is a kind of ball-shaped pancake, slightly smaller than a ping-pong ball, with a tiny piece of octopus at its core.

81. Ibid., p. 304.

82. Ibid., pp. 410–411.

83. Ibid., p. 434.

84. Ibid., pp. 502–503.

85. Ibid., p. 512.

86. Ibid., p. 520.

87. Murakami Ryū, *Murakami Ryū jisen shōsetsu shū*, vol. 3, pp. 60, 69, 95, 110.

88. Ibid., pp. 149–150.

89. Ibid., p. 100.

90. Ibid., p. 580.

91. Saitō Minako is one of the most vocal critics of the inanity of metaphors in this and many other contemporary gourmet novels. See *Bungakuteki shōhingaku*, pp. 87–97, 109.

92. Nanjō Takenori, *Shusen*, pp. 165–169.

93. Nanjō Takenori, *Mankan zenseki*, p. 16.

94. Also known as Empress Dowager Cixi, Western Empress Dowager (1835–1908).

95. Nanjō, *Mankan zenseki*, p. 115.

96. Nanjō Takenori, *Juen*.

Chapter 6. Food and Gender in Contemporary Women's Literature

1. See, for example, the section "Gendered foods," in Lupton, *Food, the Body and the Self*, pp. 104–111. See also Michael Ashkenazi and Jeanne Jacob, *The Essence of Japanese Cuisine: An Essay on Food and Culture*, pp. 105–111; and Pat Caplan, "Approaches to Food, Health and Identity," in Caplan, ed., *Food, Health and Identity*, pp. 9–11.

2. Ishige, *Shokuji no bunmeiron*, p. 57.

3. Miyashita Kikurō, *Taberu seiyō bijutsushi: "Saigo no bansan" kara yomu*, p. 225.

4. Caplan, ed., *Food, Health and Identity*, p. 10, citing Amartya Sen.

5. "Reading Brillat-Savarin," in Barthes, *The Rustle of Language*, p. 253.

6. Miyashita Kikurō, *Taberu seiyo bijutsushi: "Saigo no bansan" kara yomu*, pp. 224–225.

7. Beardsworth and Keil, *Sociology on the Menu*, p. 2.

8. Luce Giard, "Doing-Cooking," in Michel de Certeau, Luce Giard, and Pierre Mayel, *The Practice of Everyday Life*, vol. 2: *Living and Cooking*, pp. 151–152.

9. Caplan, ed., *Food, Health and Identity*, p. 11.

10. I do not mean, of course, that all women characters created by men are submissive. Many of Hisao Jūran's female characters, for instance, are subversive.

11. An earlier version of some parts of this chapter was published as "Food and Gender in Contemporary Japanese Women's Literature" in *US-Japan Women's Journal*, no. 17 (1999): 111–136. The discussion of *Indian Summer* overlaps in part my chapter "Transgendering *Shōjo Shōsetsu*: Girls' Inter-text/sex-uality," in Mark McLelland and Romit Dasgupta, eds., *Genders, Transgenders, and Sexualities in Japan*; and a conference paper, "The Peach Girl Views: Appropriating the Gaze," in Robert Crib, ed., *Asia Examined*.

12. This term refers to a person who does Western-style flower arrangement rather than traditional ikebana (and takes it seriously as an artistic genre).

13. This was only very briefly mentioned in chapter 3. For more detail see Aoyama, "Literary Daughters' Recipes," pp. 104–112.

14. See Honda Masuko's chapter "Hirahira no keifu" in her *Ibunka to shite no kodomo*, pp. 135–170. "Freedom and arrogance" are from Takahara Eiri's *Shōjo ryōiki*, whose introductory chapter is translated into English and included in Copeland, ed., *Woman Critiqued*, pp. 185–193. For a succinct definition of the term *shōjo*, see Orbaugh's entry in Sandra Buckley, ed., *Encyclopedia of Contemporary Japanese Culture*, pp. 458–459. See also Aoyama, "Transgendering *shōjo shōsetsu*," pp. 49–50.

15. Kanai uses katakana "indian samā" as the reading of the kanji for *koharu biyori*. The Japanese word sounds very much like a film by Ozu Yasujirō, which is apt for the title of this novel, whose protagonist and her friends are all connoisseurs of cinema.

16. Satō Takako, "Kaisetsu," in Haitani Kenjirō, *Shōjo no utsuwa*, p. 298.

17. Haitani, "Atogaki," ibid., p. 291.

18. Katō Tokiko, "Kaisetsu," in Haitani Kenjirō, *Umi ni namida wa iranai*, pp. 261–264.

19. Maki, *Oishii hanashi tsukutte tabete*, p. 12. The claim men make about the superiority of men's cooking is evident in the 1973 dialogue between Yoshiyuki Junnosuke and Dan Kazuo, "Danseiteki hōchō dangi," in Yamamoto Yōrō, ed., *Seihin no shokutaku*, pp. 243–258.

20. This is poignantly depicted in Ōba Minako's short story "Yamanba no bishō" (The Smile of the Mountain Witch, 1976). For a detailed discussion of this particular

story, see the chapters by Susan Fisher and Hirakawa Sukehiro in Hirakawa Sukehiro and Hagiwara Jakao, eds., *Nihon no haha: hōkai to saisei*, pp. 412–445; and Meera Viswanathan's chapter "In Pursuit of the Yamamba: The Question of Female Resistance," in Schalow and Walker, eds., *The Woman's Hand*, pp. 239–261. For more references, see note 6 on *yamanba* in chapter 4.

21. Kirishima, *Sōmei na onna wa ryōri ga umai*, p. 18.

22. Uno Chiyo, "Watashi no hatsumei ryōri," first published in 1981, included in Yamamoto, ed., *Seihin no shokutaku*, pp. 11–35.

23. As mentioned earlier, these are the key terms in Takahara's *Shōjo ryōiki*, which has a chapter on Mori Mari. For more detailed discussion of food in Mari's writing compared to that in Kōda Aya's, see Aoyama, "Literary Daughters' Recipes." Mori Mari's male homosexual romance published in the 1960s is now regarded as the forerunner of the theme in *shōjo manga*.

24. Yagawa, "*Chichi no musume*"-*tachi: Mori Mari to Anaisu Nin*, pp. 64–66.

25. "Ryōri to watashi," in *Mori Mari zenshū*, vol. 3, p. 6.

26. Ibid., pp. 6–7.

27. Yoshimoto Banana, *Kitchen*, trans. Megan Backus, p. 3; *Kitchin*, p. 7. In the following references, the page numbers in the Japanese text will be given in parentheses. Saitō Minako cites this first line of *Kitchin* to point to the grammatical or stylistic awkwardness that is part and parcel of Yoshimoto's writing (*Bundan aidoru ron*, pp. 63–64). Eiji Sekine's translation of this chapter, "Yoshimoto Banana and Girl Culture," is included in Copeland, ed., *Woman Critiqued*, pp. 167–185. Saitō's discussion of the style and grammaticality is omitted, however, from this translation.

28. Yoshimoto, *Kitchen*, p. 10 (p. 17).

29. Ibid., p. 43 (p. 70).

30. Ueno Chizuko, "Collapse of 'Japanese Mothers,'" and idem, "'Nihon no haha' no hōkai," in Hirakawa and Hagiwara, eds., *Nihon no haha*, p. 213.

31. Yoshimoto, *Kitchen*, p. 69.

32. Ibid., p. 11 (p. 18).

33. Ibid., pp. 101–102 (pp. 158–159).

34. For an insightful study of shopping in contemporary Japan see Jan Bardsley and Hiroko Hirakawa, "Branded: Bad Girls Go Shopping," in Laura Miller and Jan Bardsley, eds., *Bad Girls of Japan*, pp. 110–125.

35. Yoshimoto, *Kitchen*, p. 52 (pp. 84–85). The femininity of Eriko's language is much more marked in the Japanese text than in the translation.

36. Ibid. (p. 84; emphasis in original). In the Japanese text the first sentence is less gender laden: *Datte watashi, karada o hatte akaruku ikite kitanda mon* (Because I have lived cheerfully with my body [i.e., life] at stake). Similarly, "wages of beauty" is *zeikin no yō na mono* (something like tax) in the original.

37. Treat, "Yoshimoto Banana's *Kitchen*, or the Cultural Logic of Japanese Consumerism," in Lise Skov and Brian Moeran, eds., *Women, Media and Consumption in Japan*, pp. 280–281.

38. Saitō Minako, *Bundan aidoru ron*, pp. 62–65.

39. Kawasaki Kenko, *Shōjo biyori*, p. 195. Kawasaki's emphasis.

40. Ibid., p. 211. Kawasaki is referring here not only to *Kitchen* but also to *Utakata* and *Shirakawa yofune*.

41. Ibid., p. 217.

42. In her "Kaisetsu" for Tsutsui Yasutaka's parody of her tanka ("Karada kinenbi" [Body Anniversary]) Tawara recalls the headline in a sports paper "Kuwata kinenbi" after the victory of the baseball team the Giants and its pitcher Kuwata. Tsutsui Yasutaka, *Yakusai hanten*, p. 248.

Kanchūhai is a canned cocktail of *shōchū* (distilled spirits) and soda water (i.e., highball). It appears in Tawara Machi, *Sarada kinenbi*, p. 34: *Yomesan ni nare yo da nante kanchūhai nihon de itte shimatte ii no* (You say "Be my wife" after only two cans of *kanchūhai*, but are you really sure?). Shimamura Teru mentions the sudden sales increase prompted by this tanka in Kanai Keiko et al., *Bungaku ga motto omoshiroku naru*, p. 22.

43. Tawara, *Sarada kinenbi*, p. 127. The English is Juliet Winters Carpenter's translation, *Salad Anniversary*, p. 136. Hereafter the page number of the translation will be shown in parentheses.

44. As Saitō Minako mentions in her chapter on Tawara Machi (*Bundan aidoru ron*, p. 58), Kanai Mieko was one of the earliest critics to point out the conservative nature of *Kitchen* and *Salad Anniversary*. Kanai's review of *Sarada kinenbi* (first published in July 1989) is included in Kanai Mieko, *Hon o kaku hito yomanu hito tokaku kono yo wa mama naranu*, pp. 236–238. Kanai also makes one of her characters caustically remark that the eponymous salad is probably dressed with commercial salad dressing (*Dōkeshi no koi*, p. 170).

45. The intended novelty of this commercial must have been the anomalous use of "[*tsukuru/taberu*] *hito*" for the first person. The commercial was withdrawn after feminist protests. See Murakami Motoko, "Masu media to shoku," in Ishige Naomichi, ed., *Kōza shoku no bunka*, vol. 5, *Shoku no jōhōka*, p. 291.

46. Tawara, *Sarada kinenbi*, pp. 21, 154.

47. Ibid., p. 18.

48. Ibid., p. 15 (p. 14).

49. Ibid., p. 16 (p. 15).

50. Ibid., p. 151. See also p. 120.

51. Ibid., p. 25 (p. 24).

52. Ibid., p. 34, cited above in note 42.

53. Ibid., p. 156.

54. Ibid., p. 180 (p. 191).

55. For instance, Rose, *Parody*, and Linda Hutcheon, *A Theory of Parody: The Teachings of Twentieth-Century Art Forms*.

56. This is shared by many other women's works in a variety of genres, including, for instance, Jean Fraser's 1990 photographic parody of Manet's "Luncheon on the Grass" (discussed in Miyashita, *Taberu seiyō bijutsushi*, pp. 227–228).

57. The book has not been translated into English. The translation of the title is Janet Ashby's, which is a fair attempt to render the pun in Ogino's title, namely *doku* meaning "poison" instead of "reading." See Aoyama, "The Love that Poisons," pp. 40–46, for more information about this masterpiece of parody.

58. Ogino, *Watashi no aidokusho*, p. 60.

59. Ibid., pp. 97–134.

60. Ibid., p. 118.

61. Ibid., p. 109. Mishima's comments quoted in this parody include "The interior of a virgin is essentially unsuitable for expression. A man who violates a virgin can never understand a virgin. Neither can a man who does not violate a virgin understand a virgin well" (ibid., p. 108).

62. "Kuenai hanashi," in Ogino Anna, *Seoimizu*.

63. "Warau Bosshu," in Ogino Anna, *Buryūgeru tonda*, and idem, *Taberu onna* (The Eating Woman).

64. Ogino, *Taberu onna*.

65. Quoted and translated by Donald Keene, *Dawn to the West*, vol. 2, p. 607.

66. Ogino Anna, *Madonna no henshin shikkaku*, p. 21. ("Chanchiki Okesa" is a hit song by Minami Haruo, which typically combines the *enka* conventions with traditional folk music, in this case *okesa*.) *Tetchiri* is a blowfish dish. *Dote-yaki* is pork offal stewed in red miso; *takoyaki*, as mentioned in chapter 5, is a small, ball-shaped pancake with a piece of octopus inside; and *okonomi-yaki* is a flat pancake that contains vegetables, seafood, and meat.

67. Kathryn Pierce and Mika Endo's translation of this essay, which includes Kobayashi's comments on *Snow Country* as well as a quotation of Kawabata's remarks on women writers, is included in Copeland, ed., *Woman Critiqued*, pp. 47–52.

68. Ogino Anna, *I Love Ango*, pp. 13–14.

69. Mizuta Noriko et al., "Symposium Women's Culture: Postmodern Expressions," p. 70. For more detailed discussion of Rabelais' impact upon Ogino's fiction, see Midori McKeon's chapter "Ogino Anna's Gargantuan Play in *Tales of Peaches*," in Copeland and Ramirez-Christensen, eds., *The Father-Daughter Plot*.

70. Mizuta Noriko et al., "Symposium Women's Culture: Postmodern Expressions," p. 70.

71. Okamoto, *Rōgishō*, p. 49.

72. Kaikō, *Saigo no bansan*, pp. 16–17.

73. As Orbaugh notes (Orbaugh, "The Body in Contemporary Japanese Women's Fiction," p. 157, footnote 11), Ōigimi's starving herself to death in *The Tale of Genji* to resist a liaison with Kaoru may be considered an early example, written by a woman, of a female character's resisting male domination by not eating. The jury is still out, though, on whether to interpret Ōigimi's death as suicide. Ōno Susumu and Maruya Saiichi, for instance, express disagreement with Imai Gen'e, who believes that it should be interpreted as suicide (Ōno and Maruya, *Hikaru Genji no monogatari*, vol. 2, pp. 277–279).

74. Kaikō, *Saigo no bansan*, p. 359.

75. Tanizaki, *Tanizaki Jun'ichirō zenshū*, vol. 6, pp. 142, 189.
76. Hayashi Mariko, *Bishoku kurabu*, p. 88.
77. Saitō, *Bundan aidoru ron*, pp. 108–109.
78. Ibid , p. 104.
79. Ibid., p. 110.
80. Ibid., p. 120, citing Ogura Chikako.
81. Shimada Masahiko's short stories such as "Danjiki shōnen, seishun" (The Fasting Boy: Adolescence, 1990) and "Miira ni naru made" (The Diary of a Mummy, 1990) have anorexic male protagonists who are either totally uninterested in eating or determined to reject food. Gender is not an issue in these stories. Both stories are included in Shimada, *Arumajiro ō.* "The Diary of a Mummy" is the title of Judy Wakabayashi's English translation, which was commissioned for the Sydney Writers' Festival.
82. As a translation of this title Ogino suggests "Tomorrow Is Not Another Day for Bulimic Me" (Mizuta et al., "Symposium Women's Culture," p. 70).
83. In her review of five major studies of eating disorders published between 1978 and 1983, including Chernin's *The Obsession: Reflections on the Tyranny of Slenderness* and Susie Orbach's *Fat Is a Feminist Issue: The Anti-Diet Guide to Permanent Weight Loss,* Carole Counihan identifies four principal themes: "confusion over sexual identity and sexuality; struggle with issues of power, control, and release; solitude and deceit; and family strife" (*The Anthropology of Food and Body*, p. 79). While we are cautious not to confuse fiction with the North American case studies discussed in these studies, these four elements are clearly discernible in the two works under discussion.
84. Matsumoto, *Kyoshokushō no akenai yoake*, p. 45.
85. Ibid., pp. 53–54.
86. See Aoyama, "Literary Daughters' Recipes," pp. 104–112.
87. Matsumoto Yūko, *Kyoshokushō no akenai yoake*, pp. 40–41.
88. Ibid., p. 78. The permeation of this "womb = woman" myth is evidenced, for instance, in Mishima Yukio's essay on narcissism, in which he claims, "The woman's mind is unable to divest itself of the flesh because it is subject to the constant pull of both the brain and the womb." *Mishima Yukio zenshū*, vol. 32, p. 376; translation by Tomoko Aoyama and Barbara Hartley in Copeland, ed., *Woman Critiqued*, p. 83.
89. Ogawa Yōko, *Shugā taimu*, p. 14.
90. Matsumoto, *Kyoshokushō no akenai yoake*, p. 30.
91. Eagleton, *Literary Theory*, p. 23, quoting George Gordon.
92. This reminds us of one of the readings of *Tsuchi* Waswo mentioned (quoted in chapter 2, note 8), namely, as a text used in a university entrance examination question.
93. Nakajima Azusa, *Komyunikēshon fuzen shōkōgun*, pp. 119–120.
94. Wolf, *The Beauty Myth*, p. 211.
95. Matsumoto, *Kyoshokushō no akenai yoake*, p. 126.
96. Ogawa, *Shugā taimu*, pp. 9, 12.
97. Mizuta et al., "Symposium Women's Culture," p. 70.
98. Wolf, *The Beauty Myth*, p. 188.

99. An interesting comparison can be drawn between this text and Margaret Atwood's *Edible Woman*. In Atwood's novel, chapters 1–12 are recounted from the first person point of view, and chapters 13–30 from the third person perspective; the final chapter returns to the first person. As Alan Dawe points out in his introduction (ibid., n.p.), this shift corresponds to the state of the protagonist Marian's self: it is maintained in the first part, lost in the second, and regained in the third.

100. Tokiko's conflict with her mother seems to support some theories about eating disorders: Susie Orbach, for example, "'reads' women's fat as a statement to the mother about separation and dependence," and Kim Chernin "gives a psychoanalytic reading of fear of fat as based on infantile rage against the all-powerful mother" (Wolf, *The Beauty Myth*, p. 188). See also Asano Chie, *Onna wa naze yaseyō to suru no ka: sesshoku shōgai to jendā*, pp. 219–228. As Counihan notes (*The Anthropology of Food and Body*, p. 86), the heroine of Margaret Atwood's *Lady Oracle* "stuffs herself like 'a beluga whale' as a way of waging war against her mother and demanding autonomy."

101. I refer here to the publication dates of the two novels in book form. *Indian Summer* was first serialized in *Ansanburu* (Ensemble) between October 1985 and April 1987, whereas "Kitchin," the first part of *Kitchin*, appeared in *Kaien* as a new writer's prizewinner in 1987.

102. Kanai Mieko, *Indian samā*, p. 62. In the text of *Kitchin* Mikage actually uses *daidokoro* more frequently than *kitchin*. The translation of this quotation is mine (to indicate the Japanese words used in the original text). For most of the longer quotations from *Indian Summer* in the following I use the draft translation I made in collaboration with Barbara Hartley.

103. For more detailed discussion of food in Kōda Aya's work, see Aoyama, "Literary Daughters' Recipes."

104. Yoshikawa Yasuhisa, *Kaku koto no senjō*, pp. 107–138. Yoshikawa's reading, insightful though it is, does not include any gender perspective.

105. Ibid., p. 113.

106. Kanai Mieko, *Indian samā*, p. 67.

107. Ibid., p. 46.

108. Ibid., p. 116.

109. Ibid., p. 69.

110. Ibid., p. 158.

111. Ibid., p. 175.

112. Momoko is not bulimic as such, but it is mentioned especially in the sequels to *Indian Summer* that sometimes she eats too much and suffers from stomach upset.

113. For instance, "Funiku" (Rotting Meat) and "Usagi" (Rabbits), both published in 1972. See Orbaugh's chapter in Schalow and Walker, eds., *The Woman's Hand*, and Mary Knighton's "Writing the Body—as Meat: Kanai Mieko's 'Rotting Meat' as Surreal Fable," in James C. Baxter, ed., *Japanese Studies around the World*, for a detailed discussion of some such stories. Yoshikawa's *Kaku koto no senjō* also includes analysis of these stories.

114. Ogino Anna, *Kenage*, pp. 28–29. The second sentence parallels the notion of men's cooking as a hobby, rather than an everyday necessity.

115. Ibid., p. 265.

Conclusion

1. See chapter 10 of *Wagahai wa neko de aru* (in Natsume Sōseki, *Sōseki zenshū*, vol. 1), or Aiko Itō and Graeme Wilson's translation, *I Am a Cat*, vol. 3, p. 140 onwards.

2. Ishihara Chiaki's *Sōseki no kigōgaku* (A Semiotic Study of Sōseki) includes a chapter that specifically discusses the significance of illnesses. For a discussion of mental illness in Japan circa 1900, see Shiba Ichiro's chapter "'Kyōki' o meguru gensetsu" (The Discourses on "Insanity"), in Komori Yōichi et al., eds, *Media, hyōshō, ideorogii: Meiji 30-nendai no bunka kenkyū*, pp. 98–126.

3. The old woman in Niwa Fumio's "Iyagarase no nenrei" (The Hateful Age, 1947), for example, is treated by her family as nothing but a burden—a rice-eating monster. The story captures not only the physical and mental deterioration of old people but also the collapse of social morals and mores in the chaos of the immediate postwar period. Ariyoshi Sawako's *Kōkotsu no hito* (The Twilight Years, 1972) depicts another society— Japan once it had achieved the "economic miracle." Ariyoshi warns the reader—just as she did about compound pollution in another work—about the serious lack of welfare and support for the aged and their carers, who are usually women. Sakagami Hiroshi's short story "Daidokoro" (Kitchen, 1997) has a male narrator-protagonist who enjoys caring for his eighty-four-year-old mother—including shopping and cooking for her after work.

4. In Itami Jūzō's film *Tanpopo*, an old man (played by Ōtaki Hideji), surely a parody of Tanizaki and his "mad old man," cannot help eating his favorite food, even at great risk to his life.

5. Murase Manabu's *Miyazaki Hayao no "fukami" e* includes insightful "readings" of the food chain and the environment in Miyazaki's *anime*. As exemplified by Ōkōchi Shōji and Aoyama Kōji, there has also been a move against the gourmet boom.

6. Kubota Jun, ed., *Bungaku to shoku*, includes Kumei Teruko's essay on food that appears in the *senryū* (comic/satirical haiku) written by Japanese Americans.

7. Kubota, ed., *Bungaku to shoku*, also includes Takahashi Hirofumi's close reading of "Kozō no kamisama" (discussed in chapter 2 herein). The March 2004 issue (no. 21) of *Gengo bunka* (Language Culture, a journal of Meiji Gakuin University) features a number of extremely interesting essays on food culture and language, some of which, including Miyauchi's article on "Flower-eating" and Amazawa's tribute to Miyazawa Kenji, have been mentioned in earlier chapters. As already mentioned, there are studies of food in other genres such as Miyashita's *Taberu seiyō bijutsushi* and Murase's study of Miyazaki's *anime*.

8. Saitō Minako, *Bungakuteki shōhingaku*, p. 6.

9. Brillat-Savarin's aphorism was quoted in chapter 5 (note 79), when I discussed Kaikō's gourmet novel *Atarashii tentai*.

10. Mori Ōgai, "Tsuina" (Exorcizing Demons, 1909), in *Ōgai zenshū*, vol. 4, p. 588. The "shackles" are an allusion to Shimamura Hōgetsu's 1906 essay "Torawaretaru bungei" (Literature in Captivity).

11. Kanai Mieko, *Obasan no disukūru*, p. 58, and idem, "*Kyōsō aite wa baka bakari*" *no sekai ni yōkoso*, p. 297. See also Kanai's novel *Bunshō kyōshitsu*, pp. 41, 153–154, and her dialogue with Hasumi Shigehiko, ibid., pp. 339–340. As mentioned earlier, Yoshikawa's *Kaku koto no senjō* includes an interesting and sustained discussion of eating and writing. Although I had to abandon the analogy of reading = eating (and writing = cooking) for this book, Yoshikawa's argument informed by French theories is both inspiring and inviting for further studies of this theme.

12. Ishige Naomichi, for example, calls Japanese literature "a literature of diminished appetite" (Ishige, "Shoku to bungaku ni tsuite," in Nakayama and Ishige, eds., *Shoku to bungaku: Nihon, chūgoku, furansu*, p. 17).

Bibliography

"Akutagawa-shō senpyō." *Bungei shunjū,* March 1983, pp. 394–398.

Amazawa Taijirō. "Sugame yomi *Chūmon no ōi ryōriten* ron: *Chūmon no ōi ryōriten* no naka no 'Chūmon no ōi ryōriten' no naka no (Chūmon no ōi ryōriten)." *Gengo bunka,* no. 21 (March 2004): 43–51.

Andō Kyōko, ed. *Miyazawa Kenji.* Nihon bungaku kenkyū ronbun shūsei, vol. 35. Tokyo: Wakakusa Shobō, 1998.

Angles, Jeffrey. "The Heritage of Symbolism: The 'Aesthetic' Style of Kitahara Hakushu and Murayama Kaita." In Eiji Sekine, ed., *Japanese Poeticity and Narrativity Revisited,* pp. 237–263. Proceedings of the Association for Japanese Literary Studies, vol. 4. West Lafayette, Ind.: Association for Japanese Literary Studies, Purdue University, 2003.

Aoki Masaru. *Kakoku fūmi.* Tokyo: Iwanami Shoten, Iwanami Bunko, 1984.

———. "Tōzentei." In Nanjō Takenori, ed., *Bishoku,* pp. 22–38. Tokyo: Kokusho Kankōkai, 1998.

Aoki Tama. *Koishikawa no uchi.* Tokyo: Kōdansha, Kōdansha Bunko, 1998.

Aoyama, Kōji. *Tabenai hito.* Tokyo: Chikuma Shobō, 2006.

Aoyama, Tomoko. "Cannibalism, Gastronomy, and Anorexia: A Short History of Eating in Modern Japanese Literature." In A. Skoutarides and A. Tokita, eds., *Japanese Studies: Communities, Cultures, Critiques.* Vol. 5: *Power and Culture,* pp. 119–124. Papers of the 10th Biennial Conference of the Japanese Studies Association of Australia. Clayton: Monash Asia Institute, 2000.

———. "The Cooking Man in Modern Japanese Literature." In Kam Louie and Morris Low, eds., *Asian Masculinities: The Meaning and Practice of Manhood in China and Japan,* pp. 155–176. London and New York: Routledge Curzon, 2003.

———. "The Divided Appetite: 'Eating' in the Literature of the 1920s." In Elise K. Tipton and John Clark, eds., *Being Modern in Japan: Culture and Society from the 1910s to the 1930s,* pp. 154–169. Honolulu: Australian Humanities Research Foundation, University of Hawai'i Press, 2000.

————. "Food and Gender in Contemporary Japanese Women's Literature." *US-Japan Women's Journal* 17 (1999): 111–136.

————. "Literary Daughters' Recipes: Food and Female Subjectivity in the Writings of Mori Mari and Kōda Aya." *Japanstudien*, Band 12 (2000): 91–116.

————. "The Love That Poisons: Japanese Parody and the New Literacy." *Japan Forum* 6, no. 1 (April 1994): 35–46.

————. "The Peach Girl Views: Appropriating the Gaze." In Robert Cribb, ed., *Asia Examined: Proceedings of the 15th Biennial Conference of the ASAA, 2004, Canberra, Australia*. Canberra: Asian Studies Association of Australia (ASAA) and Research School of Pacific and Asian Studies (RSPAS), The Australian National University, 2004. http://coombs.anu.edu.au/ASAA/conference/proceedings/Aoyama-T-ASAA.pdf.

————. "Romancing Food: The Gastronomic Quest in Early Twentieth Century Japanese Literature." *Japanese Studies* 23, no. 3 (December 2003): 251–264.

————. "Transgendering *Shōjo Shōsetsu*: Girls' Inter-text/sex-uality." In Mark McLelland and Romit Dasgupta, eds., *Genders, Transgenders, and Sexualities in Japan*, pp. 49–64. London: Routledge, 2005.

Aramata Hiroshi. *Puroretaria bungaku wa monosugoi*. Tokyo: Heibonsha, Heibonsha Shinsho, 2000.

Arashiyama Kōzaburō. *Bunjin akujiki*. Tokyo: Magajin Hausu, 1997.

Arens, William. *The Man-Eating Myth: Anthropology and Anthropophagy*. New York: Oxford University Press, 1979.

Ariyoshi Sawako. *Fukugō osen*. Tokyo: Shinchōsha, Shinchō Bunko, 1979.

————. *Hishoku*. Tokyo: Chūō Kōronsha, 1982.

————. *Kōkotsu no hito*. Tokyo: Shinchōsha, 1972.

Asano Chie. *Onna wa naze yaseyō to suru no ka: sesshoku shōgai to jendā*. Tokyo: Keisō Shobō, 1996.

Ashkenazi, Michael, and Jeanne Jacob. *The Essence of Japanese Cuisine: An Essay on Food and Culture*. Richmond, Surrey: Curzon Press, 2000.

Ashley, Bob; Joanne Hollows; Steve Jones; and Ben Taylor. *Food and Cultural Studies*. London and New York: Routledge, 2004.

Attali, Jacques. *Kanibarizumu no chitsujo: sei to wa nani ka, shi to wa nani ka*. Trans. Kanezuka Sadafumi of *L'ordre cannibale: vie et mort de la médecine*, 1979. Tokyo: Misuzu Shobō, 1994.

Atōda Takashi. *Mayonaka no ryōrinin*. Tokyo: Kōdansha, Kōdansha Bunko, 1989.

————. *Taberareta otoko*. Tokyo: Kōdansha, Kōdansha Bunko, 1982.

Atwood, Margaret. *The Edible Woman*. Toronto: McClelland and Stewart, 1973.

Austen, Jane. *Volume the Second*. Oxford: Clarendon Press, 1963.

Barker, Francis; Peter Hulme; and Margaret Iversen, eds. *Cannibalism and the Colonial World*. Cambridge: Cambridge University Press, 1998.

Barthes, Roland. *Elements of Semiology*. Trans. Annette Lavers and Colin Smith. New York: Hill and Wang, 1967.

————. *The Rustle of Language.* Trans. Richard Howard. New York: Hill and Wang, 1986.

Beardsworth, Alan, and Teresa Keil. *Sociology on the Menu: An Invitation to the Study of Food and Society.* London and New York: Routledge, 1997.

Beichman, Janine. *Masaoka Shiki.* Tokyo: Kodansha International, 1986.

Bellei, Sérgio Luiz Prado. "Brazilian Anthropophagy Revisited." In Francis Barker, Peter Hulme, and Margaret Iverson, eds., *Cannibalism and the Colonial World*, pp. 87–109. Cambridge: Cambridge University Press, 1998.

Bloom, Harold. *A Map of Misreading.* Oxford: Oxford University Press, 1975.

Boscaro, Adriana, and Anthony Hood Chambers, eds. *A Tanizaki Feast: The International Symposium in Venice.* Michigan Monograph Series in Japanese Studies, no. 24. Ann Arbor: Center for Japanese Studies, University of Michigan, 1998.

Brillat-Savarin, Jean Anthelme. *Bimi raisan.* Trans. Sekine Hideo and Tobe Matsumi. 2 vols. Tokyo: Iwanami Shoten, Iwanami Bunko, 1967.

————. *Physiologie du goût avec une lecture de Roland Barthes.* Paris: Hermann, 1975.

————. *The Physiology of Taste, or, Meditations on Transcendental Gastronomy.* Trans. M. F. K. Fisher. Washington, D.C.: Counterpoint Press, 1999.

Brown, Janice. "De-siring the Center: Hayashi Fumiko's Hungry Heroines and the Male Literary Canon." In Rebecca L. Copeland and Esperanza Ramirez-Christensen, eds., *The Father-Daughter Plot: Japanese Literary Woman and the Law of the Father*, pp. 143–166. Honolulu: University of Hawai'i Press, 2001.

Buckley, Sandra, ed. *Encyclopedia of Contemporary Japanese Culture.* London and New York: Routledge, 2002.

Caplan, Pat, ed. *Food, Health and Identity.* London and New York: Routledge, 1997.

Certeau, Michel de; Luce Giard; and Pierre Mayol. *The Practice of Everyday Life.* Vol. 2: *Living and Cooking.* Trans. Timothy J. Tomasik. Minneapolis and London: University of Minnesota Press, 1998.

"Chosha ni kiku: Inoue Hisashi san." In *Sankei shinbun*, March 28, 1999. http://www.sankei.co.jp/databox/paper/9903/28/paper/today/book/28boo001.htm.

Cixous, Hélène. "The Laugh of the Medusa." Trans. K. and P. Cohen of "Le rire de la méduse." In Elaine Marks and Isabelle de Courtivron, eds., *New French Feminisms*, pp. 254–264. Brighton: Harvester, 1980.

Cohn, Joel R. *Studies in the Comic Spirit in Modern Japanese Fiction.* Cambridge and London: Harvard University Asia Center, Harvard University Press, 1998.

Colette. *The Vagabond.* Trans. Enid McLeod. London and New York: Penguin Books, 1960.

Colligan, Karen. "The Emergence of Environmental Literature in Japan." Ph.D. dissertation, Stanford University, 1986.

Copeland, Rebecca. "Mythical Bad Girls: The Corpse, the Crone, and the Snake." In Laura Miller and Jan Bardsley, eds., *Bad Girls of Japan*, pp. 15–31. New York: Palgrave Macmillan, 2005.

————, ed. *Woman Critiqued: Translated Essays on Japanese Women's Writing.* Honolulu: University of Hawai'i Press, 2006.

————, and Esperanza Ramirez-Christensen, eds. *The Father-Daughter Plot: Japanese Literary Woman and the Law of the Father.* Honolulu: University of Hawai'i Press, 2001.

Counihan, Carole M. *The Anthropology of Food and Body: Gender, Meaning, and Power.* New York and London: Routledge, 1999.

Cuddon, J. A. *A Dictionary of Literary Terms.* Harmondsworth: Penguin Books, 1982.

Dan Kazuo. *Danryū kukkingu.* Tokyo: Chūō Kōronsha, Chūkō Bunko, 1998.

————. *Kataku no hito.* 2 vols. Tokyo: Shinchōsha, Shinchō Bunko, 1981.

————. *Ritsuko sono ai, sono shi.* Tokyo: Shinchōsha, Shinchō Bunko, 1993.

Eagleton, Terry. "Edible Écriture." In Sian Griffiths and Jennifer Wallace, eds., *Consuming Passions: Food in the Age of Anxiety*, pp. 203–208. Manchester and New York: Mandolin, 1998.

————. *Literary Theory: An Introduction.* Oxford: Basil Blackwell, 1983.

Edogawa Ranpo. *Ankokusei, Yami ni ugomeku.* Tokyo: Shun'yōdō, 1988.

Eguchi Yūsuke. *Hisao Jūran.* Tokyo: Hakusuisha, 1994.

Enchi Fumiko. *Yō, Hanakui uba.* Tokyo: Kōdansha, Bungei Bunko, 1997.

Endō Shūsaku. *Umi to dokuyaku.* Tokyo: Shinchōsha, Shinchō Bunko, 1985.

Ericson, Joan E. *Be a Woman: Hayashi Fumiko and Japanese Women's Literature.* Honolulu: University of Hawai'i Press, 1997.

————. "The Origins of the Concept of 'Women's Literature.'" In Paul Gordon Schalow and Janet A. Walker, eds., *The Woman's Hand: Gender and Theory in Japanese Women's Writing*, pp. 74–115. Stanford, Calif.: Stanford University Press, 1996.

Eubanks, Charlotte. "Re-Writing the Myth of Motherhood: Short Stories by Okamoto Kanoko and Hirabayashi Taiko." *Critical Asian Studies* 33, no. 2 (June 2001): 287–300.

Fessler, Susanna. *Wandering Heart: The Work and Method of Hayashi Fumiko.* Albany: State University of New York Press, 1998.

Fowler, Edward. *The Rhetoric of Confession: Shishōsetsu in Early Twentieth-Century Japanese Fiction.* Berkeley: University of California Press, 1988.

Furukawa Roppa. *Roppa no hishokuki.* Tokyo: Chikuma Shobō, Chikuma Bunko, 1995.

Genette, Gerard. *Palimpsestes: La littérature au second degré.* Paris: Seuil, 1982.

Gengo bunka, no. 21, *Tokushū: Shoku to gengo* (March 2004).

Glants, Musya, and Joyce Toomre. *Food in Russian History and Culture.* Bloomington: Indiana University Press, 1997.

Haitani Kenjirō. *Shōjo no utsuwa.* Tokyo: Shinchōsha, Shinchō Bunko, 1992.

————. *Umi ni namida wa iranai.* Tokyo: Kadokawa Shoten, Kadokawa Bunko, 1998.

Hall, Robert King. *Education for a New Japan.* New Haven, Conn.: Yale University Press, 1949.

Hayama Yoshiki, Kobayashi Takiji, and Nakano Shigeharu. *Hayama Yoshiki, Kobayashi*

Takiji, Nakano Shigeharu shū. Gendai Nihon bungaku zenshū, vol. 67. Tokyo: Chikuma Shobō, 1967.

Hayashi Fumiko. *Hayashi Fumiko shū.* Shōwa bungaku zenshū, vol. 19. Tokyo: Kadokawa Shoten, 1953,

———. *Hōrōki.* Rev. ed. Tokyo: Shinchōsha, Shinchō Bunko, 1979.

———. *I Saw a Pale Horse and Selected Poems from Diary of a Vagabond.* Trans. and introduction Janice Brown. Ithaca, N.Y.: Cornell University East Asia Program, 1997.

Hayashi Mariko. *Bishoku kurabu.* Tokyo: Bungei Shunjū, Bunshun Bunko, 1989.

Henmi Yō. *Mono kuu hitobito.* Tokyo: Kyōdō Tsūshinsha, 1994.

Hijiya-Kirschnereit, Irmela. *Rituals of Self-revelation: Shishosetsu as Literary Genre and Socio-cultural Phenomenon.* Cambridge: Harvard University Press, 1996.

Hirabayashi Taiko et al. *Hirabayashi Taiko, Sata Ineko, Amino Kiku, Tsuboi Sakae shū.* Gendai Nihon bungaku zenshū, vol. 39. Tokyo: Chikuma Shobō, 1955.

Hirakawa Sukehiro and Hagiwara Takao, eds. *Nihon no haha: hōkai to saisei.* Tokyo: Shin'yōsha, 1997.

Hisao Jūran. *Hisao Jūran zenshū.* 7 vols. Tokyo: San'ichi Shobō, 1969–1970.

———. *Pari no ame.* Tokyo: Shuppansha, 1974.

Honda Masuko. *Ibunka to shite no kodomo.* Tokyo: Kinokuniya Shjoten, 1982.

———. *Kōkan nikki: Shōjo-tachi no himitsu no pureirando.* Tokyo: Iwanami Shoten, 1996.

———. *Kowakare no fōkuroa.* Tokyo: Keisō Shobō, 1988.

Honda Shūgo, ed. *Miyamoto Yuriko kenkyū.* Tokyo: Sinchōsha, 1957.

Huizinga, Johan. *Homo ludens: A Study of the Play Element in Culture.* Trans. anon. London: Paladin, 1970.

Hutcheon, Linda. *A Theory of Parody: The Teachings of Twentieth-Century Art Forms.* New York: Methuen, 1985.

Huysmans, Joris-Karl. *Against Nature.* Trans. Robert Baldick. New York: Penguin Classics, 1959.

Ibuse Masuji. *Black Rain: A Novel by Masuji Ibuse.* Trans. John Bester. Tokyo; Palo Alto, Calif.: Kodansha International, 1969.

———. *Kuroi ame.* Tokyo: Shinchōsha, Shinchō Bunko, 1970.

Inose Naoki. "*Kuroi ame* to Ibuse Masuji no shinsō." Originally published in *Bungakukai* (August 2001). Included in the Japan P.E.N. Club, Denshi Bungeikan. http://www.japanpen.or.jp/e-bungeikan/study/inosenaoki.html (accessed July 15, 2007).

Inoue Hisashi. *Dō shite mo kome no hanashi.* Tokyo: Shinchōsha, Shinchō Bunko, 1993.

———. *Jikasei bunshō dokuhon.* Tokyo: Shinchōsha, 1984.

———. *Kome no hanashi.* Tokyo: Shinchōsha, Shinchō Bunko, 1992.

———. *Tōkyō sebun rōzu.* Tokyo: Bungei Shunjū, 1999.

Inuta Akira. *Haha, Sumii Sue no yokogao.* Tokyo: Yamato Shobō, 1999.

Ishige Naomichi, ed. *Kōza shoku no bunka.* 7 vols. Tokyo: Ajinomoto Shoku no Bunka Sentā and Nōsangyoson Bunka Kyōkai, 1998–1999.

———. *Shokuji no bunmeiron.* Tokyo: Chūō Kōronsha, 1982.

Ishihara Chiaki. *Sōseki no kigōgaku.* Tokyo: Kōdansha, 1999.

Ishikawa Takuboku. *Jidai heisoku no genjō, Kurau beki shi.* Tokyo: Iwanami Shoten, Iwanami Bunko, 1978.

———. *Takuboku: Poems to Eat.* Trans. Carl Sesar. Tokyo: Kodansha International, 1966.

———. *Takuboku zenshū.* 8 vols. Tokyo: Chikuma Shobō, 1967–1968.

Ito, Ken K. *Visions of Desire: Tanizaki's Fictional Worlds.* Stanford, Calif.: Stanford University Press, 1991.

Itō Sei et al., eds. *Meiji bungaku zenshū.* 99 + 1 vols. Tokyo: Chikuma Shobō, 1965–1980, 1989.

Itō Shinkichi et al., eds. *Nihon no shiika.* 31 vols. Tokyo: Chūō Kōronsha, 1967–1970.

Iwasa Sōshirō. *Seikimatsu no shizen shugi: Meiji yonjūnendai bungaku kō.* Tokyo: Yūseidō, 1986.

Jameson, Fredric. *Postmodernism, or, The Cultural Logic of Late Capitalism.* Durham, N.C.: Duke University Press, 1991.

Kaikō Takeshi. *Darkness in Summer.* Trans. Cecilia Segawa Seigle. Tokyo: Tuttle, 1974.

———. *Kaikō Takeshi zenshū.* 22 vols. Tokyo: Shinchōsha, 1991–1992.

———. *Nihon sanmon opera.* Tokyo: Shinchōsha, Shinchō Bunko, 1971.

———. *Saigo no bansan.* Tokyo: Bungei Shunjūsha, Bunshun Bunko, 1982.

———. *Shōsetsuka no menyū.* Tokyo: Chūō Kōronsha, Chūkō Bunko, 1995.

Kanagaki Robun. *Agura nabe.* In Okitsu Kaname, ed., *Meiji kaikaki bungakushū.* Meiji bungaku zenshū, vol. 1, pp. 138–166. Tokyo: Chikuma Shobō, 1966.

Kanai Keiko. *Mayonaka no kanojo-tachi: kaku onna no kindai.* Tokyo: Chikuma Shobō, 1995.

——— et al. *Bungaku ga motto omoshiroku naru.* Tokyo: Daiyamondosha, 1998.

——— et al., eds. *Kōda Aya no sekai.* Tokyo: Kanrin Shobō, 1998.

Kanai Mieko. *Bunshō kyōshitsu.* Tokyo: Fukutake Shoten, Fukutake Bunko, 1987.

———. *Dōkeshi no koi.* Tokyo: Kawade Shobō Shinsha, Kawade Bunko, 1999.

———. *Hon o kaku hito yomanu hito tokaku kono yo wa mama naranu.* Tokyo: Nihon Bungeisha, 1989.

———. *Indian samā.* Tokyo: Kawade Shobō Shinsha, Kawade Bunko, 1999.

———. *"Kyōsō aite wa baka bakari" no sekai e yōkoso.* Tokyo: Kōdansha, 2003.

———. *Obasan no disukūru.* Tokyo: Chikuma Shobō, 1984.

Kanehara Hitomi. *Hebi ni piasu.* Tokyo: Shūeisha, 2003.

Kaneko Hiroshi. *"Kuroi ame (Ibuse Masuji)." Kokubungaku kaishaku to kanshō* 50, no. 9 (August 1985): 81–85.

Kara Jūrō. *Sagawa-kun kara no tegami.* Tokyo: Kawade Shobō, Kawade Bunko, 1986.

Karatani Kōjin. *In'yu to shite no kenchiku.* Tokyo: Kōdansha, Kōdansha Gakujutsu Bunko, 1989.

———. *Nihon kindai bungaku no kigen.* Tokyo: Kōdansha, Kōdansha Bungei Bunko, 1988.

Kawabata Yasunari. *Kawabata Yasunari shū*. Gendai Nihon bungaku zenshū, vol. 66. Tokyo: Chikuma Shobō, 1967.

———. *The Sound of the Mountain*. Trans. Edward Seidensticker. New York: Knopf, 1970.

Kawai Hayao. *Mukashi-banashi to nihonjin no kokoro*. Tokyo: Iwanami Shoten, 1982.

Kawakami Hiromi. *Sensei no kaban*. Tokyo: Heibonsha, 2001.

Kawamoto Saburō. *Taishō gen'ei*. Tokyo: Chikuma Bunko, 1997.

Kawasaki Kenko. *Shōjo biyori*. Tokyo: Seikyūsha, 1990.

Keene, Donald. *Dawn to the West: Japanese Literature of the Modern Era*. 2 vols. New York: Henry Holt, 1987.

———. *Modern Japanese Diaries: The Japanese at Home and Abroad as Revealed through Their Diaries*. New York: Henry Holt, 1995.

———, ed. *Modern Japanese Literature: An Anthology*. New York: Grove Press, 1956.

———. *Travelers of a Hundred Ages*. New York: Henry Holt, 1989.

Kilgour, Maggie. *From Communion to Cannibalism: An Anatomy of Metaphors of Incorporation*. Princeton, N.J.: Princeton University Press, 1990.

Kirishima Yōko. *Sōmei na onna wa ryōri ga umai*. Tokyo: Bungei Shunjū, Bunshun Bunko, 1990.

Kirkup, James, trans. *Modern Japanese Poetry*. Ed. and intro. A. R. Davis. Asian and Pacific Writing 9. St. Lucia: University of Queensland Press, 1978.

Kitaōji Rosanjin. *Rosanjin midō*. Ed. Hirano Masaaki. Rev. ed. Tokyo: Chūō Kōronsha, Chūkō Bunko, 1995.

Knighton, Mary. "Writing the Body—as Meat: Kanai Mieko's 'Rotting Meat' as Surreal Fable." In James C. Baxter, ed., *Japanese Studies around the World*, pp. 161–188. Observing Japan from Within: Perspectives of Foreign Scholars Resident in Japan. Kyoto: International Research Center for Japanese Studies, 2004.

Kobayashi Hideo. *Mōtsaruto, Mujō to iu koto*. Tokyo: Shinchōsha, Shinchō Bunko, 1961.

Kōda Aya. *Kōda Aya zenshū*. 22 vols. Tokyo: Iwanami Shoten, 1994–1997.

Komori Yōichi. *Dekigoto to shite no yomu koto*. Tokyo: Tōkyō Daigaku Shuppankai, 1996.

Komori Yōichi et al., eds. *Media, hyōshō, ideorogii: Meiji 30-nendai no bunka kenkyū*. Tokyo: Ozawa Shoten, 1997.

Kōno Taeko. *Tanizaki bungaku no tanoshimi*. Tokyo: Chūō Kōronsha, 1993.

———. *Tanizaki bungaku to kōtei no yokubō*. Tokyo: Bungei Shunjū, 1976.

Kosuge Keiko. *Guruman Fukuzawa Yukichi no shokutaku*. Tokyo: Chūō Kōronsha, Chūkō Bunko, 1998.

Kosugi Tengai et al. *Kosugi Tengai, Okamoto Kidō, Oguri Fūyō, Mayama Seika shū*. Gendai Nihon bungaku zenshū, vol. 56. Tokyo: Chikuma Shobō, 1958

Kubota Jun, ed. *Bungaku to shoku*. Tokyo: Geirin Shobō, 2004.

Kurahashi Yumiko. *The Adventures of Sumiyakist Q*. Trans. Dennis Keene. St. Lucia: University of Queensland Press, 1979.

———. *Atarimae no koto*. Tokyo: Asahi Shinbunsha, 2001.

———. *Kurahashi Yumiko no kaiki shōhen.* Tokyo: Shinchōsha, Shinchō Bunko, 1988.

———. *Sumiyakisuto Q no bōken.* Tokyo: Kōdansha, Bungei Bunko, 1988.

———. *The Woman with the Flying Head and Other Stories by Kurahashi Yumiko.* Trans. Atsuko Sakaki. Armonk, N.Y.: M. E. Sharpe, 1998.

Kuroiwa Hisako. *"Kuidōraku" no hito Murai Gensai.* Tokyo: Iwanami Shoten, 2004.

Kusano Shinpei, ed. *Miyazawa Kenji kenkyū. Miyazawa Kenji zenshū,* Bekkan. Tokyo: Chikuma Shobō, 1969.

Kyū Eikan. *Shoku wa Kōshū ni ari.* Tokyo: Chūō Kōronsha, Chūkō Bunko, 1996.

Lévi-Strauss, Claude. *The Raw and the Cooked.* London: Jonathan Cape, 1969.

Lippit, Noriko, and Kyoko Iriye Selden, eds. *Japanese Women Writers: Twentieth-Century Short Fiction.* Armonk, N.Y.: M. E. Sharpe, 1991.

Lippit, Seiji M. *Topographies of Japanese Modernism.* New York: Columbia University Press, 2002.

Lofgren, Erik. "Christianity Excised: Ichikawa Kon's 'Fires on the Plain.'" *Japanese Studies* 23, no. 3 (December 2003): 265–275.

Lupton, Deborah. *Food, the Body and the Self.* London: Sage Publications, 1996.

Lu Xun (Rojin). *Rojin bunshū,* vol. 1. Trans. Takeuchi Yoshimi. Tokyo: Chikuma Shobō, 1976.

Maeda Ai. *Bungaku tekusuto nyūmon.* Tokyo: Chikuma Shobō, 1988.

———. "Kodomotachi no hen'yō: Kindai bungakushi no naka de." *Kokubungaku* 30, no. 12 (October 1985): 32–41.

Maki Yōko. *Oishii hanashi tsukutte tabete.* Tokyo: Bungei Shunjūsha, Bunshun Bunko, 1995.

Marin, Louis. *Food for Thought.* Trans. Mette Hjort. Baltimore and London: Johns Hopkins University Press, 1989.

Maruya Saiichi. *Shikō no ressun.* Tokyo: Bungei Shunjū, 1999.

Masaoka Shiki, Itō Sachio, and Nagatsuka Takashi. *Masaoka Shiki, Itō Sachio, Nagatsuka Takashi shū.* Gendai Nihon bungaku zenshū, vol. 11. Tokyo: Chikuma Shobō, 1967.

Matsumoto Yūko. *Kyoshokushō no akenai yoake.* Tokyo: Shūeisha, Shūeisha Bunko, 1991.

McDonald, Keiko I. *From Book to Screen: Modern Japanese Literature in Film.* Armonk, N.Y.: M. E. Sharpe, 2000.

Mennell, Stephen. *All Manners of Food: Eating and Tasting in England and France from the Middle Ages to the Present.* Oxford: Basil Blackwell, 1985.

———, Anne Murcott, and Anneke H. van Otterloo. *The Sociology of Food: Eating, Diet and Culture.* London: Sage Publications, 1992.

Miller, Laura, and Jan Bardsley, eds. *Bad Girls of Japan.* New York: Palgrave Macmillan, 2005.

Mishima Yukio. *Mishima Yukio zenshū.* 35 + 1 vols. Tokyo: Shinchōsha, 1975.

Miyamoto Yuriko. *Miyamoto Yuriko shū.* Gendai Nihon bungaku zenshū, vol. 64. Tokyo: Chikuma Shobō, 1967.

Miyashita Kikurō. *Taberu seiyō bijutsushi: "Saigo no bansan" kara yomu.* Tokyo: Kōbunsha, 2007.

Miyauchi Junko. "Hamo to satōgashi: Kindai bungaku no naka no 'hitokui' to 'hanakui.'" *Gengo hunka,* no. 21 (March 2004): 52–64.

Miyazawa Kenji. *Kōhon Miyazawa Kenji zenshū.* 15 vols. Tokyo: Chikuma Shobō, 1973–1977.

———. *Miyazawa Kenji zenshū.* 12 vols. Tokyo: Chikuma Shobō, 1967–1968.

Miyoshi Yukio and Sobue Shōji, eds. *Kindai bungaku hyōron taikei.* Vol. 6: *Taishō-ki III, Shōwa-ki I.* Tokyo: Kadokawa Shoten, 1973.

Mizuta Noriko. "In Search of a Lost Paradise: The Wondering Woman in Hayashi Fumiko's *Drifting Clouds.*" In Paul Gordon Schalow and Janet A. Walker, eds. *The Woman's Hand: Gender and Theory in Japanese Women's Writing,* pp. 329–351. Stanford, Calif.: Stanford University Press, 1996.

———. *Nijusseiki no josei hyōgen: Jendā bunka no gaibu e.* Tokyo: Gakugei Shorin, 2003.

——— and Kitada Sachie, eds. *Yamauba-tachi no monogatari: Josei no genkei to katari-naoshi.* Tokyo: Gakugei Shuppan, 2002.

——— et al. "Symposium: Women's Culture: Postmodern Expressions." *Review of Japanese Culture and Society,* no. 4 (1991): 62–76.

Mori Mari. *Mori Mari zenshū.* 8 vols. Tokyo: Chikuma Shobō, 1993–1994.

Mori Ōgai. *Ōgai zenshū.* 38 vols. Tokyo: Iwanami Shoten, 1971–1975.

Mostow, Joshua S. "Mother Tongue and Father Script: The Relationship of Sei Shōnagon and Murasaki Shikibu to Their Fathers and Chinese Letters." In Rebecca L. Copeland and Esperanza Ramirez-Christensen, eds., *The Father-Daughter Plot: Japanese Literary Women and the Law of the Father,* pp. 115–142. Honolulu: University of Hawai'i Press, 2001.

Murai Gensai. *Hana: A Daughter of Japan.* Trans. Kawai Unkichi. Tokyo: Hochi Shinbun, 1904.

———. *Kuidōraku.* 4 vols. and Appendix (*Fukkokuban Kuidōraku kaisetsuhen*). Tokyo: Shibata Shoten, 1976. The electronic version of the complete set is available on the Shibata Shoten Web site: http://www.yumyumtown.com/lib/shokudoraku/index.html (accessed April 9, 2003).

———. *Kuidōraku no reshipi.* Rentier Collection. Tokyo: Kadokawa Haruki Jimusho, Rantie Sōsho, 1997.

Murakami Ryū. *Murakami Ryū jisen shōsetsu shū.* Vol. 3: *Gūwa to shite no tanpen.* Tokyo: Shūeisha, 1997.

Murase Manabu. *Miyazaki Hayao no "fukami" e.* Tokyo: Heibonsha, Heibonsha Shinsho, 2004.

Nagatsuka Takashi. *The Soil: A Portrait of Rural Life in Meiji Japan.* Trans. Ann Waswo. London and New York: Routledge, 1989.

Nagayo Yoshio and Nogami Yaeko. *Nagayo Yoshio, Nogami Yaeko shū.* Gendai Nihon bungaku zenshū, vol. 56. Tokyo: Chikuma Shobō, 1967.

Nakajima Azusa. *Komyunikēshon fuzen shōkōgun.* Tokyo: Chikuma Shobō, Chikuma Bunko, 1995.

Nakano Miyoko. *Kanibarizumu ron.* Tokyo: Fukutake Shoten, Fukutake Bunko, 1987.

Nakayama Kazuko, Egusa Mitsuko, and Fujimori Kiyoshi, eds. *Jendā no nihon kindai bungaku.* Tokyo: Kanrin Shobō, 1998.

Nakayama Tokiko and Ishige Naomichi, eds. *Shoku to bungaku: Nihon, chūgoku, furansu.* Tokyo: Fūdiamu Komyunikēshon, 1992.

Nanakita Kazuto, ed. *Jinniku shishoku.* Ryōki bungakukan, vol. 3. Tokyo: Chikuma Shobō, Chikuma Bunko, 2001.

Nanjō Takenori, ed. *Bishoku.* Shomotsu no ōkoku, vol. 14. Tokyo: Kokusho Kankōkai, 1998.

———. *Juen.* Tokyo: Kōdansha, 2002.

———. *Mankan zenseki.* Tokyo: Shūeisha, Shūeisha Bunko, 1998.

———. *Shusen.* Tokyo: Shinchōsha, Shinchō Bunko, 1904.

Natsume Sōseki. *I Am a Cat.* 3 vols. Trans. Aiko Itō and Graeme Wilson. Rutland, Vt.; and Tokyo: Charles E. Tuttle, 1972, 1979, 1986.

———. *Sōseki zenshū.* 16 vols. Tokyo: Iwanami Shoten, 1965–1967.

Niwa Fumio. *The Hateful Age.* Trans. Edward G. Seidensticker. Tokyo: Hara Shobō, 1965.

Nogami Yaeko. *Kaijinmaru.* Rev. ed. Tokyo: Iwanami Shoten, Iwanami Bunko, 1970.

———. *The Neptune, The Foxes.* Trans. Ryōzō Matsumoto. Tokyo: Kenkyūsha, 1957.

Noguchi Takehiko. *Ichigo no jiten: Shōsetsu.* Tokyo: Sanseidō, 1996.

———. *Sakka no hōhō.* Tokyo: Chikuma Shobō, 1981.

———. *Tanizaki Jun'ichirō ron.* Tokyo: Chūō Kōronsha, 1973.

Numa Shōzō. *Kachikujin yapū.* 5 vols. Tokyo: Gentōsha, Gentōsha Outlaw Bunko, 1999.

Ōba Minako. *Ōba Minako zenshū.* Vol. 3. Tokyo: Kōdansha, 1991.

Ogawa Yōko. *Shugā taimu.* Tokyo: Chūō Kōronsha, Chūkō Bunko, 1994.

Ogi Masahiro. *Rekishi wa gurume.* Tokyo: Chūkō Bunko, 1986.

Ogino Anna. *Buryūgeru tonda.* Tokyo: Shinchōsha, 1991.

———. *I Love Ango.* Tokyo: Asahi Shinbunsha, 1992.

———. *Kenage.* Tokyo: Iwanami Shoten, 2002.

———. *Madonna no henshin shikkaku.* Tokyo: Fukutake Shoten, 1993.

———. *Seoimizu.* Tokyo: Bungei Shunjū, 1991.

———. *Taberu onna.* Tokyo: Bungei Shunjū, 1994.

———. *Watashi no aidokusho.* Tokyo: Fukutake Shoten, 1991.

Ohnuki-Tierney, Emiko. *Rice as Self: Japanese Identities through Time.* Princeton, N.J.: Princeton University Press, 1995.

Okamoto Kanoko. "The Love of Kishimo." Trans. Charlotte Eubanks. *Critical Asian Studies* 33, no. 2 (June 2001): 289–294.

———. *Okamoto Kanoko zenshū.* 15 vols., 3 supplementary vols. (Hokan; Bekkan 1, 2). Tokyo: Tōjusha, 1974–1978.

———. *Rōgishō.* Rev. ed. Tokyo: Shinchōsha, Shinchō Bunko, 1968.

Ōkōchi Shōji. *Anchi-gurume dokuhon.* Tokyo: Fukutake Shoten, Fukutake Bunko, 1989.

———. *Soshokuha no kyōen.* Tokyo: Shōgakukan, Shōgakukan Bunko, 1998.

Onfray, Michel. *Tetsugakusha no shokutaku.* Trans. Kōda Norimasa of *Le ventre des philosophes*, 1989. Tokyo: Shinhyōron, 1998.

Ōno Susumu and Maruya Saiichi. *Hikaru Genji no monogatari.* 2 vols. Tokyo: Chūō Kōronsha, 1989.

Ōoka Shōhei. *Fires on the Plain.* Trans. Ivan Morris. Tokyo: Charles E. Tuttle, 1967.

———. *Ōoka Shōhei shū.* Nihon bungaku zenshū, vol. 80. Tokyo: Shūeisha, 1967.

———. *Ōoka Shōhei zenshū.* Vol. 3. Tokyo: Chikuma Shobō, 1994.

Orbaugh, Sharalyn. "The Body in Contemporary Japanese Women's Fiction." In Paul Gordon Schalow and Janet A. Walker, eds., *The Woman's Hand: Gender and Theory in Japanese Women's Writing*, pp. 119–164. Stanford, Calif.: Stanford University Press, 1996.

Ōtsuka Shigeru. *Tabemono bunmei kō.* Tokyo: Asahi Shinbunsha, Asahi Sensho, 1978.

Poole, Gaye. *Reel Meals, Set Meals: Food in Film and Theatre.* Sydney: Currency Press, 1999.

Pollack, David. *Reading against Culture: Ideology and Narrative in the Japanese Novel.* Ithaca, N.Y.; London: Cornell University Press, 1992.

Pollan, Michael. *The Omnivore's Dilemma: A Natural History of Four Meals.* New York: Penguin Press, 2006.

Reichert, Jim. "Deviance and Social Darwinism in Edogawa Ranpo's Erotic-Grotesque Thriller *Kotō no oni.*" *Journal of Japanese Studies* 27, no. 1 (Winter 2001): 113–141.

Reiter, Rayana R., ed. *Toward an Anthropology of Women.* New York and London: Monthly Review Press, 1975.

Rose, Margaret A. *Parody: Ancient, Modern, and Post-Modern.* Cambridge: Cambridge University Press, 1993.

Sagan, Eli. *Cannibalism: Human Aggression and Cultural Form.* Santa Fe, N.M.: Fish Drum Magazine Press, 1993.

Saitō Bun'ichi. *Miyazawa Kenji to sono tenkai.* Tokyo: Kokubunsha, 1976.

Saitō Minako. *Bundan aidoru ron.* Tokyo: Iwanami Shoten, 2002.

———. *Bungakuteki shōhingaku.* Tokyo: Kinokuniya Shoten, 2004.

———. *Senka no reshipi: Taiheiyō sensōka no shoku o shiru.* Tokyo: Iwanami Shoten, 2002.

Sakagami Hiroshi. "Daidokoro." *Shinchō*, June 1997, pp. 246–257.

Sakaki Atsuko. *Kōi to shite no shōsetsu: naratorojii o koete.* Tokyo: Shin'yōsha, 1996.

———. *Recontextualizing Texts: Narrative Performance in Modern Japanese Fiction.* Cambridge and London: Harvard University Asia Center, Harvard University Press, 1999.

Sanday, Peggy Reeves. *Divine Hunger: Cannibalism as a Cultural System.* Cambridge: Cambridge University Press, 1986.

Sata Ineko and Tsuboi Sakae. *Sata Ineko, Tsuboi Sakae shū.* Nihon gendai bungaku zenshū, vol. 88. Tokyo: Kōdansha, 1964.

Satomi Shinzō. *Kenja no shokuyoku.* Tokyo: Bungei Shunjū, 2000.

Schalow, Paul Gordon, and Janet A. Walker, eds. *The Woman's Hand: Gender and Theory in Japanese Women's Writing.* Stanford, Calif.: Stanford University Press, 1996.

Sekine, Eiji, ed. *Love and Sexuality in Japanese Literature.* Proceedings of the Midwest Association for Japanese Literary Studies, vol. 5 (Summer 1999).

Shea, G. T. *Leftwing Literature in Japan: A Brief History of the Proletarian Literary Movement.* Tokyo: Hosei University Press, 1964.

Sherif, Ann. *Mirror: The Fiction and Essays of Kōda Aya.* Honolulu: University of Hawai'i Press, 1999.

Shibusawa Tatsuhiko. *Hanayakana shokumotsushi.* Tokyo: Kawade Shobō Shinsha, Kawade Bunko, 1989.

Shiga Naoya. *Shiga Naoya shū.* Gendai bungaku taikei, vol. 21. Tokyo: Chikuma Shobō, 1963.

Shimada Akio. "*Kuroi ame.*" *Kokubungaku kaishaku to kanshō* 50, no. 4 (April 1985): 86–90.

Shimada Masahiko. *Arumajiro ō.* Tokyo: Shinchōsha, Shinchō Bunko, 1994.

———. *Donna Anna.* Tokyo: Shinchōsha, Shinchō Bunko, 1990.

Shimazaki Tōson. *Tōson zenshū.* Vol. 1. Tokyo: Chikuma Shobō, 1966.

Shimizu Tōru. *Kagami to erosu to: dōjidai bungaku ron.* Tokyo: Chikuma Shobō, 1984.

Shōno Yoriko. *Yūkai Mori musume ibun.* Tokyo: Kōdansha, 2001.

Stam, Robert; Robert Burgoyne; and Sandy Flitterman-Lewis. *New Vocabularies in Film Semiotics: Structuralism, Post-Structuralism, and Beyond.* London and New York: Routledge, 1992.

Sumii Sue. *Hashi no nai kawa.* 7 vols. Tokyo: Shinchōsha, Shinchō Bunko, 1981, 1992.

———. *The River with No Bridge.* Trans. Susan Wilkinson. Rutland, Vt.; Tokyo: Charles E. Tuttle, 1990.

Suzuki Sadami. *Nihon no "bungaku" o kangaeru.* Tokyo: Kadokawa Shoten, Kadokawa Sensho, 1994.

Suzuki, Tomi. *Narrating the Self: Fictions of Japanese Modernity.* Stanford, Calif.: Stanford University Press, 1996.

Swift, Jonathan. *Gulliver's Travels.* Ware, Hertfordshire: Wordsworth Editions Limited, 1992.

Tabata Masahide. "Kaisō to genzai: Ōoka Shōhei *Nobi.*" In Kitaoka Seiji and Mino Hiroshi, eds., *Shōsetsu no naratorojī: Shudai to hensō,* pp. 30–51. Kyoto: Sekai Shisōsha, 2003.

Takahara Eiri. *Shōjo ryōiki.* Tokyo: Kokusho Kankōkai, 1999.

Takahashi Gen'ichirō. *Bungakuō.* Tokyo: Kadokawa Shoten, Kadokawa Bunko, 1996.

Takahashi Mutsuo. *Shijin no shokutaku.* Tokyo: Heibonsha, 1990.

Takamura Kōtarō. *Takamura Kōtarō zenshū.* Tokyo: Chikuma Shobō, 1957.

Takeda Taijun. *Hikarigoke.* Tokyo: Shinchōsha, Shinchō Bunko, 1964.

———. *This Outcast Generation, Luminous Moss.* Trans. Yusaburo Shibuya and Sanford Goldstein. Tokyo: Charles E. Tuttle, 1967.

Tanaka, Yukiko, ed. *To Live and to Write: Selections by Japanese Women Writers 1913–1938*. Seattle: Seal Press, 1987.

Tanizaki Jun'ichirō. *The Gourmet Club: A Sextet*. Tokyo; New York; London: Kodansha International, 2001.

———. *Some Prefer Nettles*. Trans. Edward G. Seidensticker. Tokyo: Charles E. Tuttle, 1981.

———. *Tade kuu mushi*. Tokyo: Shinchōsha, Shinchō Bunko, 1969.

———. *Tanizaki Jun'ichirō zenshū*. 28 vols. Tokyo: Chūō Kōronsha, 1972–1975.

Tanizawa Eiichi. *Kaisō Kaikō Takeshi*. Tokyo: Shinchōsha, 1992.

Tansman, Alan M. *The Writings of Kōda Aya: A Japanese Literary Daughter*. New Haven, Conn.; London: Yale University Press, 1993.

Tatsumi Takayuki. *Nihon henryū bungaku*. Tokyo: Shinchōsha, 1998.

Tawara Machi. *Salad Anniversary*. Trans. Juliet Winters Carpenter. Tokyo: Kōdansha, Kodansha International, 1990.

———. *Sarada kinenbi*. Tokyo: Kawade Shobō, Kawade Bunko, 1989.

Treat, John Whittier. *Pools of Water, Pillars of Fire: The Literature of Ibuse Masuji*. Seattle and London: University of Washington Press, 1988.

———. *Writing Ground Zero: Japanese Literature and the Atomic Bomb*. Chicago: University of Chicago Press, 1995.

———. "Yoshimoto Banana's *Kitchen*, or the Cultural Logic of Japanese Consumerism." In Lise Skov and Brian Moeran, eds., *Women, Media and Consumption in Japan*, pp. 274–298. Richmond, Surrey: Curzon Press, 1995.

———. "Yoshimoto Banana Writes Home: Shōjo Culture and the Nostalgic Subject." *Journal of Japanese Studies* 19, no. 2 (1993): 353–387.

Tsubouchi Shōyō. *Tsubouchi Shōyō shū*. Meiji bungaku zenshū, vol. 16. Tokyo: Chikuma Shobō, 1969.

Tsuchida Tomonori. *Kantekusutosei no senryaku*. Tokyo: Natsume Shobō, 2000.

Tsushima Yūko, Inoue Hisashi, and Komori Yōichi. "Josei sakka: Nogami Yaeko, Sata Ineko, Enchi Fumiko o chūshin ni." *Subaru*, January 2002, pp. 272–312.

Tsutsui Yasutaka. "Hitokui jinshu." In Bungei Shunjū, ed., *Mono kuu hanashi*, pp. 139–157. Tokyo: Bungei Shunjūsha, Bunshun Bunko, 1990.

———. *Yakusai hanten*. Tokyo: Shinchōsha, Shinchō Bunko, 1992.

Uchida Hyakken. *Gochisōchō*. Tokyo: Chūō Kōronsha, Chūkō Bunko, 1996.

Ueda Akinari. *Ueda Akinari shū*. Nihon koten bungaku taikei, vol. 56. Tokyo: Iwanami Shoten, 1959.

———. *Ugetsu Monogatari: Tales of Moonlight and Rain*. Trans. Leon Zolbrod. Tokyo: Charles E. Tuttle, 1977.

Ueno, Chizuko. "Collapse of 'Japanese Mothers.'" *US-Japan Women's Journal*, no. 10 (1996): 3–19.

Ueyama Tochi. *Kukkingu papa*. Vol. 10. Tokyo: Kōdansha.

Unger, J. Marshall. *Literacy and Script Reform in Occupation Japan: Reading between the Lines*. New York: Oxford University Press, 1996.

Vialles, Noélie. *Animal to Edible.* Trans. J. A. Underwood. Cambridge: Cambridge University Press, 1994.

Washburn, Dennis. "Toward a View from Nowhere: Perspective and Ethical Judgment in *Fires on the Plain.*" *Journal of Japanese Studies* 23, no. 1 (1997): 105–131.

Watson, James L., and Melissa L. Caldwell, eds. *The Cultural Politics of Food and Eating: A Reader.* Malden, Mass.; Oxford: Blackwell Publishing, 2005.

Wolf, Naomi. *The Beauty Myth.* London: Vintage Books, Random House, 1991.

Yagawa Sumiko. *"Chichi no musume"-tachi: Mori Mari to Anaisu Nin.* Tokyo: Shinchō-sha. 1997.

Yamada Yūsaku. "Fetisshu na nikki: shoku, yume, sei." *Kokubungaku kaishaku to kyōzai no kenkyū* 41, no. 2 (February 1996): 20–26.

Yamamoto Yōrō, ed. *Seihin no shokutaku.* Tokyo: Chūō Kōronsha, Chūkō Bunko, 1998.

Yamato Hiroyuki. *Kyoshokushō to kashokushō: konwaku suru arisu-tachi.* Tokyo: Kōdan-sha, Kōdansha Gendai Shinsho, 1998.

Yano Ryūkei. *Yano Ryūkei shū.* Meiji bungaku zenshū, vol. 15. Tokyo: Chikuma Shobō, 1970.

Yasuoka Shōtarō. *Yasuoka Shōtarō shū.* Shin Nihon bungaku zenshū, vol. 35. Tokyo: Shūeisha, 1963.

Yomota Inuhiko. *Bungakuteki kioku.* Tokyo: Goryū Shoin, 1993.

Yoshida Ken'ichi. *Hontō no yō na hanashi.* Tokyo: Kōdansha, Bungei Bunko, 1994.

———. *Kanazawa, Shuen.* Tokyo: Kōdansha, Bungei Bunko, 1990.

———. *Sake ni nomareta atama.* Tokyo: Chikuma Shobō, Chikuma Bunko, 1995.

———. *Sanmon shinshi.* Tokyo: Kōdansha, Bungei Bunko, 1991.

Yoshikawa Yasuhisa. *Kaku koto no senjō.* Tokyo: Sōbi Shuppansha, 2004.

Yoshimoto Banana. *Kitchen.* Trans. Megan Backus. London: Faber and Faber, 1993.

———. *Kitchin.* Tokyo: Fukutae Shoten, 1988.

Yue, Gang. *The Mouth That Begs: Hunger, Cannibalism, and the Politics of Eating in Modern China.* Durham, N.C.: Duke University Press, 1999.

Yumeno Kyūsaku. *Yumeno Kyūsaku.* Chikuma Nihon bungaku zenshū. Tokyo: Chikuma Shobō, 1991.

———. *Yumeno Kyūsaku zenshū.* 11 vols. Tokyo: Chikuma Shobō, Chikuma Bunko, 1991–1992.

Index

About the Author

Tomoko Aoyama is senior lecturer in Japanese language and literature at the University of Queensland in Australia. She has published journal articles and book chapters on topics ranging from male homosexuality in women's texts and contemporary parody to father-daughter love and representations of young women in modern and postmodern Japanese literature. Her article "Appropriating Bush Tucker: Food in Inoue Hisashi's *Yellow Rats*" (2006) was awarded the Inaugural Inoue Yasushi Award for Outstanding Research in Japanese Literature in Australia.

Production Notes for Aoyama | *Reading Food in Modern Japanese Literature*

Text design by the University of Hawai'i Press production staff with display in Souvenir and text in Minion

Text composition by Santos Barbasa Jr.

Jacket design by Julie Matsuo-Chun

Printing and binding by The Maple-Vail Book Manufacturing Group

Printed on 55 lb. Glatfelter Offset B18, 360 ppi